THIS VERY GROUND,
THIS CROOKED AFFAIR

A Mennonite Homestead on Lenape Land

THIS VERY GROUND,
THIS CROOKED AFFAIR

A Mennonite Homestead on Lenape Land

John L. Ruth

Foreword by Raylene Hinz-Penner

Publishing House
Telford, Pennsylvania

Cascadia Publishing House orders, information, reprint permissions:
contact@CascadiaPublishingHouse.com
1-215-723-9125
126 Klingerman Road, Telford PA 18969
https://www.CascadiaPublishingHouse.com

This Very Ground, This Crooked Affair:
A Mennonite Homestead on Lenape Land
Copyright © 2021 by Cascadia Publishing House,
a division of Cascadia Publishing House LLC
Telford, PA 18969
All rights reserved.
ISBN 13: 978-1-68027-019-8 ISBN 10: 1-68027-019-2
Book, cover, and map design by Philip Ruth.

Library of Congress Cataloging-in-Publication Data

Names: Ruth, John L., author.
Title: This very ground, this crooked affair : a Mennonite homestead on
  Lenape land / John L Ruth.
Other titles: Mennonite homestead on Lenape land
Description: Telford, Pennsylvania : Cascadia Publishing House, [2021] |
  Includes bibliographical references and index. | Summary: "Ruth's volume
  connects the centuries-old history of the author's Pennsylvania
  Mennonite homestead with that of the land's indigenous Lenape
  inhabitants, interweaving documented Pennsylvania history with the
  national pursuit of a Doctrine of Discovery, and the story of Mennonites
  who had themselves fled suffering and landlessness with the fates of
  Native Americans continent-wide"-- Provided by publisher.
Identifiers: LCCN 2021029805 | ISBN 9781680270198 (paperback)
Subjects: LCSH: Stauffer, Hans, 1644---Family. | Sassoonan, -1747. | Penn,
  William, 1644-1718. | Delaware Indians--Land
  tenure--Pennsylvania--Perkiomen Creek Region--History. | Indian land
  transfers--Pennsylvania--History. | Frontier and pioneer
  life--Pennsylvania--Perkiomen Creek Region. |
  Pennsylvania--History--Colonial period, ca. 1600-1775. |
  Mennonites--Pennsylvania--Perkiomen Creek Region--History. | Perkiomen
  Creek Region (Pa.)--History, Local.
Classification: LCC F152 .R97 2021 | DDC 974.8/02--dc23
LC record available at https://lccn.loc.gov/2021029805

27 26 25 24 23 22 21   10 9 8 7 6 5 4 3 2 1

Contents

FOREWORD	*Raylene Hinz-Penner*	1
PREFACE	This Book Is a Musing	9
ONE	The Story Begins 1643–1644	15
TWO	Precedents 1644–1666	21
THREE	Changing Scenes 1667–1672	31
FOUR	The Thames, the Rhine, the Delaware 1673–1680	39
FIVE	Whose Woods These Were 1681–1683	49
SIX	Friendship Begun, and Interrupted 1683–1684	61
SEVEN	Province, Capital, and Colony 1685–1698	73
EIGHT	Land, Land, Land 1699–1701	87
NINE	Earth for Dwelling and for Selling 1702–1707	101

CONTENTS Continued

TEN	"Fix Them … for They Are … Minonists" 1707–1709	111
ELEVEN	Fewer Natives, More Mennonites 1709–1710	121
TWELVE	Pennsylvania's Best Bargain 1710	131
THIRTEEN	Home on the Earth 1711–1712	135
FOURTEEN	A Voice Silenced, A Voice Raised 1712–1716	145
FIFTEEN	A Mass Migration and a Crooked Affair 1717-1718	151
SIXTEEN	Two Concerns, Two Endings 1718	159
SEVENTEEN	Naming the Land 1719–1726	167
EIGHTEEN	The Branch, the Brandywine, Durham, and Tulpehocken 1727	173
NINETEEN	Gunfire 1728	185
TWENTY	Pain 1729–1732	201

TWENTY-ONE	Late Payment 1732–1733	215
TWENTY-TWO	Honored and Bypassed 1734–1736	225
TWENTY-THREE	The Crookedest Affair 1737	241
TWENTY-FOUR	Brethren? Uncles? Friends? 1738–1741	249
TWENTY-FIVE	"What Ground You Stand On" 1742–1743	259
TWENTY-SIX	Publication, Pathos, Profit 1744–1747	275
TWENTY-SEVEN	Still "Brethren"? 1748–1755	287
TWENTY-EIGHT	Vengeance 1755–1758	301
TWENTY-NINE	Peace Lost and Re-Attempted 1758	313
THIRTY	Competing Narratives 1759–1762	325
THIRTY-ONE	"Our Hearts Are Good" 1762–1768	332
EPILOGUE	This Has Been a Musing	353

CONTENTS Continued

About the Author   364

Acknowledgments   365

Selected Sources and Readings   367

Index of Characters and names   379

MAPS

1: Southeastern Pennsylvania   8

2: Pennsylvania   164-165

FOREWORD

by Raylene Hinz-Penner

IN LIGHT of the current climate for immigrants in the United States, how should I tell the stories of my immigrant ancestors? They came to farm land in Kansas in 1874 with shiploads of other Mennonites, most of them feeling entirely welcome and noble as they took the land cheap from the railroad, divided and settled it, tore up the grassland to farm it, established churches and community. Where does this story begin and who is included? I have wrestled with this question for the past decade, especially as I learned of the long history of rights and privileges assumed by my European ancestors. It was known as the Doctrine of Discovery, codified rights to the land in place for hundreds of years in the Americas, falsely declaring the land vacant and for the taking for European colonizers. Today, especially as I work for human rights for immigrants who seek a new home in this country, I need a reckoning, an acknowledgment.

There is, indeed, a movement underway in the U.S. and Canada to dismantle the Doctrine of Discovery, to begin this reckoning with the first step of "land acknowledgment," the recognition that the land we live on was available to us because of the genocide, deaths in battle, treaties broken, forced removal, atrocities committed against those whose homeland we carved up and commodified. We start by learning their names and their stories. We acknowledge their existence in the invisibility we took for granted. We find them among our neighbors and hear them. These are small acts of restorative justice.

Here, John Ruth, approaching the end of a long life, hears in his head the echoes of the stories he has told, and is dissatisfied with his omissions, the gaps, the acceptance of invisibility. This book is his vow to do better. His deep history is no dutiful, perfunctory, or obliging land acknowledgment, some chastened convert's newfound understanding of the Doctrine of Discovery and its error of *terra nullius*—the settler's fantasy of "vacant land" or "uninhabited terrain." Rather, this history is the working out of Ruth's lifelong wrestling with his realization that his tiny homestead is an Original People's homeland. Why were his people in the earliest Mennonite communities established in the U.S. not more curious to know the history of the land? Whose footsteps still haunt the land alongside the artifacts he finds? Who were the players in dividing the land? Why are there no records of encounters with Native neighbors?

Ruth admits that he must often work from his mind's own "musings," giving him the liberty to speculate from where he stands on the land, where "stones still cry out from the last of the fields cleared by my ancestors along the East Branch of the Perkiomen Creek, 29 miles northwest of Philadelphia" (Preface). These are not just anybody's musings, but rather the well-studied creativity of a respected Mennonite historian and commentator long known for his keen observations and probings of Mennonite faith heroes, community, and denominational politics. An earlier book Ruth wrote is a narrative account of life in the oldest Mennonite community in America. He knows of the things he imagines. Ruth is especially interested in the possible convergences among the families of three characters around whom he weaves his story: his Swiss Mennonite ancestor Hans Stauffer, the Lenape leader Sassoonan, and William Penn.

First, William Penn, the English Quaker and utopian dreamer who sought to begin Christian society over again on a new continent. "Historians should not neglect," writes Ruth, "to factor into the prehistory of Pennsylvania its founder's overwhelming sense that decadent Europe was no friendly place for people of his radical convictions" (21-22). To this end Penn parleys the British Crown's debt to his family into the gift of a forested expanse larger than Ireland which will become Pennsylvania.

Penn's is the easiest story for Ruth to imagine as he follows a well-documented life, sermons, travels, Quaker ministry, consorts with royalty, prison stays, and Penn's brief time on the land he is given. There is plenty of ink devoted to Penn for Ruth to quote, analyze, conjecture over, and interpret. He ends up as disappointed with Penn as Penn will be with his own children who have no interest in his utopian experiment save for the money they can make selling the land. Penn's final lament: "O Pennsylvania, what hast thou cost me? 30,000 pounds more than I ever got by it, two hazardous fatiguing voyages, financial straits, my son's soul."

Contrast Ruth's story of Sassoonan, a young Lenape boy perched at the feet of his elders as they deal with William Penn; from Ruth's point of view, the boy carried those early impressions of friendship between their peoples to his grave. The Lenape people were considered by other Native groups to be the Original People, the Grandfathers, like those "in the beginning" of Genesis, before corruption, before alcohol. Ruth traces the Lenape story through tribal meetings, treaties, and their forced displacement.

Here is Ruth's most speculative writing as he seeks the Lenape point of view, puzzles over their generosity toward Penn himself, their loyalty to him. A historian has scant records and dates, meetings, treaties, and translated speeches to trace an original people's movements, their real history available only in oral culture long lost to Ruth, though he tries to connect with Lenape people still alive. Ruth must use the colonial filters through which much of the Lenape story comes to him, desperate to know what his ancestors may or should have known through their even minimal interactions with their Lenape neighbors. He attempts to read the artifacts left by Native peoples buried in the land and struggles to posit to what extent the Lenape people comprehended what their readiness to sell or give land would lead to. At times Ruth seeks a Lenape point of view with regard to, for example, Mennonite worship habits: "Did white people need to gather so often in order to keep from forgetting their God?" Sassoonan's relationship with alcohol, his warnings to the intruders destroying Native communities with rum, his laments, and then his appeal for gifts of alcohol, create for Ruth a tragic figure.

The third principal thread in the interweaving story is the genealogical one: Ruth's ancestor, Hans Stauffer. Ruth is interested in denominational history, how European Mennonite communities got word about Penn's project, how they might have decided to go to his colony. He is eloquent when he describes their instinct for farming, e.g., "the neighboring grape-girdled villages" in the homelands of the Swiss immigrants (107) or "They nursed the soil with manure and clover, and introduced crop rotation, but 'felt only shallow land-rootage for their children'" as they rented from a local lord (108).

About his vine-growing ancestors' departure from the land in the Palatinate, Ruth writes of the harsh spring of 1709: "Hans and son-in-law Gerhart Clemens at Niederflörsheim found their wine turning into blocks of ice and their vines frozen dead in the ground. Birds, it was said, fell stiff from the air, and if a person spit, the saliva crackled before hitting the ground" (121). He traces these poor Palatines from Rotterdam to London where the indigents became part of a group growing to 15,000 souls, and eventually boarded a Philadelphia-bound boat on the Thames to migrate to a place of welcome (124-125).

Uniting the three strands of this story and creating its central tension is each principal character's need "to have land for their children's dwelling." Penn needs land for his utopian dream of freedom for Quakers, the freedom of new life for his own family; Sassoonan needs for his people a place on the land and access to water where they might continue the Lenape way of life, undeterred by encroachment; Stauffer and his fellow Mennonites, like Penn's persecuted Quakers, praise the rich land and celebrate their new entitlement to settle their descendants on land free from the State's harassment.

And so we readers follow Ruth's convergences in 31 short chapters, spanning the period 1643-1768, that divide the years into key events, many with provocative titles like "Whose Woods These Were"; or "Fix Them . . . for They are . . . Menonists"; or "A Mass Migration and a Crooked Affair" followed by "The Crookedest Affair"; or "What Ground You Stand On." Each chapter covers a relatively brief timespan, sometimes only a single year, noting historic dates and times that situate the principals of the story. For example, in Chapter 14, "A Voice Silenced, A Voice Raised," during the four years of 1712-1716, Penn suffers a stroke and disappears into dementia: "The public life of this friend of kings, Quakers, and Indians was over." Meanwhile, the Palatines are hacking out plantations in Pennsylvania, sometimes using the labor of their nearby Native neighbors. Surveyors and land plotters amass huge acreages to sell to trusting Mennonites who can't read the language of the contracts. Ruth reminds readers that much of what we can hear of the emerging voice of the Lenape spokesman Sassoonan is filtered through the prose of James Logan, secretary to the Pennsylvania Governor's Council and Commissioner of Property. His notes will carry Sassoonan's history the next 35 years.

At the heart of this book is the settlement history that haunts us as Mennonite inheritors of land today: the beginnings of the commodification of the land. If Penn is the English dreamer, he is also the greatest real estate agent in history, Ruth tells us. One of the distinct fascinations to be found in this story is Ruth's careful technical research, historical documentation, and imagination of how the land was carved up. How does the pristine earth of Pennsylvania come to be owned land? "[W]e templated it with field, pasture, fence, yard, lane, road, and township line" (Preface). Or, later, "White mussel shells dotted the banks of the new Clemens mill pond, eels still wriggled past the rocks of the new dam breast, and snapping turtles waddled annually to lay their eggs in creek-side muck. But upstream from such a dam there could be no migrating shad" (179-180). Ruth records the repeated requests of the Lenape people that the dams be removed, as well as the "wave of Mennonite Palatine immigration resurging in 1727, persisting for nearly three decades, [which] all but completed the transfer of the land of Sassoonan's people."

The most obvious offenders in this story are the land-grasping dividers, surveyors, and money changers who seized the moment to take theirs. Penn was only briefly (twice) on the continent to oversee the operation of dividing and selling the land; some of his greedy associates, in positions of power to deal the land they didn't live on, do not escape Ruth's critique: "What for centuries had been favorite earth under Lenape feet and wigwams . . . had become in European mentality, vendible as private property. . . . To the Natives, of course, the terms by which Europeans understood land ownership were a meaningless jargon."

Ruth's carefully researched details make for rich story. For example, there are Penn's gifts to the Lenape people, suggesting the biblical 30 pieces of silver. "'Let them know,' Penn directed, 'that you are come to sit down lovingly among them'" (51). For his own plantation on the banks of the Delaware, Penn gave the Indians "money, nearly a half-mile of wampum, 20 white blankets, 20 fathoms of quality red cloth to be worn over the shoulder, 60 fathoms of coarser fabric called duffels, 20 kettles, 20 guns, 20 coats, 40 shirts, pipes, scissors, shoes, combs, hoes, tobacco, knives, and—significantly—some 20 gallons of rum, cider, and beer" (54). Ruth sees the Mennonite immigrants with their "genetic ability and will to produce a new agricultural *Gottesgarten*" (137). as one of Penn's best bargains. "Generations of land cultivation in their memory had prepared them to recognize the fecundity under the stupendous oaks just west of the Brandywine and Octorara watersheds."

The Lenapes continue to move away. More than once Ruth notes that the Lenapes' dream of Penn "was not about private property but shared friendliness" (148). Sometimes Ruth even feels called to step into his own story to address the Lenape people, for example, as he responds to a Lenape promise to his people that they would be left unharmed: "After 336 years at this writing, thank, you, Maughoughsin. Living and worshiping on the East Branch of the Perkiomen, we have never been molested on your land" (69).

In the last chapters of the book, beginning with "Vengeance, 1755-1758," the reader follows the poisoning of the dream of friendship: "Seventy-two years after the boy Sassoonan had watched William Penn celebrate brotherhood with the Lenape sachem Tamany at Perkasie, that dream had turned into a nightmare" (307). Sassoonan's nephews have taken to violence against the landed families. In the Delaware and Schuylkill Valleys of their grandfathers, where Mennonite families are thriving as millers and distillers, only small groups of Lenape people linger along the creeks.

Settlers are violently attacked. "The bloody procedure was thick with symbolism, with a chain left on one corpse mocking the work of surveyors of this land never ceded by the Delawares or Shawnees" (p. 309). This "French and Indian War" will torment Pennsylvania for seven years. Ruth describes the divisions among Natives, among Quakers, Moravians, and Mennonites, between the British and French—the unruly politics in Pennsylvania over the closing years of his story. To "weave a narrative of Perkioma's first half-century of the post-Lenape era" that will be "realistic," it was necessary to draw on sources without reference to the Indians.

Finally, Ruth turns to the notes of a young Moravian missionary, John Heckewelder, living among Lenapes in Ohio's Muskingum River watershed, 300 miles west of Perkioma. The young man meticulously records his service as a pallbearer for the Lenape funeral of the wife of his friend Shingas, the burial clothing, face paint, ceremony, giveaway, feasting. He is profoundly moved by the Natives' expressions of tender feelings toward him and all humanity. This is a reminder that for all the sins of Christian missionaries against Native peoples in stripping them of language, culture and religion, because they lived among and observed Native peoples as fellow humans, missionaries have often served as important chroniclers of Native life and humanity. Ruth then concludes his story with "[a] last flickering of the old council fire" at a treaty in Lancaster, Pennsylvania, where Sassoonan's nephew Tamaqua returned his people's last prisoners, and the governor responded with gifts.

Mennonites telling settlement stories in the U.S. have been quick to emphasize the heroics of persecution and martyrdom, rescue of the land through an exceptional work ethic, and the stalwart communal upholding of the faith. Our omissions tell another story we can no longer disregard. In this Mennonite story haunted by a stern conscience, Ruth vows at the end of a long life to "do better" as a storyteller and historian, to attend to the usually inaudible voices. Why haven't we sought out the stories of those we have displaced? Why haven't we as Mennonites looked more critically at our long agrarian history of displacement? Those of us settled in the Plains states can easily trace back to the hundred years in Russia and our neighbors, the Nogai people. Do we have the right to aggrandize our immigration journeys without some critical look at the agrarian tradition and norms we brought to the land?

In his Epilogue, Ruth confesses that he wrote these pages in recognition of all the shallow or unsatisfying stories he has heard himself tell over the years. What Ruth has done in this examination is arduous and difficult, being so far removed in time from the settlement events. It has demanded that Ruth rethink Mennonite identity. As a gesture toward integrity as a historian and storyteller, he models courageous self-criticism in this humble deep history of land acknowledgment that we need in the current reckoning. Some Mennonites in my (western) region are working on land acknowledgments as faith communities engaged in restorative justice in league with their Native neighbors who have not disappeared and are not invisible. Here, too, the first step is a sincere investigation which asks, "Whose homeland do I inhabit?"

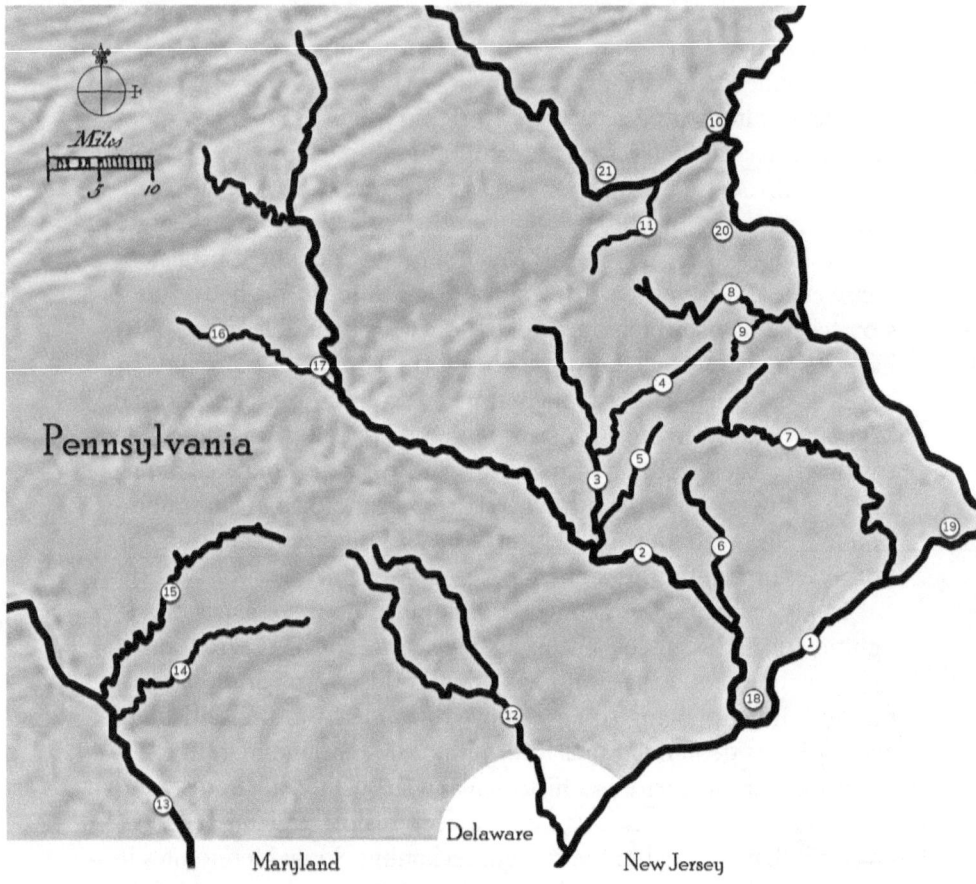

Map 1: Southeastern Pennsylvania

1. Delaware River
2. Schuylkill River
3. Perkiomen Creek
4. East Branch Perkiomen Creek
5. Skippack Creek
6. Wissahickon Creek
7. Neshaminy Creek
8. Tohickon Creek
9. Deep Run
10. Forks of Delaware, Lehigh Rivers/ Easton
11. Saucon Creek
12. Brandywine Creek
13. Susquehanna River
14. Pequea Creek
15. Conestoga River
16. Tulpehocken Creek
17. Tulpehocken/Reading
18. Philadelphia
19. Pennsbury Manor
20. Durham
21. Bethlehem/Allentown

Map Prepared by Philip Ruth, 2021

PREFACE

This Book Is a Musing

Harvesting her sweet potatoes, my neighbor picks up—a large one? No, it's heavier. A pestle, a hominy-pounder once grasped in other women's hands.

Stones still cry out from the last of the fields cleared by my ancestors along the East Branch of the Perkiomen Creek, 29 miles northwest of Philadelphia. It was from this forest-laid loam, instructed by genetic European algorithms, that my people have been shaped in utero for a third of a millennium. After William Penn "bought" *Perkioma* in 1684, and speculators leveraged it, we templated it with field, pasture, fence, yard, lane, road, and township line. In Ralph Waldo Emerson's idiom, this had become ours to measure, till, celebrate, and entail:

> *Clemens, Kratz, Bergey, Lederach, Landis, Ruth*
> Possessed the land which rendered to their toil
> Hay, corn, roots, hemp, flax, apples, wool and wood.
> Each of these landlords walked amidst his farm,
> Saying, 'Tis mine, my children's and my name's.

"As a boy," wrote a late-twentieth-century Mennonite farmer, "I recall hearing the prayers of gray-headed preachers acknowledging that our lines had fallen in pleasant places. There was a sense of awe and humility conveyed with those prayers. Now those same prayers, if prayed at all by us moderns, seem to smack of arrogance."

I heard a Lancaster County Mennonite bishop, gesturing toward a stand of corn so thick it could be reaped only in low gear, declare with unconscious irony, "God got no glory from this land when the Indians lived on it." On YouTube, another plain farmer charmed German tourists in his Pennsylvania Dutch patois, explaining that when his ancestors arrived in the Conestoga Creek watershed in 1741, "*Es wor nix do* (there was nothing here)." Ignorant, certainly, but hardly more dismissive than hymnist Isaac Watts had been in 1719:

> Where nothing dwelt but Beasts of Prey,
> Or Men as fierce and wild as they,
> [God] bids th' Oppress'd and Poor repair,
> And builds them Towns and Cities there,

or a Colonial Virginian imitator in the same meter:

> This Wilderness, so long untill'd,
> An hideous Waste of barren Ground,
> [God's] care has made a fruitful Field,
> With Peace and Plenty richly crown'd.
>
> [The] Gospel spreads an heav'nly Day
> Throughout this once benighted Land,
> A Land once wild with beasts of Prey,
> By impious Heathen rites profan'd.

Not to speak of a "Christmas Hymn" written before the land of my birth was deforested:

> Where roam'd the savage race,
> In cruelty and blood,
> He form'd this sacred place,
> A temple for our God.

Descendants of the Moyers on our Indian Creek, finding at the dawn of the twentieth century almost no lore saved by their own immigrant forebears, filled the gap with family reunion panegyric. The humble sires, it was intoned, had

> bravely plunged into the wilderness, erected their cabins amidst the howling of the wild beasts and the yells of the treacherous savages; carved out their homes, subdued the land, and made the wilderness to rejoice and blossom as the

rose; built up altars of the Lord in their midst and praised Him from whom all blessings flow, with hearts overflowing with gratitude to Him who had led them out of the house of bondage into the land of universal liberty and freedom . . . where they could worship the God of their fathers around their own altars without fear or restraint.

Have I done any better than that?

On the living room wall of our restored ancestral farmhouse glows a motto in antique German: *"Die erd ist des HERRN"*—"The earth is the Lord's." We have braided this Hebraic dictum, by which our Anabaptist forebears lived and died in Switzerland, with a dated sequence of owners' initials, beginning with those of "W P 1684." Only in old age are we wondering why we omitted reference to ownership far prior to that of the English Quaker who sent the first surveyors through the woods of what he'd wished to rename "Sylvania."

All right. Half a century ago the sense of our living from and with this ground faded sharply. As the trees began to burgeon back, my farming father mused, "Everything's growed up." Having had our seven-generation turn, we were surrendering those once-so-painfully cleared fields to monetizers, with little or nothing of our intervening story having been told. Are we, too, as incurious or overbusy as our predecessors who lived and died here without recording what they experienced? Did they think no one would need their thoughts? Will I, too, in my lifetime not have bothered to ask who carried compass and measuring chain through this creek-blessed arboreal dreamscape, who the previous dwellers had been, what *they* said, where they went, what we said then . . . or didn't say?

As Kathleen Norris observes, "The fact that one people's frontier is usually another's homeland is mostly overlooked." But why should the lament of the displaced be any less of the story's music than the grateful praise of the displacers?

In 1908, when my grandparents—responding to a crisis of ownership triggered by a pre-marital pregnancy—suddenly had a chance to return to my grandmother's homestead, jealous old Moyer cousins pronounced this "the nicest place in Montgomery County." It was surely a reference to its being embraced by the Branch Creek. Though I'd not heard this until I moved back here myself eight decades later, when I did hear it I felt blessed by that praise. On the other hand, a sacredness had dissolved: my birth home had suddenly become real estate. Initially, a wealthy neighbor, member of President Ronald Reagan's cabinet, had offered to buy it and preserve it at the center of a larger traditionally open space, to be kept as farmland. While he was away, though, on international business for the president, a local Mennonite, recognizing a speculative opportunity, suggested a slightly higher price. Annoyed to hear this, the famous earlier applicant abandoned his deal. The new participant, with no initial investment, went at once to the township with a plan to cover the creek-side acreage with 67 houses and, when that was declined, settled for 17. Amazingly, my family (helped by my sympathetic Salford Mennonite congregation) was allowed to buy the nine acres around the two crumbling farmhouses along the creek.

Gazing down beside me across tilth I had plowed as a boy, while I mused, "The memories!" a developer exclaimed, "The potential!" A young employee drove his pickup across a swell I had helped to seed and cultivate, stepped out onto the meadow and, standing blankly facing me, urinated. I sensed no intention to insult. Like the Indians before me, I did not register in his vision of the coming improvements.

My cousin Walt Hackman worked as a conscientious objector prior to the Vietnam War years at a mission among Ojibwas in Ontario. On Sunday evenings, he recalled, while his volunteer colleagues had dutifully gone to church, he had hung out in Native homes. There he heard stories that "went back," as he put it, "to Creation." He was not the same after that, sensing that the narratives we entertain must come not just from those who would newly seed the land, but those who had to cede it. When I described the first bulldozer rumbling across what had been my grandfather's apple orchard, he commented, "Now you know how the Indians felt."

I've indeed meditated on how it felt to be ordered off the creek-bank path where I led Sunday school children in memory of my youth, by a quarry-owner who later took his Branch Valley equity to another state and died there. Another cousin tells me of being scolded during a walk past our grandfather's largest field, by a man from another country who had recently built a house on it. (That man later proved friendly, and his daughter reported, to my astonishment, hearing cheerful ancestral voices drifting up from the Branch at night.)

It was humiliating to realize, after giving talks about the Original People of our region, that I really knew nothing about them. My people's mentality does not readily translate theirs. So what do I know, and why should I write? Yet, the less time remaining for me on this land, the more compulsively I reflect on how "we got" it. The best I can do is to tell the little I know from the European newcomers' point of view. That will be fair to neither them nor the Lenapes they displaced, but it is what is possible for me.

I am by no means innovating. In recent years Mennonites with names such as Landis, Hostetter, and Stutzman have offered penetrating looks at my subject—in fiction. Though I find this mode important, it is not what I will use. And while telling, I hope, like them, not be soft-headed. Why sentimentalize the people of the Lenape remnant? They had enough in their traditional attitudes to commend without our earnest compliments. Wasted by the human tsunami from Europe, they were fragile—why wouldn't they have been? And the loss of their land is of course irreversible. Some of their children's idea of returning to Lehigh land with a casino does not appeal to me. Still, evoking the memory of their fraught departure is at least a gesture—toward feelings that live on in the hearts of Lenape descendants. Among whom I claim, if only by local legend, $1/512^{th}$ of my own ancestry.

While being written, my struggling account attempts *a triple view from a specific location* at what took place where one family sank roots into another's homeland, and rested there for a third of a millennium. It is less a "history" than a pondering, from the very ground of my birth, a story becoming clearer as some of today's long-quiet Native descendants speak up, and as documents in archives from Philadelphia to Amsterdam are digitized and made instantly available online. For decades a persistent scholarly corps, in a growing library of remarkable books, has been unveiling a more detailed colonial scenario than the vague one that had entertained our grandparents. We are at a threshold of feeling.

As I zigzag from London to European *hofs* and the American woods, I am asking: Who were the characters in the story of this land's transition, and what were they thinking? Hardly knowing what to ask, can I at least consider some simple facts? I proceed by what English poets just before William Penn's time called "conceits": imaginative yokings of otherwise unrelated things, places, and ideas. I apologize to both the professional historians whose facts make such musing possible, and readers who would prefer a fictional approach. It's just an attempt to share viscerally the experience of gaining and giving up a home on this land.

    John L. Ruth
    Branch Valley, Lower Salford Township
    Harleysville, Pennsylvania
    September 2021

CHAPTER ONE

The Story Begins
1643–1644

THREE CENTURIES after William Penn set foot on the west bank of the Delaware River, young Lee Hallman strolled along the East Branch of the south-flowing Perkiomen Creek. A disc-shape on the ground caught his eye. Gently brushed, the numerals *1643* glowed silver beside a rampant lion encircled by a Latin slogan: "Trusting in God we shall not be moved." On the other side strode the figure of William of Orange, royal Dutch hero of escape from imperial oppression in 1581. To us Mennonites, it is even more important that a few years earlier this prince had tolerated our people's refusal to swear oaths.

We have archived the coin. Could it have been a fur trader, in this undulating piedmont forest of "New Sweden" or "New Netherlands," who had dropped his Dutch "Lion Dollar" by the Branch? Many like it must have ridden along with Europe's maritime empires competing so far east and west that by 1620 they had lapped into this watershed known to its natives as *Perkioma*.

As early as the arrival of New England's Pilgrims, commerce in three European languages had been probing the lithic culture of what we call the "Delaware Valley." First had come a few Dutch adventurers settling on an island in the Delaware in 1620. Four years later some northern Lenapes "sold" a rocky, mosquito-ridden peninsula called *Manhattan* to the Dutch for 60 guilders. After another decade an English dreamer, without any knowledge of the Natives, claimed to be awarded by his King Charles ownership of a region sweeping from the forthcoming New Jersey down to Virginia. The forgettable grantee, a Sir Edmund Plowden, choosing the legendary name "New Albion" for his "county palatine," designated for each of his 18 children a "manor." One, named "Kildorpy," was to be set at the falls of the river where Trenton would appear, and across from which William Penn would raise a mansion.

Absolutely nothing of Plowden's fantasy would be realized, as, while he was scheming in 1638, the landscape was claimed on site by adventurous Swedes. Astoundingly, within five years of their takeover they had published their Lutheran confession of faith in a Lenape language. But their occupation, it must be remembered, had been Old Testament style, with a bellicose Governor John Printz requesting soldiers from home to "break the necks" of any Natives who made trouble. And since his Christian compatriots, he explained in 1644, had "not only bought this river but also won it with the sword," no "Hollander or Englishman" could "pretend in any manner to this place either now or in coming times."

Already that year some 2,000 beaver furs were reportedly shipped outward from the Delaware River, averaging a pelt for every two or three of the valley's possibly 7,500 "Original" or "Common People": the Lenapes. The broad, fish-rich stream they knew as their *Lenapewihittuck* was being renamed, by both Dutch and Swede traders, the "South River." Its fur trade drew the jealousy of Susquehannocks just to the west, who fiercely attacked and partially subjugated the Lenapes. The latter had their own worries, with their leader Mattahorn ominously questioning whether it would be better to exterminate the Swedes. Fortunately, friendship won out. Then, in 1675, the Susquehannocks, reduced by smallpox, were defeated by a still larger force from New York, the Five Nations (called *Iroquois* in French parlance), who took over both their fur trade and overlording of the Lenapes.

The name "Delaware" had been given by the English when they seized the region back from the Dutch in 1664. The main tributary known to the Lenapes as *Manayunk* or *Passyunk* kept a recently coined Dutch name: "Schuylkill" (hidden river). Only the names of smaller streams on whose banks the Natives had movably camped for ages would join the European vocabularies: Neshaminy, Pennypack, Perkiomen, Saucon, Tohickon, Towamencin, Unami, and Wissahickon. So that now, when we mention our creeks, we too speak Lenape.

As the white wave crashed in, the wampum-making women kept on tending their beans, maize, and squash, but their men's hunting and trapping were skewed by the commercial peltry option. Within a generation, they needed the guns, hoes, and awls proffered by traders, and wanted blankets, combs, and scissors. To get them, they were willing to share their places on the ground.

Not that they found everything admirable about their pale, land-hungry guests who, for all their power to cross seas and send words on a skin, had strange ignorances. Laughably prone to getting lost in the woods (which they called "wilderness"), they had to calculate their way, and move with horse-drawn wagons loaded with provisions. They had only one generic word for a bear. They could not read much in a footprint, or in the pantry and pharmacy of the forest. They were irreverent and cruel, not even thinking to weep before skinning a fellow creature they had killed for food. They spoke of an unknown God, to whom the Original People had no access without dropping their own stories of Creation.

Surprisingly, as a European observer would write, the "savages" could "relate the most trivial circumstances, which have happened in their councils many years ago, and tell the exact time of former meetings, with the greatest precision."

Foreign pathogens and the Trojan gift of rum! It has been variously estimated that by the time William Penn arrived to treat for land, there may have been only a fifth as many Lenapes as the first Dutch and Swedes had found. In eight decades the grandchildren of the race that had millennially sown our slopes with points and pestles had become a hurting remnant. Remembering that holocaust must throw a sympathetic light on the faces emerging as we reconsider their—and our—living on, by, and with this land.

Reader alert: The multiple perspectives in this telling are awkward. Spatially, it looks around from the very plot of my genesis and the adjacent field which birthed a Mennonite meetinghouse to be called "Salford." Temporally, it moves forward from the months of the Swedish governor's cruel warning in 1644. For this was also the birth year of two of the story's main characters: England's famous William Penn, and a simple farmer in Switzerland named Hans Stauffer. It would be the latter's daughter and son-in-law who would "buy" the very ground on which these words are written.

The careers of these two European characters' fathers could hardly have been more different. Whereas Penn's had won naval celebrity, Stauffer's was jailed as an obscure pacifist minister. And while the Penns would be awarded lucrative family estates in Ireland by their English king, the Stauffers would be denied their own simple farmstead in their natal Emmental valley.

Another contrast: Whereas the infant Penn was christened in London's aristocratic All Souls Barking Church by the Thames, Stauffer, of Eggiwil on the little Emme River just north of the Alps, was intentionally *not* baptized in a "church," and *not* before he could think for himself. When a neighboring Anabaptist was asked why his people didn't "go to church," he jibed, "What would I want in that pile of stones?" But there was also a remarkable parallel. Penn, in his mid-20s, would likewise reject "steeple-houses," and refuse, as Hans Stauffer's people did, to fight or swear an oath.

What a burden Christendom, whether Catholic or Protestant, was laying on people who wanted "freedom of conscience" to live by the Sermon on the Mount! By 1644 the issue had already leaped the Atlantic. America's millions of Baptists look back to this very year as the publication date of Roger Williams' protest: the *Bloudy Tenent of Persecution*.

Above all, my musing links Penn's and Stauffer's bone-deep longing to have land for their children's dwelling with the same motif in the psyche of our third main character: the Lenape *Sassoonan*. Born three decades later than 1644, this headman or "sachem" was a child of the woods north of the future city of Philadelphia. He is not introduced until Chapter 5, when we find him as a boy watching Penn deal with the Natives for their land. The site of their parley, a Lenape village called *Perkasie*, is in the headwaters of the East Branch of the Perkiomen Creek which flows, nine miles downstream, between the seven-generation farm on whose soil this story is remembered, and a rise called "Salford Heights," where prayer has been made by Mennonite families for three centuries.

While Sassoonan would live with the memory of his boyish glimpse of Penn, he would never know our character Hans Stauffer, whose son-in-law and grandsons would turn the woods on either side of the Branch into a family cluster of six Mennonite farms. In fact, already by the time Stauffer would dock in Philadelphia (1710), Sassoonan had moved westward to the Susquehanna River valley. His story, unlike those of Penn and Stauffer, would then turn landless. Yet, because for another generation he would revisit the watershed of his birth, speaking forlornly for his clan, he (and his nephews of the next generation) will be heard here. Significantly, many more of his words are on record than any by Stauffer or his son-in-law Gerhart Clemens.

As a weary old sachem, Sassoonan would protest to Penn's secretary that what his Lenape people had given up was "good land, and he ought to have good Goods for it." In that he would be disappointed. Instead of his people, mine would get the land—cheap. But he was right: It was good. We, born from and living on it for three centuries, never imagined his feelings on leaving it. All his people had to do for us was to get out of the way. I never even heard of him before I was 50.

CHAPTER TWO

Precedents

1644–1666

WILLIAM AND MARGARET PENN's first child was born in the shadow of the grim Tower of London on October 14, 1644. That was the year when the 23-year-old father, a sea captain since the age of 17, was promoted to the rank of Admiral. In this he followed his own father Giles, famous for rescuing hundreds of Britons enslaved by Muslim pirates in Morocco. Admiral William had married a widow, the daughter of Jan Jasper, a "Merchant of Rotterdam," and niece of Mennonites in Krefeld on the Lower Rhine.

Substantial income from the Irish estate of Margaret Penn's first husband meant that finances were not an issue for the parents of the founder of Pennsylvania. The times, though, were insecure, Britain being at peace neither religiously with itself nor militarily and commercially with its sea-ranging Spanish and Dutch rivals. In civil war begun two years before little William's birth, Dissenters had overthrown their own King (Charles I). Under the harsh ensuing Puritan regime of "Lord Protector" Oliver Cromwell, the youthful Admiral Penn was mostly away from the home at Wanstead, just north of London, to which he and Margaret had brought their infant son. Before the boy's fifth birthday, the nation's disgraced king would actually be executed, leaving sore rivalries and suspicions in English clans. The senior Penn himself, though now commanded by Cromwell, was correctly suspected of wanting to restore rule to the beheaded King's son (the future Charles II). For this he spent time in prison.

At the age of three, William Jr. lost his hair to a case of smallpox (considerably milder than the strain that was then killing thousands of Natives in his future colony). Around his sixth birthday, he was sent from Wanstead to a Puritan grammar school in nearby Chigwell, where mother Margaret had relatives in her maternal Jasper clan. The sober discipline there contrasted sharply with the glamor of William's going at the age of eight with his mother to quayside in London, to see his admiral father leading up the Thames a convoy of a dozen captured ships, bringing for the Cromwell regime five chests of silver and gold. The boy would never forget his father's principled refusal to allow Mrs. Penn even one of the coins as a souvenir, though she offered to pay for it.

This was the very opposite of a pacifist upbringing. In the following year the Admiral won more glory in a famous battle near the Dutch port of Scheveningen, when a sharpshooter in his ship's rigging killed the fleet commander on an opposing vessel. In the jubilation that followed in England, a narrative of the victory was officially read in churches, and Admiral Penn was among the officers awarded gold chains by Parliament. William Jr. would eventually inherit his father's prize and, though becoming a pacifist himself, nostalgically bequeath it to his own son, William Penn 3rd.

Flush with public applause, Admiral Penn seized the chance to request official remuneration for the loss of income from his wife's Irish estate, which had recently been captured by rebellious Catholics. Protestant forces in Ireland having hanged a Catholic bishop at nearby Macroom, that cleric's estate was available for transfer to Scottish and English settlers. Thus Cromwell himself could order that the Penns be given the castle-dominated land in the vicinity of Cork. The Penns had now twice seen land as something to be transferred by the stroke of an official pen over the heads of the common people who lived on and from it.

While the 33-year-old Admiral's estate-request was still being processed, Protector Cromwell, eager to acquire foreign territory, sent the hero back to sea with sealed orders. To be in charge of a fleet transporting a thousand soldiers could only have flushed Penn with a sensation of power. His assignment, he discovered, was to wrest from the Spanish empire the rich western island of Hispaniola (modern Dominican Republic and Haiti). There at sea, he realized, he was in a position to switch his naval assets over to the executed King Charles' 25-year-old son of the same name, now hiding in France. Penn sent Charles, in fact, a secret offer of support, with a request for response. This was a gesture whose results would help to rename a vast woods in America. For though at this moment the future Charles II cautiously declined the clandestine offer, 21 years after he had gained back his father's English throne, the grateful memory of Penn's secret and risky loyalty would move him not only to grant the Admiral's son an overseas colony, but to insist on giving it the Admiral's family name.

With the father once again overseas, 11-year-old William Jr. was proving to be a spiritual schoolboy, "extremely tender under rebuke." In the words of an early biographer, he was often "in his meditations ravished with joy, and dissolved into tears." "Much given to reading and meditating of the scriptures," by the age of 14 he had marked up his Bible. What he would remember as the very "first sense he had of God" had "suddenly surprised" him, when alone at Chigwell, with "an inward comfort" and "an external glory in the room." From then on he would often recall that moment as when he had been given "the seal of divinity and immortality," convincing him "that there was a God and that the soul of man was capable of enjoying his divine communication." This must have been the boy's own experience, since the schoolmaster in charge of his education "was not of his persuasion."

Father Penn's return from the West Indies to London in 1655 was not glorious. The campaign to capture Hispaniola, which he had shared with a jealous land general, had collapsed, and Cromwell was not pleased with the consolation prize of the smaller island of Jamaica, which he had not given orders to take. The anxiously awaiting student at Chigwell had to learn that his father was jailed in London's infamous Tower.

Politics being what it was, soon after the Admiral apologized, he was let out and allowed to take his family to where they could live in Ireland as lords of Macroom, their recently awarded Irish estate. It was an optimistic feeling, surely, for an oldest son to be growing up in a community's first family, networked with people in power, and with financial security amidst hard times. Yet young William Penn was touched with a non-standard view of social status. When he was about 15, a London tradesman named Thomas Loe, traveling through Ireland as a Quaker missionary, was a guest in the Penn household at Macroom. Typical of the recently birthed Society of Friends, Loe had much to say about both inner faith and Christian behavior. He discoursed so tellingly in the Penns' home that young William would later recall tears on the faces of both his listening father and a slave brought back from Jamaica. "What if our family," young William himself imagined, "became Quakers?" Though this did not happen, he would eventually call this another moment when "the Lord visited me." And ten years later, when Loe would come through Ireland again, the naval hero's son would yield to the vision of a human society unendorsed by the sword.

Penn had not quite reached 15 when England's Lord Protector died. Within a year, as son Richard Cromwell's brief attempt to rule proved feckless, a majority of the British population was ready to take back the rejected royal government to which father Penn had stayed secretly loyal. His reward was to be among the officials sent in 1660 to fetch the young king from the Netherlands. The joyous fellowship on the returning flagship renamed the *Charles* brought Penn into close companionship with the new king's younger brother James, Duke of York. Ashore, as bonfires and bells welcomed Charles and James to Whitehall Palace, the social status of their Admiral friend rose steeply.

Though the newly acclaimed Penn now lost his Cromwell-given Irish estate at Macroom (which had to be restored to Catholic friends of Charles II), he was quickly given a similarly valuable replacement at nearby Shanagarry. And soon after the royal return, Admiral Penn was elevated to Member of Parliament for the district of Weymouth. Before long he would also be appointed a trustee of an overseas colony on the east side of the Delaware River in America, which in 1664 had been seized from the Dutch by his friend James, Duke of York.

Consonant with these hopeful signs of advancement, the Penns now sent their son to Oxford. There, reading widely in theology and history in classic languages, even being tutored by John Locke of future philosophic fame, the student soon made his parents proud. A Latin ode he composed for the death of the youngest brother of the King and Duke brought public commendation from them both. It was fuel for familial hope for high, even noble, position. But William Jr., no matter how faithful a son, was not to be shaped by parental social climbing. Amidst his Oxford studies, he preferred to listen to nonconformist critics of official Anglican Christianity, and was among those refusing to wear the traditional surplice of students at Christ Church College, or to attend chapel. As a result, in less than two years he was, in his own words, "banisht the college," leaving his socially ambitious father beside himself with disappointment. Never would the son forget "the bitter Usage," as he put it, "when I returned to my Father; whipping, beating, and turning out of doors in 1662." Apparently there would be, for such a scion, no future seat in the House of Lords.

Frightened by his son's nonconformity, the Admiral sent him to France to learn more conventional manners. This succeeded somewhat, but even after visiting the lavish Court of Louis XIV at Paris, William would choose to study for more than a year in a sober Protestant academy under a Huguenot promoter of religious toleration. Even after traveling in Switzerland and Italy, returning home with a noticeable French gait and costume, and enrolling in law school at London's Lincoln's Inn, he had lost little of his distaste for popular Christianity.

Interweaving our story's three families now turns us briefly westward into the transatlantic woods where, a decade before our third character Sassoonan was born, a steady trickle of Europeans had been arriving. Among the newcomers was a group of 41 idealistic Dutch Mennonites, led by a Cromwell-favoring man named Pieter Cornelisz Plockhoy, settling in 1663 on the Lower Delaware River. The site they chose for their utopian experiment, called *Zwaanandael* or *Swaanandael* (later Lewes), had a dubious history. It was the very spot where an earlier Dutch settlement had been exterminated in 1631 by Indians alarmed by the newcomers' expanding a trading post into a plantation. Precisely such concern would be evident among Lenapes as white settlement pursued them to Susquehanna and Ohio country.

There had also been, however, less discouraging news from an English missionary named George Coale. A year before the Mennonites' 1663 coming to Zwaanandael, he had scouted the area for a possible Quaker settlement in America. On his return, his report to Quaker leader George Fox of a friendly Indian reception stirred gossip in London. When it reached all the way to the ears of 17-year-old William Penn, then at Oxford, he had felt a mystic "opening of joy."

King Charles and his brother James, Duke of York, while continuously preoccupied with Dutch naval competition, also had their eyes on America. It had been in 1664, several months before William Penn had returned from France, that Charles had declared his younger sibling the ruler of the freshly reclaimed New Netherlands, turning it instantly into "New York." As the English Navy then cleared the Atlantic coast from New Amsterdam to the Delaware Bay, they wiped out the year-old Dutch Mennonite colony at Zwaanandael "to a naile." From now on anyone wanting land along the "South" (Delaware) River had to deal with James' deputy governors of New York.

The most important of the Lenape villages affected by this change of "ownership" was called *Shackamaxon*, a beach just upstream from the future site of Philadelphia. Here, on a sandy western bank of the "Lenape" or "South" (Delaware) River was a favorite place for tribal councils. On the opposite shore a little English colony called "New Jersey" had been established in 1661, with one of its trustees, Admiral William Penn, drawing up its code of laws. Mid-stream lay a fertile 350-acre island. Extending pleasantly back from the gradual beach where the Cohocksink Creek joined the river just upstream from the still unborn town of Philadelphia, the treeless marshes and meadows long enjoyed by the Lenapes had also attracted Swedish settlers with names such as Cox, Nelson, and Rambo. A deed obtained by Lawrence (Lasse) Cock for the valuable riparian tract had been signed by the Dutch government in 1664, only weeks before the English takeover. Cock, in friendly conversation with the Indians in their own language, had paid them as well as the Dutch for this acquisition.

There are places of special memory. Our story will return to this one, since it was probably under an iconic elm on this naturally friendly site at Shackamaxon that William Penn would soon exchange "great promises" of lasting friendship with the Lenape people. As an old man, Penn himself would vainly yearn to live, die, and plant his children in this specific neighborhood, where in March the river seethed so thickly with spawning shad that they could be caught by hand. Centuries later, with the once-lovely tributary Cohocksink a mere sewer under the scrim of North Philadelphia, the district would still be called "Fishtown," and a casino-owner applying for a license to build on the beach would call the site "delicious."

Meanwhile in England, a month after the newly francophone returning William Penn Jr. enrolled in law school at Lincoln's Inn, his Admiral father was once again sent to fight the Dutch. London held its breath as the enemy navy, so recently defeated in America, nevertheless cruised challengingly back and forth in the English Channel. Sir William, appointed Great Captain Commander of a war fleet of 136 ships, took his handsome son with him as personal assistant. With them on board the famous flagship *Royal Charles* rode the King's younger brother James, Duke of York, carrying the honorific title of Lord High Admiral. It was of course understood that since James was a landsman, it was the naval veteran Penn who would literally call the shots.

With battle expectation mounting, Sir William sent his son ashore with a quick personal update for their friend King Charles. Arriving at the Whitehall Palace at daybreak to ask for a royal audience, the 21-year-old courier was astonished to see the scandalously womanizing King emerging from his chambers in his nightgown, exclaiming, "Oh is't you? How is Sir William?" They talked for over half an hour, wrote William to his father, with the King asking "three several times" how the Admiral was doing. This unmistakable affection was powerfully enhanced in the ensuing huge battle just offshore from the town of Lowestoff in Sussex. A "chain shot" from a Dutch ship, tearing across the deck of the *Royal Charles*, wiped out the two men standing just beside the King's brother James. Meanwhile, Penn's fleet was destroying or capturing 32 Dutch ships with the loss of only two English vessels. That was glory enough. But it was especially the Duke's lucky survival, and Sir Penn's bringing him safely home to the palace of his royal brother, that welded the bond between their families. Sixteen years later, the victory of Lowestoff would be specifically cited in the charter by which Charles would convey to the younger Penn the right to be lord of his own demesne in America. When Penn would plan to move there himself, he would announce to the Lenape Natives that the woods they lived in was one which "the king of the country where I live, hath given unto me."

Any farm carved from the Lenape woods has fiery Lowestoff in its pedigree.

London, though in the throes of a horrible plague, went delirious with joy over the victory at Lowestoff. Meanwhile, the Penn family had become so obviously a royal favorite as to attract professional rivalry. Well might son William learn the lesson, from a bitter though unsuccessful attempt by rival naval officers to have his Admiral father impeached, that public success invites political jealousy. Certainly, if he did not learn it then, he would be so educated in America. In any case, the physically worn out and now retired Sir William, still only in his late 40s, had become well off. With the King being short of funds, the Admiral himself advanced his sailors' salaries, and even deferred demanding his own pay. The resultant growing royal debt would not be settled until years after the senior Penn's death.

Just then the celebration-damping plague hit London. The King and his retinue quickly fled the city, where bells tolled continuously for as many as 7,000 deaths per week. The smoke of bonfires set to quell the stench of contagion brought young William Penn a "deep sense of the vanity of this world." Fortunately, having gained a legal education, he could be sent away by his father to use it in managing the family estate at Shanagarry in Ireland. By living there in the following year, he was spared the experience of the Great Fire of London, which on the heels of the plague consumed some 13,000 houses and 87 churches. Even the monumental six-century-old St. Paul's Cathedral collapsed, and only Admiral Penn's calling up of his navy yard workers to break down buildings around All Hallows Barking kept the church where his son had been baptized from the same fate. The blackened ruins greeting William on his return from Ireland may well have still smoldered in his imagination years later when, designing a new city in a new world, he would prescribe that its houses be built far enough apart that they would "never be burnt."

Since this story of a homestead in Pennsylvania also harks back along the line of Hans Stauffer's family, it must touch down briefly where, in 1658, their spiritual community in the hills along the Emme River in Bern was under severe stress. Much as England was persecuting its Quakers, Bern had run out of patience with rural Anabaptist dissidents whose refusal to swear oaths or carry weapons had preceded that of the Quakers by over a century. In 1653 Bern's ruling lords ordered up a special penitentiary for their "stiff-necked" *Wiedertäufer* (rebaptizers). On Pennsylvania farms today Amish congregations still sing of how paid vigilantes broke up a farmhouse-meeting in 1659, on a hill just above Eggiwil where Stauffers lived on a farm called *Glasshütte*. Anabaptist preachers were carried off to prison in the capital town of Bern, and some were expelled from the canton (after which they repeatedly crept back). Whole families were giving up and walking northward across the Jura Mountain range, past Basel into Alsace. Others from the Canton of Zurich had already migrated even farther, into a South German region called *die Pfalz* (the Palatinate). The ruler of that fertile but war-ravaged realm spreading on both sides of the Rhine was a first cousin of William Penn's royal friends, King Charles and Duke James. A moderate Protestant, Elector Karl Ludwig was more favorable to Swiss Anabaptist refugees than were his minor officials. He found the Anabaptists so valuable as restorers of his war-stricken hofs that in 1664 he issued a "Concession" by which, if they agreed not to proselytize, they would be tolerated in his regime.

News of this opportunity must have drifted quickly south to Hans Stauffer's tormented Anabaptist community in Bern. But the reluctance of a people's involuntary leaving an immemorial homeland must not be underestimated. There was in the psyche of Stauffer's people a genetic urge to stay both who and where they were. It would take them and their spiritual siblings seven years after the news of toleration in the Palatinate before they were tearfully willing to abandon their *Erdboden* (ground) along the Emme, where they had expected their children to dwell, and flee northward to other soil.

CHAPTER THREE

Changing Scenes
1667–1672

A MUTINY BY UNDERPAID SAILORS at Carrickfergus, Ireland, in 1667 brought a quick reaction from William Penn, the 23-year-old manager of his family's neighboring estate. So impressive was his spontaneous leadership in retaking a stone tower from the rebels that he was promptly offered a local commission as military commander. Pleased with himself, he wrote for approval from his father back in London. But there was no answer; a son's career as a soldier would have ruled out the Admiral's jealous family dream of advancement to the peerage.

The son, on the other hand, was proud enough of his newly minted military reputation to have his portrait painted in armor. His frank, handsome face looks out serenely above the carapace, suggesting potential military glory. Then suddenly, in the summer of 1667, that equanimity glowed into spiritual enthusiasm. Thomas Loe, the traveling Quaker whose preaching had stirred the Penn family a decade earlier at their previous Irish estate, had turned up again at Cork. His text this time—"There is a Faith Which Overcometh the World, and There is a Faith Which is Overcome by the World"—blew away the young soldier. Whether his response was a sudden paradigm shift, or a fulfilment of the spirituality incubating from his elementary school days on through studies at the French seminary and Oxford, it was now radical—and definitive. The upward-bound socialite soldier would henceforth identify with the Truth as witnessed to by Britain's despised Quakers. However we may view this conversion, had it not happened, there would be no Pennsylvania, nor would this story be told from a certain farm on the East Branch of the Perkiomen Creek.

Many millions of words have been written about the young man who swiftly became the Quakers' best public voice, eclipsing in this regard even their founder George Fox. The often-retold story of a young itinerant preacher is one of a half-dozen arrests and prison terms, during which Penn never stopped writing passionate pamphlets and books. He could quote from an astonishingly broad acquaintance with the classic authors he had read at Oxford, and cite scripture after scripture. Before long he was refusing, as a Quaker Christian, to swear civil oaths, carry a sword, socially remove his hat, desist from public preaching, or accept early release from prison via his family's social standing. Remarkably too, his spiritual fervor flowed together with confidence in his family's politically powerful friends in London, including, intimately, King Charles himself. In a strange way the King's Catholic younger brother James, Duke of York, wanted what the despised Quakers also longed for—freedom from the Anglican establishment. For two decades the oddness of a Quaker's close friendship with a Catholic Duke (who also became King) would bring preposterous accusations that the Quaker preacher Penn must be a secret Jesuit!

Yielding to his worried father's repeated demands for a visit, William traveled back to London in the company of the Quaker missionary, Josiah Coale. It had been news of Coale's scouting the American woods from Maryland to New York that had quickened Penn's pulse as a student at Oxford. Perhaps he read then of how the Susquehanna Natives had "entertained" Coale's party "in their huts, with much respect," and had guided the visitors 200 miles on their explorative journey. In a second journey at George Fox's prompting, Coale asked the Natives about buying some land for a possible Quaker settlement along the Susquehanna. Surely, as Penn conversed with this veteran missionary as they traveled, and soon afterward as they sat imprisoned together in the Tower of London, there was conversation about the new land and its possibilities. And this must have been a main topic as both men then talked with Fox himself in London.

Admiral Penn, embarrassed and humiliated by his son's new Quakerly appearance, seems to have made a scene at William's visit. Yet there was no long estrangement. The passionate young preacher was shortly on another missionary tour, at his own expense, and, when not interrupted by stays in prison, lodging in appreciative Quaker households. One of them was the home of a former playmate, the now grown-up Gulielma Springett. She too was well-connected, being the admired stepdaughter of affluent Quaker Isaac Pennington, whose own father had been Lord Mayor of London. Her tutor, who considered her a jewel, had served as secretary to the blind John Milton, when the famous poet had lived in nearby Chalfont to escape the plague in London. Besides being a tenderly spiritual young lady, Guli had a comfortable income from her deceased father's Warminghurst estate in Sussex, south of London.

Newly betrothed to Quaker William Penn, Guli saw him off to preach all across Ireland. He wrote urgently to awakened young converts, "Let us no more look back on our ancient pastimes and delights, but with holy resolution press on, press on." Defying laws he considered unjust, the ardent young preacher was soon arrested for not doffing his hat before authorities. After publishing a tract, *The Sandy Foundation Shaken*, and enduring a nationally sensational trial, he landed again in prison. Undeterred, the 24-year-old prophet wrote furiously in the gloomy Tower of London, producing a book entitled *No Cross No Crown* that has seldom if ever gone out of print. Penn was no Freethinker. As piously as any modern "Evangelical" could wish, the book's very title page argued that *"the Denial of Self, and Daily Bearing of Christ's Cross, is the Only Way to the Rest and Kingdom of God."* A later edition was autobiographical, telling how it was

> first written during my confinement in the tower of London in the year 1668, now reprinted with great enlargement of matter and testimonies—that you may be won to Christ; or if won already, brought nearer to Him. It is a path which God, in His everlasting kindness, guided my feet into in the flower of my youth, when about twenty-two years of age. He took me by the hand, and led me out of the pleasures, vanities and hopes of the world.

"Hear me once," exhorts the future founder of Pennsylvania,

> Can Christ be your Lord and you not obey Him? Or, can you be His servant and yet not truly serve Him? Come now, what has He saved you from? Has He saved you from your sinful lusts, your worldly affections and vain conversations? If not, then He is not your Savior. For though He be offered a Savior to all, yet He is actually a Savior to those only who are saved by Him; and none are saved by Him who still

live in those evils by which they are lost to God, and from which He came to save them.

"Right is right," argues the preacher, "even if everyone is against it, and wrong is wrong, even if everyone is for it." And perhaps the book's most often-quoted passage, wherever the English language has gone, is the creed-like declaration: "I expect to pass through this world but once. Any good therefore that I can do, or any kindness or abilities that I can show to any fellow creature, let me do it now. Let me not defer it or neglect it, for I shall not pass this way again."

William's father, whose health was rapidly giving way at the age of 49, was of course eager to get his son released, but that son demanded—and would eventually win—nothing less than a public reversal of the verdict that had sent him to prison. Sprung from jail with anonymous help, he made it to his father's bedside with only 10 days to spare. Years later, he would recall that it had been to none other than King Charles and his brother James, Duke of York, that his father and he owed the "particular favour in getting me released out of the Tower of London." Now the royal brothers came to see their dying friend. Young William would never forget his father's "humble request . . . upon his death bed . . . [to Charles and James] to protect me from the inconveniencies and troubles my [Quaker] persuasion might expose me to." This elicited from the King not only a "friendly promise to do it," but an "exact performance of it from the moment I addressed myself to him." There was certainly no need to discuss with the dying Admiral the substantial debt which the King still literally owed him, and which, 13 years later, would become the hinge of one of history's great land transfers.

However different the younger Penn's convictions were from his deceased father's, the son had no hesitation to accept the family's financial legacy, or even the gold chain that had been awarded by Oliver Cromwell for the Admiral's naval exploits. Just as filial are the pacifist son's sentiments inscribed on the armorial escutcheon for his father installed in the St. Mary Redcliffe Church of Bristol, the city of Penn ancestry. On it, the junior William cited no fewer than 13 stages of his father's military career. The proud conclusion—"and in Anno 1664, was chosen Great Captain Commander under his Royal Highnesse in ye signal and most evidently successful fight against the Dutch Fleet"—was yet another foreshadowing of the transaction that would plant the family name, a decade later, on a sweep of woods in North America containing more land than in Britain itself.

Before long William had preached himself into jail again, this time at Newgate, the notorious penal venue for gross criminals. But even there he kept on writing, whether to his plighted Gulielma, or to the public, in *A Serious Apology for the People Called Quakers*. More than 40 titles from his pen were published in his first six years as a Quaker.

After release from jail in August of 1671 Penn saw George Fox off to America, and went on a mission trip of his own to the European Continent. No record was kept to let us know whether he saw any of his mother's relatives in the Netherlands, or of the details of his visit to a German princess who had been kind to Pietist dissidents. But he saw enough that fall to make him want to return. Astonishingly, the trajectory of this and a later more extended European journey would geographically intersect with that of our story's Swiss Mennonite character, Hans Stauffer.

In 1671 both the famous Quaker and the simple Anabaptist farmer, still bachelors in their late 20s, were living in tension with their governments. A few years earlier Hans Stauffer had even been reported as "hiding" in "Germany." Now, in fact just as Penn was visiting Germany, events in the Emmental were triggering a sorrowful emigration. Authorities had made hostages of 12 of the wealthiest farmers from around Eggiwil, where the Stauffers lived, holding them in the capital city of Bern until the village would give up the local Anabaptists, and they would leave the canton. As a result, Hans Stauffer was among a three-generation refugee cluster walking northward with some 600 other *Täufer* (Baptists), toward the only community they knew of that might receive them as fellow Christians.

Whereas the Emmental-born Stauffers were among those fleeing unofficially, a Täufer preacher who had come to the Emmental from Zurich, and had been living for years at the village of Hasle, was openly and forcibly driven to the border with France. Henrich Funck, having been flogged to make him promise never to return, and with pus draining from the letter "B" branded on his back, wandered for days among people whose French language he could not understand. Before long, with help from Mennonites in Alsace, he managed to join the hundreds of other Swiss refugees turning up in the Palatinate. There he could display to sympathetic Mennonite deacons the official sign of the Bernese Bear singed onto his body. This was a story, we should note, that would be told one day in Pennsylvania by descendants living along a little stream called "the Indian Creek," joining the East Branch of the Perkiomen a few farms upstream from plantations of the grandsons of Bernese Hans Stauffer.

It was late in 1671 (while Penn was sojourning in Europe) when some 450 of the Bernese refugees showed up across a 12-mile-wide territory west of the city of Worms. Here was where most of the Mennonite Kolb and Clemens families had been living. Among the arriving exiles, wrote an alarmed deacon to Holland, "you will find those who need crutches, being 70, 80 and 90 years old. Most are in desperate need of clothes, having not brought along more than what they were wearing. With little bedding, we don't know how to keep them warm." Old Christian Stauffer in particular, who had 78 living descendants, and was near death from the journey, had "brought nothing with him." The only possessions that could be inventoried for his entire set of four families were three duvets (comforters). Some local Mennonite families now had "seven, eight or nine [refugees] living with them." It was heart-rending to hear them speak of having gone from immemorially familiar landscape to landlessness.

The Stauffers' first experience was of trying to find lodging in an abandoned castle near the Ibersheimerhof (nicknamed *Mennonistenhof*) on the west bank of the Rhine. It was frightening to have to wait overnight in the bushes until a gang of bandits was chased out of the ruins. A letter from deacon Valentyn Hütwohl and an assistant named Johannes Clemens reported both young and old exiles arriving in the village of Kriegsheim. Some had come there "lame," with bundles on their backs and children in their arms. There was a couple with 12 children. Hans and Anna Roth, with five, had only "one quilt." Some were in good spirits, but others, forced in their advanced old age into an alien scene, were weeping. Even Hans Stauffer's 90-year-old grandfather, the minister Christian Stauffer who had been jailed in Bern in the year Hans and William Penn were born, was not the oldest of the refugees.

None of the now overwhelmed Mennonites already living in the Palatinate had expected such a flood of helpless spiritual relatives. Though they themselves had been officially tolerated on their well-kept *hof*s (farmsteads), they too were not legal citizens. It was seven years since the "Elector" Karl Ludwig (first cousin of England's present King Charles) had given Anabaptists in the Palatinate the privilege of farming in his realm. That had allowed the stable little "Mennist" community at Ibersheim to thrive, along with members in villages such as Alsheim, Dirmstein, Kriegsheim, and Niederflörsheim. But had wealthy Dutch Mennonites now not quickly sent substantial funds for food and bedding, it would be hard to imagine how the Palatine Mennonites could have supported the Swiss refugees through the oncoming winter. Deacon Hütwohl and Johannes Clemens wrote from Kriegsheim to Amsterdam "with tears" that even though farms might be leased for the newcomers, every family taking one up would need a plow and a wagon, as well as a cow, and that even those who would have to "sleep in the straw" would "still need duvets or blankets."

"They sigh," reported Hütwohl and Clemens, at the thought of leaving their lands and homes, and having to start new ones. Not surprisingly, in a few months old Christian Stauffer passed on, never dreaming that his grandson Hans would someday make another epic move, into an unknown forest across the sea, to where immigrant Clemens and Ruth families would own farms with a mutual border.

Soon after Penn's return from his travels in Germany, a Quaker meeting near Gulielma Springett's home at Warminghurst endorsed the childhood friends' decision to marry, which they did in April 1672. Their comfortably blended inherited estate incomes and deeply united faith supported the bridegroom's going out, only a few months later, on yet another mission tour. Preaching at 21 locations in as many days, the aristocratically handsome, articulate, and fearless prophet was increasingly a hero to Quakers longing for freedom of conscience. With their founder George Fox away on a two-year exploratory mission in America, William Penn had become their chief hope.

Fox, struggling "through the woods" of the Delaware Valley, hired Native guides to lead him northward toward New England. While passing "through many Indian towns," he recorded, "We declared the day of the Lord to them." Some of the Indians, fortunately, proved "very loving." On a cold night, they helped to make fire as the missionaries reached "the head of Delaware Bay." Farther up the river, in an area now known as "New Jersey," the missionaries "swam our horses over a river about a mile ... to an island called Upper Tineconk [Burlington Island] and then to the mainland, and hired Indians to help us over in their canoes, and our horses." Many Natives seemed to listen respectfully as Fox explained that if they did God's will they would go to heaven, and if not, would be "burned." A few who were less friendly included some "Indian men eaters [who] lay in wait for some of our company that had separated from us."

Fox would not remember with any pleasure the "great swamps, bogs, and wildernesses" he passed through. He described them, rather, as full of "perils of wolves, bears, panthers, cougars [and] rattlesnakes." "Great bays of water, creeks, and rivers" had to be crossed with only "small open boats and small canoes." It got so cold at night "when sleeping in the woods and wilderness" that several of the missionaries "had their hands and fingers numbed." Of course, on the other hand, this forested scene, described by English hymnists as a "howling wilderness," was the very livable home of the Natives listening to George Fox's strange words.

Somewhere among these Indian "towns" in the Delaware Valley, possibly even while Fox was on tour, was born a Lenape boy who would be named Sassoonan. Though too young to have met Fox, he was destined to know—and appreciate—Fox's famous friend William Penn, who would bring his dream of a Quaker colony into Sassoonan's woods, give it another name, and parcel it out to foreign purchasers.

CHAPTER FOUR

The Thames, the Rhine, the Delaware
1673–1680

WORSE THAN THE PERILS George Fox faced in the American woods were the political dangers he encountered upon his return to England. Refusing to take an oath when arrested for preaching in public, he was jailed in Worcestershire (where he wrote eight books) until William Penn influenced his Catholic King Charles to grant a release. Penn himself was scribbling on mightily, whether in a letter to Quakers Fox had met in Maryland, or in the latest of the 36 books he had written since his conversion. He addressed large topics head-on, as in *England's Present Interest Considered* (1675), which argued that the religious tolerance Quakers wanted was not only at the root of English law, but the best way to national welfare.

Also in 1675 came a book with lasting consequences, entitled *A Treatise of Oaths, containing several weighty reasons why the people called Quakers refuse to swear*. Addressed to the King and Parliament, it cited not only Jesus' directive to "Swear not all," but also 120 authors from classic to recent times, in an impassioned appeal for the removal of "the heavy clog of Swearing" from Quaker consciences. The 31-year-old author, who had ancestors and relatives in the Netherlands, knew that, a century before the Quakers had appeared in England, Dutch "Menists" had been given this exemption, and that it was still the case that "magistrates in Holland do take the Solemn Affirmation of such as cannot swear instead of an Oath." Whether or not this was the first time Penn would connect Mennonite and Quaker convictions, it was certainly not the last. In fact, 34 years after his book against swearing appeared, he would recommend that a group of Mennonites (including a stepdaughter of Hans Stauffer) be given special entrée into Pennsylvania, as Mennonites who he knew would "neither swear nor fight."

Penn's growing reputation among Quakers now brought him a special American assignment: to resolve a bankruptcy dispute among well-known Quakers to whom James, Duke of York, had granted land east of the Delaware River. The 30-year-old preacher proved up to the task. Not only did he negotiate a satisfactory settlement; he actually wrote most of a "Charter of Fundamental Laws" for the emerging colony of West New Jersey. That document's Quaker-flavored values were prophetic: fair trial by jury, freedom of conscience, freedom from unjust imprisonment, an assembly elected by the people, and true trial by jury. The quickly adopted constitution helped to stimulate a rush to Jersey of 3,000 more English Quakers in the four-year interval leading up to the founding of Penn's own colony.

In the years just previous, both New England and Maryland had been frightened by Indian warfare. Whereas in Massachusetts, Indians had attacked whites, south of the Chesapeake region once-powerful Susquehannocks were being humiliated by the larger Five Nations. News of such Indian "grudgings" having reached London, William Penn, who had never been to America, had been careful to write into the Jersey "Charter" a standard of fair dealing. Before any land was surveyed, he directed, someone was to

> go to the chief of the natives concerned in that land . . . to acquaint the natives of their intentions, and to give the natives what present they shall agree upon . . . and take a grant of the same in writing. . . . Which grant is to be registered in the publick register, allowing also the natives (if they please) a copy thereof.

This, especially with reference to the topic of presents, was a far more respectful method than other colonies had practiced with their "Natives."

The Lenapes of the Delaware Valley were proving friendly themselves, as they saw some of the first white newcomers in "Jersey" forced to weather the winter in wigwams, and supplied them with Indian corn and venison. But neither the Natives nor perhaps Penn himself could then have imagined that the next few years would bring into the Lenape homeland two or three times as many Quakers as there remained Lenape survivors of imported smallpox.

A month or two after the first of the Jersey-bound English boatloads arrived in March 1677, an unusual assemblage of Natives took place at Shackamaxon, the traditional seat of council just upstream, as we have noticed, from the future Philadelphia. This conferring had nothing to do with the Europeans arriving on the opposite shore. It was fallout from the Five Nations' recent conquest of the once-powerful Susquehannocks. Senecas from the Five Nations had come down with English officials from New York to talk with "River Indians" (Lenapes) over where to settle remnants of the defeated Susquehannocks. This may have been the last time the almost sacred old Shackamaxon ground saw an important Native-Native council. For at least a generation—since before the British takeover in 1664—Swedes had been farming on this pleasantly situated riverside ground. Recently, more of the Indian-cleared scene had been surveyed and bought, under the regime of William Penn's friend James, Duke of York, by the German Julian Hartsvelder. And now the land on the east bank, too, just across from Shackamaxon, was taken up by a boatload of Quakers from Hertfordshire, where William Penn had lived as a boy at Wanstead.

In these same months in 1677 Penn was again traveling on the European continent as a Quaker missionary. His itinerary this time brought him all the way into the Rhineland countryside where Hans Stauffer, still a bachelor, and his Bernese relatives had been getting an economic foothold since their arrival six years earlier. The aim of Penn's touring party, which included George Fox, was to promote a fellowship that Quaker missionaries had brought to the Continent in their movement's very first years (1650s). Already then itinerant preachers had founded Quaker "meetings" among Mennonite communities from the Netherlands to the Palatinate, up to Hamburg on the Elbe and as far as Danzig on the Baltic. On this latest tour Penn, while helping to organize a Quaker system of monthly, quarterly, and yearly meetings centered in Amsterdam, conversed with some of that city's leading Mennonites. Then, while Fox kept sojourning in Holland, Penn took a translator and a few other members of the missionary party eastward into the Rhine-divided Palatinate (*Pfalz*) region. There, he knew, lived people who were spiritually "tender"—an adjective Quakers sometimes applied to Mennonites.

Always eager for conversation with top officials, Penn headed south for Mannheim on the Rhine and a hoped-for visit with the Prince-Elector (*Kurfürst*) of the Palatinate. Penn well knew that this Karl Ludwig was a cousin of his own close friends, the British King Charles and his brother James. Disappointingly, when the Quaker party arrived in Mannheim, the Elector was in Heidelberg. Penn had to make do with a long letter admonishing the "Great Prince" to be tolerant to people of conscience, such as the recently arrived Bernese Anabaptists. Then he set out on a Sunday morning from ancient Worms on a six-mile walk west to the vine-growing village of Kriegsheim on the Pfrimm River.

Penn would have known about Kriegsheim (adjacent to the village of Niederflörsheim) because it had a little Quaker congregation, established 22 years earlier when English missionaries had won some of the local Mennonites to the Friends' persuasion. Surely it was a sensation for them to welcome another English visitor. Intriguingly to us, there had been a family with the English name of Clemens in the community as early as the original Quaker visit, and we have noticed a young Johannes Clemens assisting Deacon Valentyn Hütwohl in registering refugees from Bern in 1671. Clemens descendants in Pennsylvania cite strong DNA evidence of English ancestry. It has been theorized that a Jacob Clemens at Niederflörsheim (father of this story's Gerhart) was a son of the wealthy, scandal-ridden English regicide Clement of Toft, executed at London in 1660 (eight years later than the first mention of the Clemens name among German Mennonites). Had members of the troubled Clemens family fled to tiny connections in the Palatinate? In any case, three years after Penn's visit to Kriegsheim, the wife of Jacob Clemens would bear a son named Gerhart, who would one day purchase from Penn's officials the land on which this story is written.

The first worship service on this historic morning at Kriegsheim lasted five hours, with Penn doubtless the main speaker through an interpreter. Listening suspiciously from behind a door was a Lutheran clergyman, officially responsible for monitoring any illegal religious activity. He was able to report hearing nothing for which anyone should be arrested. Penn himself was memorably touched by the spiritual atmosphere of this Lord's Day fellowship. And when he regathered in the evening with "a more retired meeting" of only the Quakers (which did not include members of the local Clemens and Kolb families), his spirit rose farther. The mood of the "little handfull" of formerly Mennonite Cassels, Hendrickses, and Schumachers proved, he would recall, "very weighty and tender." As the Quaker meeting progressed, "the power rose in a high operation among them, and great was the love of God that was in our hearts." Here in the midst of a landscape dominated by what Penn called the darkness of a "great and mighty" state-enforced (Catholic) religion, he was finding "a lovely, sweet, and true [Quaker] sense. We were greatly comforted in them," he journaled, "and they were greatly comforted in us."

Penn pitied these formerly Mennonite Friends at Kriegsheim, ten miles south from the later home of our story's Swiss-born Hans Stauffer. "Poor hearts!" Penn called them; "it is the Lord's great goodness and mercy to them, that they are so finely kept in the seed of life." Doubtless the Kriegsheim Friends had told him about their cattle and other property being confiscated when, as newly convinced Quakers, they had declined to pay what they now objected to as a religious tax. In any case, Penn's compassion was not merely theoretical. It would take very concrete form in the following decade, in the Lenape woods of America to which all the Quakers of Kriegsheim—and some of their Mennonite-remaining cousins—would move at the invitation of their impressive English guest of 1677.

It may seem strange to genealogists that Penn's itinerary made no contact with another, somewhat larger Mennonite-turned-Quaker fellowship that was then emerging in a region generally referred to as the "Lower Rhine," in the textile-weaving town of Krefeld. Though there is no record that he stopped anywhere nearer there than the neighboring town of Mühlheim, in Krefeld too English missionaries had been making "Friends" out of part of another old Mennonite congregation. Among the converts there were a family of op den Graeffs, whose father Isaac was a first cousin of William Penn's Dutch-born mother. Unfortunately, no record of this relationship exists outside of genealogical files, not even in accounts of the op den Graeffs' move as Quakers six years later to Germantown, where they would live side by side with other (likewise ex-Mennonite) "Palatines" from the village of Kriegsheim.

We can sense the warmth of Penn's evangelistic mood as he approached the end of his three-month missionary tour. His passion glows in a letter exhorting a devout sister of the Elector, "Princess Elizabeth," to a Quaker-type commitment. And that epistle is outdone in a more general one Penn wrote to her from Amsterdam on the day before leaving for home. Its apocalyptic title announces an urgent "Summons, or Call to Christendom In An Earnest Expostulation with her, to prepare for that great and notable Day of the Lord, that is at the Door." Historians should not neglect to factor into the pre-history of

Pennsylvania its founder's overwhelming sense that decadent Europe was no friendly place for people of his radical convictions. An excursus from his rolling jeremiad will make that clear:

> O how hath Christ's religion been prophaned, and his holy name blasphemed, by the lewd life of professed Christians!. ... O what tremendous Oaths and Lyes! What Revenge and Murders, what Drunkenness and gluttony! What Pride and luxury! What Chambering and Wantonness! What Fornications, Rapes, and Adulteries! What Masks and Revels! What Lustful Ornaments, and Enchanting Attires! What Proud Customs, and Vain Compliments! What Sports and Pleasures! What Plays and Romances! What Intrigues and Pastimes! Again, what Falseness and Treachery! What Avarice and Oppression! What Flattery and Hypocrisy! What Malice and Slander! What Contention and Law-suits! What Wars and Bloodshed! What Plunders, Fires and Desolations! And it is not only committed by Christians in *general* one against another, but by Christians of the *same Faith, Sect* and *Church* one against another; praying to the same God to *destroy* one another; and singing Psalms to God, when they have wickedly destroyed one another. O the Rapes, Fires, Murders, and Rivers of Blood, that lie at the doors of professed Christians! If this be *godly*, what is *devilish*? If this be *christian*, what is *paganish*?

What worse provocation than such an iniquitous world could there be to a born leader, to consider the option of beginning Christian society over again—if some neutral landscape were available?

As we have seen, one of the prettiest unspoiled landscapes across the Atlantic—the Delaware Valley's riverside Shackamaxon—had immediately caught the attention of arriving Quakers. Whereas most of them were buying land east of the river in New Jersey, one man, an affluent Hertfordshire friend of Penn and former prison-mate of George Fox, had his eye on the pleasant meadows on the opposite bank, next upstream from the mouth of the Cohocksink Creek. Though this Quaker, John Kinsey, died before completing his purchase, it was carried out in the name of his unmarried daughter Elizabeth, who in March of 1678 bought 300 of the 1,800 Swede-domesticated riverside acres at Shackamaxon. What for centuries had been favorite earth under Lenape feet and wigwams—now known as "a great place to gather blackberries and huckleberries" and "for shooting wild ducks"—had become, in European mentality, vendible as private property. The 1678 deed at Shackamaxon, addressed "to all Christian People," certified that the Swedish Lawrence and Martha Cock "of Sachamexing in Delaware River" had "fully absolutely and clearly ... Given Granted bargained Sold assigned aliened Transported made over and confirmed" their farm to the English "Elizabeth Kinsey her heirs and assigns." To the Natives, of course, the terms by which Europeans understood land-ownership were a meaningless jargon.

With more than enough inherited money to spend, Miss Kinsey also had eyes for the grassy mid-river island just across from her new purchase—perhaps the most desirable of the 86 islands scattered up and down the river. It too was a favorite Lenape site. And Swedes who had paid the Natives for the right to farm it knew well that the Natives did not feel themselves "aliened" from land they had "sold." Miss Kinsey therefore had to pay not only the Cocks for their Swedish "interest" in the island, but also the Natives whose own prior claims to it had clearly not, in their minds, been all "extinguished." Evidence of this was the understanding of four Lenape "chiefs" who agreed to the sale that, while promising to be careful not to kill Miss Kinsey's hogs or burn her hay, they could continue to hunt and fish on the island, and dig there for "tuckahoes," a tuber traditional in their diet. Further, to keep the deal alive, she was to provide them annually a modest bonus of gunpowder and rum. Although both sides seemed satisfied with this deal, 20 years later still another Swede, Gunnar Rambo, would demand to be paid for what he called a "Right and title" *he* had "of in and to the greate Island opposite to Shackamaxon," which he claimed had been "assigned" to him by four Lenape sachems. Even more irritating, as far as Elizabeth Kinsey was concerned, was the fact that some of her fellow Quakers on the east bank thought the island belonged to *them*.

Special to this story of land is the first appearance, as a witness signing the deed for Elizabeth Kinsey's island purchase, of another Hertfordshire Quaker. Young bachelor Thomas Fairman, having been among the first arrivals in Jersey, would soon marry the newly fatherless Elizabeth. He would then not only take over ownership, with her, of the "dwelling house barns, stables, stalls, [and] fences" of the Swedish farm she had purchased at Shackamaxon, but launch a career as the most often-recorded surveyor of land in the Delaware Valley through the following three decades. The substantial house that the newly married couple would immediately build at Shackamaxon would radiate an influence as notable for European immigrants as the beach under it had been for generations of the Lenape "River Indians."

Surveyors! They were appearing, with compasses, sextants, and chains, marking trees with nicks along both sides of the Delaware River, from where Swedes had a Lutheran church at Wicaco (future south Philadelphia) near the juncture with the Schuylkill, all the way 30 miles upstream to above the Delaware Falls (across from future Trenton). English purchasers wanting the "conveniency" of frontage on the west side of the Delaware were buying it from officials under the governor of New York. This was confusing and unsettling to the most sensitive of the Lenape sachems. Though losing thousands of their people to the white man's diseases had already made them feel vulnerable, their sense of what was fair remained acute. They did seem to trust the Swedish Lawrence ("Lasse") Cock when he came among them, fluent in their language, as interpreter for the incoming English.

We now return to England, where in 1680 Guli Penn, after losing her first three children in infancy, is raising two more: Springett and Laetitia. Their father, as active as ever, and staying in touch with his royal friends Charles and James, has two burning issues on his mind: the religious persecution in Europe, and the possibility of a haven for the persecuted. He has heard that his recently converted (formerly Mennonite) op den Graeff cousins are in trouble in Krefeld. At least one of them has been beaten and expelled from town, simply for acting like a Quaker. Fortunately, William has more than genetic connections. William of Orange, the young Prince of the Netherlands from which Krefeld is ruled, is the son-in-law of the Duke of York—Penn's close friend James at Whitehall. So, with the approval of both the Catholic Duke and his royal brother Charles, Penn writes a protest letter on March 26, 1680, to the Protestant Dutch ruler. Addressing the latter respectfully as "Great Prince," he admonishes that it would make no sense to reproach the Catholics "with persecuting Protestants, if Protestants themselves will persecute Protestants." Penn pleads nobly: "Indulge these poor inoffensive [Mennonite-turned Quaker] people [at Krefeld], it is Christian, it is Protestant, it is human." The Prince should direct the governor "of those parts to suffer these dissenting inhabitants of *Crevelt* now exiled, to return quietly to their habitations [so] that the great God who is King of kings and Lord of lords, may bless and prosper thy affairs."

If Penn could feel this way about a tiny community on the Rhine, how much more must he have grieved for the thousands of Quakers in his own Britain, harassed, impoverished, and jailed for three decades now? What other religious group would have organized, as they had in London, a regular "Meeting for Sufferings"? What a contrast between their lot and that of Quakers who were now, under a charter largely written by Penn himself, freely "meeting" for worship in the woods of New Jersey! It made Penn wonder about the land on the west side of the Delaware River, also in possession of King Charles and his brother, the Duke. Could not that wilderness, with its few friendly Indians and Swedish farmers, be a sanctuary for England's tormented Quakers? And might not Charles himself, who had promised Penn's father to be good to the son, be willing to grant some of that unmapped American landscape to pay off the burdensome £16,000 he still owed—with growing interest—to the Penn estate?

The royal answer would be a ready Yes. A month or two after writing to the Prince of Orange, William Penn submitted a petition to his own King for payment of the long overdue family debt. Instead of money, Penn would accept a tract of land north of Maryland, extending as far west of the Delaware River "as plantable." This would give the Penn family a forested expanse larger than not only their Irish estates, but of the whole of Ireland. While his most important motive was a spiritual dream, Penn made it sound economically attractive to the King. The project envisaged, he wrote shrewdly to Charles, would be "a profitable Plantation to the Crown."

CHAPTER FIVE

Whose Woods These Were
1681–1683

IN LATE MARCH 1681 the Lenapes returning to their summer camps along the creeks in the Delaware watershed knew that in its welcoming bay the roe-swollen shad were collecting to spawn. Within weeks the clear upriver tributaries would turn silver with the crowding, fattened backs of this largest species of herring. There would be netting and feasting for both Natives and the Swedes whose plantations focused on their Lutheran church at Wicaco, a mile or two downriver from Shackamaxon.

No special tremor, on the first day of spring, ran through Passayunk, Playwicky, Perkasie, Tinicum, or other villages scattered through the unbroken woods extending northward across the endless Kittatinny or Blue Mountain range toward Five Nations (Iroquois) territory. But on that day, 3,500 miles eastward at the Palace of Whitehall in London, the signature of William Penn's friendly King Charles II was renaming those rolling forests. "WHEREAS ... WILLIAM PENN, Esquire," began the charter, "Sonne and heire of Sir WILLIAM PENN deceased ... hath humbley besought Leave of Us to transport an ample Colonie ... in the Partes of America not yet cultivated and planted,"

Wee ... haveing Regard to the Memorie and Meritts of his late Father ... perticulerly to his Conduct, Courage, and Discretion under our Dearest Brother JAMES Duke of York, in that Signall Battell and Victorie fought and obteyned against the Dutch Fleete [in 1665]: Doe give and Grant unto the said William Penn ... that Tract ... bounded on the East by Delaware River [with] all the Soyle, lands, fields, woods, underwoods, mountaines, hills, fenns, Isles, Lakes, Rivers, waters, Rivuletts, Bays, and Inletts. ...

As to how the said soil, lands and fields had become the English King's to grant to anyone, there was not a syllable. Any notion of a doctrine of discovery was taken for granted. And by this sovereign rhetoric, the earth under the moccasins of Lenape Natives, including a "little lad" to be known as Sassoonan, was forever renamed. The document's only reference to Sassoonan's people called them "Savage Natives" whom, it was hoped, grantee Penn might "reduce ... by gentle and just manners to the love of civil Societie and Christian Religion." As the greatest real estate agent in history, the English dreamer was hereby not only declared the "absolute Proprietarie" of their "Countrey," but was also authorized to divide and retail it for personal profit. All he owed to his royal donor were "Two Beaver Skins, to bee delivered at [the] Castle of Windsor on the First Day of January in every Year."

Beyond this vast ownership and the power to rule, undying British honor had been assigned to the Proprietor's family lineage. "We have thought fitt," stated the carefully vetted deed, to "call itt PEN-SILVANIA, and soe from henceforth we will have itt called." This embarrassed Penn. While viewing the transaction as a repayment of his father's massive loans, he feared giving the land grant a family name would be seen as "a vanity" he himself had requested. His own first choice, considering Penn to be a Welsh name, had been "New Wales," and when that was refused, he had proposed "Sylvania" (Latin for "forest"). When "They added Penn to it," he reported to a friend, "I was much opposed ... and went to the king to have it struck out." But the king "said 'twas past." Finally, after even a substantial bribe had failed to change the officials' minds, Penn accepted the naming of the huge grant. "My God that has given it to me," he wrote, "will, I believe, bless and make it the seed of a nation."

In European feudal terms, the 37-year-old Quaker missionary had been vouchsafed "Absolute power" to "Divide" a vast foreign landscape "into Townes, Hundreds and Counties, and to erect and incorporate Townes into Borroughs, and Borroughs into Cities." As a "True and Absolute Proprietary" or lord, he was specifically empowered to map out "manors"—estates of multiple thousands of acres—to sell to affluent purchasers or give to family members and employees. The new owners could then, at least theoretically, levy their own laws within their little domains.

Working urgently with friends at writing a constitution or "Frame" for his colony, Penn immediately went commercial, advertising both in Britain and on the Continent in the German and Dutch languages. Many affluent Quakers from southern England responded as "First Purchasers" of land before Penn himself could visit his new colony or have its land surveyed. In that brief interval his agents would sell the rights to over half a million acres of Native-occupied woodland west of the Delaware River. Out of every 100,000 acres he reserved a manor of up to 10,000 acres for members of his own family (Guli had just given birth to their fourth child, a second William, or "Billy"). A group of Welsh Quakers asked for 40,000 acres in one tract. Even a few of Penn's friends in the Netherlands bought in, and a group of Pietists he had visited four years earlier in Frankfurt, Germany, asked for 25,000 acres.

Quickly naming a non-Quaker cousin, William Markham, as his deputy governor, Penn sent him and four land "commissioners" ahead to begin dealing with the Natives, particularly choosing and surveying "a convenient tract of land" for Penn's personal family "settlement." Within four months Markham had arrived on the Delaware at the Swedish settlement of Upland (which Penn would rename "Chester"). Among a governing "Council" Markham chose from the mixed Swedish, Dutch, and English inhabitants along the river was the recently married Thomas Fairman who had immigrated four years earlier. From his substantial new house at Shackamaxon (already the venue designated for a Quaker monthly meeting), the young Fairman found himself recruited for several "weary" 15-mile journeys downriver to Upland, to help Markham in "Taking the Courses & Soundings of the Channel of [the] Delaware." This seven-week project launched a surveying career that would give Fairman, over the next three decades, an unmatched acquaintance with the wooded landscape between the Schuylkill and Delaware Rivers.

Still in England, Penn issued broadsides of preliminary instructions, such as that his overseas representatives should be "tender of offending the Indians." Anticipating the dynamics of his taking over their land peacefully, he was concerned to prevent anyone from advising the Natives "not to sell" him land. Making a good first impression was necessary in order to "soften" the Natives to their unknown new friend. "Let them know," Penn directed, "that you are come to sit down lovingly among them." Before he himself would arrive, the commissioners were to begin reimbursing Natives, in his name, for specific tracts, being careful not to pay more than once for the same tract. "Be grave," added Penn, somehow already knowing that the Natives "love not to be smiled on." Meanwhile, the commissioners were "by no means [to] sell any land" to European settlers until Penn himself would come. He would then become one of the greatest land-dealers of all time.

Penn sent along a letter to be read in the Lenape language—doubtless at Shackamaxon—by Thomas Fairman's earlier-settled Swedish friend Lasse Cock. Making sure that the Natives understood the letter, and presenting "their kings" with a large pile of gifts, Markham was to carefully "get them to comply" with Penn's terms. The letter itself, which has become famous, began in Quaker spirit, "My Freinds":

> There is one great God and Power that hath made the world and all things therein, to whom you and I and all People owe their being and wellbeing, and to whom you and I must one day give an account, for all that we do in this world; this great God hath written his law in our hearts, by which we are taught and commanded to love and help and do good to one another, and not to do harme and mischief one unto another.

What was the effect of such words on the silently listening Lenapes seated around Markham and Cock at the Shackamaxon beach in the spring of 1682? It may have been possible for them to accept some of Penn's thought of God and an inner sense, but just what did it mean to be told that "this great God" had "Now ... been pleased to make me concerned in your parts of the World, and the king of the country where I live, hath given unto me a great Province therein"? Would any dismay over this announcement be lessened by the claim, "But I desire to enjoy it with your Love and Consent, that we may always live together as Neighbors and friends"?

Certainly, adds the unknown friend, he is "very Sensible of the unkindness and Injustice that hath been too much exercised towards you" by unethical people. He knew well of the recent "great grudgeings and Animosities, sometimes to the shedding of blood" in New England and Virginia. But he, they would find, was "not such a man, as is well known in my own Country: I have great love and regard toward you, and I desire to ... Winn and gain your Love & Freindship by a kind, just and peaceable life." It was in that spirit, they should understand, that he had sent his commissioners on ahead to "treat" with them "about land and a firm league of peace." And it was in line with this that he had sent along for them a truly impressive pile of "Presents and Tokens."

By the time Markham and Cock read this letter to the Natives in the spring of 1682, Penn, still in England, was choosing a "Surveyor General" for his colony. Thomas Holme, having served in both Admiral Penn's navy and Cromwell's army, had been rewarded like the Penns with a grant of formerly Catholic-owned land in Ireland. After Holme, like Penn, had become a well-known Quaker minister, he had seen enough persecution to write a book on the *Sufferings* of their adopted fellowship. Thus in him Penn felt he had a man sensitive about land, and who could be described to the Natives as "sober, wise and loving." Promising Holme the reward of a 5,000-acre manor, in addition to a third of the fees collected by any deputy surveyors under him, Penn saw Holme's family and servants off in April 1682, with another letter for the Indians.

Arriving on the Delaware in August, the eight-member Holme party took up residence in the best facility available: Thomas and Elizabeth Fairman's house at Shackamaxon. This made it necessary for the Fairmans to move out (Governor Markham, too, had lived there since the previous year). As had Markham before him, Holme promptly hired his experienced landlord as a deputy, to help him survey around the junction of the Schuylkill and Delaware Rivers. Familiar now with the landscape for half a decade, Fairman was annoyed to have to loan horses for the newcomer Holme to "ride into the interior of the land and see what it held." With much less knowledge than Fairman, Holme was receiving better compensation for the work that his deputy, in practice, was leading. However that may or may not have suited either Fairman or Holme, the advance knowledge they were gaining in the dense woods let both surveyors—employer and servant—identify choice tracts for their own speculation. At Holme's heels meanwhile was an urgent demand from William Penn for an official map to guide the vast sales campaign.

The land deal most impressive to the Natives that spring was overseen by Penn's cousin, Governor Markham. He had chosen for Penn's personal country estate a 10,000-acre spread nestled 30 miles northeast from Shackamaxon in a bend of the Delaware at its "Falls," across from the site of future Trenton, New Jersey. With a mid-river island much like Fairman's at Shackamaxon, this was the farthest upriver location that could still be reached by tide-floated barge. Although already, under the post-1664 ownership of the Duke of York, four Native headmen had "sold" the woods eight or nine miles northward and southward of this spot, and there had been a dispute over the deal, Markham now got 13 Natives to sign again. Here, reaching west from the river to the head of the south-flowing Neshaminy Creek, was where it was dreamed the great Proprietor would dwell and die, passing on to his children a copious American estate.

For half a century, the forest-embraced Pennsbury Manor would be an interface or fault line between two peoples' dreams of dwelling. The deed for its purchase on July 15, 1682, confirmed a survey from a white oak on land "against the falls of Delaware River . . . up the river for five . . . miles . . . then overland to the Native village of Playwickey" (just west of future Langhorne) and "from thence westward to the creek called Neshammony's Creek," and down the Neshaminy to its mouth on the Delaware.

The goods listed as payment for the manor of Pennsbury must have been overwhelming to the Indians (which was the impression Penn intended to make). Never had they experienced such a bonanza, which included not only money, but nearly a half-mile of wampum, 20 white blankets, 20 fathoms of quality red cloth to be worn over the shoulder, 60 fathoms of coarser fabric called duffels, 20 kettles, 20 guns, 20 coats, 40 shirts, pipes, scissors, shoes, combs, hoes, tobacco, knives, and—significantly—some 20 gallons of rum, cider, and beer. Here was the unimaginable bounty of Europe, in the name of a man who had yet to arrive in the country he was coming to govern. Giver of this avalanche of goods, how could he be anything but a uniquely gracious benefactor? In fact, this and shortly following gifts would help to seat in the Lenape mind a powerfully lasting initial impression.

The sensation of largesse was repeated when Surveyor Holme arrived and, doubtless again at Shackamaxon (where he was lodging in the Fairman home), had another letter from Penn read to the Natives. It too began by invoking divine favor, and promised that when "the Great God brings me among you, I intend to order all things in such a manner that we may all live in love and peace one with another."

Penn had already taken care to protect Natives from wrong by drawing up "good laws" in his proposed "Frame." On the touchy and already serious issue of alcoholism he now promised never to "allow any of my people to sell rum, to make your people drunk" (we have just seen him giving them rum). And just as in the earlier letter sent via his cousin Markham, this one via surveyor Holme closed with a promise to "bring you some things of our country that are useful and pleasing to you."

While preparing to sail himself, Penn urgently wrote and revised not only a constitution for governing his colony, but a charter for a group of investors who would do business there. He himself, he noted, would not participate in trade, because he wanted to keep his motives godly rather than commercial. Of course, through land sales and continuing "quitrents," he expected to become quite wealthy. He was in fact so confident about his forthcoming cash flow that he was paying bills by borrowing heavily from his secretary, Philip Ford. This was to have long-term serious consequences. As the fellow Quaker Ford watched Penn getting ready to cross the ocean (possibly never to return), he became nervous, and asked for some kind of legal guarantee of repayment in case something would happen to Penn. For this Penn let Ford draw up a strangely simple promise: that if the loan were not repaid, Ford would receive 300,000 acres of land in Pennsylvania. "Pressed for time," and confident in Ford's loyalty, Penn signed the agreement without even reading it. Casual business behavior like this was unfortunately typical of Penn; some people he dealt with had to wait and complain for years to bring him to pay ordinary bills.

This is a story about concern for descendants. With his ship almost ready, Penn, at home with a pregnant Gulielma and their three living children, took time to write them a long farewell letter of admonition. Recognizing the possibility of never seeing them again, he spelled out fervent hopes for their spiritual future. Guli was to have daily devotions with the children, teach them to read their father's recently re-issued book, *No Cross No Crown*, learn useful skills, dress and live plainly, and participate in the Friends Meeting. Depth of fatherly feeling led Penn to dream that son Springett, daughter Laetitia, 17-month-old "Billy" (William Jr.), and the child now in Guli's womb might well someday, grown up after their father was gone, become involved in governing Pennsylvania. If that were to happen, he wrote them, "I charge you, before the lord god and his only Angles, that you be lowly, diligent, and tender, fearing god, loving the people, and hating covetousness, letting justice have its impartial course." If they did thus, Penn believed, God would make them "bless'd instruments . . . for the Settlement of some of those desolate parts of the world." This kind of attitude in his posterity, Penn wrote, was what "my soul desires above all worldly honours and Riches."

On August 30, 1682, the 300-ton *Welcome*, captained by Robert Greenway, sailed out of the harbor at Deal carrying just over a hundred souls, mostly Quakers. William Penn had left his family behind, but brought along several of his best horses. The *Welcome* was only one of nearly two dozen such ships optimistically bringing to Pennsylvania that year some 2,000 immigrants—possibly as many or even more persons than the total population of Lenapes that had survived the onslaught of smallpox. That Europe-sourced scourge would also accompany the whole incoming fleet, killing an average of four persons weekly on Penn's own vessel. As the bodies of a third of his shipmates were dropped overboard, he himself, protected by the inoculation of his mild case as a child, helped to nurse the sick and dying. No wonder that he would remember how, after seven weeks of this pestilent atmosphere, as the *Welcome* came within 30 miles of land, the first whiff of American air "smelled as sweet as a garden new blown."

Entering the Delaware Bay, the ship's first pause was at the town of 300 mostly Swedish inhabitants called "New Castle" (later Wilmington). Ready with documents of ownership from his friend the Duke of York, Penn invited local officials aboard. They came acknowledging Penn's lordly status with a ceremonial piece of "turf," a bowl of water, and a twig—feudal tokens of land, river and woods. But this was not yet what would become Pennsylvania, and on the next day a 16-mile upstream sail brought the *Welcome* to a smaller settlement, likewise Swedish-founded. It was here at "Upland" (from the Swedish "Optland") that Penn's cousin and deputy William Markham had gathered a governing Council. Its little meetinghouse, courthouse, and jail made it evident that this was his colony's first "town." Unsatisfied with its name, Penn immediately changed it from Upland to the Roman-based "Chester."

We have no written record of the *Welcome*'s final sail up the forest-lined Delaware, to its docking at the mouth of a creek half a mile south of the well-known Shackamaxon beach. We do find Penn making himself immediately at home, moving into the same dwelling that Surveyor Holme had commandeered—none other than the house of Elizabeth Kinsey and her surveyor husband Thomas Fairman. Now, again, the Fairmans had to move out until Penn could find something better. Perhaps the promise of rent payment eased this inconvenience for the surveyor, but in a short time he was again annoyed. With rental yet unpaid for the horses he had loaned to Holme, he now had to provide them for a Proprietor too busy to keep up with paying petty bills.

Understandably consumed with bigger matters, Penn traveled quickly northward to see the governor of New York (since it was from the Duke of York's holdings that Pennsylvania had been divided), and then southward to Maryland to pay his respects to its Catholic Governor, Lord Baltimore, with whom there was border-disagreement. Immediately, too, Penn's new "Frame" of government had to be ratified by a local Assembly, a town founded and named, and many thousands of acres of land surveyed. This meant that Fairman had to be "taking the courses of Schuylkill," along which lived many Swedish families. Penn was asking them to move to other properties so that his own "First Purchasers" could have the advantageous riverside locations he had advertised. And as urgent as anything was Penn's desire to talk with the Natives.

Elate in his new environment, the 39-year-old Proprietor pronounced the local "soyle good," with "springs many & delightfull." He boasted to English readers that in a week's time both "poor & rich" families could pack barrels of fish for winter storage. Lying in bed at the Fairmans' house at Shackamaxon, "a bow shot from the River," he could hear huge, caviar-crammed sturgeons leaping. They tasted like veal when roasted, he wrote, and were gourmet fare when pickled. Strawberries, cherries, and mulberries grew in the woods, and almost every Indian village had a set of peach trees. "I like it [here] so well," mused Penn after a few months, "that a plentiful Estate & a great Acquaintance on th' other side" of the ocean could not tempt him back to the familiar English landscape. In fact, if his family had come with him, he would already be considering himself "an adopted American." In a burst of good humor he sent over to King Charles and his brother James several beaver and otter pelts to be used "for Hatts & Muffs."

As Penn's first American spring blossomed, the 80 houses that had already sprung up at the emerging town he named "Philadelphia" included a new one for himself at Front and Market Streets. In the surrounding woods were 300 "farms" or plantations, with 60 petitions for more surveys on Surveyor Holme's desk. It was thus urgent to free up more salable land from Indian ownership. The 10,000-acre Pennsbury deal at the Falls of the Delaware that William Markham had concluded before Penn arrived reached westward only to the Neshaminy Creek. Any land above and beyond this was of course considered unsold by both the Natives and Penn.

In late May 1683 Penn's need for further purchases brought him 30 miles north from Philadelphia for an undocumented but significant parley. This meeting with several "Kings of the Natives" marks a memorable threshold in our story. While neither its precise location nor the names of the Lenape participants would be officially recorded, they were recalled half a century later by an old Native who, as "a little lad," had been there. The participating sachems he could still name in 1730 were *Tamany*, *Hetkoquean* (possibly Tamany's son), and *Mananget*. The place, which he identified with the Lenape name Perkasie, was in the vicinity of the later village of Silverdale in Hilltown Township, Bucks County. From just south of an east-west ridge later called "Nockamixon," the water flowed in two directions—southward from the headwaters of the Tohickon and Neshaminy Creeks to the Delaware River, and southwestward, via a 12-mile-long eastern tributary of the Perkiomen Creek, toward the Schuylkill. Somewhere in that leafy scene—in what Penn might describe as "a Green seat by a Spring, under some shady Trees"—came the only convergence of the lives of two of our story's main characters: 39-year-old William Penn and the "little lad" Sassoonan. While it was indeed only a friendly moment that produced no written deed, that meeting prefigured something more permanent to come, nine miles downstream on the East Branch of the Perkiomen. That was where a lasting home would be found for three other "little lads," grandsons of our third main character, Swiss Hans Stauffer. But that would not happen until 1718—the year when Penn would die back in England—and Sassoonan, troubled by deals that had sent him and his children westward from the ground of their birth, would return from a wigwam on the Susquehanna to Philadelphia, to complain about non-payment for Lenape land.

We may treasure words written some two months after the Perkasie meeting by Penn to England's secretary of state, reporting that he had laid out six counties. Whereas the Lenapes, he mused, "are Savage to us," and "in their Persons & furniture . . . rude," they are admirable in counsel." They are grave, speak seldom [with] interspaces of silence, Short, elegant, fervent. The old sitt in half moon upon the Ground, the middle in the same manner behind them. None speak but the Aged, they haveing Consulted the rest before .... I must Say, that their obscurity consider'd, wanting tradition, example & instruction; they are an extreordinary people.

CHAPTER SIX

Friendship Begun, and Interrupted
1683–1684

WILLIAM PENN felt a "grandeur" in the sound of Lenape names like "Shackamaxon" (where he lived in Thomas Fairman's riverside house) and "Tamany." He learned enough of the Lenape language for simple conversation. In letters to England he attributed to the Natives "a deep natural sagacity." While "careless" in regard to daily provision, they were dignified in speech, instinctive with sense of the landscape, and precise in what they considered fair.

Most striking, by European standards, was the Native mutuality. "Nothing is too good for a friend," wrote Penn;

> give them a fine Gun, Coat, or other thing, it may pass twenty hands before it sticks; light of Heart, strong Affections, but soon spent; the most merry Creatures that live, Feast and Dance almost perpetually; they never have much, nor want much: Wealth circulateth like the Blood . . . and though none shall want what another hath, yet [they are] exact Observers of Property.

Particular about land as they may have seemed, the friendly sachems at Perkasie had surprised Penn by offering to *give* him land beyond what he was asking them to *sell*. He responded quickly to their unusual logic by adding impressive "presents" to the "pay" he agreed on. This was a language that Indians cherished.

The frequent dances, employing "Words, sometimes Songs, then Shouts," which Penn called "canticos," struck him as a form of worship. Two persons sitting "in the middle" led the rest by "Singing and drumming." While all was "done with equal Earnestness and Labour," there was "great appearance of Joy." Penn's reciprocal delight lends some credence to an elderly settler woman's comment that he himself had been known to rise up with the dancers and "beat them all."

Conversation with the headmen at Perkasie left Penn, who had been intimate with British royalty, impressed with "how Powerful the Kings are, and yet how they move by the Breath of their People." They always consulted with their "Old and Wise men" before deciding issues of war, peace, or "Selling of Land." At one land transaction, a sachem sitting in "the middle of an half moon" of his council, with an imitative formation of younger people just behind them, had ordered a man to rise and take their decision to their new friend. "He took me by the hand," wrote Penn, "and told me, That he was ordered by his King to speak to me, and that now it was not he, but the King that spoke, because what he should say, was the King's mind." First explaining his concern for a clear meaning, the Native speaker then described both "the Bounds of the Land they had agreed to dispose of, and the Price." Meanwhile, there was not a whisper or a smile from the other listening Natives. What they had heard here would never be forgotten, and it would take a shrewd person indeed, observed Penn, to outwit them "in any Treaty about a thing they understand."

But to what extent *did* the Natives, whose consciousness included a sentience of being in non-human things, comprehend what their readiness to "sell" or "give" land would lead to in the long run? That is our obvious modern question. Their deeply symbolic wampum, gifts of furs, and approving cheers were not the same coin as the inked inscriptions on parchment which their white counterparts asked them to sign. Of course, their pleasure was evident as they exchanged "Great promises . . . of Kindness and good Neighbourhood" with the friendly English bargainer. "Many Governors," they commented, "had been in the [Delaware] River" before, but none of them "had come himself to live and stay here before." Looking back across seven generations of our own farming on this land, and having at last, like the Lenapes, given it up, we must at least try to imagine both their feelings and how it sounded in William Penn's hearing when, after every sentence of the pledges of mutual respect, the Natives "shouted, and said, Amen, in their way."

Penn's optimistic accounts included, however, an ominous note: the endemic Indian "drunkenness," for which he generically blamed the example of "the Dutch, English and Swedes" who had preceded him. Though ordinarily tractable, when intoxicated, the Natives became erratic and dangerous. A Delaware chief himself had put it roundly: Drink "makes us mad; we do not know what we do, we then abuse one another; we throw each other into the Fire." Liquor could actually become "so dear" to an Indian "that for 6 penny worth of Rum" he would part with five shillings worth of furs. Penn sounds like a personal (and sadly prophetic) witness:

> If they are heated with Liquors, they are restless till they have enough to sleep; that is their cry, Some more, and I will go to sleep; but when Drunk, one of the most wretchedest Spectacles in the World, often Burning & Sometimes killing one another, at which times the Christians are not without danger as well as fear.

In fact, continues Penn, "Because in thos fitts they mischief both themselves & our folks too, I have forbid to sell them any [rum]." This was an overly optimistic statement; no laws then or later proved anywhere nearly effective in stanching the flow of the white man's strong drink to Natives who wanted it. As a Moravian would ruefully observe, "All Indians are excessively fond of rum, and will be drunk whenever they can get it." It would play a very melancholy role in the life of Delaware leader Sassoonan himself.

A month after the memorable woodland conversation at Perkasie in 1683, its substance was confirmed by at least five land-transferring deeds signed in one day at Philadelphia. Busy as that kept Penn, he hosted Tamany and another Lenape leader overnight in his town residence on Front Street. The receipt of items he paid the Natives shows how dependent their people had already become on traders for the tools of their subsistence: lead, gunpowder, awls, hoes, fishhooks, knives, and axes. Women, makers of the sacred wampum, now needed needles, scissors, and kettles. Less absolutely necessary but just as significant were stockings, shirts, combs, hats, caps, blankets, and bells. Only two guns are on the list, which ended with "20 handfulls of wampum."

Strangely, though Tamany had inked this transaction with his own coiled mark, he would soon and repeatedly complain that it had not been followed with full payment. The often-cited legend of Tamany's affability is countered, in fact, by blunt complaints he made in subsequent land dealings. At the early Philadelphia signing, though, all seemed pleasant. On the following day, a Sunday, Penn had six sachems as guests for the midday meal, and afterward took them to the nearby Quaker meetinghouse, where they stayed for most of the First Day gathering.

Agitated that summer of 1684 by political pressures from New York, West Jersey, and Maryland, Penn nevertheless kept his land-purchase program in motion. He rode out from Philadelphia on Thomas Fairman's horses to lay out manors for persons such as his wife Guli, one of her brothers, or another soon-to-arrive Quaker purchaser. In the unmapped woods along the Wissahickon Creek east of the Schuylkill that would soon be called "Whitemarsh," Natives watched surveyors coming to a village they knew as *Umbilicamence*. Here Penn, on behalf of a purchasing family he expected from Ireland, "marked the place and the tree with his own hands." Another manor, which he designated for his namesake son, came from land Fairman was sent to explore just south of the "Perkeaoming" Creek, near its confluence with the Schuylkill from the east. Since not all of that land (future Norriton) was considered valuable, Fairman was allowed to use his own "discression" if he found any "conveniencies" (i.e., desirable features). However, Penn would be annoyed with some of Fairman's decisions in this region, when they seemed made to please other buyers or even himself more than Penn. Indeed, dealing with unsurveyed land could become quite informal. To record the location of the manor designated for wife Guli Penn (future Springfield), the best Fairman could note was that it was at "the Spring where we ate our dinners on a Tree the Indians Chopped a Bough in." Fairman had also been the surveyor for some "Germans" who arrived in October 1683 and, led by Franz Daniel Pastorius, chose 6,000 acres along an Indian trail (future Germantown Avenue) near the Wissahickon Creek.

There was so much land-related activity that Surveyor General Thomas Holme employed another deputy, David Powell, a Welsh Quaker living at "Blockley" (future West Philadelphia). Powell's first main work was to survey a "Welsh Tract" that was to comprise 40,000 acres in "one barony," running "two miles backward" from "the west side of Skoolkill river." He was also soon called into districts in Philadelphia and Bucks Counties where Thomas Fairman had been active. As a result, the two Quaker deputy surveyors became long-term friends. The inexactness of their calculations would sometimes become embarrassingly evident, when it would turn out that they had surveyed the same tract with quite different results in both size and shape. And they almost always measured out more acreage than was specifically called for in the warrants issued to them by the Surveyor General. The "overplus" acreage, after a resurvey, could be sold to later buyers. Having personally walked the ground, Fairman and Powell gained more precise knowledge of all such acreage than anyone else, giving them the option of speculatively leveraging it to their own advantage. From this practice, both men (as well as Surveyor General Holme) were well known to be frequent profiters. Annoying as this was to Penn, he continued employing the two deputies because of their unrivaled and thus invaluable knowledge of the terrain.

It would be none other than the Welsh David Powell who, after 34 years of surveying and the death of his friend Fairman, would both survey and speculate on the Perkiomen land at the center of this story.

In the early 1680s, German-speaking immigrants were a tiny minority around Philadelphia. Penn, wanting them to feel welcome, said nice things about them, and wrote to the Netherlands inviting other Mennonites to "Come here, and serve God with me in a virgin wilderness, which already begins to blossom like the rose." Did he recognize among Germantown's arrivals from Krefeld a cousin of his mother, the widow Grietgen op den Graeff, or her three sons (his own second cousins) Dirk, Herman, and Abraham op den Graeff, living side by side in the infant community? It would be fascinating to know whether he attended a funeral for the aged great-aunt Grietgen, who died six weeks after arriving (a week or two after the death of Surveyor General Thomas Holme's son William).

Germantown's recently-arrived leader Franz Daniel Pastorius, erudite as he was, could lose his way home from the Delaware's bushy bank and, whichever way he looked, could see nothing but "ancient forest." He too was fascinated by its friendly Natives, several of whom, as his arriving ship had paused at Upland (Chester), had rowed out in greeting. When he gave them a drink of liquor, he wrote, they called him "Brother." "Many" of them showed up at the crude, cave-like first house he had dug into the Delaware's bank at Front Street. While at table with William Penn and an Indian "king," Pastorius heard Penn speaking in the Lenape language, describing Pastorius as a *Deutschmann* (German). Later, not only a "king and queen," but other Natives who came visiting "very often," called their host

"Teutschman" (German) and "Carissimo" (most beloved). "I almost always show my regard," observed Pastorius, "by a piece of bread and drink of beer, by which an affection is in turn aroused in them." It was evident that he had "nothing at all to fear from them." The ones he saw first, he noted, "went about naked ... and wore only a cloth about the loins." Later they were "beginning to wear shirts," but continuing to "shave the head, smear the same with grease, and allow a long lock to grow on the right side." Within a very short time, disturbingly, as a cold winter descended, the Natives seemed to be daily decreasing in numbers, leaving Pastorius with the vague impression that they were withdrawing "several hundred miles farther into the country." They were actually said to "hold certain superstitions that just as many Indians must die annually as there are Europeans who come here."

A charming anecdote of Native-white goodwill survives from the hand of another Germantowner, Penn's second cousin Herman op den Graeff. Writing descriptively back to Europe in the same wintry weeks as Pastorius, he reported that "The Indians show themselves very amiable and friendly, and we live together with them very quiet and peaceable. We travel day and night through the forest without the least fear of them." As though in apt illustration of this amity, just as Herman was writing about it, several Natives, including a woman "with her child wrapped in the skin of a wild animal," entered the simple cabin. Her people, being typically mystified by the art of writing, punned with their word for feather or quill as a name for Penn. Observing his visitors' fascination with his penmanship, Herman responded by playfully inviting them to try it for themselves. When this proved impossible, he "took the hand of one" and "guided" it through several German syllables—doubtless imagining the exotic effect on the letter's curious recipients at their Rhenish hearths.

A personal moment with the Natives in that winter of 1683-84 proved particularly memorable for Penn himself. Though a "great frost" had locked the river the Natives called *Manayunk* or *Passyunk* (the Schuylkill) in ice, the Proprietor's urge to know his land took him with surveyor Fairman over 50 miles upstream from Philadelphia, past the Perkiomen and Manatawny tributaries, north to a Lenape "town" called *Monocacy* (just above the later Douglassville in Berks County). With an eye on salability, Penn was glad to find land there that was "generally good, well watered and not so thick of woods as imagined." More importantly, there were "many open places that [had] been old

Indian fields." Later Penn would persuade several Swedish farmers along the Schuylkill at Philadelphia to move up to Monocacy from their plantations whose river-frontage Penn wanted for his English first-purchasers. But in 1684 the population at Monocacy was purely Lenape, with a headman called *Tenoughan* living a stone's throw from the Schuylkill's eastern bank.

Tenoughan's happening to be "ill of a fever" when Penn and Fairman arrived at his riverside wigwam gave his guests a special opportunity for close observation of a Native tradition. The sachem's wife had prepared what Penn called a "bagnio" that looked like an "oven," which she heated with "red hot stones." Creeping in at a little opening, Tenoughan began to sweat and sing, as his wife chopped a hole in the thick ice on the nearby river. Emerging after less than half an hour, drenched with sweat and steaming with vapor, the sachem ran almost naked to the river and repeatedly dunked himself. A brief stay to recover in the bath-house followed, and then he came to his hut, which was large enough to contain his visitors. Wrapping himself in a "woolen mantle," he lay down beside a "long (but gentle) fire in the midst of his Wigwam." After "turning himself several times, till he was dry," remembered Penn, "he then rose, and fell to getting us our Dinner, seeming to be as easie, and well in Health as at any other time."

Penn must have thought he understood the meaning of Tenoughan's song in the wigwam, since he later told a friend in England that it had been a recital first of the exploits of the sachem's people, then of his ancestors', and finally of his own deeds. After which, went Penn's memory, Tenoughan had fallen "into this Rhapsody":

> What is the matter with us Indians, that we are thus sick in our own Air, and these Strangers well? 'Tis as if they were sent to inherit our Lands in our steads; but the Reason is plain, they love the great God, and we do not.

Even if this was merely Penn's interpretation, shaped by the editing of an English friend (in a book appearing 25 years later crediting Penn with having "heard" the song and personally "attested it to be Matter of Fact"), its themes concur with the great land-transferring drama at the core of our story.

Much to Penn's regret, the stubborn competing claim of Lord Baltimore that his ownership extended even north of Philadelphia had not abated, and in the summer of 1684 it became known that Baltimore was about to go to England to seek royal backing for his demands. Penn knew right away that in order not to lose his own claim he would have to end what was only his second summer in Pennsylvania by hurrying back to London. This meant a crush of business: to take care of unsold land (he needed the money!), the mansion partly built at Pennsbury, uncollected quitrents, dissatisfaction in the Pennsylvania Assembly, and an unpopular governing "Frame" (constitution) badly in need of updating and revision. With the Natives, too, negotiations that had seemed finished were re-opening. The influential Tamany, proving unsatisfied with the payment he had been given for land in the previous summer, had to be dealt with. That Penn must have agreed with his claim is evident in a new release he had Tamany sign on June 2, 1684: "Received more severall Matchcoats, Stockings, Shirts, & blanckets besides several Guilders & I acknowledge I have Sold all my land as above said." Even this assurance, however, would prove less than firm. In subsequent dealings with Tamany, Penn would find it necessary to emphasize, in the receipt Tamany signed, the adjective "all." The same word would appear on a deed signed on the following day by another Lenape sachem.

And now, inauspiciously enough, on June 3, 1684, came the threshold in our story when the Perkiomen land at its epicenter—with a certain future farm, mill, and meetinghouse—was to pass out of Lenape possession. The signing group for this transaction was modest, including only Surveyor General Thomas Holme, Penn's personal secretary Philip Lehnman, and two more witnesses meeting at Philadelphia with a lone Lenape sachem. This was no parley on the scale of the previous year's sessions with Tamany at Perkasie on the Perkiomen's East Branch, but a kind of release-signing by a Lenape sachem who had a family interest in the land in question. To be sure, the statement he would agree to sign called it "my land." He seems to have come down alone from somewhere in the watershed referred to by Thomas Fairman as "Perkioma," extending 30 or 40 miles to the north of Philadelphia, to give his consent to the seventh sale of land since Penn had arrived on the Delaware.

And what were the terms for this sale of the 17,000 acres so foundational for future thousands of residents in the Perkiomen watershed? "Upon my own Desire and free offer," read the prepared document,

I Maughoughsin in consideration of Two Match coats, four pair Stockings, and four bottles of sider, do hereby grant and make over all my land upon the Pahkehoma, to William Penn, Prop[rietor] and Governor of Pennsylvania and territories his Heirs and Assigns forever with which I own myself satisfied and promise never to molest any Christians so called yt shall seat thereon by his orders. Witness my hand and seal at Philadelphia ye third day of ye fourth month, 1684.

To these congenial words—which he could not read—the otherwise unrecorded but legally "satisfied" sachem whose name included a Lenape word for "bear," dutifully suffixed his mark:

Done. There would be a home in this land for the "Christians" in the family of Hans Stauffer. After 336 years at this writing, thank you, Maughoughsin. Living and worshiping on the East Branch of the Perkiomen, we have never been molested on your land.

If William Penn had not been present for the Perkiomen deal, it was likely that he was still too busy. The next purchase, coming a day later (for land along the Pennypack Creek in Bucks County), would prove the last to be arranged before he would take ship for London. Hastily writing to his friend James, the Duke of York, that since Lord Baltimore had "gone for England . . . I am following him as fast as I can," Penn asked "that a perfect stop be put to all [Baltimore's] pleadings till I come."

Instructions had to be left with the steward at Pennsbury, where the great manor house in which Penn hoped to raise his family was still under construction. Pressed as he was, he could write, "I would have a kitchen, two larders, a wash-house, a room to iron in, a brew house, and a Milan oven for baking, and a stabling for twelve horses."

Though the Proprietor's overseas absence was meant to be temporary, its approach seemed to dampen the colony's mood. Complaints were coming from prospective land-purchasers worried whether the releases obtained from the Indians were secure. Worse, as already noted, some of the Lenapes themselves were proving dissatisfied with what they had received as payment. Also, Penn's attempts to settle Indian claims out in the Susquehanna Valley were foundering in New York, where Onandagas and Cayugas of the Five Nations would "not consent that the great Penn should settle" on the Susquehanna land they claimed to have won by their own "sweat" in recent warfare. "We have no other lands," they argued, "to leave our wives and children."

For Penn, who by now had sold 700,000 acres of land, it was time to head back to London. Boarding the *Endeavour* in early August 1684, he made the ketch his harbor-keeping office for a flurry of last-minute operations. These included multiple instructions for surveyors, gardening directions for Pennsbury, unwritten oral promises to purchasers of land in the hearing of his secretary, directives that if he died the Proprietorship was to pass to his then eight-year-old son Springett, emotional written farewells to Pennsylvania and Philadelphia, and, in case of his death at sea, a letter to his wife Guli ("the true & great Joy & crown of my life"). He also wrote a hasty but sweeping new will to designate a manor for each of his children, 50,000 acres for "poor families," 10,000 acres for a hospital, and the same amount for a school, totaling approximately 300,000 acres.

The 300 houses in the rapidly expanding Philadelphia that Penn was departing now held, he boasted, over 2,500 residents. His estimate of 6,000 for the colony's Indian population, on the other hand, was perhaps treble the actuality. Though by now Thomas Fairman was surveying far up into Perkioma, neither Penn nor later myth-makers paid serious attention to the unresolved dissatisfactions he was leaving behind among the Lenapes clustering above Penn's manor at the great bend in the Delaware. Already now, and soon after Penn set sail, some of those indigenous people were jealously criticizing the creeping presence of settlers, especially on land never agreed to, north of Pennsbury in the direction of the Tohickon Creek, and still farther north to the "Forks of the Delaware." The Lenapes were especially sensitive about where the Pennsbury property line ran (one of them even marking it angrily with an ax). Within months of the *Endeavor*'s departure there would be letters following Penn, telling that Tamany, with whom there had been such congenial negotiations at Perkasie in the previous spring, was very unsatisfied. He had actually "played the rogue," opined an alarmed Surveyor General Holme, "in hindring our people to plant and settle" on some lands for which Holme had issued survey warrants. In fact, threats by the widely known sachem "to fire their houses" had "so discouraged [potential purchasers] that we cannot get them to go into Bucks County to settle." Holme had checked Penn's papers to see whether or not Tamany had actually acknowledged selling "all his land" between the Pennypack and Neshaminy Creeks. Now the surveyor asked urgently for Penn's opinion on that score. A letter from a neighbor of Pennsbury was in the same vein. "The Indians," it reported, were proving "Much displeased at our English settling upon their Land, and seeme to Threaten us, saying that William Penn hath deceived them not paying for what he bought of them." Some of the northern (Five Nations) Indians who had found out about the deals had "rebuked" the Lenapes for "what they . . . sould so Cheape."

An unusually swift and healthy homeward voyage brought Penn in only seven weeks to the coast of Sussex and the mouth of a creek up which he could be rowed almost to where his Gulielma and three children waited at their Warminghorst estate. To hear him tell it, things in Pennsylvania had been going "sweetly," with no fewer than 18 Quaker meetings thriving in the Province. By the end of October 1684 the man who had conferred with "Indian Kings" in the woods at Perkasie was back along the Thames in one of Europe's grand palaces, sharing his fascinating story with his friend King Charles, James the Duke of York, and an aristocratic circle of Londoners who were proving, he reported, socially "very kind" to their adventurous returning Friend.

CHAPTER SEVEN

Province, Capital, and Colony
1685–1698

HANS STAUFFER, who in his 20s had fled from Bern's Emme River Valley with his aged grandfather, became a grape-grower in the Palatine neighborhood where he had arrived in 1671. His eventual residence, unlike that of his famous "twin" William Penn now in metropolitan London, was in the village of Alsheim, eight miles north of ancient Worms, scene of Martin Luther's epochal *Hier stehe ich*! on the western bank of the Rhine River. Also unlike Penn, whose Gulielma had given birth to seven children (three surviving), it seems that our transplanted Bernese farmer had remained single until his 41st year. Perhaps he had noticed few possible spouses among the Swiss refugees still sifting northward. In any case, in 1685 he married a Zurich-born Anabaptist widow whose husband, Michael Reiff, had died shortly after they had migrated to a village near Stauffer's new location. Küngold Hiestand Reiff brought to her second husband not only money sent up that year from her mother back at the Zurichsee, but her little fatherless daughters Elizabeth and Anneli. Kinget (as she was familiarly known) was still young enough to bear her Bernese Hans three sons whose future migration would take them into the woods of our story's Perkiomen watershed. That move, though, would not come until a quarter-century after the Stauffer-Reiff wedding.

While their little family was young, the Stauffers were not dreaming, as was William Penn, of moving to another homeland. They could viably rent land belonging to the aristocratic owners of the ancient *Schloss* (castle) of Alsheim. Their reputation was likely in line with an official report on Alsheim, noting that three Anabaptist couples in the village had "all demonstrated a neighborly attitude and industry in their work." This was "like their ancestors." Good managers, they were said to "turn everything into money." Recognizing them as having been denied respect in Switzerland, their neighbors had "only heartfelt words of praise for them, which is indeed rare."

On the other hand, there were Mennonites in the village of Kriegsheim, eight miles south of Alsheim, who had been converted into Quakers, whose new manners made them economically unpopular. The convictions they had adopted against paying certain taxes were being punished by official confiscation of their cattle and even furniture. Repeated visits of encouragement by English Friends, including William Penn himself in 1677, had kept them in a network by which they quickly heard of the Quaker settlement begun in 1683 in faraway Germantown. Within two years of the founding of Pennsylvania (and in the year of Hans and Kinget Stauffer's marriage), the oppressed ex-Mennonite Quakers of Kriegsheim had applied for permission to emigrate. Elderly widower Peter Schumacher, whose Mennonite Kolb grandchildren were not following him into the Quaker fellowship, was the senior figure among the Kriegsheimers who in 1685 left for Pennsylvania. Was this departure connected with another visit of Penn to the Palatinate that year? In any case, as the Schumachers passed through the port of Rotterdam, Penn's agent Benjamin Furly, who had known them since visiting Kriegsheim with Penn in 1677, personally helped them to make a small land purchase in the infant Germantown. In London, elderly George Fox was glad to encourage these Schumachers called "German Friends" on their way to a new life. By the following year (1686) almost the entire circle of Mennonites-turned-Quakers in little Kriegsheim had regathered across the Atlantic, six miles north of Philadelphia.

As for Penn, multiple public commitments had him residing, apart from his family, in the Kensington district of London. Here, close to the Palace of Whitehall, he could continually remind his friendly King Charles that more than 1,500 Quakers were languishing in English prisons. Penn had found time to concentrate on their lot when Lord Baltimore temporarily dropped his campaign to establish his northern Maryland border above Philadelphia. This break had also made a quick transatlantic return for Penn seem possible. Meanwhile, he had gone right back to the kind of preaching he had done in his pre-Pennsylvania days, with the familiar result of being arrested twice even before leaving Gulielma and their little children at their country estate. Now in London he was being accused for having suspicious gatherings of Friends at his low-profile residence.

How was it possible, critics wondered, for a Quaker preaching moral behavior to be socially familiar—even intimate—with a King known for having had at least 15 mistresses and a dozen illegitimate children, and who was an undeclared Catholic? And when Charles suddenly had a stroke and died in February 1685, why could Penn remain so close to the new king, Charles' outright Catholic brother James, who attended mass?

There was national danger in the poisoned political atmosphere only a month after James was installed, when the oldest of his deceased brother's illegitimate sons brought a force of 150 soldiers to demand the crown for himself. Quickly defeated and executed, this unfortunate "Duke of Monmouth" had led many of his supporters to his own stern fate. Penn successfully begged pardon from James for 20 of the condemned, but after witnessing a hanging, had to hurry to see a well-known Baptist woman who had given shelter to another rebel gruesomely roasted at the stake. How could the pacifist Quaker stomach the unwillingness of his royal friend James to pardon such a person? Penn did describe to others the weeping of the crowd watching kind-hearted Elizabeth Gaunt arranging the straw around her feet in order to make it burn her more "speedily." Could such a scene be even dreamt of in Penn's Woods?

Hoping meanwhile for good reports from his Province, the busy Proprietor was disappointed. Ship after ship, he complained, brought unpleasant news of expense and dissension back in Philadelphia. Even the trusted Surveyor General Thomas Holme was accused of a troublesome drinking habit. The same issue involved Indians impatiently waiting for payment for land Penn had personally marked for surveying six miles north of Germantown at Whitemarsh. Natives there complained that white "servants" clearing a plantation for purchasers still in England had caused trouble by "making the Indians drunk, then Lying with their Wives, and . . . beating both men and their wives." Disgusting confusion followed: A messenger sent to summon the accused white "servants" to a hearing in Philadelphia got lost in the woods. The Natives themselves, needing time to hunt, asked for a different date, then mistook the new one. Finally, after the misbehaving "servants" appeared before a council presided over by Surveyor Holme, the Indians were reported too "drunk in the woods" to attend, while the accused "servants" were afraid to return to their work.

Holme had recently been bargaining with other Lenape "sachamakers" for land running westward—from the Delaware River at Chester "back into the woods . . . as far as a man can go in two days." The price the increasingly hard-bargaining Natives now expected for land had risen well beyond what had sufficed at the first purchases in 1683, when Tamany had been a friendly negotiator. News that this supposedly affable sachem himself had gone negative triggered an overseas comment from the absentee Proprietor not in line with his legendary reputation of benevolence. "You must make them keep their word," he wrote, treating the Indians "severly when Rogueish and kindly when just." He had given Tamany's people, in a pre-payment, "many matchcoats, stockings & some Guns." If now they proved "rude and unruly," Penn directed, "you must make them keep their word by Just course. . . . The vast number of Matchcoats & other things that I have given . . . should compel them to a better & easier compliance." Since a document Tamany had signed stated definitely that he had "sould all" the land in question, "if the Indians will not punish him, we will & must, for they must never see you afraid of executing the Justice they ought to do." What kind of "justice" the pacifist Penn wished to be "executed" here is not clear. As for Tamany's complaint, it could hardly have been idle, since Penn's agents soon conceded twice, giving additional payments for the land in question.

Nor was Tamany the only Lenape becoming difficult. The land in Bucks County just north of the manor at Pennsbury between the Neshaminy Creek and the Delaware River could not be surveyed or sold, reported Holme to England, because "some of the chief Kings refuseth to sell." Yet Penn persisted in painting an optimistic picture for further purchasers. "So far are we from ill terms with the natives," he wrote, "that we have lived in great friendship." "Our humanity" to them is such that "they generally leave their guns at home, when they come to our settlements; they offer us no affront, not so much as to one of our dogs. If any of them break our laws, they submit to be punished by them, and to this they have tied themselves by an obligation under their hands. We leave not the least indignity to them unrebuked, nor wrong unsatisfied. Justice gains and awes them."

Penn's mood was different regarding the reluctance of land-buying settlers to pay him any quitrent. As already noted, his dream had been that this would have been a continual income stream for his family. It was dismaying, to say the least, while spending another

£1,000 of his own funds for Pennsylvania expenses, to be losing financially instead of gaining from his project. It was unfair, he complained, not only to himself but to the children to whom he dreamed of leaving estates. The lavish manor house at Pennsbury was a case in point. Penn had engaged a good young Quaker manager, James Harrison, but was concerned for the project's finances, and sent agricultural instructions. "Ashes and soot," he imagined, would be "excellent for the ground, grass and corn . . . . I suppose it should be sowed pretty thick for corn; in spring, not so thick. Let me desire thee to lay down as much as thou canst with English grass, and plough up new Indian fields."

Watching "fields" and woods measured and marked out by ever-advancing, chain-marking surveyors, Lenape sachems in what were now called "Philadelphia" and "Bucks" Counties were increasingly uncooperative. And in London, Penn's joy at the King's release of 1,300 Quakers from prison was diluted by reports of dissatisfaction among would-be land purchasers in Pennsylvania. Where a valuable streak of limestone discovered in the Wissahickon watershed just above Germantown promised economic development, rum-stoked Native dances were making nearby newcomers nervous. One night, after a tussle broke out over the rum supply, a terrified young English immigrant unfamiliar with fireflies spread the false news of an attack by Indians "coming with firebrands to sett [a] House on fyre." Making inquiry, Surveyor Holme found only disgruntled Natives still waiting for payment for their land. Their disappointed chief, Swanpees, who had readily signed up to sell land before Penn had even arrived in 1682, had now given up and retreated 35 miles back into the woods of Bucks County. Even there some of his people were threatening to kill Quaker surveyor Israel Taylor if he measured "any more land before it be bought." Holme had to report to Penn in London that his current transactions with "the Bucks Indians" were "long and chargeable." The Lenape were confirming their reputation, which Penn himself had acknowledged, of being exact negotiators. Sensing the growing monetary value of their land, they were demanding a higher rate of payment which Holme confessed "could not be avoyded." He asked Penn's secretary for immediate shipment of the goods agreed on for payment, since the Natives would now allow "no lines run" over their land until "all is paid." At the same time, any delay increased pressure on Holme from the opposite direction—the would-be settlers and speculators accusing Pennsylvania of not laying out tracts for which they had paid.

Indeed, the process of land acquisition in Pennsylvania that would later be lyrically celebrated could be anything but amicable. In the words of a later Quaker surveyor, it was "always attended with contest." Poor Holme, while speculatingly acquiring quite a few acres for himself, caught it from all sides. The Natives bargained hard; his deputy Israel Taylor failed to hand in the required share of the surveying fees; deputy Thomas Fairman was jealous of his position; and potential land-buyers were bitter at his delays. "Didst thou but know," Holme wrote to Penn in London, "what hard speaches I have met with from many about Lands (thy selfe not escaping their Lashes)." "Must lands be kept waste," a frustrated buyer had demanded, while "we . . . cannot have lands to settle upon?" Others who had paid Penn years earlier were likewise angry at not getting their grants laid out. He could tell much more about all this, Holme wrote, but knew "it would not please" his employer.

Meanwhile, Lenapes along the Neshaminy and the Perkiomen, hardly considering their unsold woods to be "kept waste," were as concerned about fairness to their children as Penn was about his.

Penn continued his promotional efforts, with another tour in Holland and the Rhineland in 1686. "A great many Dutch and Germans," he predicted, would come to Pennsylvania in the following year. As if in fulfillment of this, in 1687 the Mennonite families of Amsterdam businessmen Dirck Keyser and Willem Ruttinghuýsen (Rittenhouse) bought house lots in Germantown. Meanwhile, Penn admitted knowing that his absence was "extreamly uneasy to [his] Province." He wanted his people to know that "I pray with my whole Soul to God, my father, that he would please to bring me among them." But how did they think he could "budge" from England until he was completely sure Lord Baltimore's takeover claim had been ruled out? Should he hurry abortively over to Pennsylvania only to have to rush "soon back" to London? That would defeat his own cherished aim to permanently "Americanize" his family. And wasn't it better for both Pennsylvanian and English Quakers that he stick close to King James who, though a strong Catholic, continued to be, as Penn claimed, "perticulerly Kinde to me"? Quakers should be glad for this strategic friendship which enabled Penn to be "an instrument to open the Prison Dores for our Brethren all over the nation."

It was increasingly annoying to get "bills for famely matters" at the Pennsbury manor, while of the £500 from quitrents Penn considered already due, he could not "gett a penny." Never exact in financial figures, he could certainly express indignation. Coming as close to an oath as a Quaker might, he wrote, "God is my wittness, I lye not, I am above Six thousand pounds out of pocket." The Pennsylvania people "think not about my supply." If they would only do the decent thing, providing a "table, cellar and stable with a barge [on the Delaware River] for the service of [their] Governor," he could consider trying to come. But to be "so baffled" by people he had helped was "hot to put up" with. "Now I desire thee," he wrote to his Pennsbury steward, "to draw no more upon me for one penny." There was actually nothing he wanted more in the world, "next to my dear family's life, than that I may see poor Pennsylvania." Gulielma too, having recently birthed another child, was willing to come this time. But Penn was not going to plan a return while there was so little encouragement from the people of his colony.

In England, Penn had at least some respect. "The King is kind to me and friends," he reported, "and [Quaker] Meetings [are] open again." James had in fact so trusted Penn as to send him to negotiate personally with William, King of Holland (and James' own son-in-law). It was also due to Penn's influence that in April 1687 the Catholic James proclaimed a (short-lived) liberty of conscience to all English citizens, removing the hated loyalty tests and penalties. The King was even known to have attended when Penn preached to an audience of thousands, perhaps when it was reported that a large meetinghouse could "not neare hould ye people that came to heare him."

Unfortunately for Penn, the political critics of the King were growing so suspicious of his Catholic sympathies that they were ready to replace him with his Protestant son-in-law and daughter, William and Mary of the Netherlands. And this did happen. When the new King actually made his landing in Britain in 1688, James fled, coming back only briefly before slipping into France, and later mounting a futile landing of his own in Ireland, to retake the throne. When it was soon reported that the exiled King had written a letter back from France to his old Quaker friend, Penn was accused more hotly than ever of being a secret Catholic. Again and again he had to protest his innocence, and for several years had to avoid public notice. Though after some delay the new King William acknowledged Penn's harmlessness, he was in continuous danger of arrest by jealous officials, especially after he preached at George Fox's funeral in 1691.

Though essentially in hiding, Penn kept on writing, and in 1690 proposed a second economic venture in Pennsylvania. Philadelphia, he exaggerated, had "advanced from a wood, to a good forwardness of building" with over "one thousand houses finished in it." He was now proposing "another City" 70 miles west near the Susquehanna, a branch of which, when linked to the headwaters of the Schuylkill, provided "the Common Course of the Indians with their Skins and Furr's into our Parts." That was a note meant to attract businessmen. More important for settlement was what Penn called "the known goodness of the soyll" in this future "Garden Spot" to be named "Lancaster County." Not to be overlooked was "the Pleasantness, and Largeness of the [Susquehanna] River," which was "broader than the Thames at London bridge," and ran, according to the Indians, from "many miles above the Place intended for this Settlement." And even beyond that, for consideration by investors, were the commercial implications of the potential "Traffic and Intercourse" resulting from Pennsylvania's being geographically "the Center of all the English colonies upon the Continent of America."

To encourage a quick response, Penn promised—"if God please"— to return to his colony "with what speed I can, and my Family with me, in order to [establish] our future Residence." But as his affairs in England intervened, the Susquehanna proposal failed to take immediate form. Still, Philadelphia speculators stayed alert: for them, land dealings were the main possibility of big money. And for surveyors, too, the land radiating out from Philadelphia was not only something to measure, but real estate to leverage. An example of this in 1688 was the equal partition of a tract Thomas Fairman had bought four years earlier among a set of four young Quaker brothers—the Waltons— who named their settlement after their ancestral Byberry in England. As noted earlier, Fairman, whose personal lifetime purchases would total over 20,000 acres, was notorious for including more space ("overplus") in a survey than called for in a warrant issued by the Surveyor General. Inside knowledge of where such surplus patches of woods remained unbought gave a surveyor personal advantage in speculation. Penn, hearing of some of Fairman's maneuvers, remained suspicious of his fellow Quaker, as well as of the Welsh David Powell, the main surveyor in and around the huge Welsh Tract west of the Schuylkill. Yet, as noted, because of their valuable knowledge, Penn would call on both of them for important tasks, such as laying out a manor along the Schuylkill for his 15-year-old namesake son William.

Nine years after Tamany's people had given Penn a receipt for his payment for their land, they impatiently demanded that they were still owed nine guns, 10 matchcoats, and 10 blankets. Once again Pennsylvania's Commissioners of Property, sensitive to the seriousness of this claim, responded with two dozen rolls of bread and two gallons of rum, followed soon thereafter with "six guns of a grade better than ordinary, ten Dutch blankets, ten kettles," and more bread and beer. Another "King" from the Neshaminy watershed, Hetkoquean (possibly Tamany's son), was also officially recorded as resenting "the unkindness of the English to the Indians here," and saying that recent settlers were not likely "to hold the land much longer," because the Natives had not been "satisfied for it." Only after receiving the new payments would he and three others again sign away "all their right to lands lying between the Neshaminy and Poquessing from the river Delaware."

The Natives' insistence on exact agreement was so strong, remarked an observer, that if a person dealing with them would try to change a "first offer or Bargain, it would be very difficult for that Party to get any Dealings with them any more, or to have any farther Converse with them." This seemed admirable to observer Gabriel Thomas, who remarked further that "they never interrupt or contradict one another 'til two of them have made an end of their Discourse; for if never so many be in Company only two must discourse at a time, and the rest must keep silence."

In 1694 it was finally a relief for Pennsylvania officials, after the repeated dealings with Tamany, to find him more satisfied. "Wee and the Christians of this [Delaware] river," he was now recorded as saying, "have allwayes had a free rode way to one another, & tho' sometimes a tree has fallen across the rode yet wee have still removed it again, & kept the path clean, and wee design to Continou the old friendshipp that has been between us and you." Three years later, signing his last land deal known to historians, the famous sachem mentions that his son Andrew "is to be king after my death." This directive, however, was not to be fulfilled. And the longest-term follower in Tamany's role, the "little lad" Sassoonan who had watched Tamany converse with Penn at Perkasie in 1683, would be of a much less challenging temperament than Tamany.

Not only in Bucks County, but northward up the Schuylkill and along the Brandywine Creek in Chester County, "Indian" tensions were recurrent. Observers were reporting that the Native population was shrinking and retreating. "Many of these savages have died," wrote Pastorius in Germantown, "so that there are hardly more than a fourth part of the number existing that were to be seen when I came to the country ten years ago." In 1694 the sachem Hetkoquean called his people "week and verie few in number." Gabriel Thomas claimed that "The Indians themselves say, that two of them die, to every one Christian that comes here." In 1697 a Swedish pastor near Philadelphia wrote vaguely that the Natives, though friendly, had become "very scarce, so that only a few times do they appear. Here at Passyunk, where my parsonage is, there were formerly many thousands, but now there are none. God has exterminated them through contagious diseases, war among themselves, etc."

As the woods above Philadelphia echoed increasingly with the thud of axes, the Natives were withdrawing northward to Schuylkill tributaries such as the Manatawny, Allegheny, and even the Tulpehocken Creek. While this might reduce tensions, Philadelphia officials were nervous in regard to fur traders in the Schuylkill Valley. Names such as Bezaillion and Letort made their French identity obvious, hinting at potential disloyalty to the British during a currently raging "Nine Years' War" or "King William's War" in both Europe and Canada. Officials in Philadelphia sent the Swedish farmer Lasse Cock, conversant in Lenape language, up the Schuylkill Valley to investigate. As it would turn out, the retreating Native presence would send the French traders west from the Schuylkill to the Susquehanna, leaving behind a name-change for the Schuylkill's main western tributary, the Lenape *Sacknack*, now called "French Creek."

The war's international impact was felt by the Lenapes themselves, as they were invited by belts of wampum to follow the leadership of the larger Five Nations (Iroquois), whose location was closer to the British-French military maneuvers in Canada. But there was no Lenape enthusiasm for war. "Having allwayes been a peaceable people, & resolving to live so, & being but weak and verie few in number," they declared at Philadelphia, they could not "assist" the Five Nations'

Senecas and Onondagas in warfare; "and having resolved among ourselves not to goe, doe intend to send back this their belt of Wampum." In fact, for another half-century the issue of how the Lenapes were related to the larger northern tribes would remain sensitive, and would eventually leave with the Lenapes a painful memory of manipulation.

Happily for Pennsylvanians, the currently transpiring "Nine Years' War" did not physically visit them. Not so fortunate, in its European phase, were the Swiss-born Mennonites who had moved northward into the Rhineland. In 1689 hundreds of them lost their painfully restored *hofs* to French soldiers sent by a vengeful King Louis XIV to torch the Palatinate. Worms, just south of Alsheim, lost to the flames even the horizon-defining cathedral beside which Luther had defied Pope and Emperor, and similar destruction left Oppenheim, a two-hour walk north of Hans' and Kinget's home, in decades-long decay. In such a landscape there was reduced hope for a peaceful domestic future.

William Penn, too, living, writing and preaching in London, had an agenda of problems. Bitter complaints of political squabbles and moral conditions in Pennsylvania were taming the joy of his "Holy Experiment." In 1692 King William's officials took the Pennsylvania governorship away from Penn, transferring it to the governor of New York. Meanwhile, whether in prison or remaining as much as possible out of daily notice, Penn kept on writing, adding ever more apothegms to a new edition of his earlier book, *Some Fruits of Solitude*. He had this collection of aphorisms, written while maintaining a low public profile, published anonymously to keep himself out of jail. Readers to this day can find in these proverbs the spiritual understandings of Penn's dream for his republic. He could write, for example, from his American experience (in his #268), "When the poor Indians hear us call any of our Family by the Name of Servants, they cry out, What, call Brethren Servants! We call our Dogs Servants, but never Men."

In 1693 the dreamer who had visited Paris, Amsterdam, Heidelberg, and the woods of Perkasie addressed the whole international military debacle with an *Essay towards the Present and Future Peace of Europe*. Quoting Cicero's *cedant arma togae* ("let military yield to civilian power"), he suggested a "European dyet" or parliament to overcome the endemic curse of Christian wars which, he asserted, were basically "the duels of princes." His unpopular passion on this subject kindled a prophetic eloquence that can stir answering emotion when read three centuries later along the East Branch of the Perkiomen Creek in Pennsylvania.

> Not only Christians against Christians, but the same Sort of Christians have embrewed their Hands in one another's Blood: Invoking . . . the Good and Merciful God to prosper their Arms to their Brethren's Destruction: Yet their Saviour has told them, that he came to save, and not to destroy the Lives of Men: To give and plant Peace among Men . . . . Of all his Titles this seems the most Glorious as well as comfortable for us, that he is the Prince of Peace . . . . And it is very remarkable, that in all the New Testament he is but once called Lyon, but frequently the Lamb of God; to denote to us his Gentle, Meek and Harmless Nature; and that those, who desire to be the Disciples of his Cross and Kingdom, for they are inseparable, must be like him.

With no reference to its Christology, this prescient proposal was destined to be cited at the founding of the League of Nations, and again in the formation of the United Nations organization.

Soon after the *Essay* appeared, its author's lost governorship was restored. Since, however, this story of Pennsylvania land is only partly William Penn's, it can only briefly record events in his family such as the death of his beloved Gulielma in his arms in 1694. Their three surviving children—Springett, Laetitia, and William—were still in their teens. The grieving widower was of the same age (49) as that of his own father at death, but was far from being retired, and still expecting to return to his troubled Province. Within two years he had found a second affluent Quaker bride, Hannah Callowhill of Bristol. Only half his age and only six years older than her stepson Springett (who died a few weeks after the wedding), Hannah Callowhill was young enough to give birth as often as had Gulielma. If less devoutly tempered than Guli, she was just as loyal a Quaker, and an excellent manager of familial economy. This would become important, as disturbing demands for debt-repayment increased from the family of Philip Ford, the aging secretary to whom Penn owed an enormous, interest-expanding debt now 15 years old. He kept begging Pennsylvanians to send him money he felt they owed him, insisting, "This is no Anger, tho I am grieved, but a cool & resolved thought." In 1696 he wrote, "I have not seen Six pence these twice six years." His "Plantation" at Pennsbury, though "a lovely place and good beginning," was already "ruinous." Before long he would complain that the colony had cost him £20,000.

In Pennsylvania, surveyors were pushing northward from Philadelphia through the woods toward the eastern shoulder of the Schuylkill Valley, an area called Perkioma. Thomas Fairman, working in 1694 on behalf of an absentee English speculator, laid out what he claimed were 7,280 acres in what Welsh settlers would name "Gwynedd Township." The frequently troubling inaccuracy of his hasty work would be illustrated when his friend David Powell, who had laid out the much greater Welsh Tract west of the Schuylkill, was called to "resurvey" the same tract, and calculated it to contain 4,169 acres more than Fairman had found. This meant that Fairman had left an "overplus" of more than 4,000 acres, clearly showing his speculative interest in this northward advance. In 1699 he sold 1,100 acres to a newly arrived Quaker, while surveying up into what would become a township with the indigenous name *Skippack* ("Wet Land"). The Gwynedd area's lack of any large stream may have made it less of a Native-favored place (though there was a trail through it). The Lenape withdrawal up the Schuylkill watershed had already become so complete that Gwynedd's future historian Howard Jenkins, looking for "evidence . . . concerning the Indians in Gwynedd," would find "next to nothing."

For two years after the elderly Surveyor General Thomas Holme died in 1696, Fairman, who probably knew the Delaware Valley terrain better than any other white man, entertained the possibility that he might be Holme's replacement. But Proprietor Penn, disappointed with Fairman's unpredictability, instead sent news from England that he had chosen Edward Penington, a stepbrother of his deceased wife Gulielma, for the position. Fairman complained bitterly. In his own opinion, he was one of the most deserving and original settlers in Pennsylvania, not to speak of his children, who in his incorrect claim had been the very first white babies born on land in Penn's colony. Before long Fairman would designate another of his purchases, this time of 5,000 acres, for one of his own two little sons. Indeed this concern (land for one's posterity) is a transatlantic motif uniting all the families in our story—those of Penn himself, his future secretary James Logan, surveyors Fairman and Powell, Hans Stauffer and, most poignantly of all, Sassoonan, the future titular head of the Indians now regathering along the upper Schuylkill and its western tributary, the Tulpehocken Creek.

Penn consented to reside with his new wife in her hometown of Bristol, a hundred miles west of London. Though Hannah soon lost their first child in infancy, she proved willing during her next pregnancy to move to her husband's overseas plantation. Meanwhile, Penn's outlook remained exceptionally broad, as when conversing earnestly with the young Russian Peter Alexeyevich (future Peter the Great) then visiting England, or in a publication anticipating by eight decades the formation of the United States of America: *A brief and plain scheme how the English colonies in the North parts of America . . . may be made more useful to the crown and one another's peace and safety*. He also traveled diplomatically again to the Rhineland to look into reports of persecution of the Mennonites there, after which King William sent a letter in their defense to the Palatine Elector.

Crowds, realizing that Penn was planning to leave again for Pennsylvania, kept coming to hear him preach, and the local Quaker meeting gave him a very complimentary testimonial. God had given him, they testified, not only unique "wisdom" but a remarkable "Interest in the hearts of princes and our Rulers Even in time of Sore persecution and great Sufferings." In return Penn issued a devout *Epistle of Farewell*, urging "the people of God called Quakers" in Europe to "Let your eyes be to the Lord, and wait upon Him; walk with Him; and He will walk and dwell with you."

By the time his ship was ready to sail, Penn had found in Hannah's town a secretary, a bright young Quaker schoolmaster named James Logan. And in a brisk move between spiritual and economic poles while waiting for the *Canterbury* to embark, Penn arranged for a major land sale, this time of 60,000 acres to be laid out by Thomas Fairman on the east side of the Perkiomen Creek. The result, to be called "Gilbert's Manor," would be only a few miles south of where the grandchildren of Hans Stauffer, who had tended castle grounds by the Rhine, would deforest new soil in America.

CHAPTER EIGHT

Land, Land, Land
1699–1701

On September 9, 1699, 15 years after William Penn had rushed back to London from his half-built mansion in Bucks County, the 55-year-old Proprietor boarded the *Canterbury* at Cowes for what he thought might be his final return to his colony. This time he had the companionship of young second wife Hannah (six months pregnant) and flirtatious daughter Tishe. His recently married son William had declined to come along. A young steward-and-housekeeper couple had been found for Pennsbury Manor. And, as on Penn's first western voyage, there was horseflesh on board, this time a magnificent white stallion named Tamerlane. Most significantly for Pennsylvania's future was the shrewd daily attention of the recently hired secretary less than half Penn's age, a brilliant Scotch-Irish bachelor schoolteacher named James Logan. "Before I was 13 years of age," as he put it, he had "learned Latin, Greek, and some Hebrew" in his own father's school.

While the employer and secretary shared Quaker affiliation and great personal confidence, they were of contrasting spiritual tonality. This was illustrated in an entertaining if possibly exaggerated anecdote told many years later by none other than Benjamin Franklin. When an unknown vessel approached the west-bound *Canterbury*, went the tale, the captain, fearing the worst, cleared the decks and told Penn's party to go into the cabin. All obeyed except Logan, who was then told to man a cannon until it was clear that the other ship was not hostile. Afterward, according to the tale, Penn asked Logan why he hadn't acted according to Quaker pacifism. In return Logan asked why, since he was Penn's servant, Penn hadn't ordered him to leave the deck. "But thee was willing enough," jibed the young secretary, "that I should stay and help to fight the ship when thee thought there was danger." Whether or not such an exchange happened, the attitudinal difference between the two loyally friendly men would be obvious in their future careers.

There was joy and booming cannon at Chester on the Delaware when the *Canterbury* arrived in December. An unfortunate young celebrant lighting the antique gun lost an arm in the resultant explosion, moving a sympathetic Penn to pay both medical and funeral bills. At Philadelphia, a crowd streaming "down to the water-side" included Shackamaxon's Thomas Fairman. The veteran surveyor, by whom Penn had considered himself "basely injured" in the laying out of a manor along the Schuylkill, now "denied it," Penn would remember, already "on the Canterbury." Henceforth, James Logan would never respect Fairman. On the other hand, Fairman was dazzled by the general welcome to his employer, writing back to William Jr. that "The highest terms I could use would hardly give you an idea of the expectation and welcome that thy father received." Even the "ringleaders" of Penn's political opposition appeared glad to welcome him back.

For the long-absent Proprietor, it was emotional to see his beloved "greene country town" stripped of its aboriginal trees. Whereas on his first coming to the Delaware there had been only one good house (Fairman's, just upstream at Shackamaxon), 17 years later there were hundreds. For his own part, Penn was eager to live in his woods-surrounded mansion now finished at Pennsbury, thirty miles up the Delaware. But with Hannah nearing her time, they stayed in town for a month with an affluent friend, Edward Shippen, and then in the best house in town, owned by merchant Samuel Carpenter, where Hannah gave birth to her "Johnne" (Johnny). As the only Penn child born outside of England, he would be sometimes called, in dealings with the Natives, "the American."

When Johnny was only a few months old, he was taken with his family upriver to Pennsbury, probably on his father's cherished little tide-borne "barge" to avoid the otherwise necessary rough land-journey. The expansive red brick manor house, squarely facing the Delaware and a mid-river island like the one downstream at Shackamaxon, was without comparison for luxury in Pennsylvania. It was in pattern a gracious English manorial country seat, framed in a village of smaller structures. Living in family clusters in the surrounding primeval woods were the Lenapes from whose relatives Penn's cousin William Markham had bought Pennsbury's land 18 years earlier. Here, Penn dreamed, where his young Hannah, waited on by slaves, began ordering many genteel amenities, was where their progeny would live and thrive for unfolding American generations. And beside them the Lenapes expected to be their friendly neighbors.

Wanting extra living space, and quite ready to pay the Indians for it, Penn looked around into the adjacent forest. Just north of Pennsbury, the area called Tohickon had "rich land . . . much cleared by the Indians." When Penn found that Thomas Fairman had never yet surveyed that far, he was greatly disappointed. But "the Indians have been with me about it," he noted, while ordering a supply of "match coats" and rum with which to treat them.

Philadelphia politics and Lord Baltimore's still-threatening claim kept Penn busy, though not enough to prevent him from ordering a resurvey of the Pennsbury acreage. This time not Thomas Fairman, but fellow Quaker David Powell, living at Wicaco near Philadelphia, was employed. Fairman himself was continuously discontent, complaining that Penn's young secretary Logan was allowing most of the hay on the Schuylkill island owned by the Fairmans at Shackamaxon to be harvested by other parties, leaving the Fairmans only enough to feed two cows. The aggrieved deputy surveyor, whose "Famely of Children" he incorrectly claimed to be the "First borne English" in Pennsylvania, demanded of Penn, "Have I no merrits"? Unimpressed, the Proprietor ordered several compasses brought up to Pennsbury where he himself could see the surveying done satisfactorily. "Take care," he instructed secretary Logan, "that I have five hundred acres in every township that is laid out, and that the surveyor do me right therein."

What "the Indians" felt and said to each other as they watched Fairman's or Powell's chain carriers leaving unwelcome marks on tree trunks is not on record. Penn himself, concerned that the Natives be satisfied, was troubled to hear of a trader named "Captain Hans" treating them with rum just north of Tohickon along the Lehigh River. Summoning Hans for an accounting, Penn also invited the Indians to come and discuss this at Pennsbury. He told his secretary to look into an incident down at Shackamaxon, the traditional Native site of diplomacy where the Fairmans now lived, and where some Senecas from the Five Nations had come down to talk with the Lenapes. These visitors, Penn heard, had been alarmed by the sound of gunfire beside the Delaware—the last thing he would approve of because of his concern for good relations with the Five Nations. If the shooting had been done intentionally to scare them, wrote Penn, whoever was responsible should be "severely punished."

While temporarily home-bound with a leg injury, Penn stayed in daily written correspondence with officials in 30-mile distant Philadelphia, eagerly following what was transpiring across his great surveying campaign. A legal struggle had broken out over a 22,000-acre tract in the Manatawny watershed, 40 miles up the Schuylkill. Called "Falckner's Swamp" after a German who had gained ownership, this was the future site of Pottstown and the townships of Frederick and Hanover (named for German royalty). Here, too, before long, Indians were protesting that they had not been paid. A few miles on upstream, where Penn had visited Indians in 1684 and the future Douglassville would appear, David Powell now surveyed 10,000 acres for a special grant to Swedish families Penn had asked to surrender their farms along the Schuylkill near Philadelphia so that he could allot that favorable space to some of his English Quaker "First Purchasers." Though not many Swedes would actually move up to the village called *Morlatton* by the Indians, those who did got along so well with the Natives that a future township laid out there would be called "Amity."

As the grid of surveys and land sales crept steadily up the woods north and west from Philadelphia, Lenapes having moved as far west as the Susquehanna River were feeling their own tremors. Two sachems brought their concerns all the way east from Conestoga (future Lancaster County) to Pennsbury on the Delaware, where Penn rewarded them with gifts for agreeing to his purchase of their land jointly from the governor of New York and the Five Nations. Nearer than Conestoga, in the upper Brandywine Creek watershed of Chester County, a manor called "Springtown" (future Wallace Township, near Downingtown) had been laid out by Penn's brother-in-law, Surveyor General Edward Penington. Still closer to home, in Bucks County, was another fertile "Swamp," the future Richland Township and Quakertown area. Purchasing 6,000 acres there in 1701 was a Welshman named Griffith Jones. Having paid for land before immigrating, Jones had been assigned acreage with his people in Gwynedd, only to find when he came over that it had been surveyed for other buyers. The meadowland-type bottom he now received in the Swamp neighborhood looked so promisingly "rich" that before long secretary Logan would send both Fairman and Powell there to lay out "ten thousand acres of good land" for the Penn family. Logan himself, already acutely sensitive to the monetary element in any news of land transactions, asked for 2,000 acres at what was now called "Richland."

Two other deals at this time, one in Bucks and the other in Philadelphia (later Montgomery) County, sped the Lenape retreat from old watersheds. Directly north of the Pennsbury mansion, between the Tohickon Creek and Delaware River (future Tinicum Township), a 5,000-acre tract was surveyed in 1701 for a manor in the name of a Lower Rhenish German investor named Johannes Strieper. Eighteen years earlier, as one of Penn's "first Purchasers," Strieper had paid for that much acreage, but a manor had not been laid out. The tract had since been surveyed, but the Tohickon location proved still too sensitive to the Lenapes to allow subdivision for resale to settlers. Another 25 years later the official explanation offered was that there was "a claim made to the land by the Indians, who say they never yet sold it."

By comparison, in the very months of the undevelopable Strieper deal in 1701, one of Strieper's early co-First Purchasers from the Lower Rhine was having no Indian issues in unloading his long-idle grant of 6,000 acres. This was Dirk Sypman, whose allotment was now laid out in the woods at Skippack, directly northwest of Philadelphia, to a Dutch-speaking speculator named Matthias van Bebber. In contrast to what was going on in the woods around Tohickon, hardly a trace of Indian presence would thereafter be recorded in documents of "Bebberstaun" (Skippack), considerable acreage of which was being taken up by Mennonites now spilling beyond filled-up Germantown.

This sampling of the wave of surveys radiating out from Philadelphia represents only a fraction of the irreversible rolling back of the Lenape land-base. One can only imagine what the unfamiliar chop and crash echoing northward across those memory-haunted woods felt like to those whose home it had been.

Now came a threat to Penn's own dream, newly disturbed by an attempt by his King's advisors to have all of the English colonies placed under direct royal administration. This would have ruled out the unique role Penn had been promised in his original charter of 1681, since it would leave him, though *still owner* of the land, without the right to *govern* its people. In alarm, he wrote home to his undependable 21-year-old son William, instructing him to defend the original agreement in court. He was to argue, wrote the Proprietor, that his family's basic motivation for taking up Pennsylvania in the first place had been the opportunity of having the "government" of it. The very vision of a noble experiment had been predicated on this chance to *oversee* a new kind of society. "As to Land," Penn now wrote, "it is the Natives" (which was why, morally, he had to pay them for it). Why, after all, would he have come "3,000 miles off to convert a mere Desert into an improved and faithful country"? It had been one thing to own domesticated real estate in England, "but here [there] was nothing but mere Creation"—a woods that was not turning out to be the economic prize he had imagined. It was precisely having "the government," wrote Penn, that "was our greatest inducement," and it was on this promise that "we have buried our blood and bones, as well as our estates, to make it what it is." To be a proprietor now "without powers" to govern would be like having a ring with no jewel in it.

If son William would hear any objection that Quakers should not govern at all because they would not fight to protect their King's colony, he was to quote his father. "King Charles, King James & King William," he would argue, "knew that we are a Quaker colony, it was so intended." And if the military issue proved a sticking point, Penn would be willing to let the armed defense of his Province be handled by the adjacent non-pacifist "government of New York."

The aging Proprietor devoutly hoped that his Quaker purchasers who had "come so far and . . . endured and spent so much" to live "with more ease [of conscience] than at home" would not be persecuted here too simply because "our consciences are tender." And, just as certainly, strange as this pacifist ideal may have seemed in most venues of Europe, it was beginning to wave like a banner of hope for pockets of religiously dissident people. Within a decade, the tender consciences of Mennonites renting *hof*s in the Rhineland would find unprecedented surcease at hearths they would carve from Penn's Indian-cleared Woods.

Frustrated by his purchasers' stubborn non-payment of the quit-rent he had expected, carped at by Philadelphians considering his constitution too restrictive, alarmed by demands for repayment of his large loans to his English secretary Philip Ford, and regretfully realizing that he must quickly leave Pennsylvania again to defend it from political enemies in London, Penn could at least take pleasure in his frequent "treating" with the Natives for land. In April 1701 he personally welcomed to Philadelphia 40 "Indians Inhabiting upon and about the River Sasquehannah," to further his claim on their land. The language used in the resultant treaty, recorded by Penn's officials, breathed fraternal optimism. Since "hitherto there hath always been a good understanding & Neighbourhood," ran the statement, "there shall be forever hereafter a firm and lasting peace Continued between Wm. Penn, his Heirs & successors, & the [Native] Kings and Chiefs, & their successors." The new and old inhabitants of Pennsylvania "shall forever hereafter be as one Head & One Heart, & live in true friendship & Amity as one People." On the one hand, the Indian "Kings" (nine of whom "signed" their marks) promised to allow no European inhabitant "to be Hurt, Injured or defrauded by any of their Indians," and on the other, Penn's government would not allow "Any Act of Hostillity or Violence wrong or Injury, to or against any of the Said Indians, but shall on both sides at all times readily do Justice." The friendliness of this rhetoric, obviously still animated by the Proprietor's Quaker dream, was cheerfully confirmed by the Indians' treaty-concluding shout of "Joha!"

Following up the favor of this visit from Susquehanna Indians, Penn "traversed the wilderness" westward into the woods of future Lancaster County. There are varying local traditions on this subject. One has to do with Penn's visit in the autumn of 1700 to a village, near the Gap and future Sadsburyville, of Shawnees led by a headman named *Opessah*. Having just migrated northward to flee the incursion of settlers on their former land, they were appreciative of Penn's welcome to a new home in the woods now in his name. Here, according to local folk memory, Penn witnessed a "dancing of the squaws in the 'Shawnee Garden'" where, "according to the traditions of [the later] oldest inhabitants who lived during the last century, he danced a jig along with them in the garden, and partook of a feast of roast deer and green Indian corn baked in the ashes."

Farther west at Conestoga, Penn left an even more lasting and intimately favorable impression. A traveling companion recorded, "We lived nobly at the king's palace in *Conestoga*." This meant that they had spent at least one night on the ground floor of a wigwam in a forested landscape that within two decades would be cleared for farms of German-speaking Mennonites. An unusual memory that Penn would take back to England was his being visited during the night by one of the Indian women, whose obvious attentions he of course declined. (A later Moravian missionary would observe that this could almost be expected. Penn himself would later be distressed to hear that one of his deputy governors, visiting the same Native community, would not observe the same personal code.)

Penn's associating with the Natives in the summer of 1701 evoked a long-remembered critical comment from a notable character, the Pietist hermit Johannes Kelpius who lived in the woods along the Wissahickon Creek near Philadelphia. Theorizing that the Indians might be one of the lost tribes of Israel, this German mystic was too otherworldly for land ownership himself, but concerned enough to address the subject prophetically. Four years after Penn's Conestoga visit, Kelpius wrote to Germany that Penn, while present at a Native "cantico" (dance celebration), had taken the opportunity to preach to the Indians on "faith in the God of Heaven and Earth." While the Indian response, as Kelpius renders it, is told in his own German wordage, the critical ring of it speaks to our story's theme of land and Indians. "You bid us," begins the Native answer,

> [to] believe in the Creator and Preserver of Heaven and Earth, though you do not believe in Him yourself, nor trust in Him. For you have now made your own the land we held in common amongst ourselves and our friends. You now take heed, night and day, how you may keep it, so that no one may take it from you. Indeed, you are anxious even beyond your span of life, and divide it among your children. This manor for this child, that manor for that child. But we [Natives] have faith in God the Creator and Preserver of Heaven and Earth. He preserveth the sun, He hath preserved our fathers so many moons (for they count not by years). He preserveth us, and we believe and are sure that He will also preserve our children after us, and provide for them, and because we believe this, we bequeath them not a foot of land.

Whether or not such a conversation literally occurred, the favorableness of the Conestogas toward Penn, and even his preaching, remained evident. Five years after his visit, a Conestoga woman told a Quaker friend of Penn's that she had dreamed about the Proprietor. She had been in London, she said, where after walking by several streets she had come upon a crowd listening to William Penn preach. They were both glad, she said, to see each other again. He had even promised to accept her invitation to preach again to her people—as he had apparently done during his Conestoga visit in 1701.

Penn was quite pleased with his western tour. He reported to friends that at "divers meetings with [Shawnee], Susquehanna, Schuylkill and Delaware Indians" he had admonished them "not to war one with another and other Indians under Governments that are under the Crown of England." This was a very relevant topic, since the general Susquehanna area was becoming a place of refuge, with permission of the northern Five Nations (Iroquois), for a miscellany of Native remnants displaced by European immigrants.

Also increasingly sensitive was the topic of drunkenness, especially among the Delawares newly clustering along the Tulpehocken tributary of the upper Schuylkill watershed. It was encouraging to have their elderly chief Manangy (who had met Penn at Perkasie in 1683), come to Philadelphia in the summer of 1701 to talk about the worrisome increase in rum traffic impacting his people. This, sadly, would remain a perennially unsolved problem. As mentioned earlier, it would in fact deeply injure the life of our story's Sassoonan.

It hardly seems right not to include another folk-glimpse of Penn from the years 1699-1700. Quaker Hugh Evans of Gwynedd, then about 12 years old, would remember that the Proprietor, his daughter Laetitia, and a servant "came out on horseback to visit father Thomas Evans" in his debarked log home near the Gwynedd Friends meetinghouse. At nighttime, when Penn clambered up an exterior stair to his "chamber," he was curiously followed by the young Evans son who, peeking into the room, saw the famous guest "on his knees praying, and giving thanks to God for such peaceful and excellent shelter in the wilderness."

Back at the Pennsbury mansion on the Delaware, which Penn realized he must leave in a few months, he was anxious to get a better grip on his disappointing income flow. So was his surveyor and fellow Quaker Thomas Fairman, whose "abilities" (including speaking "Indian pretty well") Penn valued, but whose self-serving manners were annoying. When Penn now demanded an updated accounting, Fairman complained of being too busy. He hadn't had even enough personal time, he complained, to resell 6,000 acres he had purchased for his own use. While it may seem questionable for a surveyor to also have been a speculator, Fairman would buy and sell during his professional career at least 20,000 acres that he had surveyed. No doubt he felt justified in making money that way, since he felt cheated in the amount of income he had expected from surveyor's fees. He had not received payment of the £140 he had charged for house rent and services from his now deceased employer Thomas Holme, nor had he been reimbursed for service to Penn himself, starting with Penn's initial visit 16 years earlier. "At my own charge for hands, horses, and provisions," he reminded Penn, "I laid out many manors for the Proprietor, and never had a penny consideration; and also, besides all that, the Proprietor may remember how I have been as his boy, as I may say at a whistle, viz.: go show this and that man, such and the other piece of land, riding my own horse and sometimes two,—one for the person to be showed." Indeed, Penn's carelessness toward paying his bills throws an uncomplimentary light on his religious reputation. Surveyor General Holme, for his part, had felt that he, not Fairman, had been the one cheated.

Fairman's disappointment went beyond finances. "I confess I have took it a little hardly," he complained, that a person "less capable" than he had "been preferred to offices of profit, and myself overlooked." This was a reference to Penn's recent appointing of his wife Guli's stepbrother Edward Penington to replace the deceased Holme in the office of Surveyor General, even though Fairman's knowledge of the counties of Philadelphia, Bucks, and Chester was far superior. "Pray, governor, excuse me," wrote Fairman; "methinks I see myself angry, but I know not with whom, and therefore I think I must close." Such words, when Secretary Logan was allowed to read them, remained unconvincing. "Thou fully knows my opinion of the man," Logan wrote to Penn, "and time does not alter it . . . . There is no dependence upon him." Only a careful reading of the sources by modern historians would reveal Logan's own obviously self-enriching motives.

Actually, Quaker Fairman and his wife Elizabeth must have been living decently well for two decades at Shackamaxon, across from the island she had brought to their marriage. With two sons and two daughters to raise, they were accruing a household that included, in addition to an Indian girl named Betty, five slaves: "Negroes" Cuff, Peter, Jane, Hannah, and Molle. (There were slaves at Pennsbury, too, serving Quaker Hannah.)

Penn's looming departure was an abortive disappointment to everybody but his own little family. The Assembly in Philadelphia was demanding a more liberal constitution, to which Penn responded with a hastily constructed "Charter of Liberties." Influential Quakers wanted an explanation as to what his absence would mean for them.

Unpaid personal bills were accumulating. With the ocean travel season drawing to a close in the summer of 1701, Penn barraged his secretary with instructions. Since it was "absolutely necessary" to find income, he was eager, "while land is high and valuable . . . to dispose of many good patches that else I should have chosen to have kept." Logan was to summon surveyors Fairman and Powell quickly, whether or not they were ideal for the work, because of "all they know." Wealthy Welsh immigrants just then moving into Gwynedd would likely "want quantetys" of land. Fairman had the knowledge sufficient to "accommodate them handsomely," and Powell, who was Welsh himself, could beat other speculators to the punch, so that Penn himself, selling off parts of his manors, would get the income.

Hannah Penn was with child again, and though her husband insisted he would quickly return from England, was refusing to stay and wait for him. Daughter Tishe, engaged to a man she didn't like and preferring town to country life, was "still less" willing to stay. "I know not what to do," Penn confessed to his secretary. To anybody who talked about this, Logan was supposed to explain that Penn would not need to stay long in England. Since it was only while living in his own colony that he could build up a financial inheritance for his second family, he would be highly motivated to come back. He would *have* to return to Pennsylvania, they should understand, in order to sell land, pay down debts, "and lay up for posterity." Anyone who knew him well would know that his "inclinations" were "strongly to a country . . . life." All that, together with Hannah's "promise to return whenever I am ready," should set Pennsylvanians at ease.

The Indians, too, were disappointed by the puzzling second departure of their friend whose unexpectedly lavish gifts had captured their imagination. On this topic, a comment by one of the French fur traders who had moved from the Schuylkill to the Susquehanna was very complimentary. The Indians, he noted to Penn, "have always been well entertained at your house with food and drink," and beside "all the other trouble that these sort of people give, they have never given you presents that you have not repaid them doubly." This was the background for a gathering of Natives with Penn at Philadelphia to discuss "their former covenants, now again revived by his going away for England." The meeting's atmosphere was recorded by a Quaker traveling minister, John Richardson, who was struck by the "calmness of temper, and . . . amicable way" of the Natives' proceedings.

They claimed, he noted, that they "never first broke covenant with any people; for, as one of them said, smiting his hand upon his head three times, they did not make [covenants] there in their heads, but smiting his hand three times on his breast, said, they made them there in their hearts." When Penn then, as usual, gave them "match-coats and some other things," the Indian speaker directed that the gifts be "put into the hands of one of their Kings, for he knew best how to order them." Particularly fascinating was their refraining from speaking two at a time, and their "eating and drinking . . . in much stillness."

By what "Terms or Words," wondered this visiting preacher, could the Natives' hearts be reached with the spiritual truths of Christianity? Could they have "a Sense of the Principles of truth, such as Christ's manifesting himself to the inward Senses of the Soul, by his Light, Grace or Holy Spirit?" Was it possible to "come to the Substance of this in their own Language?" Though Penn "much pressed . . . the Interpreter to do his best, in any Terms, that might reach their Capacities," Richardson reported no particular success. What he could recognize in the Natives was a clear "satisfaction, both for themselves and their people, in keeping all their former [promises] inviolate." No "differences" that might arise, they agreed, should be addressed by war. Rather, "justice" should be practiced so "that all animosities might be prevented on all sides for ever."

After the parley, the Natives went outdoors for what the minister considered their own kind of worship. The men sat around a small fire, singing a "very melodious hymn, which affected and tendered the hearts of many who were spectators." Beating "upon the ground with little sticks" (because they had no drum?), they would pause briefly until one of the older men renewed the song for a few minutes, and then repeat the procedure. It "seemed exceedingly to affect them and others," noted Richardson. Finally, "they rose up and danced a little about the fire, and parted with some shouting like rejoicing."

Whereas the dancers recorded here were probably Lenapes, another Native delegation came east again from Conestoga to register their own farewell. Having learned that Penn, "to our great Grief and the trouble of all the Indians of these parts [was] obliged to goe back for England," they declared him "not only alwayes just but very kind" to them, giving, "as is well known, his House for our Home at all times and freely entertaining us at his own Cost and often filling us with many presents of necessary Goods." Whoever wrote this down in English (almost certainly James Logan) was making Penn look good to the authorities of the Crown in England. In turn, Penn, remembered Logan, "at his leaving in a most solemn manner at a great meeting with them recommended me [!] to them as the person particularly intrusted to take care of them in his behalf and likewise them to me."

As the ketch *Dolmahoy* loaded for a return voyage to England, Penn found "many matters of moment Crowding at once." Surveyor David Powell wanted land to resell for profit; a cousin of Penn named Robert Asheton got a personal promise of 500 acres; a Swedish woman who claimed that although both Fairman and Powell had surveyed land for her family, she had never gotten possession of it, now got an oral promise from the busy Proprietor, in his secretary's hearing, that the deal would be completed. At Perkasie (where Penn had met "King" Tamany 18 years before), a new manor of 10,000 acres was laid out in the name of baby Johnny, who would also get 12,000 acres east of the Schuylkill, at Manatawny. His stepsister Laetitia was allotted a manor named "Mount Joy" west of the Schuylkill and just south of the future Valley Forge.

By the time the Assembly had received Penn's new Charter of Liberties, he was aboard ship at New Castle on the Delaware, preparing to write a pre-voyage will. Most of that was about land in Pennsylvania. In case of Penn's death, the faithful caretakers at Pennsbury, John and Mary Satcher, were to have 300 acres; "old Sam," one of the slaves to be freed at Penn's death, was to get 100 acres; and Logan 1,000. Son William, who had remained in England, was named as executor, but not given any American land. His inheritance was to be limited to the English estate of his deceased mother Gulielma, a condition which, when he discovered it, would dismay him. He was singled out, near the end of his father's hastily drawn-up testament, as the recipient of a special heirloom, the "Gold Chain and Medal" Penn still treasured in memory of young William's admiral grandfather—awarded for naval derring-do 36 years earlier by Oliver Cromwell, when there had been no thought of pacifism in the Penn family. But though the military memory was thus honored, the Quaker attitude was just as evident in the will. "I do hereby charge all my children," it stipulated, "as their loving dying Father's last command and desire, that they never goe to law [among themselves over the conditions of the family estate], but if any difference should arise which I would hope will not, that they be concluded by the Judgement of F[rien]ds to be chosen by the meeting of sufferings of the people called Quakers." All in all, it appeared that daughter Laetitia was to receive a total of 100,000 American acres, and her baby stepbrother Johnny 150,000 acres. Hannah's next child, if it turned out to be a boy, would get 100,000 acres, but if a girl, only 70,000. Their mother herself, if widowed, would get 5,000.

As to the Indians, or their children, there was no mention in the will.

Finally aboard the *Dolmahoy* on November 3, a reflective Penn addressed his secretary: "I have left thee in an uncommon trust . . . with a singular dependence on thy justice and care. . . . Use thy utmost endeavors . . . to receive all that is due to me. Get in quit-rents; sell lands . . . ; look carefully after all fines . . . that shall belong to me as proprietor or chief governor. Get in the taxes . . . , and use thy utmost diligence in making remittances to me. . . . Draw up an estimate of my estate, and of what may be raised from it, which send over to me [in England] as speedily as possible. In conclusion, "Cause all the province and territories to be resurveyed in the most frugal manner."

Then the anchor was lifted, and the *Dolmahoy* departed on its eastward sail. Little Johnny, innocent of the 150,000 acres of Lenape land newly in his name, was cheerful throughout the voyage. He would only return once, at the age of 34, and would stay less than a year.

We have gone a chapter without mentioning Hans and Kinget Stauffer, renting the castle vineyard in their German village. Since the oldest of their children, Kinget's daughter Anneli, was now about to marry, there were plans for her dowry. The bridal home of her imagination was doubtless in her lover Gerhart Clemens' crowded nearby village of Niederflörsheim, adjacent to Kriegsheim, in the broad Palatine landscape green with the viniculture brought north in the days of the Caesars. The transatlantic soil of her actual future, still forested in 1701, was the floor of a little valley, 30 miles northwest of Philadelphia. There, where eight generations of Anneli's progeny would live, farm, and die, only a few Natives lingered in 1701. But seeded in the forested sod on either side of the Perkiomen's East Branch, the millennia-laid deposit of their people's simple stone mementoes was older than Rome's. It is from that specific ground, three centuries after Gerhart and Anneli Clemens would take it over, that our story gazes affectionately back at their immigration, and the undocumented departure of their Lenape predecessors.

CHAPTER NINE

Earth for Dwelling and for Selling

1702–1707

TENDING THE CASTLE VINEYARD at Alsheim near Worms, Hans and Kinget Stauffer were the only Mennonites included in a census of the village in 1702. But other family names of their faith-fellowship—such as Bliem, Cassel, Clemens, Hackman, Hiestand, Kolb, and Stauffer—gathered from lands both north and south, were listed frequently in the neighboring grape-girdled villages, especially at one called the Ibersheimerhof (or Mennonistenhof) on the western Rhine-bank. Mostly Swiss immigrant families, these refugees had been fairly well received by the older residents. "Everyone must give them the testimonial," reported a local official, "that they live quietly and peaceably . . . in harmony with their neighbors, and have proven themselves more industrious than others, obedient to the government, true and constant in all things." In future years the region's farmers would credit the lushness of their crops to the agricultural methods brought north by Swiss Anabaptist émigrés with names such as Brubacher and Mellinger. They nursed the soil with manure and clover, and introduced crop rotation.

Still, since as neither Catholic nor Reformed, they were not actual citizens, the recently arrived Mennonites could feel only shallow land-rootage for their children. From time to time they had to renew appeals for the privilege of meeting for worship. Whereas a Palatine declaration of 1664 had limited the size of their gatherings to 20 persons on one farmstead, by 1683 suspicious officials complained of assemblies of 100. Mennonites who had turned Quaker at the Palatine village of Kriegsheim, where William Penn had visited and preached in 1677, had been harassed until they left in 1685 for Pennsylvania.

As William Penn observed two decades after the fact, Quaker preaching in 1655 had divided the Mennonites at Kriegsheim. Thirty years later the family of the foremost Quaker convert, elderly widower

Peter Schumacher, had crossed the Atlantic. Back home, his daughter Agnes and her husband Thielman Kolb were still loyal Mennonites, raising six sons—Peter, Henrich, Martin, Jacob, Johannes, and Thielman Jr. The oldest, Peter, a bishop like his father, still lived in Kriegsheim, near the Mennonite Cassel and Clemens families of adjacent Niederflörsheim. It was from there in 1671 that we have noticed Johannes Clemens helping to register the weeping Swiss refugees, including the Stauffers. And it was from Niederflörsheim, 30 years after that influx, that young weaver and vinedresser Gerhart Clemens, a nephew of Johannes, had learned to know a girl from nearby Alsheim: Anneli Stauffer, daughter of Kinget from Zurich, and stepdaughter of Hans from Bern.

The fabulously long-sloping fields, among which vine-villages such as Alsheim, Kriegsheim, and Niederflörsheim still bask, draw sighs of admiration from modern visitors to the Palatinate west of Worms. What an enviably fecund *Erdboden* to dwell on for generations! But who owned that land? Only a fraction of the grapes Hans Stauffer harvested at Alsheim—nine miles north of the Clemens vineyard—were his own, and the fertile castle ground at their roots could only be rented from a local "lord." The taxes, Rhine-tolls, Mennonite "protection money," fees, and dues paid to this landlord and the mayors of both Alsheim and Geisenheim, 12 miles downstream, to which Hans boated his lord's grapes, left his own family only a barely net profit. At best, a good Mennonite farmer could be allowed a feudal *Erbpachtrecht* (leasehold)—to pass on to his children the right to rent a particular hof. This was nothing like the incredible freedom from taxation of which news was drifting back from Pennsylvania, where in 1704 and 1707 Peter Schumacher Jr., Quaker cousin of the eager young Kolb brothers, was serving as the burgess of tiny Germantown.

Six miles southeast of Alsheim, Mennonite minister Christian Bliem of the Ibersheimerhof stayed in written correspondence with supportive Mennonites in Holland. Now and then he felt he must caution these sophisticated, generous Dutch friends against exporting their liberal church manners into the Palatinate, even while gratefully accepting their aid for the Swiss-born families still recovering from their loss of homeland. Their economic difficulty was not necessarily shared by Hans and Kinget Stauffer, whose careful family records note inheritances brought up from relatives in both Bern and Zurich. There was even money from Kinget's deceased first husband, Zurichian

Michael Reiff, to be kept for his daughter Anneli. Another entry was for funds from Bern—from the Stauffer family inheritance, coming to Anneli's adoptive father Hans via his brother Ulrich, whose Dutch-aided migration had deflected him to Groningen in the Netherlands. Internationally scattered and tentatively renting as these Mennonite émigrés were finding themselves, they kept their Swiss-born family network. So when Anneli Hiestand Stauffer married Gerhart Clemens in 1702, there were substantial gifts from her parents at Alsheim, as noted in her stepfather's records: money for the wedding itself, a young ox, a sheep, a pig, a cow with its calf, linen and woolen cloth, and later, a horse. More gifts following gave the newlyweds a modest financial boost, and a chance to work the rich Palatine soil. Yet, before long both the young Clemens family and their elderly Stauffer in-laws would abandon their Palatine lands. Their future lay across the sea, just north of Philadelphia in woods cheaply "bought" by William Penn from its Original People.

By the time Penn had returned a second time to England in late 1701, most of the Lenape remnant were fading west and north from the Perkiomen watershed. Secretary Logan reported, "Our own [Lenape] Indians for this last year have seldom come near us." Even those regathering up the Schuylkill at Falckner Swamp (near future Pottstown), were heard to be "uneasy." As earlier Natives had done along the Delaware in Bucks County, these were threatening to "disturb . . . the new German tract, which they clamor is not purchased." There was no such tension, fortunately, farther northwestward in Tulpehocken ("place of turtles" in the Unami dialect spoken by southern Lenapes), northwest of the confluence of Tulpehocken Creek and the Schuylkill River, where dislocated Lenapes were re-clustering peaceably with other Natives. As we have seen, they were being led by Manangy, a name we may remember from the parley with Penn back at Perkasie in 1683, where the "little lad" Sassoonan, destined to succeed Manangy in due turn as leader of the "Schuylkill Indians," had been an observer.

In Chester County the inexorable sweep of surveying was still led by David Powell, the veteran Welsh Quaker of Philadelphia who would eventually survey the Clemens purchase around which our story centers. Powell's reports from the 50,000-acre Welsh Tract he had been assigned to lay out show him as active a speculator as he was a surveyor. Much like his Quaker colleague Thomas Fairman, Powell claimed to have "spent much time, Labour and money in Resurveys and Other Services" for Penn, for which he had "never yet rec'ed Any Compensation." The Commissioners of Property, knowing that Penn, just before taking ship, had granted Powell in writing 400 acres at a price "under the Value," now allowed him to pay for it in convenient installments "as he [could] raise the money before and after" signing for it. He "Craves no other Pay than Land," noted the Commissioners, while approving Powell's further purchase of seven tracts totaling over 2,000 acres in the Welsh Tract alone. Even beyond this, Powell would claim a right to 1,000 acres which, while waiting for more buyers, he would not be able to cash in for another decade.

When the office of Surveyor General was left vacant again in 1701 by the unexpected death of Penn's brother-in-law Edward Penington, Secretary James Logan, steadily resentful of both Powell and Fairman, wanted neither of them to be promoted. Thus, rather than advancing one of the two most experienced and longest-serving deputy surveyors, the Logan-led Commissioners of Property hired a young Quaker schoolmaster, Jacob Taylor, as a functionary whose work they could closely control. Logan saw to it that from then on he himself could examine all warrants to survey land. As Penn's most direct representative in the Colony, the unmarried 27-year-old now had a position of unique speculative advantage. It was he who wrote the minutes of the Governor's Council, and who was the main source of inside information to Penn in London. For better or worse, many of the most significant details of our story are sifted from his self-justifying records.

Land might now be "selling," Logan wrote ruefully to London, but the buyers were not paying up. This was "sorrowful and wounding" news to Penn, who kept vainly hoping for what he called "supplys" (income from quitrents) to offset the growing legal expenses he had to pay from his personal funds to defend his governorship from takeover by jealous royal officials. "Make returns with all speed," Penn urged Logan, "or I am undone." Two decades after his dream of a Holy Experiment had flared, it was withering under the gloom of economic and political reality. True, the newly crowned Queen Anne, remembering Penn's friendship with her ousted Catholic brother, James II, might converse favorably with him for two hours. But he was still becoming so discouraged that, in spite of his campaign that had brought him back to London to save his governorship, he was beginning to think it would be better to give up and sell the "government" (though not the land itself) back to the Crown for enough money to get him out of his alarming debt. To this prospect Hannah Penn, having now birthed a second son, Thomas, was also resigned.

"I hope thou mindest my land," Penn insisted to Logan. Living in London, he kept dreaming of Pennsbury, the steward's family there, its "fruit, corn, and improvements, and clearing particularly." He still aimed to bring back to it not only his own second family, but that of his namesake son, which had now grown to five (including a grandson "Billie"). Realizing that Pennsbury could "hardly accommodate" such a crowd "unless enlarged," Penn asked Logan to find out whether there would be Quakers in Pennsylvania who "would be so kind to build me a pretty box" on some other piece of land that remained in his own name. Or perhaps Logan could look into buying a familiar house he had once stayed in, that of Thomas and Elizabeth Fairman at Shackamaxon.

Kept by legal concerns from the quick return he had promised, Penn decided to send over his oldest son as his representative. Part of his motivation was to get William Jr. away from an unpromising behavioral pattern. A timely opportunity came with the chance to send the young father along with a newly appointed lieutenant governor—non-Quaker bachelor John Evans. Penn asked Secretary Logan to look out for the young heir when he arrived: "Possess him, go with him to Pennsbury, advise him." Instead of "rambling to New York" or hanging out with questionable company, there should be healthy activities such as fishing or "little journeys . . . to see the Indians."

When William Jr. arrived in Philadelphia in February 1704 with the likewise young governor, the first reports were hopeful. A quick letter from son to father called life at riverside Pennsbury pleasant. But his immediate request for the shipment of several hounds and a stallion was not particularly encouraging. Quakers noted approvingly that as a member of the Governor's Council, he took an "affirmation" rather than an oath, but he was otherwise proving less than devout. "He . . . sometimes comes to meeting," observed an acquaintance, and "is good-natured, and loves company, but that of Friends is too dull."

On the positive side, a hundred Indians, including nine "kings" in the Lehigh region, hearing of the arrival of a son of their great friend, came down to greet him at the mansion beside the Delaware. Having brought nine belts of wampum to solemnize their covenantal relationship, they were given gifts accordingly. News of this gladdened the heart of Penn in London, but he was soon shocked by an account of a scandalous brawl. There was gossip of at least one extramarital affair. "'Tis a pity," remarked James Logan, that "his wife came not with him, for her presence would have confined him within bounds he was not too regular in observing." "O Pennsylvania," wrote the grieving parent, "what hast thou cost me? Above 30,000 [pounds] more than I ever got by it; two hazardous and most fatiguing voyages; my [financial] straights and slavery here, and my child's soul, almost." Could it be that the Quaker heir to Pennsylvania was serving as a captain in Governor Evans' uncalled-for militia?

Fully as discouraging was the young fellow's insisting that two wealthy Philadelphia Quakers, Isaac Norris and William Trent, immediately buy from him the 7,480-acre manor on the Schuylkill that was his personal allotment. Adjacent to Plymouth and Whitpain Townships, it would first be called "Williamstadt," but that German name was to be replaced by "Norriton" and "Norristown." Only after strenuous persuasion (and against the advice of surveyor Fairman), would this transaction transpire, for a bargain price of £850. William Penn's own spendthrift son would have no interest in American land beyond the cash that could be immediately squeezed from it.

Less than a year after his arrival, the heir was back in London, handing in troublesome new bills to his father. He was no longer a Quaker, he declared, and would either join the Navy or run for election to Parliament. He remained angry that Philadelphia's officials had dared to criticize the behavior of a future Proprietor. His father wrote pathetically to "Friends" in Pennsylvania, calling his son "my greatest affliction for his soul's and my posterity's or family's sake." In fact, "Many weights & Burthens, Griefs & Sorrows" were leaving the visionary Founder and Quaker preacher in a kind of daze. Reports of other misbehavior by his appointed governor added to his woes. By now he was even retroactively suspicious of having been let down by the deceased Surveyor General Thomas Holme. Worst of all, the family of his former English secretary Philip Ford was making serious legal moves toward claiming ownership of the land of Pennsylvania to satisfy the long-standing debt to their estate. Little wonder that Penn was preparing a "Proposal for Surrender of the Government of Pennsylvania" to the royal government. As Logan put it candidly, "Pennsylvania, thy former darling, is now become thy heavy affliction."

In the midst of such frustrations arrived an irritating letter from Fairman, appealing for employment for one of his own two sons. "I beg not for my selfe," Fairman wrote, while nevertheless reminding Penn of his "grudge to see fresh hands that have never served Proprietor or Country jump into Offices of profitt and Eate the bread due to others [like himself!] by a kinde of birth right." Asserting his own professional value, Fairman claimed to "know" he could find 100,000 more acres of unsurveyed land for the cash-strapped Penn to sell to English buyers. Such a proposition (dismissed by Logan as "little more than wind") was based on a landscape that, abstracted from the thought of its Native population, meant nothing more than monetizable real estate.

Ironically, just then Indians on the Brandywine Creek in Chester County were making "a very troublesome claim." When they had made a "great sale" to Penn of their land downstream from the future Downingtown, it had been with the trusting understanding that a part of it would be "reserved" by Penn for their continued dwelling. Even with that concession, as Logan remembered, the Indians had not agreed easily. They had "insisted" on pay three times higher than what they actually received, and had been given that much only because the commissioners had felt "forced to promise them £100 of our money." (Only part of this would be paid until there were more protests a decade later.) And now they were complaining about being pressured in their living space.

This was only one incident in the unfolding story of Pennsylvania's rendering its Lenape Natives homeless. The drama would soon spread beyond Chester County northward to both the Indians regathering in the Schuylkill-feeding Tulpehocken Creek watershed, and New Jersey-born *Munsee* Delawares above Tohickon at the Forks of the Delaware. At the moment, the Tulpehocken woodland (west of future Reading) was remote enough from settlements spreading north from Philadelphia for retreating Lenapes to hunt and garden there undisturbed, and even welcome other uprooted Natives. In 1705 the old Lenape headman, Manangy, appeared again in Philadelphia, to show the willingness of the Indians at Tulpehocken to receive remnants of a tribe they called *Conoys* (Gawanese) who had lost their homes in the Potomac region.

Even friendly official responses to the Natives could prove ambiguous. When the volatile Governor Evans returned to Philadelphia from a visit to the Susquehanna, he was accompanied by rumors of unwelcome behavior by his party among Natives. What an example, fumed the Philadelphia Quakers, to the supposedly unreligious "savages"! Penn himself, hearing of his governor's "lewd ... practices with the wives & daughters of the people of Conestogo," wrote, "My Soule mourns under these things." Before long Evans had to be replaced.

Constantly hoping for a way out of the threatening Ford family's lawsuit, Penn demanded from his American secretary a fresh accounting of how much land could be expected to sell, and for how much. Logan was well up-to-date on what was left in Bucks and Chester Counties, "But for Philadelphia County," he wrote, "where we should have the exactest [records], there have I met with more difficulty than in all the rest. I have employed three surveyors upon it, but they all have their own ways. T[homas] F[airman] seldom fails of disappointing those who depend on him; D[avid] Powell is the best-natured man to talk to, but the most unmanageable to deal with that I have met with." It might have been expected that when a resurvey ordered by Penn showed that the original survey had taken in more acreage than had been "warranted," the "overplus" could be sold to later buyers, for an extra income to the Penn estate. Indeed, Fairman was himself noteworthy for leaving big "slices" of such "overplus" when he surveyed. But he only did so, complained Logan, so that he could come back himself and claim them (for his own speculation when he had a buyer). Wherever Fairman had surveyed, as Logan put it, "there [was] nothing to be expected" of profit for Penn.

The secretary's chagrin with his fellow Quaker, however, was beginning to be matched by other people's suspicion of Logan's own financial interests. Dislike of the 31-year-old bachelor by members of the Province's elected Assembly reached a peak in March 1707, when they impeached him. "Whereas," according to his political opponents, the two offices of Surveyor General and Secretary to the Proprietor "ought to be ... a mutual check upon each other" for the protection of the citizens' interests, "James Logan has, since the death of Edward Pennington, late Surveyor Genl, kept both the said Offices in his own hands or Power." Angered, Logan riposted that this had only been done for the sake of practicality and economy. In any case, he expostulated, "I never made a farthing to my self by the office." While this was technically true, his unrivaled advance knowledge of land dealings was preparing him to make a fortune. For a while he actually had under his own control four different offices: secretary to the Province, commissioner of property, receiver-general (collector of taxes and fees), and personal business agent for Proprietor Penn. With his explanatory pen ever active, it would be no wonder that it would be his version of history—whether of Indians or immigrants—that many historians of Pennsylvania would approvingly recycle for two centuries.

As steadily as the Lenape population was disappearing, their European replacements were confirming a future on the lands they had purchased in and around Germantown. In 1706, before Governor Evans was quite dismissed, his office received a "humble Petition" for naturalization from 124 "High & low Germans." The land they had paid for, they stated, had been "Rough & Uncultivated," but "by the blessing of God" on "their great Labour . . . Charge & Hazard," they had "Reduc'd" it from "a Howling Wilderness . . . to an Habitable Condicion & Tillage." They now hoped for the privilege of citizenship that would let them "Enjoy Inheritt Give Grant Alien Sell & Dispose of their Lands . . . and Estates" like "Naturall born Subjects of England." Among the applicants, it was noted, were "Certain Mennists who . . . for above One hundred & Fifty years past according to their Principle & Profession of Christian Religion can't take an Oath." Hopefully, the Governor and his Council could treat the Mennonite Gaetschalcks, Keysers, Neusses, Sellens, and Rittinghuysens with the same leniency as they had had for the Quakers who had been there for 23 years. Among the latter were old Peter Schumacher and his son Peter (Germantown's current burgess).

The appeal of 1706 was not granted, but immigration continued, leading to homesteads that began to emerge 18 miles northwest of Germantown, at Bebberstaun (future Skippack), named for its Dutch real estate investor, within three miles of the East Branch of the Perkiomen. That watershed, "bought" from Chief Maughoughsin in 1684, was still being called "Vacant Land."

CHAPTER TEN

"Fix Them... for They are... Minonists"
1707-1709

By 1707 the crash of ancient timber falling echoed up the Schuylkill watershed beyond the Wissahickon Creek, across landscapes with new European names: Norriton, Bebberstaun (Skippack), Gwynedd, and Providence. Too few Lenapes lingered this close to Philadelphia to keep the French fur traders by the Schuylkill from moving 50 miles westward, leaving behind only the name of the tributary "French Creek." Traders Peter and Ann Bezaillion, as well as Ann Letort were now out in the Susquehanna Valley, competing with fellow Frenchman Martin Chartier, who had married a Shawnee woman. The presence of so many white faces around Conestoga prompted that village's "Queen" Conguegas (who had recently dreamed of seeing her friend William Penn preaching in London) to send a messenger to Governor John Evans in Philadelphia to ask if these French newcomers were approved by Penn's government. One man in particular, she reported, was insisting that her people lead him to silver mines he had heard about.

The young governor, already aware of the exploring "Swisser" he called "Mitchell," had summoned him to explain his "traversing the Country... without permission." It turned out that this Bernese Franz Luis Michel, on behalf of investors from his native Canton, had crossed the Atlantic twice, and while pausing in London had personally looked up William Penn. Surprised to find the well-known Quaker badly embarrassed by debt and political harassment (living apart from his family in an adjunct to the Fleet Prison next to the Thames), Michel had nevertheless "contracted" with him to bring to Pennsylvania a special group of settlers—Bernese Anabaptists. These were none other than cousins of our story's 63-year-old Hans Stauffer, now living near Worms in the Rhineland. Three decades after Stauffer had abandoned their Emmental home, his relatives were being newly harassed, some imprisoned. It was the Bernese lords' wish to get rid of all their *Täufer* subjects—in chains if necessary—that had given Michel his idea of profiting via a deal with William Penn to bring to his colony a set of desirable immigrants.

The fast-talking Michel had convinced Penn that Indians west of Philadelphia knew where silver could be mined. Vague as such talk was, it was music to the discouraged old Proprietor's ears, as clouds of the debtor's suit brought against him by Philip Ford's family were darkening. Neither debt nor news of trouble in Pennsylvania (where his unpopular secretary Logan had just been impeached), could keep the 63-year-old Quaker from further fantasizing about moving with his own family to Pennsylvania. "Depend upon it," he wrote to Logan, "if God favors me and my son [William] with life, one, if not both [of us], will come as soon as possible."

Our story now provides a fascinating comparison. Dreams cherished by the Thames of establishing a Penn family homestead in the American woods were being paralleled in the rural but crowded Palatinate of our character Hans Stauffer. The Mennonite bishop of his community, 200 miles north of his native Bern, had a set of sons who, unlike the disappointing non-Quaker heir, William Penn Jr., were remaining true to their father's faith. Resisting the Quaker mission that had drawn their grandfather Peter Schumacher and his family out of the Mennonite fellowship at Kriegsheim, and led them to Germantown in Pennsylvania, three of the six sons of Thielman and Agnes Schumacher Kolb would migrate there too, and continue as Mennonites. The other three were just as inclined to follow. Eventually, while William Penn would have no sons in Pennsylvania, there would be thousands of Kolb progeny in the valleys abandoned by the Lenape people whose homeland this had been. By sad contrast, the namesake Penn heir, having been to America and back, was continuing to give his father "much grief and expense." He was "not of that service and benefit to me," mourned Penn, "that some sons are, and 'tis well known I was to my father before I married. But oh, if yet he will recommend himself, and show himself a good child and a true Friend [Quaker], I shall be pleased, and leave the world with less concern for him."

Of Penn's tender parental hope there would be no fulfilment, whether in Pennsylvania or England. In contrast, in the summer of 1707 three of Bishop Peter Kolb's younger brothers— Jacob, Martin, and Johannes—left their Palatine homes to join their Quaker-convert grandfather Peter Schumacher in Germantown, where he had been living for 22 years six miles north of Philadelphia. Since this was the very year when old Peter died, we may wonder whether he might have lived just long enough to greet his Mennonite grandsons when they arrived in the fall. In any case, the Kolb brothers must have been intrigued to find little Germantown's Quaker burgess to be their own cousin, Peter Schumacher Jr.

The population of the growing linen- and paper-making village included a miscellaneous Mennonite cluster to greet the arriving Kolbs. Did they find its spoken accents initially off-putting, in its mixture of not only the Kolbs' *Pfälzisch* but the Lower Rhenish of Krefeld, Dutch of Amsterdam, and Dutch-German of Hamburg? Certainly, as William Penn himself would put it, there were "divers" kinds of Mennonites. It took the Kolb brothers until the following spring (and after the sudden, unexpected death of Dutch-speaking preacher William Rittenhouse) to meld with the bishop-less Germantown congregation to the point where one of the brothers, Martin, accepted appointment as a preacher. During this process, the Kolbs let it be known that one of their older siblings (Henrich) was also at the point of emigrating, and that he would arrive in Germantown as a regularly ordained leader.

Meanwhile, however, a years-long-frustrated urge for regular church order was cresting in the village's diverse Mennonite cluster. In the months following William Rittenhouse's unexpected passing in 1708 the cautiously focusing group proved willing to accept that an unordained man, lathe-operator Jacob Gaetschalcks from Goch in the Lower Rhine region, although he could only "read" (without preaching), could perform the acts of a bishop. Thus, eight months after the Kolb brothers arrived in the fall of 1707, Gaetschalcks went ahead with baptisms and communion. A little log meetinghouse built that year (1708) had thus seen the historic beginning of the first permanent Mennonite congregation in America, and in fact the first such a uniting of Mennonite varieties anywhere.

The Kolb emigration was news throughout the Palatine Mennonite network west of Worms, especially in Bishop Peter Kolb's home village of Kriegsheim. It was among his flock in the adjacent village of Niederflörsheim that Anneli Stauffer Clemens and her husband Gerhart tended their vineyard. Surely, in the summer of 1708 the gossip at the wedding of Anneli's younger sister Elizabeth of Alsheim to Paul

Friedt included the topic of Pennsylvania. Perhaps few of the relatives could have imagined that within another three years not only both of the Stauffer sisters' families, but their elderly Swiss-born parents as well, would follow the Kolb brothers from their adopted Rhineland hofs to the woods of Pennsylvania.

Turning to the elderly William Penn keeping a low profile in London, we find him hotly pursued by the Ford heirs. Things became outright ridiculous when they had their famous "Friend" arrested as he left a preaching appearance at a Quaker meeting. As the civil case dragged on through 1708, he lived under a kind of house arrest that allowed him to choose his own living quarters, but away from wife Hannah and their brood of five youngsters. He was still hoping that his ingenious Swiss agent "Mitchell" would find the silver mine that might clear his debt, and let him move at last back to Pennsylvania with both sets of his hopefully to-be-Americanized children. Finally, a group of sympathetic English Quakers gave Penn a mortgage, making available enough funds to settle the Fords' suit. Without delay, the relieved dreamer sent his secretary Logan fresh orders to find him a residence near Philadelphia. His preferred location, he made clear, was the very riverside spot where he had first lived in surveyor Thomas Fairman's house at the Lenapes' traditional haunt at Shackamaxon. He made the same point in a conversation with Fairman's brother Robert, whom he chanced to meet in London. That site, reported Robert, was called by Penn "a pleasant place for situation, out of the noise of Philadelphia, but in sight of it." It was just the kind of "place" that Penn said he "would choose for his dwelling if he should return there."

A better place on the earth—was this not what Hans Stauffer's Mennonite relatives dreamed of on their rented Palatine vineyards? After all, they were only tolerated migrants, not citizens, now under the Holy Roman Empire of the German Nation. There was continuing pressure for them, pacifist as they were, to serve on defense watch with weapons, or pay extra *militzengeld* (military fees). From time to time they appealed, citing the toleration offered their parents in a *privilegium* granted them by Elector Karl Ludwig in 1664. But discrimination continued. At Kriegsheim, where Henrich Kolb lived, adjacent to the Clemenses' village of Niederflörsheim, there was even tension over whether Mennists could be buried in a church graveyard.

And then suddenly, in the spring of 1709, we reach a threshold in our story of establishing an American homestead. The previous fall's weather had been odd enough for elderly winegrower Hans Stauffer to make a special note at Alsheim. "On the apple trees," he recorded, "apples and blossoms hung together on the same tree or twig. And this was found on many trees." By January the atmosphere was even stranger, with unprecedented cold locking up the swift-flowing Rhine. Farmers like Hans and son-in-law Gerhart Clemens at Niederflörsheim found their wine turning into blocks of ice and their vines frozen dead in the ground. Birds, it was said, fell stiff from the air, and if a person spit, the saliva crackled before hitting the ground. It was so unusual that an Alsatian house would carry the carved inscription: "Seventeen hundred nine is the year counted as my building from the time of Christ's birth. In this winter, unfortunately, on hill and dale all vines [and] very many trees in Europe froze." There would be no 1709 grape harvest.

As spring came, the cold gave way to a memorable spectacle: walking caravans of panicked German-speaking families, many of them listed as vinedressers, suddenly swarmed along the Rhine-path toward Rotterdam in hopes of crossing the Atlantic. Historians have guessed that the brutal winter may have been the last straw for many non-land-owning "poor Palatines." They had read, they claimed, or heard of, a book promising a new life in Carolina or Pennsylvania. Prompted by a rumor that the English Queen Anne had offered not only free ocean passage but acreage for settlement for impoverished German Protestants, a human wave threw itself on the mercies of the Dutch authorities, requesting free transportation to London. Two local Mennonite businessmen appointed to oversee the emergency shipping were quickly overwhelmed by the unanticipated throng.

Amid an anxious initial multitude of 850 persons waiting at Rotterdam in April were reported "nine or ten" families from "near Worms," carrying "testimonies of their membership" in Mennonite congregations. One of the families was that of Henrich Kolb, whose plans to join his three brothers in Pennsylvania had been born before the current emigration excitement had broken out. Their older brother, Bishop Peter Kolb, was likewise inclined to go. In fact, just before Henrich had left home, Peter was planning to ordain him to fill the repeated request of his brothers' congregation for a bishop at Germantown. Listed next to the Kolb family at Rotterdam was that of Gerhart Clemens, son-in-law of Hans Stauffer. Gerhart and wife Anneli had also been planning to leave at least since the beginning of March, when Gerhart had recorded settling finances with his father and brother.

At this very hectic moment in April 1709, Bishop Peter Kolb had come to Amsterdam, not far north of the seaport where Henrich and the Clemenses were waiting for passage to London. Peter had been sent on his errand from his home in Kriegsheim by fellow Mennonite bishops named Landis and Moyer from the Kraichgau east of the Rhine, to visit "many locations" among the generous Dutch Doopsgezinden to bring them an apology. The wonderful Dutch aid funds, confessed the Palatine ministers, had recently not been responsibly administered among their people, and they wanted to clear the record.

That it was Gerhart Clemens' bishop who was selected to carry a delicate diplomatic message testifies to Peter Kolb's status among his own people. Even greater evidence was his authority to respond to the pleas from his younger brothers' infant overseas congregation for a bishop to oversee baptisms and communion services. It was with the knowledge of letter-writing Mennonite leaders in both Amsterdam and Hamburg that Palatine Peter now ordained his own 30-year-old Pennsylvania-bound brother Henrich, friend of Gerhart Clemens, to the office of bishop. Though for three centuries historians would overlook the evidence of this historic act in the records of Amsterdam's conservative Doopsgezind congregation at "the Zon," Henrich Kolb, now bound for England, had thus become the first Mennonite actually ordained for the bishop's role in America.

The baptisms that had been performed in Germantown in 1708 had been done by a man (Jacob Gaetschalcks) with no hands-on ordination from the unbroken European Mennonite continuum. Now the Amsterdam Mennonites with whom Peter Kolb was conferring wrote to Germantown that Peter's brother Henrich, whom they called an *oudste* (elder), was "ready to cross over to you." When he arrived, they explained, he could fill the role of bishop without repudiating what the unordained Gaetschaelcks had done before a regular bishop could be supplied.

Though the Mennonite migrant group was characterized by observers in Rotterdam as "all very poor," the Clemenses, having recently sold a cow and horse to Anneli's parents, could hardly have been as cashless as some of their fellow travelers. True, the Mennonite group had given the impression of poverty by immediately appealing to the Rotterdam Doopsgezinden for help with travel expenses. But when the Dutch bluntly declined this request and advised a return to the Palatine homes, the Kolb and Clemens family-headed cluster still managed to be included, in this memorable spring of 1709, among the first of many shipments of "Poor Palatines" from Rotterdam to London.

Arriving in England with over 800 fellow travelers, the Kolbs and Clemenses were registered next to each other by two Lutheran pastors appointed to the task. Both of the young husbands were among the 13 persons called "Baptists" (out of a total of 200 male adults), and both were listed as "husbandmen and vinedressers." With the recently ordained Henrich Kolb, age 30, was his wife and their three young daughters. Listed next to the Kolbs was 28-year-old Gerhart Clemens with his wife and two sons. Other family names registered that we can recognize as Mennonite were such as Bauer, Bien, Eshelmans, Halteman, Nusbaum, Oberholtzer, Ruth, Schrager, Wengert, and Wismar.

At first the migrants were housed in cheap rented rooms in St. Catherine's parish in London. Unlike the Clemenses and Kolbs, who had more deliberately planned their emigration, most of the refugees had little or no money. Finding themselves jammed together 20 or 30 to a room, they quickly demanded that the ships they expected to board for America be less crowded than the ones that had brought them from the Continent. Though provided with bread, cheese, and meat, they were otherwise uncomfortable, so closely packed that the smell repulsed both them and observers. A committee was formed to rent them lodging on the outskirts of London. There too they were stranded for months, as thousands more "poor Palatines" arrived, to exist at subsistence level while the initially sympathetic British Parliament now angrily debated their fate.

The extraordinary scene on London's "heath," never to be forgotten by Gerhart and Anneli Clemens while later living in the woods of Pennsylvania, deserves a lingering look. A description is available from the pen of Daniel Defoe, best-selling author of *Robinson Crusoe*, who could recognize a potential literary sensation. When the crowd at London had grown to 825 persons, he reported, some "well-disposed *private* Gentlemen" formed "a Charitable Society" aiming to reduce the crowd of the resourceless émigrés "by hiring some cheap Houses and Barns out of the Town." Meanwhile, "as the number of the Palatines encreas'd," so did the Care of these Gentlemen, in providing more Barns and Houses for them; also in procuring from the Queen Lodgings for them in her Majesty's Rope-Yard at Deptford, in the upper Rooms in the Red House in the same Place, which the Queen hir'd, and were then vacant, with the loan of a thousand Tents from her Majesty, for their reception on Black heath, Greenwich, and at Camberwell, where a Gentleman of that place gave her a Ground to set them up in. Nor did the care of these Gentlemen terminate in Lodging them, but they also supply'd them with great Quantities of bread, cheese, milk and Small Beer, with Straw to lie on, Blankets, and Cover-lids.

Other compassionate "gentlemen" included Quakers who reported finding "about Sixty Persons that have been lately obliged to Leave their Native Country the Palatinate on Account of general Poverty and Missery... being by Religion... called Minists." In addition to giving them money, the Quakers distributed "Friends' books" among at least some of the Mennonite families.

As the flow of indigents grew alarmingly to some 15,000 souls, two and a half months went by before eight of the Mennonite Palatine families, including the Kolbs and Clemenses, could finally board a Philadelphia-bound boat on the Thames. A donation of £48 toward their passage money was probably from the Quaker network that led them to their boat. Its captain, Quaker Joseph Guy, was an acquaintance of William Penn, who knew about both the sailing date and the cluster of Mennonite passengers.

The discouraged Proprietor had just been cheered by a royal confirmation of his appeal against Lord Baltimore's border claim. He placed a copy of the favorable legal decision on Captain Guy's ship, which, he noted to his wife Hannah, was the one "that carrys the Palatinats over." Feeling "easier than before, now [that Lord] Baltimore's business is dismissed," he wrote again to Logan to prepare a house at Shackamaxon for the Penn family in time for the summer of 1710. In addition, Logan was to see that the country mansion upstream at Pennsbury, with its gardens, was "put in inhabitable order [so] that we may subsist in good measure upon it; for a spare food and living suit both me and mine."

Unlike this wistful, never-to-be-fulfilled fantasy of the Penn children growing up on American soil, the dream of the embarking Clemenses and Kolbs was taking on heartwarming potential. In Penn's own handwriting in the letter on Captain Guy's ship at the time of departure was a request that Logan ensure especially favorable attention to the Mennonites on board. "Herewith come the Palatines," Penn had written, "whom use with tenderness and love." Could Gerhart and Anneli Clemens have had a warmer welcome to America? "And fix them," continued Penn, "so, as they may send over [to their people in Europe] an agreeable character."

Pennsylvania, in contrast with authoritarian Zurich, cruel Bern, and the heavily taxing Palatinate, wanted more, not fewer, of Gerhart and Anneli Clemens' people on its land. There was a place on the earth that welcomed them! How remarkable it was to be described, in the words of the famous Proprietor himself as, though of "divers" European backgrounds, a uniformly "sober people" who "will neither swear nor fight"; to be moving from under the Holy Roman Empire of the German Nation, where Christians were persecuted for not taking an oath or serving as soldiers, to a place on earth where such convictions were a recommendation; and to have a ship captain under special orders to treat his Mennonite passengers with special "tenderness"! How often in human history have poor migrants received a welcome as warm and gentle as this?

But what about Sassoonan, who, having seen all his people's living space by the Neshaminy and Perkiomen "sold," was reported this year (1709) to have moved to the Susquehanna? Who would fix him?

CHAPTER ELEVEN

Fewer Natives, More Mennonites
1709-1710

THE WARMLY WELCOMED arrival of the family whose plantation in Perkioma is this story's focus contrasts sharply with the uncelebrated withdrawal of the people being replaced. True, while the ship bringing the Clemens and Kolb families had been bearing westward, some Lenapes were hearing friendly words in Penn's name. They were offered in Philadelphia by elderly Charles Gookin, Penn's recent replacement for the erratic Governor Evans, to a group of Indians unexpectedly appearing from the Susquehanna Valley 95 miles westward. Though surprised by the visitors, Gookin adroitly assured them of his own "special Charge" from their great English friend "to be very kind to the Indians, and to treat them as his friends & brothers."

Four of the dozen visiting "chiefs" were Lenape, one of them none other than our story's Sassoonan. We had last seen him 26 years earlier as a "little lad" watching Penn dealing with the memorable chief Tamany at Perkasie. Now (in 1709) grown up, and having apparently moved on to the Susquehanna from among Lenapes who had been regathering in upriver Schuylkill woods at Tulpehocken, Sassoonan was reported as currently living at *Peshtank* (site of future Harrisburg), among other Indians called *Mingoes* (Susquehannocks or Iroquois). Not yet the main leader of his Lenape people, he was not recorded as speaking during the parley with Governor Gookin. That role was performed by fellow sachem *Scolitchy*, a successor to the more famous Tamany.

These indigenous negotiators had come from Susquehanna, they said, to reaffirm the warm relationship some of them had enjoyed with William Penn while they were still living nearer to Philadelphia. Pleasantly intrigued, the Governor asserted that "As there had been a strong Chain of friendship" in the past, it was his desire that "it might be continued and made every day firmer," in fact, "that it might never be broken." The visitors, for their part, wanted to let the Governor know that they were about to make a peaceful journey north to carry "tribute" to the powerful Five Nations to whom they considered themselves ambivalently subject. Penn had been aware of that relationship and, also urgently wanting a friendly connection with the northern tribes, had left with the Conestogas just east of the Susquehanna a wampum belt to take on such an errand. So far, however, the proposed northern journey had not been carried out.

The Governor appreciated such friendly information, but with England presently at war with France, was more eager to learn from the visitors whether the Lenapes and Susquehannocks would be willing to join in a military campaign by Britain against the French in Canada. As a non-Quaker, Gookin had been commissioned by Queen Anne to raise troops for this purpose, and had been quite disappointed a few weeks earlier when Pennsylvania's pacifist, Quaker-dominated Assembly had withheld its participation. And now the Indians, partly led by Sassoonan, also declined. Though earlier some of them had seemed ready to let their younger men fight, they proved not ready to leave their wives and children to be dragged into a "Queen Anne's war."

As the Native guests lingered several days, they were further addressed with friendly rhetoric by James Logan. Currently in deep political trouble with the elected Assembly, he knew how important peaceful Indian relations were for his famous employer's success in selling land to arriving immigrants. He thus reminded the visiting Natives of how, in all previous "proceedings," they had been "considered" by Penn's officials "as brothers," with "nothing but love and peace between them and us." Hopefully, Logan said, this relationship would "extend to all posterity," as the "aged [indigenous] fathers inform their children of the friendship that has always been maintained amongst us, so that in every generation it may continually grow stronger." Logan then quickly arranged for the unanticipated visitors to receive what he knew they expected, and he made it impressively generous: 100 pounds of gunpowder, 200 pounds of lead, 100 flints, four coats, a dozen linen shirts, a half dozen pairs of stockings, "and a large quantity of Biskitt and Loaves." An additional promise of rum pleasantly refreshed the memory of Penn's original dealings with the Natives. It was the method always used thus far, and would continue to be employed while peaceful relations persisted.

Two months later, unlike the Lenapes returning to their wigwams in their adopted Susquehanna Valley, the Clemens and Kolb families arriving at the Philadelphia docks quickly found promising room in the mostly Native-emptied woods north of Norriton. For seven years already, along the first Perkiomen tributary above the Wissahickon, there had been land for sale in Bebberstaun (Skippack). In 1702, as we have noted, Dutch Mennonite speculator Matthias van Bebber had bought from one of Penn's disappointed Lower Rhenish "First Purchasers," Dirk Sypman of Krefeld, the rights to 6,000 acres. Over the next seven years van Bebber had sold off many parcels from his purchase to families, including Mennonites, moving out of filled-up Germantown. It was here along the Skippack Creek that Henrich and Barbara Kolb, arriving in 1709, found Henrich's younger brothers Martin, Jacob, and John buying land. Also acquiring 100 acres there within a few years were Gerhart and Anneli Clemens with their sons Johannes, Jacob, and American-born brother Abraham. New as they were on the scene, they could readily reconnect with some of the domestic network of their youth, with Gerhart almost immediately buying a horse from a fellow Palatine Mennonite, Germantown deacon Henrich Cassel.

The woods northeastward up the Skippack Creek toward Bucks County were also alive with speculation and settlement. Among the investors there was veteran surveyor Thomas Fairman of Shackamaxon, whose latest purchase, immediately prior to the Clemenses' settling at Skippack, had been a 1,000-acre tract at the head of the Skippack Creek. This was where, in what would become Franconia Township, the town of Souderton was to appear.

The departures of the Clemens and Kolb families from the Palatinate in 1709 had quickened emigration awareness in their neighborhood. We have seen Henrich Kolb's older brother, Bishop Peter, making it clear that he wished to follow Henrich, whom he had just ordained to a similar office, to their brothers' home in Pennsylvania. This had not pleased Amsterdam's learned physician-pastor of the conservative Doopsgezind Zon congregation, Dr. Hermanus Schijn, who was all too aware just then of what he called the "large group" of Pennsylvania-bound Palatine refugees still descending on Rotterdam. He had heard rumors that "about ten thousand" more were stranded in London. Since the leadership needs of the Mennonites at

Germantown, Schijn wrote to Peter Kolb, were now "taken care of by the coming of your brother, we again advise you absolutely against the journey."

The cautious Dutch advice must have been accepted, since neither Bishop Kolb nor any more of his brothers would leave for Pennsylvania before 1717, when the youngest, Thielman Jr., would complete the familial move. This was not the feeling, however, in the parental circle left behind by Anneli Clemens. Before she and her husband Gerhart could settle into the Pennsylvania forest, her elderly parents Hans and Elizabeth Stauffer had decided to follow them. With their three young sons, a daughter Elizabeth with husband Paul Friedt, and a little granddaughter Maria, they made a traveling party of eight. Unlike most of the resourceless Palatines swarming to Rotterdam in the previous spring and summer, the Stauffers, like their Clemens son-in-law already in Pennsylvania, had money to pay their way. And so, unadvisedly late in the year (November 1709) for such a journey, and on their own, their family party left the castle grounds at Alsheim to launch on the Rhine from the nearby town of Weissenau.

What could induce an elderly grandfather to move across an ocean? For 38 years the Swiss-born Hans Stauffer, born in the same year as William Penn (who was also still itching to emigrate!), had been a Palatine farmer near the Rhine. Now, leaving hearth and home again at the age of 66, he was still a generation younger than his grandfather Christian had been in 1671 when in his 90s his family and clan had been frightened from their native Bernese valley. The present trip, though voluntary, must have been another lonely one—down the widening Rhine, past Bingen and Neuwied, and into the Netherlands. It took two months, with Stauffer noting at least 14 landings. For unrecorded reasons, the family concluded their river voyage not at the shipping nexus of Rotterdam, where the Clemenses and Kolbs had joined the thousands of "Poor Palatines" six months earlier, but in Amsterdam. Did old Hans know of connections there, and was he hoping for support from the city's famously sympathetic Doopsgezinden? He had certainly never forgotten how, nearly four decades earlier, the Dutch from Amsterdam had sent money to help his weary folk coming by foot from Switzerland to the Palatinate.

Although Stauffer's notes include nothing about contacts in Amsterdam, his family's two-week stay there could easily have caught the attention of the influential Pastor Schijn, who in the previous spring had conversed about migration with the Stauffers' bishop Peter Kolb. In any case, a few days after the Stauffers arrived in town, Dr. Schijn submitted a proposal from his affluent home on the *Heerengracht* (Gentlemen's Canal) to the more liberal Lam and Toren Doopsgezind congregations. The current refugee emergency, he declared, just as the one back in the 1670s, was a calling to the otherwise estranged Dutch congregations to form a joint committee to serve "on behalf of our fellow believers from the Palatinate, who are here, or who would yet come." The newly "urgent needs" for help, he stated, "could not easily brook any delay for many." In response, a collection of 50,000 florins flowed in quickly.

Other Mennonite news of "needs" on Dr. Schijn's mind was pouring in from beyond the Palatinate. Pathetic inquiries from the Stauffers' old home in Bern were reminding the Dutch of hundreds of Anabaptists in mounting trouble there, with some of them having been in prison for two years. (There was even now *another* Hans Stauffer—a nephew?—with three children in hiding at Eggiwil, the village Hans had left in 1671.) A second Dutch Mennonite relief operation was organized, this time overseen by the new "Committee for Relief" that Pastor Schijn had called for while the Stauffer family party was pausing in town. Fortunately, the Stauffers themselves (helped in Amsterdam?) had enough funds and contacts to continue on their own Pennsylvania-bound way toward London.

Years of suppression of Anabaptists in Bern's Emme River Valley were now culminating in a forced expulsion. The canton's lords had ordered hostages brought from Eggiwil to the city. They were particularly angry with the minister Benedicht Brechbühl, who, after being expelled twice, had stubbornly stolen back to his hillside farm at Aeschau. A widely aware man, he had taken the opportunity of his forced absence to visit Mennonites both west of the Rhine where our story's Hans Stauffer lived, and in the Kraichgau, the adopted home of other Emmentalers such as Hans Ruth or miller Theodorus Eby. In January 1709, paid vigilantes flushed Brechbühl out of a haystack on his upland farm. Jailed with other Emmentalers for a year in the city of Bern, he was the most notable passenger of a boatload of chained *Täufer* sent down the Rhine in the spring of 1710.

The official expulsion was turned into a business venture by young Bernese entrepreneur Franz Luis Michel. We have noticed him stopping, on his way to Philadelphia, to converse with William Penn in London, regaling him with talk of Indians who knew where to find silver, and suggesting that the Anabaptists evicted from Bern would be valuable as immigrants to Pennsylvania. Penn agreed eagerly, and while the chained Emmentalers were coming down the Rhine, informed the English ambassador in Amsterdam that he had "contracted" with Michel to bring "fifty or Sixty Swissers, called Menonists," on their way to emigration to Pennsylvania. Urging that they not be delayed in the Netherlands, the Proprietor explained that "Menonists or Menists" were called "Annabaptists" in England.

In spite of Penn's promotion, the project fizzled as soon as the prison boat stopped in Dutch territory. Set free by sympathetic Mennonites, the prisoners, still stiff from their chains, became instant celebrities. Several were invited to preach, and Brechbühl to describe their experience to an indignant Doopsgezind audience in the Hague. Bemused as they might be by the humble folk manners of the freed prisoners, the spellbound listeners carefully recorded Brechbühl's story. After all, they were grandchildren of people who, for a century, had likewise suffered gruesomely for conscience's sake, from Flanders to Friesland.

The Dutch Mennonite experience had produced multiple books of stories, culminating in 1660 in a huge volume entitled *The Bloody Spectacle of the Baptism-minded and Defenseless Christians*. The great tome, subtitled *Martelaers Spiegel* (*Martyrs' Mirror*), made a lasting impression on Brechbühl. It was in another language than his, but nearly a hundred of the stories in its sumptuous edition of 1685 were made vivid with drawings by one of Holland's finest artists. It must have been a sensation for the unusually imaginative Bernese Anabaptist to find, in the book's closing pages, a brief account of his own community's troubles, including the refugee outflow to the Palatinate in 1671. Reading this helped to bond the unschooled farmer with his urbane Dutch benefactors. And they, though toleration had allowed them to become successful merchants with children in the arts and professions, felt a reciprocal, overwhelming identity with the roughshod, long-bearded refugees. Benedicht Brechbühl asked for three copies of the great *Mirror*.

William Penn probably never heard of the Hans Stauffer family. As in the previous year, though, in April 1710 he was again hoping for more Anabaptist emigration to his colony. But the aging Proprietor was otherwise in a melancholy mood. On his 65th birthday he wrote to his embattled secretary Logan in Philadelphia that he had run out of patience with landowners in the Delaware Valley who ignored his requests for financial support. Those stingy "numsculls," he wrote, "vile pack of brutish spirits" that they were, had better not underestimate what he, though like a weakened Samson of old, was still capable of legally doing to them. Such language, unfitting to the image of a benevolent Quaker, was actually no worse than the barrage of criticisms Logan was personally receiving in Philadelphia. As Penn's old friend Isaac Norris reported, members of the Pennsylvania Assembly were politically polarized, displaying what he called "A strange unaccountable humour . . . of Straining & resenting Everything." Animosity toward the constantly manipulating Logan had metastasized. Instead of rejoicing in Pennsylvania's tolerant atmosphere, its lawmakers had descended into "Voluminous" argument about "Everything that is said or done . . . always remonstrating, and valluing the last word highly." In such an atmosphere, wrote Norris, "I See no room to Expect much effectual business." In fact, things had reached such a point that Logan, under threat of impeachment, fled Philadelphia in the fall of 1709, taking a wheat-loaded boat for Portugal. By the time the Stauffer family reached London, the secretary, carrying an Indian remedy for snakebite, was on the high seas sailing for the same city.

To the confusion of future historians, in the very same week of the arrival of the Bernese prison-boat in the Netherlands, *another* small party of emigrating Mennonites appeared at Rotterdam. These were a set of self-motivated "29 Palatines" whose Swiss Anabaptist grandparents had migrated northward after 1650 from both Zurich and Bern to the Kraichgau region east of the Rhine, midway between Heidelberg and Heilbronn. As a group of mostly siblings and cousins traveling on their own initiative, they had decided to emigrate to the "Charolina" invitingly described in a recently published book. Having apparently no prior contact with William Penn, they checked in at Rotterdam with Hendrik van Toren, the Mennonite businessman-minister who in the previous summer had been in charge of shipping thousands of "poor Palatines" to London. At this point, they changed their destination to Pennsylvania, appealing successfully to Dutch Mennonites for a travel subsidy. By the time they wrote their thanks for this heartwarming aid, they were in London, where, on June 24, 1710, they boarded the unarmed Pennsylvania-bound *Mary Hope*. As in the previous summer, a weary Penn was well aware of who was going.

Old as he was, Penn was having a busy time of it. A few weeks before the departure of the *Mary Hope* he had entertained four Mohawk "Indian kings" then making a sensational visit in London. This must only have intensified his feelings—then very gloomy—regarding his own part of the American scene. The pressure of debt had brought him to the point of submitting a proposal to sell back to the English Crown the government (not the land) of Pennsylvania. Though the original debt owed by King Charles II to William Penn Sr. had been estimated at £16,000, the son had never received a penny beyond the grant of the land itself. He now agreed to accept £12,000 for the surrender of the colony's government. This would enable him to pay off the heavy mortgage he had taken out from Quaker friends in order to satisfy the long-standing Ford suit.

With relief at last in sight, Penn should have been able to take more satisfaction in his colony. But a letter he was sending over with the Mennonite-carrying *Mary Hope* was again suffused with bitter irony. "It is a mournful consideration," he wrote to his "ould Friends" among Pennsylvania's legislating Assembly, "and the cause of deep affliction to me that I am forced . . . to speak to the people of that province in a language I once hoped I should never have had occasion to use." He had heard too much from his currently visiting secretary Logan about how members of the Assembly had disrespectfully opposed his ideas of governance. "When it pleased God," he reminisced, "to open a way for me to settle that colony, I had reason to expect a solid comfort from the services done to many hundreds of people." He had rejoiced "in seeing them prosper, and growing up to a flourishing country, blessed with liberty, ease, and plenty, beyond what many of themselves could expect." "But, alas! as to my part, instead of reaping [similar] advantages, some of the greatest of my troubles have arisen from thence." Having by now "exhausted" most of his own funds to support the Pennsylvania dream, what was his reward? An "undeserved opposition" even by Quakers in the Assembly that was threatening to "sink me into sorrow."

> The attacks on my reputation; the many indignities put upon me in papers sent over . . . ; the secret insinuations against my justice . . . ; my lands entered upon without any regular method; my manors invaded (under pretence I had not duly surveyed them) . . . , a right to my overplus land

unjustly claimed by the possessors of the tracts in which they are found . . . , the violence that has been particularly shown to my secretary. . . . In short . . . I cannot but mourn the unhappiness of my portion.

When this long, passionate, Logan-informed epistle arrived in Philadelphia with the Mennonites on the *Mary Hope* in September 1710, it was published as *A Serious Expostulation With the Inhabitants of Pennsylvania*.

CHAPTER TWELVE

Pennsylvania's Best Bargain

1710

Two DAYS after the Conestoga Indians had conferred with the governor in Philadelphia, the Mennonite passengers of the *Mary Hope* arrived in town. Already, while sailing up the Delaware, these Herrs, Kendigs, Müllers, and Mylins from the German Kraichgau had gotten their first taste of America. The apples and peaches they were offered were, they said, "the largest and finest fruit they had ever seen." Several of the most eager chose to walk along the river's banks. Their emotions were not lost on a fellow traveler—the very Quaker who four years earlier had preached to the Indians at Conestoga, and on Thursdays had done the same for the "Palatines" on board. Though they, like the Indians, did not understand Thomas Chalkley's English, they had seemed "satisfied" with his sermons, he recorded. From their body language, as they gazed out from the ship's deck, he judged that these Mennonists were "wonderfully pleased with the country, greatly admiring the pleasantness and fertility of it."

Like their Swiss grandparents after the Thirty Years' War, these immigrants carried a genetic ability and will to produce a new agricultural *Gottesgarten*. Eager for good, plentiful, and cheap land, they chose a location momentous for their future in Pennsylvania. Instead of joining their predecessors (including fellow Kraichgauan Hans Groff) at now-filled-up Germantown—or even Bebberstaun, where the Kolbs and Gerhart Clemens had settled—or probing into the woods northward into the still "vacant land" of the Lenapes' Perkioma, they looked west toward the Susquehanna. As early as 1684 William Penn had advertised the "goodness" of the limestone soil there. Now, with the shrewd James Logan being away in London, there were no complicated dealings. It took only three weeks after the *Mary Hope* had docked for its Mennonite passengers to get a warrant for surveying a manor-sized 10,000 acres at the head of the Pequea Creek in future Lancaster County. Generations of land cultivation in their memory had prepared them to recognize the fecundity under the stupendous oaks just west of the Brandywine and Octorara watersheds.

Whereas, while passing through Rotterdam the "29 Palatines" had felt it necessary to apply for monetary aid, they now proved able to pay Quaker surveyor Jacob Taylor's fee for laying out their grant. Hearing of this after returning from England, Secretary Logan commented, "Never was a surveyor in this province better paid for any other claim." It had certainly been a worthwhile investment, since the acreage laid out for them along the Pequea would eventually be considered one of the best land bargains in Pennsylvania history. Inexpensively acquired, it was the nucleus of what would eventually be called Pennsylvania's "Garden Spot."

As the Palatines came to Conestoga, a reshuffling was transpiring among the colony's Native population. Lenapes were withdrawing westward, and other dislocated groupings were seeking safety by moving northward toward the protection of the Five Nations. A discouraged Shawnee ("southern") chief named *Opessah*, whose people had recently abandoned their homes near the Potomac River, came to consult with the Conestogas near the Susquehanna. Lenapes clinging to the Brandywine Creek, west of Philadelphia, decided "not to plant corn this year" (1710), with one of their old women reporting "ugly talk" among her men. A worried Governor Gookin, repaying a Native visit of 1709 by traveling to the Susquehanna, found the Conestogas friendly enough, but also complaining of traders who got their young men drunk so they could buy their pelts cheaply.

Also arriving unexpectedly at the Conestoga village were three headmen of another troubled southern grouping: the Tuscaroras. Their home in what was now called "Carolina" was being overwhelmed by European immigrants, with more shiploads anticipated. Like the similarly displaced Conoys and Shawnees, the Tuscaroras were appealing for a safe home by the Susquehanna under the Five Nations umbrella. Coming to Conestoga, they laid down over two dozen wampum belts, speaking emotionally about peace, safety, and domestic dwelling. The first belt, "sent from their old women," carried the wish "that without danger or trouble they might fetch wood & water" in a new home by the Susquehanna. The fourth, from their older men, requested that "the Wood . . . might be as safe for them as their forts," and the seventh, a hope that in a new home their people might "not be afraid of a mouse, or any other thing that Ruffles the Leaves."

This was the very moment when the worried Conestogas found that yet another home-seeking family cluster—this one not Indian or even English—was about to settle beside them on their rich Susquehanna watershed soil. Though their recent experience with fur traders as neighbors had not been positive, in less than a year, upon being "required" in William Penn's name to accept the Mennonite settlers as neighbors, they acknowledged them to be "safely seated." Before long the newcomers, without having to take an oath of loyalty, were given legal ownership of their epochal purchase. And soon larger groups of their people would be leveling the woods all around the Native Conestoga village. Logan himself, immediately after returning from London, established a mill among the Mennonite plantations, as other Philadelphia speculators sprang with him into action around "Mill Creek."

CHAPTER THIRTEEN

Home on the Earth

1711-1712

A LL OF OUR story's main characters—Lenape, English, German, Quaker, or Mennonite—dreamed of passing on to their families a place to dwell in America. Aging William Penn, while his mind remained clear, never let his own hope for this die, not even when, after his financial troubles had eased, he bought for his young second family a broad country house at Ruscombe, near Reading just northwest of London. His 39-year-old still-unmarried secretary Logan, ready to return to Pennsylvania after two years in London, was intimate with his employer's sunset dream, and shared his own version of it. But he was pensive in December 1711, waiting on a rocking ship at Spithead for a calmer wind to carry him back to Philadelphia. The "vast troubles and Disappointments" his employer had suffered, he noted, had taken a "visible" toll on "the usual strength and brightness of his great Genius."

In Logan's hands was a prized commission, signed by Penn at "Tom's Coffee House," that put him in direct charge of selling the Proprietor's lands. Actually, the secretary was now just as determined to make his own land-based fortune. When not collecting and reading among the classics during his English sojourn, he had been buying up (cheaply) from some of Penn's long-frustrated "First Purchasers" the rights to Pennsylvania acreage they had paid for a quarter-century earlier, but which had never been settled on or even surveyed. It was evident that the weary Penn, discouraged by disrespect from his two oldest children, was still clinging to the hope of taking both them and his second family to Pennsylvania. But Logan noted frankly: there were "so little hopes of matters going right" with the namesake heir in the first family that there was no point in writing "anything in relation to him."

Logan had already learned well that dealing with both land and "the skin [fur] trade" involved three groups of Indians: the local Delawares ("our Lenappys"), the Conestogas of the Susquehanna Valley, and the much more numerous and stronger Five Nations (Iroquois) of New York. Of the Lenapes, only family remnants were left 25 miles northwest of Philadelphia, where the towering oaks, chestnuts, and hickories around Skippack were being leveled by Gerhart Clemens and four Kolb brothers. Most of the local Natives, including the now grown-up Sassoonan, had sought new hunting ground either as far up the Schuylkill Valley as Tulpehocken, or west at the forks of the broader Susquehanna. Still, an opportunity for Logan to meet their main leaders came within months of his return from London.

Governor Charles Gookin had been unexpectedly asked by four Lenape "kings" living in the Susquehanna Valley to come up the Schuylkill above Manatawny (later Douglassville area) for a special meeting. The location they named was the recently built home of a Swedish settler, Mounce Jones. When the busy governor requested instead that the Natives confer with him in Philadelphia, the "kings" countered with an offer to meet 15 miles above town, at the familiar house of their miller friend Edward Farmar on the Wissahickon Creek at Whitemarsh. Having lived there since boyhood, before most of the Lenapes had moved out to Tulpehocken or farther west, Farmar had grown up speaking their language, and had thereby become a trusted interpreter in treaties.

Significantly, the Indians were not returning to the traditional riverside Shackamaxon site where their ancestors had negotiated in 1677 and as late as 1700 with their northern Five Nations "Uncles." Not only had that immemorial meeting site been domesticated into the estate of surveyor Thomas Fairman; by now it was neighbor to a mushrooming town of European immigrants.

It was thus to the Wissahickon, rather than the Cohocksink, that on May 19, 1712, Governor Gookin with his council, including Logan, took horse, to hear what the dozen visiting Natives had in mind. It became evident that their main leader was now Sassoonan, the "little lad" who 29 years earlier had watched William Penn deal with Tamany at Perkasie, and whom we shall later find named by his Lenape people "Keeper of the Wampum." Among the three fellow sachems accompanying him was Scolitchy, who served as their "speaker."

This visit, Scolitchy explained to the officials, was to inform them that the Lenapes, after long delay, were about to carry wampum on a very special northward journey. Its purpose was to refresh and keep friendly their traditional relationship to their Five Nations "Uncles." Any Indian politics—in these years of Queen Anne's War when British and French soldiers were sparring for control in Canada and Nova Scotia—was of acute interest to Pennsylvania's officials. Their concern was: to which of the competing European empires would the powerful Five Nations lend their loyalty and lucrative fur trade? No wonder the Governor, the Council, and Logan were keen to learn just what the Lenapes had in mind.

The visit's importance was apparent in the ritual dignity with which the Natives laid out on the floor of Farmar's house no less than 32 wampum belts of varying "figures," which they were going to carry northward. They also presented "a long Indian pipe" or "Calumet," recorded Logan, with "a stone head" and "a wooden or cane shaft [with] feathers fixt to it like wings." They said it had been given to them years ago by their northern "Uncles" as a sign of their relationship. That these Lenapes, displaced westward from the Neshaminy and Perkiomen watersheds, had not lost the immemorial sense of their identity was evident in the carefulness of Scolitchy's comments regarding each of the belts. His interpretations were closely parallel to those of the previous year's southern Tuscaroras seeking a place to live at Conestoga. Here by the Wissahickon, too, three-fourths of the Lenapes' belts had been made by women whose theme was the longing for a livable relationship with the Five Nations, ensuring them a safe home in the woods between the Schuylkill and the Susquehanna to which they had recently moved. Their feminine litany of peaceful dwelling on the earth was more than poignant. Ironically, whereas the Mennonites taking over Lenape land at Skippack could write, but would leave for our story no record of their feelings, words of the non-writing Lenapes (recorded by Logan) remain to remind us of their emotions in the time of land transition.

It was not that land-losing Mennonites could have no words on the theme. Back in the Rhineland, their Bishop Benedicht Brechbühl, recently caught hiding in a mountainside haystack and expelled in chains from Hans Stauffer's native Bern, was writing to Dutch friends that, though "I do not know of any place where I can live with my little flock," he was trusting "that the Lord . . . is preparing a place for me to live." Meanwhile, he had found room for his little family in the Kraichgau region south of Heidelberg, from which the Mennonite settlers at Conestoga had recently emigrated. Around him, in the village of Weiler and the neighboring Immelhaus and Birkenau *hof*s at the foot of the Lutheran-owned Steinsberg tower, lived many Mennonites whose families had come, a generation or two earlier, from Zurich and Bern. Their future homes, all unknown to them, would be clearings in woods north of Philadelphia: Derstein, Funck, Frey, Graff, Hagey, Landis, Meyer, Musselman, Oberholtzer, Rosenberger, Ruth, Sauter. All of them, as Brechbühl's family moved in, were feeling increasingly restless, now that the knightly land-owners who had welcomed Anabaptists up from Alsace after the Thirty Years' War were becoming less hospitable. And now that the Bernese lords of Benedicht's "earthly fatherland" were trying to root his people out of it, he could only pray that the "almighty God [would] awaken the hearts and minds of kings and princes of other places to be favorable to us." As told in ancient scripture, Benedicht believed, God would let an oppressed family have a home. Amazingly, this hope would soon be fulfilled in the form of a Pennsylvania plantation he would acquire amidst the Pequea Creek settlement. What sense, though, would such a divinely certified story make to people driven from the land taken over by the God-blessed invaders? The Tuscarora Indians, for example, were outraged to be finding their land in Carolina—renamed "New Bern"—flooded in 1711 with German-speaking immigrants. And how was that all understood by one of the Mennonite newcomers, Jacob Wismar, a fellow camper in London with the Clemenses and Kolbs, who had then sailed with the migrants to New Bern? Did he have time for such a question as he ran for his life from angry Tuscaroras in whose land he wished to claim his own new home?

Our stories are conveniently simple. The theme of a safe earthly dwelling was certainly stressed at the Wissahickon parley, as Scolitchy explained the thoughts that were to be carried with wampum to the Lenapes' northern superiors. The first belt was from a woman who desired "peace, that she may eat & drink in Quiet," and another from one hoping to "plant and reap in quiet." "The fifteenth [was] by a woman . . . glad that they can enjoy peace so quietly to bed and rise in the same manner. . . . The nineteenth That they may build their houses firm, as to continue there long, and not be obliged to make them slight, as if they were on all occasions to fly. . . . The twenty-fifth that they may make Racoon & other Blanketts to clothe them, & sett Down in them in peace. . . . The Twenty Eight that they are glad their young men have the Privilege of going far from their own habitacons to hunt abroad in peace, & that they can return home & Eat & Drink & Enjoy themselves.... The Thirtieth that they are Glad they can hunt & bring home relief to their poor relacons." And finally, that "They hope [the Five Nations] will be pleased with the presents now offered, and that their children will have it in Everlasting Remembrance."

Was there a single thought here that the European-born listeners would find primitive or different from their own sense of home?

There were also two special wampum belts, one of which had been strategically left by William Penn 11 years earlier for the Lenapes to take to the Five Nations. They now said they were not sure what those belts signified. Why was that so, if, as Penn had once observed, Indians kept very exact memory of the contents of their treaties? It must certainly have meant that the Lenapes neither fully understood the motives of the officials to whom they had "sold" much of the land of their birth, nor were they comfortable with their relation with the superior Five Nations. It was now explained to them, probably by Secretary Logan, that the special belts from Penn were to have been invitations (one *from* him personally and the other *by* him on behalf of the Lenapes) to the Five Nations to accept the same good relations that Pennsylvania had had with the "nearest Neighboring [Lenape] Indians ... ever since William Penn first came into this land." When Governor Gookin wondered why the Lenapes hadn't ever followed through with such important belts, they could only claim that the man who had intended to carry them northward (possibly a son of Tamany) had died "very soon after" Penn's departure in 1701. This was less than a full explanation. In any case, the Lenapes were now told to be sure to take the two belts along with their own wampum, in order to make Pennsylvania's offer of friendship "fully known" to the northern Nations, so that "nothing but peace & Love might reign" between them. Once the belts had been shown to the Iroquois leaders, they were to be brought back to Pennsylvania for keeping in covenantal remembrance.

Though perhaps not fully grasping the meaning of Governor Gookin's directive, the Lenapes presented him in closing with "a Bundle of Drest Deer Skins," followed by a second bundle meant to apologize for the smallness of the main gift. This hint of poverty was then replaced by a rich memory of peoplehood, as, after filling their "long winged pipe" with tobacco, they lit and presented it to the Governor and his Council, "to smoak a few blasts of it" one by one, "as the token of the greatest friendship that could be shown." In return, the Governor, Logan, and the rest of the Council, concerned to establish relations with the far more powerful Five Nations, resolved to send along on the Lenape mission "a fine Laced . . . coat and a fine white shirt for each king or Chief of the five nations." At this, the Lenape delegation "Expressed a great satisfaction," and were themselves ritually given the usual "presents" in appreciation for their friendly pre-journey visit.

Five months later—again led by Sassoonan and Scolitchy, and again with miller Edward Farmar interpreting—the Lenape travelers reported back, this time at Philadelphia rather than Farmar's mill, with an optimistic account of their journey. Their diplomatic success was evident in wampum belts they had received from the Five Nations, along with gifts of beaver, bear, and deer skins. Their northern hosts, they reported, were ready to consider shifting their fur trade away from Albany to Philadelphia. That was very welcome news for James Logan. In fact, it was becoming his long-standing passion to court the powerful Iroquois in preference to the Lenapes, while always giving the latter the impression that he was only helping them.

It has been worthwhile to pause over the dual courteous Lenape visits of 1712 because they began a 30-year-long series of encounters between two of our story's central characters: Sassoonan, future titular head of his Lenape people, and James Logan, main mover of Pennsylvania's Indian policies. Surely neither of these men—nor any other participant, European or Native—would forget the delicate atmosphere of this initial conversation. Of course, though it meant everything to the ceremonious Natives, it probably was not even heard of by settlers like the Mennonite Stauffers, Clemenses, and Kolbs, gratefully establishing their new homes in the nearby Native-abandoned woods. It was not their story. Their story was that Gerhart and Anneli Clemens, with new baby Abraham to go with brothers Johannes and Jacob, were taking only two years to pay off their 100-acre purchase at Skippack. Although they had no meetinghouse, they had church leadership from three of the four neighboring Kolb brothers: Jacob as a deacon, and Martin a minister, serving with the oldest, Henrich, as bishop. Only 29-year-old Johannes, who with wife Sarah and growing family was also prospering, would not remain part of the local story.

Busy with forest-clearing relieved only by the weekly sabbath, these settlers needed any available economic advantage. None of them or their neighbors welcomed the idea of an extra expense like the (so far neglected) annual quitrent that William Penn had dreamed would give his wife and children a comfortable continuing income. This was an unpleasant lesson for Receiver Logan, who had hardly been back in Philadelphia when one of his deputies complained of "spight and mallice," "Redicule," and "hypocritticall Laughter" from landowners when they were asked to pay up. They seemed actually surprised at the collectors' "Insolence to demand Quitt Rents." Before long Logan passed the unpleasant duties of Receiver General to a younger Philadelphian, James Steel.

Whereas only a few anecdotes would survive concerning the last Lenapes living just north of Philadelphia, an echo of their presence lived on permanently in their names for creeks such as Neshaminy, Perkiomen, and Wissahickon. In both the future-named Hilltown and Franconia Townships there were "Indian Fields," and an "Indian Creek" flowed into the Perkiomen's East Branch just above the Clemens purchase. A township next to Skippack would take the creek-name of Towamencin. An unwritten family story from that neighborhood, where both Thomas Fairman and David Powell surveyed and speculated, would carry into the twenty-first century a claim for a peaceful encounter between arriving settlers and lingering Natives. It took place on a 200-acre land grant surveyed by Powell, and bought by Fairman in 1712 for his son Thomas Jr., at whose death it passed to younger brother Benjamin. Moving onto this ground while it was still in the Fairman name was the family of immigrant Henry Frey, who had lived for 20 years near Germantown. Two of the Frey sons, runs the tale,

> walked up from the Wissahickon, a distance of eighteen or twenty miles, on Monday mornings, bringing their provisions along with them for the week, for the purpose of making a clearing and erecting a house, which they completed by the following spring. A few Indians, who appeared friendly, were still lingering here, having a couple of wigwams on the banks of the stream. The chief, who visited the scene of [the Freys'] labors, observed them eating bread, when they gave him a piece, which he ate and pronounced good. On the following week they brought him an extra loaf, at which he was greatly delighted, and in return the following day brought them a saddle of venison.

Another account had Henry Frey talking into the night with a Lenape couple. Before the conversation ended, the woman left, only to appear the next morning carrying a baby she had birthed during the night.

Such idyllic co-dwelling would be the theme of similar anecdotes told by generations of those who inherited and farmed land named for those who had been compelled to leave it. Our story will continue to show, on the other hand, that already while William Penn was still living, wherever in southeastern Pennsylvania the tide of actual settlement lapped against Native hunting grounds, there were tensions. Before the Lenapes had been back from their journey to the Five Nations, another delegation—this one of Conestogas from the Susquehanna Valley—had brought to Philadelphia a complaint about French fur traders who had moved from Lenape territory along the Schuylkill to the Susquehanna. Hogs and horses belonging to trader Ann Letort, they complained, were repeatedly invading the maize of the Conestogas' "Queen" Conguegas. Worse, when Natives had wished to pay Letort a "friendly visit," she had, "without any provocation," not only "turned them out of doors," but told them "very rudely" that her "house was her own," and that the "Land was hers, for she had bought it" from William Penn. Such talk was a shock to Natives whose dream of Penn was not about private property but shared friendliness.

Penn's dream at this time was still of returning to his province. He made it plain to his Governor's executive council at Philadelphia that Pennsylvania was the "place of the whole earth, that . . . I long the most to be at, & where I pray and hope my god will graceously please to bring me in his time." He was still trying to pull off one of his greatest deals: getting out from under his huge mortgage debt by "selling" Pennsylvania's "government" (though not its land, which he considered his second family's financial legacy) back to the English Crown. Some parts of the deal were already in place, and he took in an early down payment from Queen Anne's treasury. But the weakness of age was so evident that, even while telling Pennsylvanians to "depend upon" his return, Penn re-wrote and revised his will. Leaving nothing of his American estate to his dissolute son William, who, however, still expected to inherit all of Pennsylvania, he optimistically designated for his wife Hannah £300 a year from the American "rents" he himself had so far not succeeded in collecting. This was to enable her to raise their still-young children properly, fulfilling their father's "desire [that] they may settle at least in good part in America where I leave them [an] Inheritance from Generation to Generation which the Lord serve and prosper. Amen."

CHAPTER FOURTEEN

A Voice Silenced, A Voice Raised
1712–1716

WE HAVE NOTED that when a vigorous 46-year-old William Penn sailed home from his colony for the second (and last) time in 1701, he had left wampum belts for the Lenapes to take to their Five Nations superiors. He had also promised a quick return for himself, but this would never happen. Nor had the westward-fading Natives then carried out his diplomatic gesture to their northern "Uncles." By 1712 both Penn and the Lenapes had relocated—he with his young second family to the newly purchased gracious house at Ruscombe just northwest of London, and his Lenape friends from the Delaware Valley 90 miles northwestward to the Forks of the Susquehanna.

By the time the Lenapes had finally made their visit to the Five Nations in 1712, Penn, no longer in touch with them, was describing himself as "ould and infirme." His first child by second wife Hannah, the American-born Johnny, was only 13. Though a mild stroke had prompted Penn to make a new will, he had not stopped imagining his children becoming "americanized," with "good Tracts of Land . . . to clear and settle upon, as Jacob's sons did." He implored Quaker friends to pray fervently for his health, so "that I may see pennsylvania once more before I die"—"if I dye not suddenly."

The aged Proprietor was both worn out from trying to pay his debts by selling his colony's government to Queen Anne's officials, and increasingly discouraged by the lack of sympathy from the settlers to whom his colony had given a home. There was no joy from the surviving children of his first family. William Jr. had proved undependable at best, and Laetitia's husband Aubrey was "bullying" his declining father-in-law for more inheritance money. To these troubles were added, in the summer of 1712, the deaths of both of Hannah's parents at Bristol, 70 miles west of Ruscombe. The "great business" of settling their estates kept William, Hannah, and three of her children at Bristol for months. Feeling greatly stressed there, a frail Penn sat down on October 4 to vent his frustrations to his American secretary. It would be his last letter. Suddenly, as Hannah watched, her husband stopped writing. As he tried again in vain, it became evident that he was having another stroke. This one was serious, taking away for good his mental strength, with its vast power of personality. There would be six more years of a pleasantly declining dementia at Ruscombe, but no more intellectual conversation, nor talk of living in Pennsylvania. The public life of this friend of kings, Quakers, and Indians was over.

News of the Proprietor's indisposition would not reach Skippack, where the Kolb and Clemens "Palatines" he had recommended three years earlier were diligently hacking out plantations. Sometimes, when grain had to be sent 16 miles to Farmar's mill on the Wissahickon, a Native might be found for the task. But even that could be frustrating, since old Indian paths were "liable to be fenced up" by new land-purchasers, and could thus be used only "upon sufferance" (permission). Wealthy Isaac Norris complained that a road planned to lead from Plymouth to the Perkiomen Creek would run "aslant more than four miles" through the manor he had bought from William Penn Jr., "obliquely cutting" across its "Severall lotts." Such were the issues as nine Mennonite settlers, including Gerhart Clemens and the Kolb brothers, joined 20 other neighbors petitioning "for a road or cartway from the upper end of [Bebber's] township down to the wid-marsh, or Farmar's mill." Even that, when granted, was not without difficulty, as it prompted complaints from settlers whose clearings would be crossed by the proposed road. Some farmers, resenting newly laid-out tracks, kept on working the ground right through them.

The improvement of a road brought real estate value to the neighboring "vacant" woodland in what would become Towamencin and Salford Townships. Gerhart Clemens, whose plantation at Skippack did not include a creek big enough to power a mill, traveled to Maryland where dealer Matthias van Bebber had more land to sell. Other active speculators included perennial surveyors Thomas Fairman of Shackamaxon and David Powell of south Philadelphia. Elderly as they were, they were signing up for land purchases scattered from Skippack and Towamencin into the future-named Salford and Franconia Townships. One of Fairman's requests was, as already noted, for a "Thous'd acres of Land back in the Woods" (on the site of the future Souderton). The dealings of both Welshmen came up for criticism in court. Fairman, involved all the way from Perkasie in Bucks County to the western bank of the Schuylkill in Chester, was accused of having "fraudulently Concealed" a transaction near Skippack involving land he had "no Right to sell." Powell drew on an unused 14-year-old grant of 1,000 acres to survey land on both sides of a Skippack tributary—the first land deal in the future-named Salford Township.

Fairman, whose surveys just south of the Skippack-Perkiomen region had by now covered over 40,000 acres, was at last "Feeling cymptoms of Mortality." Bequeathing his old plantation at Shackamaxon to his wife and two sons, he hoped that after his death she would be helped by his "good friend David Powel, of Philadelphia." When Fairman would die in the midst of his land-dealings in 1714, his estate would still claim 1,700 of the 20,000 acres that he had owned at some time over three decades.

Sizable as the two surveyors' speculative acreage was, it would be far surpassed by the estate that Philadelphia's James Logan, now marrying at last, was beginning to build. He was acquiring tracts to resell at steep markups near the new Mennonite settlement out at Conestoga. With a warehouse in Philadelphia, a mill at Pequea, a trader's store on the Susquehanna, and Mennonite-driven wagons regularly hauling pelts back to the Delaware, he was well on his way to cornering Pennsylvania's fur trade. His service as secretary for both the Governor's Council and the Commissioners of Property gave him extensive insider knowledge concerning unfolding relations with Pennsylvania's Natives. He would thus soon get to know their spokesman Sassoonan very well.

Would these two main characters in our story ever understand each other? For better or worse, most of what we try to hear of Sassoonan's emerging voice comes filtered through the secretarial rhetoric of Logan's pen, beginning with the recording of a "friendly treaty" in June 1715. A few weeks after locusts had filled the woods with a chorus so loud that the settlers could not hear their cattle's bells, a raggedly dressed Sassoonan showed up unannounced at the Philadelphia courthouse with a party of Delawares carrying diplomatic wampum and deerskins. Following the death of headman Scolitchy since the meeting three years earlier at Farmar's mill, Sassoonan had taken up the speaker's role. Now in his 40s, he claimed to be representing not just the Lenapes, but other small displaced Native groupings (except the original Conestogas) that had been re-clustering in the Schuylkill and Susquehanna valleys. With Sassoonan, but speaking little, had come the discouraged head of the recently arriving Shawnees, Opessah, and several other Lenape men recorded as "Chiefs." The officials in Philadelphia called Sassoonan the Delaware "king."

The visit had been prompted, it turned out, by economic "murmurs" among the Lenape. This was unwelcome news to Logan, who was finding fur trading personally enriching. Sassoonan, though his main subject was an economic grievance threatening all Lenape-Christian relations, began by affirming the original friendship. Secretary Logan did not consider the "great Ceremony" of introductory "Rattles and songs" interesting enough to interpret in the meeting minutes, but he did note how "Sassoonan the king" offered to elderly Governor Patrick Gookin, to all the English persons present, and "afterwards to all his Indians," the same "calamet" (decorated pipe) brought to Farmar's mill three years earlier. Then Logan transcribed what now stands as the earliest recorded commentary from Sassoonan's lips—words of hopeful friendship. The calamet, he declared, was "the bond of peace, which they had carried to all the [Native] nations round." Now, even as he was bringing a complaint, he offered it to the Governor as a "seal of peace," both among the various Native tribes, and between them and the English. "By holding up their hands," Logan recorded, they "desired . . . that the God of Heaven might be Witness to it, and that there might be a firm peace . . . forever" between them and their English friends.

Sassoonan spoke in the metaphoric idiom of his people. William Penn's "first coming"—vivid in the speaker's memory—had "made a clear & open Road all the way to the Indians." They now wished that, in spite of the recent "murmurs," a "road" of clear communication "might be kept open, and [that] all obstructions should be removed." As far as the Lenapes were concerned, they would "take care" that it would be so. Sassoonan next presented the Governor with a wampum belt symbolizing that the Indians and the English "should Joyn hand in hand so firmly that nothing, even the greatest tree, should be able to divide them a sunder." This was imagery similar to that on the most famous wampum specimen of all—a belt showing an Indian and a white man with joined hands—that Penn had taken back to England, where it would be cherished for a century and a half until returned finally to Philadelphia.

To repeat, the first time Sassoonan's spoken voice was recorded, it was asking for interracial understanding and friendship. It was in an amiable tone that he would maintain, though sometimes troubled, for the rest of the speaker's remaining 35 years. Even now, when asked to change the subject to the particular concern that had brought him to Philadelphia, he persisted with several more wampums on the theme of peace between Native and immigrant people. Then, when he did switch to the "matters of trade" that had brought him to talk, he presented bundles of deerskins instead of wampum. There was a problem, he said, of "no understanding" among his people as to how the fluctuating prices for their furs were set. This uncertainty was illustrated by his own noticeably tattered "breeches." His people, having recently received considerably less for their furs than in previous years, were disturbed by fears of being cheated. It felt as though they were "in the dark," while the "English" controlled the main entrance to a room to which the Indians were given only a separate, less public access.

As optimistic as Logan might be about the trade that was making him wealthy, he now had to record the Lenapes' complaint of being "often imposed on by the weight of our money when they came to sell." Whereas the English "certainly knew the value" of the Indians' wampum or furs, to the Natives the English system was unclear. Still, their gifts of furs were showing good will. When the session concluded, Logan tallied up the worth of the 205 pelts Sassoonan had laid down—deer, fox, raccoon, and fisher. Significantly, the beaver, basic in the previous century to the fur trade, was now missing.

The Governor responded on the following day by stating that, while he trusted the Natives' peaceful intentions, he "hoped that none of them [had] any real Cause to murmur." That would be the typical rhetoric of Philadelphia officials when confronted with Native complaints: hopefully there was no "real" reason for their unease. The Indians should understand and accept the rationale of European commerce. After all, Gookin told them, all dwellers in Pennsylvania, Native or European, were under the regime of a wise and great King (George), who ruled "more Dominions than any King of Britain ever had before him." As for their friend William Penn, he was "still living, tho' but weak in health." And regarding their specific concern about trade, they must learn to think as their "English" friends did: "All trade is uncertain." Since "sometimes a [costume] that is in fashion one year is laid aside the next," it will follow that "the skins they are made of will be of a higher or lower value. It is the same with all our other merchandise." The Indians should "trade with the safest and honestest men" who would offer them the highest price. That, said the Governor, "is our Rule in all our business, and [you] must do the same."

While this logic could have made little sense to the listening Sassoonan, he and his delegation were cheered with a hastily collected "present" of coats, blankets, shirts, gunpowder, lead, and tobacco worth considerably more than the pelts they had brought from the Susquehanna. Gifts, not trading for advantage, were a language the Lenapes could understand.

Unpleasingly, before leaving town after what Governor Gookin called their "very friendly treaty," Sassoonan and his friends bought enough rum for a binge lasting a week. Had the Governor realized that they would not take "more care of themselves," he observed, he "would have prevented their buying it." They were "valuable good men when sober," but when "overcome" by liquor, were "quite lost and become beasts." Only when sober again could they have some friendly conversation, and receive a traveling gift of bread, biscuits, and tobacco. This brought "hearty thanks with Expressions of great satisfaction" from Sassoonan's friends. Yet he himself had a parting murmur about the rum problem. It came, he complained, from the great "Quantities" brought "into the woods" by unscrupulous and unlicensed traders. It was the Governor's duty, he said, to stop this.

Unfortunately, the peace-loving Sassoonan himself would prove not only permanently ambivalent about rum, but tragically humiliated. Though his voice had now been heard at Philadelphia, the Governor's response directing the Indians simply to "stave the Casks and destroy the Liquor, without suffering any of it to be sold or Drank," would be mocked by the reality of what continually happened where Sassoonan lived at the Forks of the Susquehanna.

CHAPTER FIFTEEN

A Mass Migration and a Crooked Affair
1717-1718

SASSOONAN'S TRANSFER by 1709 from his native watershed to the Susquehanna left no written account. Similarly, the story of Mennonites replacing Lenapes on their Delaware Valley homeland is minimally recorded. Remembering this parallel evokes a larger one: DNA from this author's Bernese ancestors suggests that, like the Lenapes, Roths/Ruths had nested for millennia in one narrow Alpine valley in what became Switzerland.

Whereas Hans Stauffer had been among the Bernese refugees of 1671 settling near where they had been received at Ibersheim west of the Rhine, others, such as the families of Henrich Funck and Hans Ruth, had moved farther to the 50-mile distant Mennonite community in the Kraichgau. There they had melded with Mennonites from Zurich, Alsace, and Bern who had been accruing for two decades following the Thirty Years' War. Pleasingly to their landlords, they had been turning wasted fields into what a Lutheran historian called an agricultural *Gottesgarten* (paradise). Half a century after their coming, that landscape, sprinkled with hofs rented by a third generation of Mennonites, was still blooming. But there had been trouble. In 1689 an awful invasion of French troops had smashed many painfully rebuilt hofs, leaving 400 Mennonites homeless. Some had fled to eat snails on islands in the Rhine, and find temporary lodging as far north as Hamburg and Denmark. Afterward, as the population recovered and grew, there was no longer enough land for all of the young Mennonite farmers, who could be looked at jealously by Lutheran neighbors.

The party of Millers, Herrs, Kendigs, and Mylins now living beside Indians at Conestoga had chosen in 1710 to leave the uneasily tightening community in the Kraichgau. But in another year or two the community gained the significant new family of Benedicht Brechbühl, who had visited a few years earlier after having been expelled from Bern. Following his year in prison and expulsion down the Rhine, he had been able to inform the helpful Dutch Doopsgezinden that he had been reunited with his wife and children. They had found residence in Weiler, two miles south of Theodorus Eby's mill at Sinsheim. This village, home of vineyardist Hans Ruth, lay at the foot of the knightly von Venningen family's horizon-crowning residence, the Steinsberg, nicknamed "The Compass of the Kraichgau." Living here, Brechbühl reported to his Dutch benefactors, he could make "a bare living," but hoped and prayed it would not be his permanent address.

As a "full minister" (bishop) among his Bernese spiritual family, Brechbühl was in vigorous search on their behalf. He thought he had found for his people a suitable home in Lithuania, only to have them reject his proposal. He wrote to the Dutch Doopsgezinden that he was not giving up trust that God could find a new home on the earth for his land-robbed *Völkli*. He sent several reminders of his request for three copies of the *Martyrs' Mirror*. He must have been reading it intently, since he soon began to write letters in the Dutch language. Within a few years he translated parts of a Dutch devotional book, giving it the title *Die Wandlende Seele*. He may well have felt himself like a "wandering soul."

A positive sign for the Mennonites of the Palatinate was a favorable answer, in 1712, to their request for continued release from military service. A negative signal, two years later, was a sharp increase in the fee for this privilege. A plea on their behalf from the Dutch Mennonites was turned down by Elector Karl Ludwig's Catholic son Karl, who was calling the non-citizen Mennonites a "plague" in his realm. Not only raising the fees for the "Concession" his father had allowed the Mennonites since 1664, he tried to reduce the number of their households, refusing a request that their young men be allowed to enter trades.

Dismayed by the new levies, the Kraichgau Mennonites around Sinsheim dug up the old papers and tax receipts that had been buried during the French invasion of 1689, only to find them no longer legible. Then, according to oral tradition, just when the Elector was doubling the Anabaptist *Schutzgeld* (protective tax), they were stirred by a return visit by one of the Kendigs who had left in 1710. Certainly, any account he could give of life on the rich Conestoga land must have been sensational. Might he even have told them, as an oral tradition would imagine, that he had been able to build a house of *lauter nussbleck* (all walnut logs)?

At Mannheim, halfway between the Kraichgau and Ibersheim, 26-year-old Dielman (Thielman) Kolb Jr. was becoming restless. Destined to be a minister in a congregation to which Gerhart Clemens would belong in the woods of Pennsylvania, Dielman had been 16 when three of his brothers had gone there in 1707, and 18 when a fourth, Henrich, had followed. Married at age 22 to the somewhat older widow Elizabeth Schnebele, Dielman was in close touch with his oldest brother, the influential Bishop Peter Kolb, who had given up on his earlier wish to go to Pennsylvania. Now that hope was newly stirring his flock, and a meeting of Mennonite leaders from both sides of the Rhine in February 1717, led by bishops Hans Burkholder of Gerolsheim and Benedict Brechbühl of Weiler, expressed approval for such a move. "In the year 1717, the 21st of March," Dielman would record, he with wife and two-year-old daughter Elizabeth "left for Ibersheim" in the Palatinate on the journey to Pennsylvania.

Just then, even as both Mennonite and Lutheran emigrants were heading for Rotterdam, another French general was smashing towns in the Palatine countryside. Dutch Mennonites, long accustomed to helping their Swiss-descended counterparts, were quickly alarmed. "Dear cousin," wrote a worried Doopsgezind businessman in Hoorn on April 8, 1717, "about 200 people from the Palatinate or Switzerland are planning to come here, requesting money for travel to Pennsylvania." In response, the Dutch had "taken all the necessary measures to prevent them from coming to Holland with a view to avoiding the associated costs." Unfortunately, since the Dutch "might have acted too late," the Palatines might be in Holland by the beginning of May. "As far as I am concerned," the writer continued, "these people should be sent back again," since if help came too readily, "another 200 or 300 might come." After all, while "they do not appear to be persecuted or banished and are merely looking for a good place to live," the Dutch had "too many troubles of their own."

Eight days later came a report that 300 Palatine Mennonites had indeed reached Rotterdam, had already chartered a ship on their own, and were "waiting for a favorable wind to sail to England." Among them were four families who had no means of paying, but were requesting "most fervently to be able to go along." They "weep bitterly," it was reported, if told to go back to the Palatinate. When told that the necessary 600 guilders for their fare was too much for the local Doopsgezinden, they asked whether there were "funds remaining from those [earlier] designated for the Swiss and Palatine Mennonites." Being further admonished that such aid "might only encourage more Palatines to come down," the departing emigrants promised to write letters back, warning against any more coming.

By April 6, 1717, they were all in London with enough money to engage three ships. Vivid, if vague, in their hopes was the welcome they expected across the Atlantic, whether with Martin Kendig's people near the Susquehanna or as neighbors to the Kolb and Clemens families in the Schuylkill valley. Since there were over 300 adult souls in the party, likely, with children counted, the total was over 500. Their departures in ships with captains named Eyers, Richmond, and Tower came in mid-June. Richmond's and Tower's ships would arrive at Philadelphia in August, but the one captained by Eyers, taking another route which included stopping in the Azores at the island of Fayall, would have a different story to tell.

This Mennonite departure from London was historically as silent as the retreat of the Lenapes from the woods the immigrants would shortly take over. For they were leaving in the archives of England where they had briefly lingered hardly a shred of documentation. Whereas the "Water Music" of Georg Friedrich Händel that premiered on barges on the Thames as the three ships plowed westward might delight thousands of their passengers' descendants, their own total lack of credentials would deny that progeny so much as a bare list of their names. No letters are known from the passengers on Captain Eyer's boat, to describe for us the high winds that had caught them 70 miles from the American shore, ripping away the ship's masts and bowsprit, washing the first mate overboard, and shifting some of the ship's cargo so that "a Palantine woman" was killed.

When Captains Richmond and Tower reached Philadelphia, James Logan heard that the Eyers boat was still underway, but apparently knew nothing of the reason for its delay. Already at least 270 adults (plus how many unlisted children?) had arrived, Dielman and Elizabeth Kolb among them. This was five days before yet another boat would leave London with 120 more Palatines; they too, as it turned out, would experience an extended voyage, along with the death of their captain at sea.

In this very season, perhaps expecting the approaching increase to their community, the Mennonites in the thickening community at Skippack were buying from land dealer Matthias van Bebber a hundred acres for a meetinghouse, school, burial ground and farm for poor members. (A century earlier there had been such a farm for Anabaptists in the Canton of Zurich.) Whereas the meetinghouse (referred to with the Lower Rhenish-sounding *Vorgader Hausz*) would be exclusively "for . . . the people called Menonists," the graveyard and school were open to "all & every the Inhabitants of . . . Bebberstownship." In these same months the surrounding woods were about to spawn a legally organized township, in which Gerhart and Anneli Clemens' sons John, Jacob, and Abraham could go to school—if and when there would be a teacher available.

James Logan's prediction on August 8 was not fulfilled until the late arrival of Captain Eyers on September 4, but by that time Governor William Keith was already worried. "Strangers to our Language & Constitutions," he complained, the Palatines "daily dispersed themselves immediately after Landing, without producing any Certificates, from whence they came or what they were." On the following day two more ships unloaded. Though having embarked at London, they had come, declared Keith, "without any License" from there, and now "behaved in the same manner" at Philadelphia, "without making the least application" either to the Governor or "any of the magistrates." This could prove dangerous, "since by the same method any number of foreigners from any nation whatever, as well Enemys as friends, might throw themselves upon us." It was therefore quickly "Ordered . . . that all the masters of vessels who have lately imported any of these foreigners" should submit lists "of the number and Characters of their Passengers," and "all those who are already Landed be required . . . to Repair within the space of one month to some Magistrate . . . to take such Oaths . . . as are necessary to give assurances of their being well affected to his Majesty and his Government." If only, historians would sigh, the lists of 363 names submitted on September 9 by the three captains bringing mostly Mennonite passengers would have survived!

This was a chillier reception than William Penn (now in advanced dementia) had offered the Palatine Clemenses and Kolbs eight years earlier. But this being a Quaker-dominated government, suspicion for non-swearers was not total. The Governor ordered that "Because some of these foreigners are said to be Menonists, who cannot for Conscience sake take any Oaths," they could "be admitted upon their giving any Equivalent assurances in their own way and manner."

One of Philadelphia's wealthiest Quakers, Isaac Norris, who had just completed the town's finest mansion, observed that "thinking people here are a little Shockt to See such great numbers of forreigners." A few days later another 140 Palatines arrived. Logan made his own comment about the "Diverse hundreds" who knew "not one word of English" and brought no credentials: this was in "no way safe." Palatines who would arrive "next spring must expect to pay 10 [pounds] per head here to the government for we are resolved to receive no more of them . . . our country people are inflamed against them and we are to sell them no more land." And did the Mennonites, Logan wondered, fully realize what kind of "Disadvantage they were under by being born aliens"? Without having gotten citizenship, "according to the laws of England" they could neither sell their lands nor have their children legally inherit them.

However, the same crisis that dismayed the officials was sparking optimism in old surveyor David Powell, whose land-speculation had been sluggish ever since William Penn had awarded him a thousand acres before sailing to England in 1701. Fourteen years later, as the Skippack community was filling up, he had finally sold 800 of his acres. Now recognizing in the sudden appearance of close to a thousand immigrants a potential real estate market, a day after the three ship captains reported that they had brought in 363 (mostly Mennonite) passengers, he applied to buy 3,000 acres at the wholesale price of £300. This was to come from the "vacant" land he knew just "back of" his own "late Surveys" around and "near the branches of the Parkeawming creek." There, just beyond the newly purchased Mennonite meetinghouse ground at Bebberstown, at the advancing edge of northward-creeping settlement, both Powell and his friendly competitor Thomas Fairman had been surveying for several years. Fairman's death in 1714 had left the way clear for Powell to make a better profit from the new German-speaking immigrant wave than he had experienced for years, perhaps decades. The Commissioners of Property, of course, knew all too well what the old speculator was like. Logan had described him as "the best-natured man to talk to, but the most unmanageable to deal with that I have met with." Nevertheless, the Commissioners' agent Nicholas Scull was directed to write up an "agreement" to Powell's oral request for 3,000 acres.

If the elderly speculator would put down a third of the £300 asking price, he could have a year to pay the next £100. Having seen the wording of the agreement drawn up on September 10, 1717, Powell knew it needed his signature to be legally operative. But apparently not ready to make the down payment, he went ahead, acting only on his knowledge of the deal's terms, to survey and resell the acreage stipulated. He did not even turn in the results of his surveys nor the names of his customers. His business was so rushed that after his death one of his customers, Gerhart Clemens, would have to pay William Penn's sons for 105 more acres than the hasty first "deed" had recorded. Just as quickly measured out were the adjacent smaller tracts that Powell sold at the same time to the families of 1717 newcomers Dielman Kolb, two Lederach brothers, Hans Reiff, and Henrich Ruth. Since none of them could read English, they had no idea that the documents Powell handed them were merely his own unofficial devices. He himself knew well that without having signed the "agreement" to pay what he owed, he could not have persuaded the Commissioners to give his buyers official indentures. Instead, he got the well-known but elderly Pastorius of Germantown, a recent purchaser of land at the head of Skippack Creek in the future Franconia Township, to sign homemade "deeds" as witness. Perhaps they looked official enough to the non-English-speaking buyers. Certainly, had they been able to read English, they would have found the language sufficiently impressive, such as in the indenture given to Henrich and Magdalena Ruth:

> Two hundred Acres of Land, together with all . . . the Ways, Wasts, Waters, Water courses, Woods, Underwoods, Timber and Trees, Soil, Meadow, Marshes, Cripples, Swamps, Minerals, Quarries, Commodities, Privileges, Hereditaments and Appurtenances whatsoever . . . At and under the yearly Quitrent of One English Silver Shilling or Value thereof In Coin Curr[en]t for each hundred.

There was a basic problem: the new Mennonite arrivals did not have enough money to pay the full prices Powell was asking. In response, the canny Quaker, acting as though he had the authority of a Commissioner of Property, told them that if they gave him whatever cash they had on hand, they could simply provide promissory notes for the balance. Just as remarkable were the speed and percentage of his sudden profits. Having agreed to pay a shilling an acre himself, in the sale of 200 acres to the Ruths six months later, he charged the purchasers five times that rate. More annoying than anything to the Commissioners of Property was that, two years after his "agreement" with them, Powell had still not submitted even the down payment, let alone the further £100 due after the first year. The Commissioners were also disappointed to learn that, having spent "for his own use" the "ready money" the "Palatines" had been able to pay him, Powell now wanted to satisfy his own overdue bill with their promissory "obligations." Fortunately, since the purchasers were, in Logan's opinion, "an Honest, Industrious People," they could be asked to bring in the Powell documents, which they had assumed were legal indentures, and be supplied with official ones, so that what Logan called "this Crooked Affair" could be corrected.

It is thought-provoking, looking sentimentally back through seven farming generations to the acquisition of one's Pennsylvania homestead, to find the deal called a "crooked affair" by William Penn's own secretary. Ironically, Logan was well on his way to accruing, as cheaply as possible, a life-total of six times 3,000 acres of Lenape homeland.

Though Penn would speak of Indian "kings," this was not a term or concept in the mind of the indigenous people he dealt with. Its imposition by Europeans showed their ignorance of the role of women's leadership in Native policy-making. Just as ambiguous was the even oftener-used title "chief." It is only because "chief" became so imbedded in the American parlance that we almost helplessly use it today—as evident in the present story.

CHAPTER SIXTEEN

Two Concerns, Two Endings
1718

DAVID POWELL's hurried surveys near the Perkiomen's East Branch attracted a cluster of Mennonite families from the September 1717 immigration. Included, as we have seen, in addition to the earlier arrived Gerhart Clemens and future minister Dielman Kolb, were new neighbors such as Andreas and Johannes Lederach, Hans Reiff, and Henrich Ruth. Their mutually bordering farms would be the nucleus of a congregation called "Salford," beginning with a log meetinghouse on the Ruth plantation by 1726. Added to these would be the later-arriving families, likewise from both east and west of the Rhine, of such as Christian Allebach, Hans Ulrich Bergey, Nicholas Halteman, Valentine Kratz, and eventually Friedrich Altdörfer. The largest buyers were the earlier-arriving (1709) Clemenses, who moved over from their homestead at Skippack. Their new purchase from Powell, three miles farther into "vacant Land," and six times larger than their first one, was the ground, bisected by the Branch Creek, from which the present story is told.

Just upstream was a little tributary along which the newcomers found a forlorn familial cluster of Lenapes. Whatever the stream had been called by the Lenapes, from now on it was *Insching Grick*. Doubtless more important to buyer Gerhart were the long meadow-like opening in his new property, the gentle slopes south of the Branch, and on the eastern bank a looming hill convenient for building something Gerhart and his neighbors had not yet had at Skippack—a mill. After the hurried surveys of 1718, David Powell had computed that there were 585 acres in the irregularly shaped, creek-straddling tract he laid out and sold to the Clemenses. That would be enough to provide farms or vineyards for not only the parents, still in their late 30s, but for each of the three Clemens sons, Johannes, Jacob, and Pennsylvania-born Abraham. With the sons all situated south of the creek, there would be left on the other side, where the first Clemens house would appear, plenty of acreage for a future son-in-law brought into the family by baby sister Ann.

Meanwhile, old as David Powell was (and without turning in any of the £100 down payment he owed on the acreage he retailed to the Clemens, Ruth, and Lederach families), he joined the surveyors with chains clinking on the heels of withdrawing Lenapes. As we have noted, many of the latter, now often referred to as "Schuylkill Indians," were regathering with remnants of other tribes where they could still hunt for game in Tulpehocken.

The wigwam of the Schuylkill Lenapes' headman Sassoonan was now even farther northwest, at the Forks of the Susquehanna. Approaching the age of 50, the friendly sachem had grown into the role of his people's spokesperson, who could be cultivated as a "king" by white officials eager to find single leaders to deal with. They were somewhat nonplussed when he appeared in September 1718 in Philadelphia with a nephew named *Opekasset* and other relatives, to express Native anxiety spiked by the new surge of white settlement. However, having been well known to Pennsylvania's officials since 1712, Sassoonan was coming to them as no stranger. As his little group showed up at the courthouse to visit the recently arrived Governor William Keith, his growing importance to his people was evident, and welcome.

Once again the Lenapes' old Wissahickon miller friend Edward Farmar translated as the Governor asked what had brought Sassoonan to see him. Whereas three years earlier the Natives' worry had been the unpredictable changes in the prices received for their furs, this time it was on the far weightier theme of land. Laying down seven bundles of deerskins, Sassoonan spoke gravely. His journey "a great way out of the woods," he explained, had been prompted by fears that a tree had fallen across the path of communication between his people and Pennsylvania's authorities. Recent rumors were making the Lenapes wonder whether that path would remain as wonderfully open as it had been when gift-giving William Penn had sat at their council fires. They were hoping that there would not be the kind of deadly Native vs. settler conflicts as they had heard of happening in New England and Virginia.

Commissioner Logan was annoyed to perceive Sassoonan "under some trouble to think that [Penn's land deals had] not been hitherto complied with." Particularly, as Logan would record, the surprise visit had resulted from a "notion" that the Lenapes "had not been paid fully for their lands" (specifically at Tulpehocken). This was not the kind of thing a speculator wanted to hear from people whose former living space was now the subject—and object—of his own growing equity. It was more satisfactory to include in the minutes Governor Keith's advice that on land matters the person the Lenapes should talk to was Logan himself, "W. Penn's Agent for his Land Affairs."

The said "Agent," while not transcribing the gist of Sassoonan's speech, carefully noted his own (historically incorrect) reprimand. "For these eighteen years past," he scolded, "this is the first time [the Lenapes] had ever mentioned any such thing, and it is now strange they should have occasion to complain." Revealingly to historians, the meticulous acting Clerk of the Council left off of even his own private record the Lenapes' exact words. "They added," he noted, "that what they had said"—and there the writing stops, followed by a blank half-page.

This was not the only or last time Logan's lack of interest in a Native point of view would be evident. What mattered to him, which he took pains to discredit, was any hint of questioning the legitimacy of the great transfer of the Lenapes' homelands. After the Governor promised Sassoonan's delegation that "they would be further heard" on the following day, Logan had time to consult the files of the Commissioners of Property. Since these were under his own control, he could take out "a great number of Deeds" which Penn himself had negotiated during his two stays in the colony. There were at least 16 such documents to draw from.

On the following day Logan confronted Sassoonan's ragged delegation with his sheaf of seal-stamped parchments, marked with the runic scrawls of former Lenape sachems. Sassoonan could well recognize their names, but the intimidating way they were used here was nothing like the respectful ceremonies, with wampum and calumet, of their own culture, and ceremonial gifts of the original agreements. Perhaps the "deed" to the Perkiomen watershed, "signed" 34 years earlier, was among those now exhibited by Logan. In any case, the parchments were held up to the unlettered Lenape sachem as definitive proof that his people's ancestors "had fully conveyed, & were as fully paid for all their lands" from below Philadelphia "to near the Forks of the Delaware" (Lehigh River area).

To hear Logan tell it, this discussion in the Philadelphia courthouse left "the Indians . . . entirely satisfied with what had been shewn to them." But that was not enough. Logan wanted a definitively legal document that would "putt an End to all further Claims or demands of that Kind." His procedure, without acknowledging justification for Sassoonan's concerns, was to offer the Indian delegation, "in Consideration of their Journey & Trouble," a traditional "Present in the Proprietors Name & Behalf." After this, Logan recorded, the Indians predictably "agreed to sign an absolute Release for all those Lands."

And what a thorough quitclaim, gibberish to the inquiring Lenape delegation, Logan had written for them to endorse:

> WE, Sassoonan, King of the Delaware Indians, & [six other] Chiefs of the said Indians do acknowledge that we have seen & heard divers Deeds of Sale read unto us, under the hands & seals of the former Kings & Chiefs of the Delaware Indians, our Ancestors & Predecessors, who were owners of the Lands between Delaware & Sasquehannah Rivers, by which Deeds they have granted & convey'd unto William Penn, Proprietor & Governour in chief of the Province of Pennsylvania, & to his heirs & Assigns, all . . . their Lands, Islands, Woods & Waters, situate between the said two Rivers . . ., & had received full Satisfaction for the same. And we do further acknowledge that we are fully content & satisfied with the same Grant.

Repeatedly invoking the revered name of the Lenapes' great Quaker friend, Logan had made sure to use precise juridical language, establishing both the amount of the little gift by which the Indians were now newly "satisfied," and that this was not a payment. The Indians, stated the document, acknowledged that the current "Agents . . . of William Penn" had bestowed on them "as a free Gift . . . Two Guns, six Strowd water Coats, six Blankets, six Duffell matchcoats & four kettles."

Then came words of a legal finality, the sternness of which the "signers" had no concept: "We therefore do . . . for us, Our Heirs & Successors," Logan had dictated, "Grant, Remise, Release & forever Quit claim unto . . . William Penn, his Heirs & Assigns," all the said Lands situate between the . . . two Rivers of Delaware & Sasquehannah . . . and all our Estate, Right, Title, Interest, Property, Claim & Demand whatsoever in & to the same, or any part thereof, so that neither We, nor any of us, nor any Person or Persons in the Behalf of any of us, shall or may hereafter lay any Claim to any of the said Lands, or in any wise molest the said William Penn, his Heirs or Assigns, or any Person claiming by, from or under them . . . , in the peaceable & quiet Enjoyment of the same.

If Sassoonan even understood these words as they were interpreted to him, they could have left him with the impression that he was still dealing with the respected Friend Penn, whom his people had last seen 17 years earlier (and who, unknown yet in Pennsylvania, had died less than two months earlier in his English home).

Logan now had what he felt was an airtight quitclaim to much of the future Bucks, Montgomery, Chester, and Berks Counties to store against any more Lenape complaints. Morally, though, had his tactical overwhelming of the Lenape inquiry been any less "crooked" than the Powell deal he had characterized by this adjective? The secretary himself, when there was a question of his own land purchases, could prove quite vague about where borders ran, and righteously indignant when someone hinted at his taking personal advantage of his multiple offices.

It was a relief to have the signature of Sassoonan, whose troubled demeanor at Philadelphia had been an unwelcome questioning of the original Penn-Lenape romance. As Sassoonan had put it, when Penn "first came amongst" the Lenapes, it was with a memorable declaration that "they & the English should be as one people & one heart joyn'd together in the strictest brotherhood." The glow of the kindling friendship between Penn and Tamany, witnessed at Perkasie by Sassoonan "when he was but small," was what his people consulted in their imagination, and hoped would not fade out. But the white settlements now accelerating even up to the edges of Tulpehocken where Sassoonan's people were regathering were making him wonder whether Pennsylvania's officials might be relating, over his people's heads, to the more powerful northern Nations. Back in the days of the Perkasie meeting, Sassoonan reflected, his "nation" had been "look'd on as dependant on the five nations." But now he wanted the Governor and Logan to understand that "those nations have their own land and Countrey and these [Lenapes] here have theirs, and each of them are to manage their own concerns." The sensitivity of this topic would intensify over the coming decades, and come to bitter fruition in Sassoonan's final years. In the meantime, the quitclaim he signed in Philadelphia in 1718 would be put to good use by James Logan.

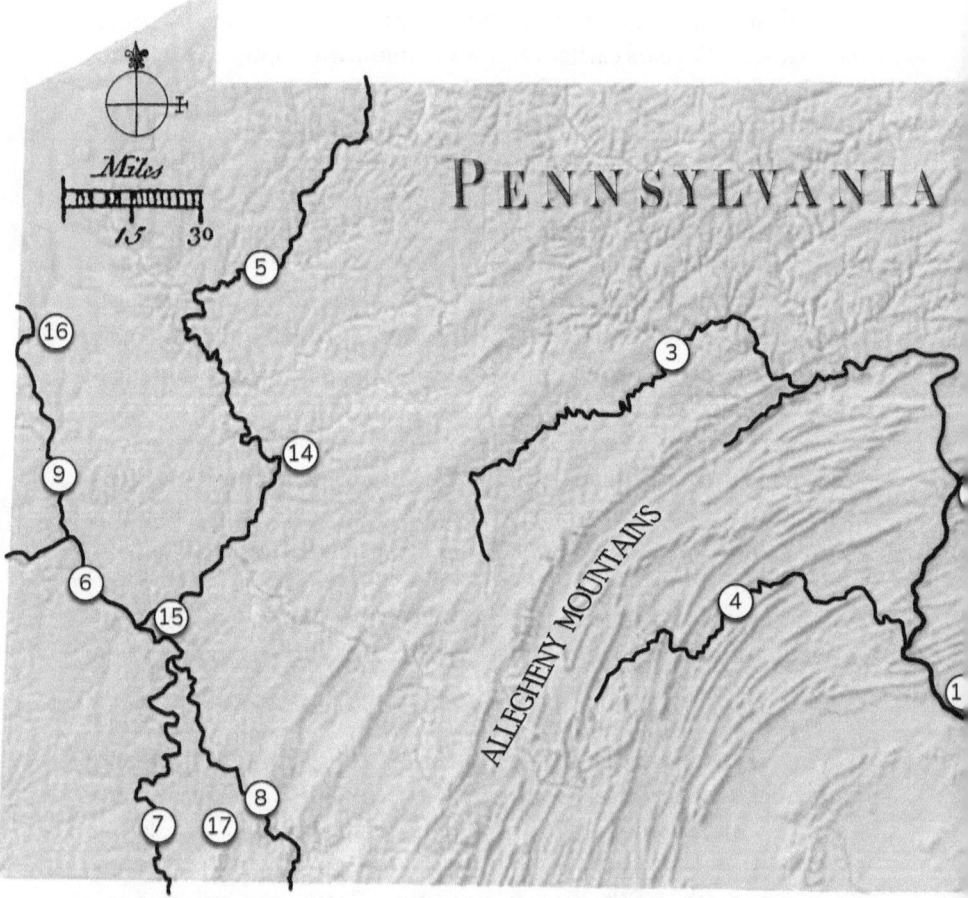

Map Prepared by Philip Ruth, 2021

Neither the Lenape delegation returning from the Susquehanna to the Delaware in concern for their place on the earth, nor the listening Governor Charles Gookin, had known that the legendary though long-silent Proprietor whose name they invoked in Philadelphia was no more. But on July 30, 1718, Hannah Penn had written to Logan from her deceased parents' house at Bristol, "My poor deare fetched his last breath this morning." Her concern was now the same

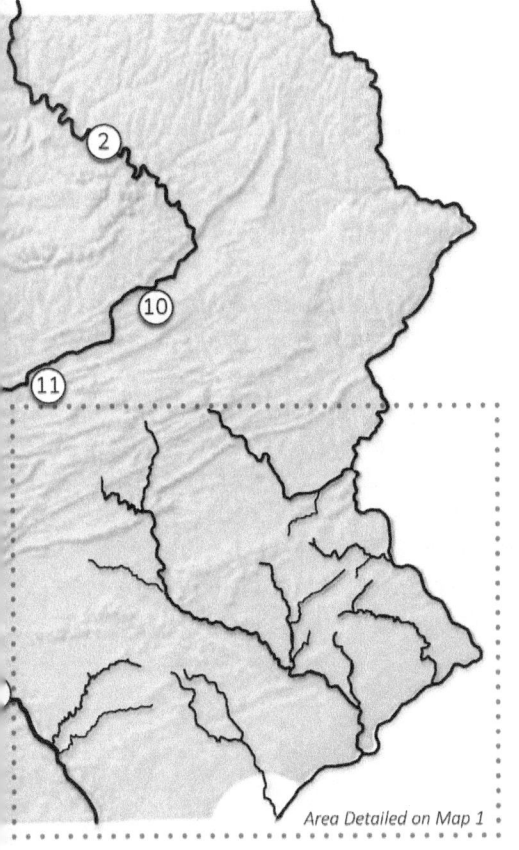

Map 2: Pennsylvania

1 Susquehanna River
2 North Branch Susquehanna River
3 West Branch Susquehanna River
4 Juniata River
5 Allegheny River
6 Ohio River
7 Monongahela River
8 Youghiogheny River
9 Beaver River
10 Wyoming
11 Nescopeck
12 Shamokin/Forks of Susquehanna
13 Paxtang (Harrisburg)
14 Kittanning
15 Fort Duquesne/Pittsburgh
16 The Kuskuskies
17 Fort Necessity

as Sassoonan's: the family's legacy to her (five surviving) children. The oldest, early teenagers John and Thomas, could already dream of a life made opulent by the vast real estate of their father. His quickly revised will of 1712, now openly read, promised each child thousands of American acres. On the other hand, the six years since his stroke had seen little income, and creditors were again threatening. The worse-than-useless stepbrother William Penn Jr., shocked to learn from the will that he would inherit nothing from Pennsylvania, was scheming to declare himself its sole owner.

Some Indians, hearing of their great friend's death, sent his widow a present of furs for a "cloak," as they put it, "to protect her while passing through the thorny wilderness without her guide." Keeping to their imagery, she responded that she would "put on" their gift to fend her way through the "wilderness of care—of briers and thorns" that had been "transplanted" into her life from Pennsylvania.

The Penn will had not pleased employee Logan, who, with a newborn son named William, was thinking of his family's future. He was perturbed by the recently arriving "great mixt multitude" of new immigrants, especially crowds of rough Scotch Irish. He did find a use for them, placing a "settlement" of them at what he called "Donegal," northwest of the pacifist Mennonites in the forthcoming Lancaster County, "as a frontier in case of any Disturbance" from the reluctantly withdrawing Indians. Regarding the "Palatines," of whom Logan thought no more should be allowed in, he wondered if they realized that those not willing to take an oath to be citizens could not legally transfer land ownership to their children.

The Mennonite immigrants, glad to have at least gotten tracts for themselves, and long accustomed to making deferential appeals to European authorities, seemed unworried about their status on the land. Surely, with sympathetic Quaker officials in charge, legal issues could be resolved as they arose. Gerhart Clemens and his Mennonite neighbors did not share the land-losing anxiety of the people they had replaced on the land.

CHAPTER SEVENTEEN

Naming the Land

1719-1726

Our story now continues without its two main characters born in 1644. William Penn has died, and no further evidence is recorded of Hans Stauffer in his new Pennsylvania home. Moving to the forefront of this narrative are the children of those men, along with nephews of our third main character, Sassoonan. Shared by all three family stories is the thread of their relation to the land. For Gerhart and Anneli Clemens in Perkioma there is the satisfaction of acquiring and starting over in their newly-bought tract divided by the Branch Creek. As we have seen, it was large enough (with 90 acres more than seller David Powell had computed) to eventually be subdivided into more than four farms, including one for each son and a son-in-law.

Penn's astute former secretary James Logan, now a successful bearskin merchant in his late 40s, regarded dubiously the German-speaking Palatines who had responded to the Proprietor's invitation and settled in Penn's Woods. Pennsylvania was an English colony, and Logan could hardly imagine it would ever be home to a significant non-English population. Though no Oxford or Cambridge graduate, he was turning out to be an exceptional book-collecting polymath, self-instructed in Greek and Latin, in epistolary touch with famous European scholars. To one of them in Hamburg he wrote in 1721, "Allow me, since what is strange and distant wins esteem not on account of its worth but because it is unusual, to address you from the wilds of Pennsylvania." With the letter he sent a dozen small skins from his warehouse, and was rewarded with a historical tome printed in Basel that had belonged to a famous European classical scholar. The Philadelphian responded with what he knew would be a sensation, "an Indian dressed buffalo skin with the wool on."

To Logan's dismay, the woods from the Delaware to the Schuylkill and beyond had begun to echo with Palatine accents. German was suddenly becoming the language of watersheds whose only reference to previous dwellers were creek names such as Neshaminy, Perkiomen, Saucon, Towamencin, or Wissahickon. As crisply put by twentieth-century Irish Nobelist Seamus Heaney (who enjoyed eating with Mennonites in Indiana): "The translation of place names into anglicized equivalents involves an emptying out of the memories embodied in the names being translated."

In 1719, two years after the departures of fellow Mennonites Henrich and Magdalena Ruth, Christian Allebach of Dühren in the Kraichgau auctioned off his property and brought his wife and six children to Perkioma. After inquiring first about land at the "Swamp" settlement, the Allebachs bought half of the Ruths' 200 acres, adjacent to the creek-divided Clemens purchase. Also in 1719, a cousin of Henrich Ruth named Johannes Roth arrived with a recommendation signed by Dielman Kolb's bishop brother Peter Kolb, and was assisted by Skippack's Michael Ziegler in finding land 15 miles west of the Perkiomen Creek. Within a few years meetinghouses would be built across the Schuylkill River on the Roth farm (Vincent) and beside Henrich and Magdalena's farm (Salford). The Roths' plantation was carved out of woods recently emptied of French fur traders and all but a few Natives. A letter from Peter Roth back in the Palatinate urged his Schuylkill settler brother Johannes: "Tell us how you got along on your journey and what it cost you, and tell us how you like it in that country and also whether you could advise me to come, or would you rather be with us again?" "Tell us the condition of the land and place. And . . . we hope you will tell us the truth."

Just up the Branch Creek from the Clemens and Ruth plantations, the family of Johann Jacob Preiss took up a tract bought from a Germantown speculator. The warrant authorizing a survey there referred to the woods as "vacant land"—an ironic term for an area where hundreds of stone artifacts would turn up under farmers' plows, bespeaking untold millennia of human habitation. At least the streamlet running through it into the Branch just above the new Clemens plantation would be named "Indian Creek." And, as already mentioned, now, even 35 years after the sachem Maughoughsin had promised "never to molest any Christians" that would "settle" in Perkioma, a few Lenapes were still lingering along the little tributary. Whether because of illness or for other reasons, they had not gone with their relatives withdrawing northwestward across the Schuylkill

River to Tulpehocken, or even farther with their sachem Sassoonan to the Delaware-Shawnee village at the Forks of the Susquehanna called *Shamokin*, site of the future town of Sunbury.

Unlike most of its new neighbors, the Preiss family was not Mennonite. However, as a minister with a recently formed *Neutäufer* (New Baptist) fellowship just north of the Mennonite-settled Kraichgau, Johann Jacob held the Anabaptist conviction that true Christians would neither fight nor swear. Equally shared with his Mennonite neighbors was the crucial belief that baptism was voluntary, and only for persons old enough to know what they were doing. But there was also an earnestly contested difference: Preiss' "Dunkers" would baptize *only* by the rite of immersion. This issue was so serious along the Branch that, 25 years after settlement there, neighboring Bishop Henrich Funck would make it the subject of the first Mennonite book written in America: *Ein Spiegel der Taufe (A Mirror of Baptism)*.

One of Perkioma's main oral Indian traditions would hold that the Preisses' only son, 17-year-old Johannes, was in dangerously weak health. How, unless he married very soon, could there be Preiss children to inherit the new plantation? And with only non-immersionists for neighbors, might he be better off taking a Lenape mate from the family found along their Indian Creek? Yes, insists the story, and from this union would come two half-Native sons, the second one born after their young father had died. Though the Lenape mother's name would never appear on written records, it would be her first son Daniel Preiss who would inherit the woods in which her people had lived, and would become, on the largest farm in the community, the undocumented father of a two-century lineage of Dunker farmers and preachers named "Price."

Nothing of the Preisses' Indian memory would be preserved in writing (and DNA testing has yet to confirm or disprove it). But the four German-speaking congregations whose land was drained by their stream echoed it in their names: Indian Creek Brethren, Indianfield Lutheran, Indian Creek Reformed, and Indianfield (later Franconia) Mennonite.

Just as agreeable as the Preiss story are memories of a Dotterer family raising their children in the woods of Goschenhoppen, a few miles closer to the larger Perkiomen Creek. In exchange for a piece of tobacco, a Lenape neighbor would "very rapidly" carry a bag of the family's grain 20 miles to Farmar's mill on the Wissahickon. Natives emerging from the woods daily, fascinated by the newcomers' pigs, fed them acorns. The Dotterers gave the visitors one of their piglets, and were amused to find a Native nursing it jointly with her own infant. More seriously, the Natives sometimes asked to take their new neighbors' baby to their own place in the woods, where they fed their little charge unfamiliar food from wooden bowls. When the anxious parents came to investigate, it would be remembered, they found their baby contentedly swaying in a sling of branches.

Regrettably, no such domestic memories would be noted in the family record book kept by Gerhart and Anneli Clemens, as two more children, Abraham and Anneli, were born, joining brothers Johannes and Jacob. Whereas, while stranded at London in 1709, Gerhart had been listed as a "vinedresser," when his new soil proved inhospitable to viniculture, his book showed him weaving linen and tow for neighboring relatives. He helped Anneli's young stepbrother Daniel Stauffer buy land from speculator David Powell up the Schuylkill Valley approaching Manatawny. And there would be extra income from renting, then selling, part of the expansive 1718 Clemens purchase on the Branch to a family of Wägeles, non-Mennonite Palatines who had found life economically difficult in their first forced settlement of 1709 along the Hudson River.

Having acquired more land in the Branch Valley than any of his fellow settlers, Gerhart Clemens became the area's leading entrepreneur. In 1726, while his Ruth and Landis neighbors were still hauling their grain 16 miles to Farmar's mill on the Wissahickon, Gerhart hired Mennonite millwright Jacob Souder to establish a mill seat along the Branch. Souder, whose familial background in Zurich was the same as that of Anneli Clemens' birth parents, oversaw the damming of the creek, the digging of head and tail races, and construction of a mill at the foot of a conveniently high southern creek bank. Upon its inauguration, Clemens' gristmill became the Branch Valley's economic and social hub. It also provided an occupation for the oldest Clemens son, Johannes, who turned 20 as the mill began operating, and was looking forward to marrying a newcomer to the neighborhood, Elisabeth Allebach.

Soon what an appeal for a new road called "a large beaten path" led from the Clemens' tail race northwestward to a mill erected along the Perkiomen Creek. Along such new patterns laid down over what had been a trail-threaded woods an equally new set of names was heard. Already (in 1725) a township named "Skippack and Perkiomen" had been surveyed by Jacob Taylor. It extended from what had been informally called "Bebberstaun" northeastward as far as the Bucks County line, at the heads of the Indian and Skippack Creeks, where the future Telford and Souderton would appear. Almost immediately this was recognized as being unmanageably large for a township bustling with "a great many families." "Your Petitioners," ran an appeal, "think it is too great a Circuit for one Constable," and "are humbly of opinion that it would be more convenient for them if there was [an additional] township laid out." Half of the two dozen signatures appended to the petition were by Mennonite settlers: Christian Allebach, Gerhart Clemens, Henrich Dentlinger, Nickel Haldeman, Dielman Kolb, Andreas Läderach, Hans Meier, Henrich Ruth, Christian Stauffer, Gaetschalck Gaetschalcks, Jan Gaetschalcks, and Jan Jans (the last three living in adjacent Towamencin). In response, a few months after the Clemens mill was completed, the surrounding district was separated from Skippack and Perkiomen Township, and set up as a township called "Salford."

Why was the new municipality not given a name from Lenape tradition, as was the case with nearby communities such as Goschenhoppen, Perkiomen, and Towamencin? Why was the name of an English town borrowed—all the more curious for having virtually no local precedent before officials in Philadelphia declared that the newly defined township was "Confirmed and called Salford"?

Suspicion rests on a man not previously mentioned in our story, an elderly member of the Governor's Council of Pennsylvania that approved and granted the new township name in 1726. He is Robert Asheton, born in Lancashire in 1666, who had come with his wife and four children to Pennsylvania when his cousin William Penn had arrived the second time in 1699. Though Asheton was not a Quaker, Penn had held him, for reasons of kinship, in continuing affection, granting him a 314-acre estate. In subsequent years Asheton had become a familiar figure as a public employee, holding so many offices—Sheriff, Town Clerk of Philadelphia, Clerk of the Peace for the County, Prothonotary for the Court of Common Pleas, and Prothonotary of the Supreme Court—that there had been criticism. His sons William and Ralph Asheton followed in the same pattern. Their Penn family loyalty had been so strong that, after the death of the Proprietor had been announced in 1718, and 52-year-old Robert Asheton had learned that William Penn Jr. wanted it declared in Philadelphia that he was the heir, he (Asheton) had secretly written a supportive message to Penn Jr. He had stuck up, he claimed, for the disgruntled older heir, against the wishes and knowledge of Governor William Keith, who rather favored the younger Penn family of widow Hannah. Angered by this information, Keith had kicked Asheton off of the Governor's Council in 1719. Yet, in three years, as tempers cooled and William Penn Jr. died, Asheton's professional value to the Council had been so obvious that he (along with son Ralph) had been invited back, and was thus again serving, in his mid-50s, on the Council when it was requested to recognize a new township.

Seldom, in naming locations in Sassoonan's woods, would the European immigrants remember the original dwellers. More typical were cases like the one unfolding just up the Branch Creek from the Clemens plantation, where the area that had briefly been called "Indianfield" was about to be renamed "Franconia," referencing the homeland of Germantown's Pastorius family that had acquired land around the headwaters of Skippack Creek. Similarly, when James Logan needed a name for the huge mansion he was building just north of Germantown, he chose not "Wingohocking" (the name he applied to the adjacent creek in honor of a Lenape chief), but "Stenton," the title of his father's estate in Scotland. And now, as the Governor's Council deliberated over the naming of the new township set off from "Skippack and Perkiomen," the winning suggestion, doubtless from council member Robert Asheton, also struck a European tone. Embedded in Asheton's Lancashire family heritage was the name of an ancient village just across the river Irwell from Manchester, where he, his first children, and most of his ancestors had been baptized: Salford.

Asheton could not have enjoyed his nominal contribution for long. In May of the following year (1727) he "died suddenly at the council table" in Philadelphia, "and was buried after the manner of people of distinction in much pomp by torch light in Christ Church." Neither the German-speaking settlers in the pomp-less municipality he had christened, nor the Lenapes who had moved westward to woods still known by "Indian" names, would have heard of Asheton's passing, or of his role in naming what they pronounced as "Sollfort."

CHAPTER EIGHTEEN

The Branch, the Brandywine, Durham, and Tulpehocken

1727

THE EUROPEAN-LIKE PATTERNS being imposed on Branch Valley's woods included a road laid out from the Welsh-speaking Gwynedd community north to *Parkeyoming* (Lenape for "where there are cranberries"). This road was described in 1728 as passing "Garret Clements Mill" as well as a nearby "Baptists Meeting House." The latter was a little log *Versammlung* and *Schul Haus* recently constructed on the edge of Henrich and Magdalena Ruth's plantation, adjoining land that brothers Johannes and Jacob Clemens stood to inherit. Within the rude walls of the *Fassamlinghaus*, Kraichgau-born Bishop Henrich Funck (miller on the neighboring Indian Creek) and Salford minister Dielman Kolb Jr., both of whom had bought tracts of land from other speculators than David Powell, could preach openly from Zurich-printed Bibles to people whose European grandparents had never been allowed a public venue of their own. And here, just as a young Johannes Clemens had served the *Gemeinde* to help needy refugees in the Palatinate in 1671, his brother's grandson Jacob Clemens would be called to the deacon's role. The adjacent Clemens mill property on the Branch Creek would be the responsibility of Jacob's brother Johannes.

Lingering Lenapes might have wondered (as did a Native observing a meetinghouse being erected near the Susquehanna River): Did white people need to gather so often in order to keep from forgetting their God? And what about the little date-inscribed brown stones planted in the ground around the meetinghouse? Indians needed no such markers. According to William Penn, they would "never forget a grave."

White mussel shells dotted the banks of the new Clemens mill pond, eels still wriggled past the rocks of the new dam breast, and snapping turtles waddled annually to lay their eggs in creek-side muck. But upstream from such a dam there could be no migrating shad. This posed a formidable problem for the region's remaining Lenapes, including those living along the Brandywine Creek where it flowed southward from future Honeybrook to a confluence with the Delaware River at Cristina (future Wilmington). The Brandywine Natives cherished four-decade-old memories of William Penn promising friendship. He had remarkably deeded back to them—from land they had just sold to him—a mile-wide strip on either side of the creek's upper reaches, where they made their home. That was before many white settlers had arrived. Then, in 1724, the Natives found "to their very great injury" two downstream dams blocking the annual migration of "the Rock & Shad fish from coming up as formerly," as they complained to both the Governor and the Logan-led Commissioners of Property. Their families' very "dependence was on these fish for food during a considerable part of the Year. They request[ed] therefore that these Dams may be removed."

The best known of the Brandywine sachems, Checochinican, had made a favorable impression on local officials. With painted face, bare head except for a lock of hair tied with a red silk ribbon hanging down his back, and draped with a blue quilt-like cloth or "stroud," he was described with adjectives such as "elegant," "haughty," and "serious," but also "mild" and "gentle." Visiting Commissioner Logan in 1725, he gravely expressed his people's feelings of existential threat. They had recently witnessed the sudden surveying of their creek-framing corridor as part of a large tract purchased by a real estate speculator. "If [we] are thrown out of this small possession," Checochinican protested to Logan (according to the Commissioner's meeting notes), "having now no more left, [our] children must be vagabonds without any home or living." Yet, as concerned as they were, the Brandywine Natives were not threatening to make trouble. Having "hitherto ever lived peaceably & . . . maintained a good understanding with [our] friends the English," they said, "[we] earnestly desire that it may ever be continued."

It was easy for Logan to agree that Penn had promised a friendly future for the Brandywines, and to tell them that "the Commissioners still desire the Continuation of the same friendship." But "small matters," he added, "ought not to make a difference between friends." *Small* matters indeed. In fact, Logan was "very Sorry to hear any complaint" regarding the aforementioned speculator—wealthy

Chester County Quaker Nathaniel Newlin—who had responded to increasing immigration by purchasing 7,700 acres along the Brandywine Creek for subdivision and sale. Since Newlin was "an old Settler in the Country" and had himself been "a good friend of W Penn," the Commissioners hoped that, if there was "any real cause" for the Natives' complaint, "Endeavors" would "be used to remove it." Logan's bland language did not ease the Natives' sense of betrayal. They recognized that Newlin was no William Penn. "They take it very unkinde," Logan recorded, that Newlin, "upon running the line of his Tract, never came to see them at their Town or acquaint them with what they were doing, but mark'd the trees with Small nicks and not great Notches which they afterward said"—and there, as he did repeatedly when he disagreed with sentiments he was responsible for recording, Logan ends his notation abruptly.

A year later, several Brandywine sachems showed up at a meeting of the Pennsylvania Assembly in Philadelphia and asked to be heard. They were invited in, given chairs and an interpreter, and questioned as to whether they had yet "received satisfaction" from Logan and Newlin. "We have not." "What is it, then, that you have to offer to the House?" The sachems answered that whereas William Penn himself had promised that they would not be disturbed on their land for at least three generations,

> it is not half the age of an old man since, and we are molested, and our lands surveyed out and settled before we can reap our corn off; and to our great injury, Brandywine creek is so obstructed with dams, that the fish cannot come up to our habitations. We desire you to take notice that we are a poor people, and want the benefit of the fish, for when we are out hunting, our children with their bows and arrows used to get fish for their sustenance, therefore, we desire that these dams be removed, that the fish may have their natural course.

The Assembly immediately reported the speech to James Logan, who adroitly replied that he was "Ready to do what he can to quiet their complaints, by granting the person who possesses the said lands, other lands in the stead thereof." That "person" (Newlin) was not so easily satisfied, however, and he warned that he would require full financial remuneration for any reassignment of his recently purchased tract.

In turn the Assembly assured the Governor that if it were not for Newlin's "too wilful resolution to hold and settle" the land, the Indian complaints "would be immediately silenced." Hopefully, then, Newlin would, "in a very short time, become sensible, that it will be as much to his own private interest as of the Province in general, to be more condescending in this affair."

Unsurprisingly, Newlin's attitude did not change, and in the following spring (1726) the Indians of Brandywine were back with another appeal. The Assembly, well aware of the Natives' dissatisfaction with Logan, summoned him to the meeting at once. He responded with the strategy he had used eight years earlier with Sassoonan, this time producing a deed signed in 1685 by 13 "Indian kings," stating that they had conveyed to the Proprietor "all the lands from Duck Creek to Upland Creek . . . as far back as a man could ride on horseback in two days." The only other relevant record Logan had found, he reported, was of the claim the Indians had made in 1705: that the land a mile on either side of their creek, from its mouth via its west branch to its headwaters (at future Honeybrook) had been returned to them by Penn. The deed for that unusual reverse grant, said the Indians, had been lost in a fire, but old neighbors remembered seeing it. To complicate matters, the Indians had more recently sold back to the Commissioners the lower part of the creek-embracing corridor, all the way from "a certain rock by Abraham Marshall's land" down to the creek's mouth on the Delaware. Embarrassingly, Logan's new research showed that of the £100 the Indians had been promised for this conveyance, only £73, 8 shillings had actually been paid. "The remainder," he now bizarrely informed the Assembly, "was paid yesterday."

Surprised and pleased by the belated payment, "the chiefs of the Indians" signed a receipt, but asked for a written document, "that they might know what was theirs and be secure in it." At that Logan became scrupulous, saying that the Commissioners themselves had no legal power (since Penn's death) to draw up such an "instrument." But the Indians were not to worry, he insisted, since the Commissioners were on their side. They had told Newlin "that it was in vain for him to pretend to that land, let the disappointment be what it would, so long as the Indians laid claim to the same, and would continue upon it." The Natives would therefore "be disturbed in their quiet possession . . . neither by Nathaniel Newlin nor by any other person."

Logan used other language in addressing the Assembly, claiming that none of the records he had researched "did amount to any certainty" as to what the lost original deed contained, "but since the Indians had an imperfect idea of it, and a strong resolution to hold it," the Commissioners were simply using "such means as they thought most likely to satisfy them, and continue them in the quiet possession of their claims." This was meaningless language, since the only "means" the Commissioners had used, along with their strange overdue pay-up, was that they had informally "agreed and accommodated the matter with Nathaniel Newlin, as far as was in their power to do at present."

Since Newlin had done nothing more than promise he would "not molest the . . . Indians in their claims," the Assembly demanded that he appear in person "to give some further assurance." After making the Assembly wait for several days, Newlin did show up, and "delivered on the table a paper" promising "that neither he nor his heirs [would], by any means, disturb or molest the Indians in their possessions or claims." With this signed statement finally in hand, the Assembly dismissed Newlin and called the Natives and their interpreters into the meeting to hear the document explained. The Natives then "declared that they were well satisfied therewith," according to the over-simplified meeting minutes, which concluded with the optimistic assertion that the Brandywines—formerly "very much disturbed in their minds"—now recognized "that this House would stand by them and see them righted," and were thus "perfectly easy." Newlin was brought back into the meeting to "orally acknowledge" his written promise, whereupon he and the Natives "shook hands together and parted fully reconciled, and then the House adjourned."

These assurances of 1726, like most official expressions the American Indians would hear in land negotiations over the next century, quickly proved empty. Newlin had already retailed many parcels of his 7,700-acre purchase, and when he died three years later the entire remaining acreage was divided among his children. In that year (1729) Checochinican sadly reported that his people were not even allowed to cut down saplings to build cabins in the two-mile-wide corridor they considered their home. Other Newlin land sales covered the Native village at the head of the creek. It would thus be Newlin's children—not Checochinican's—who inherited this section of the Brandywine valley. Later reports of the sachem's sadness would drift back from Allegheny, where he and his son continued to tell their story until the frontier burst into flames in 1755. Before the last remaining local Native, a woman named Hannah Freeman, died on the site of her old village, its Indian name would be replaced by "Newlin Township."

A similar experience awaited the last Lenape remnants in the Tulpehocken and Lehigh watersheds, where the aggressive Logan also had interests. Now Mayor of Philadelphia, and increasingly recognized as a scholar-scientist, Logan kept his fingers in land-merchandising opportunities created by Native departures, even as he prepared to build a retirement mansion for himself. In 1723 he bought land in the Hilltown section of Bucks County, from whose Neshaminy Creek watershed the Lenapes had mostly departed. Among other things, he was keenly aware of efforts to locate iron ore deposits in that region. In 1726 he wrote to the aging Hannah Penn of a project he and other investors were funding at Durham, a mile and a half back from the Delaware River, between the Tohickon Creek and the confluence of the Delaware and Lehigh Rivers (known as the "Forks of the Delaware"). The area's thick forests could finally be monetized through the harvesting of lumber to fuel a forge like the one recently established at Manatawny beside the Schuylkill River.

Holding a one-fourth share in the Durham forge project, Logan did not explain to Mrs. Penn (who died shortly after his letter arrived) that he was personally paying off a New Jersey-born Lenape sachem named Nutimus for 4,448 acres adjoining the new iron works. He had found this necessary since there had never been a deal completed between the Lenapes and their trusted friend William Penn for land north of the Tohickon Creek. Penn's policies clearly forbade buying and selling land that had not been released via treaty. Now, of course, there were no Penns in Pennsylvania to make treaties. There was a grandson and namesake Billie from Penn's first family in England, and two of Penn's sons from his second marriage, Johnny and Thomas, lived there as well. But none of those young men, troubled as they were with threats of increasing debt, was ready to cross the Atlantic. Penn's death in 1718 had left land-dealing in Pennsylvania in limbo, increasingly frustrating to deal-seeking investors like Logan. As he explained in his letter to Hannah Penn, he had "often spoken of the Confusion All Proprietary affairs are & must be [in] un till the [Penn] family [debt] Dispute is ended & proper Measures are taken." If only, Logan kept wishing, at least one Penn descendant would come and deal with the Natives, so that land commerce could be legitimized. In the meantime, Logan had personally, as a necessary gambit, paid Nutimus £60 for the forge property. Little did either buyer or seller anticipate that a decade later Logan would (1) ironically claim that Nutimus had never really owned the land he sold to Logan in 1724, and yet (2) produce "evidence" that the Lenapes had actually been paid by Penn in 1686 for all the land south of the Lehigh where it entered the Delaware.

A co-speculator little concerned with legal order in the Durham deal was a wealthy young American named William Allen, who, having studied in England, just before returning to Philadelphia, negotiated directly with sons of Penn's second family to acquire thousands of acres north of the Lehigh (the Delaware's west branch). Although this area, called "the Minisink" (home of the northern, *Munsee* Delawares), had also never been released from any Lenapes, Allen went ahead and resold the most desirable section of it to a Huguenot planter named Nicholas du Pui. The latter, to ensure good relations with the northern Lenapes, also gave them a generous payment. When James Logan heard how much he had paid, he was dismayed, since he and other speculators had been hoping to acquire the land, when legally available, at a much cheaper rate. They saw Allen's and du Pui's high-priced dealings as spoiling the Natives. Writing quickly to the Penn grandsons, Logan warned them not to sell any more land that was not "clear of Indian and other Claims."

Logan dispatched Surveyor General Jacob Taylor to persuade the Lenapes remaining in the Lehigh country to sell at a rate far lower than du Pui had paid. "It will require some caution in managing the survey," he wrote, "to prevent uneasiness to the Indians." So Taylor was to take along the kinds of high-quality gifts—"four of the best strowds, blue and red"—that had pleased the parents of the Natives in Penn's time. But after meeting with the Lenapes, Taylor reported disappointingly that "The Indians would suffer no manner of survey to be made there on any account whatsoever." They did involuntarily cheer at the mention of the name of grandson Billy Penn. But when it came to the question of selling, they absolutely refused to negotiate with anyone but Penn family members. The sachems Nutimus, Tishekunk, and Lappowinzo had no interest whatsoever in relinquishing their homeland and joining the Brandywine Lenapes and Sassoonan's people in their migration westward beyond the Susquehanna into the Ohio River watershed.

A decade after Mennonites had bought land for homesteads in the woods of Lenape-abandoned Perkioma, they were feeling no threat to their ownership. The meetinghouses at both Salford and Skippack served as schools. In 1725 the local bishops, along with several in the future Lancaster County, signed on to a Mennonite confession of faith brought over from Holland, and saw to its publishing two years later. This was just in time for a sudden large influx of Palatine relatives disembarking from ships in the Philadelphia harbor in the fall of 1727. The unprecedented surge of immigrants shocked Logan into complaining, "At this rate you shall soon have a German colony here." Among the thousands of new immigrants' names—spelled phonetically by clerks trying to decipher German signatures on loyalty pledges to the English king—were many familiarly Mennonite ones, mostly traceable back to Switzerland: Baer, Cassel, Funck, Good, Hackman, Hauser, Hiestand, Kendig, Kraybill, Landis, Martin, Meyer, Oberholtzer, Schnebele, Shenk, Souder, Stauffer, Swartz. One of the young new arrivals, crudely recorded as "Palatine Gratz" (Valentine Kratz), would become a son-in-law and neighbor of Gerhart Clemens.

The wave of Palatine immigration, resurging in 1727 and persisting for nearly three decades, all but completed the transfer of the land of Sassoonan's people. A major shock of their displacement had already registered among those having moved just west of the Schuylkill to Tulpehocken. This was the largest of the last three Lenape communities. But soon after their regathering there, already in 1720, that unpurchased land, where a hunting-supported life was still possible, had been eyed by Welsh settlers looking up from Chester County. Exploring the inviting Wyomissing, Angelica, and Cacoosing tributaries of the Tulpehocken near its mouth on the Schuylkill River, and finding only Indians there, they had begun to move in without legal process to clear trees for farms.

In the same years, just west of the Cacoosing, another and larger takeover was taking place. It had begun with a visitor from Schoharie, near Albany, New York, coming in 1721 to Governor William Keith in Philadelphia. He spoke for a group of Palatines who had lived unhappily along the Hudson River since their arrival in 1710. Struggling there with a "scanty allowance of ten acres of land to each family, whereon they could not well subsist," they had heard of German-speaking countrymen receiving a better welcome in Pennsylvania. Might there be a place for some of the Schoharie Palatines in Penn's Province?

Responding to Keith's suggestion that they investigate opportunities in his colony, five Schoharie Palatines traveled to Pennsylvania and found in "the farthest inhabited part of the province northwest of Philadelphia" just what they were looking for: the beautiful Tulpehocken valley. This expanse between the Schuylkill and Susquehanna Rivers (destined to be renamed "Lebanon") was the last place that still belonged to the Lenapes. But there was no mention of Indians in the communications between the Palatines and Governor Keith.

When Keith appeared at a diplomatic parley with the Iroquois near Albany in September 1722, several Schoharie Palatines were waiting for him with a specific request to resettle in Tulpehocken. Apparently eager to please, Keith helped them write a petition for enough land to accommodate 40 or 50 families (critics would later claim that the Governor penned the petition in its entirety). In the following spring, 33 New York Palatine families came boating and driving cattle down the North Branch of the Susquehanna River, then down the main body of the river, to the mouth of Swatara Creek below future Harrisburg, and headed upstream toward the alarmed Lenapes living in Tulpehocken. These "savens" (savages), reported a Scotch-Irish constable, protested immediately that their corn was being destroyed by the newcomers' cattle. But while the Natives waited "impatient[ly] for an explanation," the Palatine incursion proceeded unrelentingly, and there were reports that another 50 families were hoping to follow.

As the invaders from New York looked for springs among which to build cabins, they informed Governor Keith that they were ready to give "the usual prices for lands at such a distance from Philadelphia," whenever payment would be requested. Of course no deal could be made while the Penn family's legal troubles remained unresolved in England. Yet these newcomers wanted official deeds so "that our children may have some settlement to depend on hereafter; and that by your authority we may be freed from the demands of the Indians, of that part of the country, who pretend a right thereto." Those pretending Natives, whose leader Sassoonan lived several days' journey northwestward at Shamokin, were now in sustained shock. As James Logan later observed, "finding they could no longer raise Corn there for their Bread they quietly removed up the River Sasquehannah" (to its forks at Shamokin).

Within five years of the Palatines' coming, Sassoonan would be astonished to see how dramatically they had changed his people's last refuge. What would descendants think of him, he wondered, when they realized that their very last land had been taken over even without any payment? A Lutheran "meetinghouse" appeared shortly, and there were plans for a school. The Palatines who had ignored and replaced most of the Lenapes were asking for a road that would lead from their church to "Squire Boone's mill" east of the Schuylkill. New traffic would bring people all the way from Perkioma's Salford Township, home of a conscientious though unordained Reformed minister named John Philip Boehm, who came to preach, hold communion, and baptize in the new facility at Tulpehocken.

By 1724 many Lenapes were following a westward migration path. Pennsylvania's officials watched nervously as "their" eastern Natives abandoned Tulpehocken. "Most of their Hunters," observed James Logan, "retired for the Sake of better Game to Ohio" (the river, not the present state). That fateful move, he well knew, had not been made "without repining at their hard usage" at Tulpehocken. At least, on the river controlled and called *Ohio* by the Five Nations—recently expanded to Six Nations through the addition of the Tuscaroras—they could again have a town of their own, which they called *Kittanning*.

This was the situation as thousands of new Palatines arrived in Philadelphia in 1727 and the years following, all expecting land to live on. It was estimated that 100,000 acres taken up by squatters was not paid for. From the Lenapes' point of view, their forced removal from the Brandywine, Lehigh, and Tulpehocken watersheds amounted to a series of "crooked affairs."

Though they did not coordinate a response, there arose among the displaced Natives a dull realization that they might one day lose all of their land. Sassoonan, however, remained personally friendly, coming to Philadelphia in 1727 to see the new governor, Patrick Gordon. Appreciated by the authorities as pliable, he always received small courtesy gifts, which gave him, among his own people, with whom he shared everything, in spite of his growing enslavement to rum, their loyalty. They had given him a new name: *Alumapees*, meaning "Keeper of the Wampum."

With the arrival of 1,600 additional Palatines in Philadelphia during the summer and fall of 1727, tension mounted in Pennsylvania's back country. In September came news from 40 miles above Conestoga of the first murder of a white person by Native assailants since William Penn had set foot in his Province. During a drunken altercation, Indians had killed Thomas Wright, one of ten or so traders doing business with Sassoonan's people in their refuge beside the Forks of the Susquehanna.

Meanwhile all was quiet along the East Branch of the Perkiomen, where Mennonite families were fitting some of the latest immigrants into their community. There would survive one vague anecdotal hint of a man being killed on a Moyer homestead in Lower Salford. But since no record of such an event remained in any local family, it seems safe to say that there was no Indian trouble on the Branch.

CHAPTER NINETEEN

Gunfire

1728

AFTER THE HARSH WINTER of 1727-28, Native unease was growing from the Delaware to the Schuylkill and beyond. With the Brandywine watershed surveyed for sale, and Tulpehocken confiscated by the Schoharie Palatines, land around the confluence of the Lehigh River and the Little Lehigh Creek (near future Allentown) was being occupied by Scotch Irish settlers. Just north of this "Lehigh Forks" area—for which Natives had not been paid—displaced Shawnees under sachem Kakawatchy had established a village called *Pechoquealin*, but they were already looking for a better location.

In contrast, matters were more settled in largely Lenape-abandoned Perkioma, where Gerhart Clemens and his busy neighbors were absorbing some of the previous fall's flood of Mennonite Palatines. To be sure, as many as they were, they were greatly outnumbered by Lutheran and Swiss Reformed immigrants. Among the latter was a minister who ruffled feathers in the Salford vicinity by claiming that he—rather than the earlier-arrived but unordained John Philip Boehm—was the legitimate pastor of Reformed congregations as far westward as Tulpehocken. The rival pastoral claims erupted in a little tumult at the home of one of the Salford Mennonites' Reformed neighbors, Jacob Reiff.

Confusing as it was, an inter-denominational controversy like Salford's was not nearly as ominous as the tension brewing wherever European and Native cultures overlapped. From Shamokin came a warning by a worried Sassoonan that a fellow sachem named *Manahyckon* was so angry over the recent execution of a Lenape relative in New Jersey, that he was fomenting war talk. He had bragged to Sassoonan that if he would decide to go to war, "he could make a handel to his Hatsheat Seventey ffadom Long" (hatchet 70 fathoms long). Finally, in May 1728, gunshots rang out on both sides of the

Schuylkill, where Welsh-speaking and Palatine plantations had been begun among the last of the Lenapes' wigwams.

A decade earlier, while David Powell had been speculating on land along the Perkiomen's East Branch, he had also invested in real estate along the Manatawny Creek just upstream from its mouth on the Schuylkill River (near present Pottstown). He sold one of his Manatawny tracts in future Colebrookdale Township to Daniel Stauffer, who was helped in the purchase by his brother-in-law Gerhart Clemens, one of Powell's main Salford customers. Another tract in that vicinity had been bought from Powell by Germantown blacksmith Thomas Rutter, a conscientious, enterprising Baptist preacher who had protested against slavery. He was in his 50s when he moved to Manatawny and established what became America's first successful iron works, using water from the creek to power the bellows of a bloomery forge in which pig iron was smelted from ore. Partnering in that investment was the Lenapes' old Wissahickon friend, miller Edward Farmar. Before long Rutter added to his works a refinery forge whose thumping trip hammer must not have greatly disturbed the local Lenapes, several of whom found employment in the forges. In fact, it seemed that Rutter, like Farmar, was especially trusted by the Natives.

Land Commissioner James Logan, who kept abreast of land and iron ventures, disliked Rutter on political grounds, and was also not pleased with his and Farmar's relationship with the Lenapes. Logan was especially angered to hear that the Natives retreating westward from the Colebrookdale and Tulpehocken areas might have been led to suspect him of unfairly profiting by his own land dealings, and even perhaps by his handling of gifts from the Penn family to the Natives. Aging and permanently crippled that winter (1727-28) by a fall in his garden, the prosperous politician-speculator-scholar was building a mansion in which he expected to spend his golden years. Annoyed by Thomas Rutter's absences from sessions of the Pennsylvania Assembly in Philadelphia, he was also spoiling for an opportunity to defend himself in the court of public opinion. The shooting at Manatawny in the spring of 1728 would give him an occasion.

The mounting tension in April was felt westward from Rutter's "Poole Forge" across the Schuylkill into Tulpehocken, where a diminishing cluster of Indians still lived alongside Schoharie Palatines and equally invasive Chester County Welshmen such as John Roberts and the brothers John and Walter Winters. Visiting one day across the Schuylkill in Manatawny, Winters heard a man claim (falsely) "that the *Indians* had kill'd his Wife and eight Children, and they then all lay dead at his House, and that all *Tulpyhocken* was cut off by the Indians, and that he saw Fires in several Places." Badly frightened, Winters hurried back across the river to his home, only to find the Tulpehocken community unscathed. His neighbors, however, were buzzing with rumors. And the whole region had been thrown "into a strong fear," especially by the reputed remark of a Native that "the *Indians* would come and destroy the white People, and [their] Corn."

Two weeks later, on May 10, the very day when Sassoonan was sending his own warning to Philadelphia, the white neighbors of Rutter's forge were petrified by the unexpected appearance of 11 non-local Indians. Painted for war, visibly armed, and speaking an unknown language, they rudely entered houses demanding food. The settlers had no idea that these were Shawnees from Pechoquealin above the Lehigh, sent by their leader Kakawatchy not to attack local Indians, but to scout for possible Native enemies called "Flatheads." While some of the settlers' families ran to hide in Squire George Boone's mill at Oley, 20 of their men took up arms and confronted the unknown Indians. Feeling threatened, the Shawnees began to fire their own weapons, slightly wounding one of the white men. Return fire brought down one of the Indians, but he quickly recovered to scramble without his gun into the woods, and the incident was over.

The news flashed westward immediately across the Schuylkill into Tulpehocken, where all suspicion now seemed confirmed. One version of the rumor from Manatawny was that "eleven *Indians* in a Swamp . . . had killed two white Men, and wounded Three." False though this was, it convinced John Winters that war had begun. His nervous Welsh neighbor John Roberts on the Cacoosing Creek, likewise terrified, immediately sent an appeal for help to Governor Patrick Gordon in Philadelphia. The remarkable document, to be delivered "with speed," read:

> Your Excellency must know That we have Suffered and is like to sufer By the Ingians, they have fell upon ye Back Inhabitors . . . . Therefore, we . . . with our poor Wives & Children Do humbly Beg of your Excellency To Take It into Consideration and Relieve us . . . Whos Lives Lies At Stake

With us and our poor Wives & Children that is more to us than Life. Therefore, We . . . Desire An Answer from your Excellency By ye Bearer With Speed . . . from your poor afflicted People Whose names are here Subscribed. John Roberts, Jn. Pawling, Henry Pannebeckers . . . .

Of 77 purported signatures on the hastily prepared petition, many were obviously written in the same hand. Some of the names belonged to plantation-owners 30 miles away in Skippack and Lower Salford. How could Mennonite "signers" such as Gerhart Clemens, Henrich Ruth, and Dielman Kolb have instantly heard about the Tulpehocken affair, especially given that a new road from Colebrookdale to Skippack was still months from completion? However such names came to be affixed to Roberts' appeal, the document's urgency was amplified by a second "Petition of the Frontier Inhabitants of ye County of Philadelphia" sent to Governor Gordon from a son-in-law of Thomas Rutter. "Several Families," it read, "have Left their Plantations with what Effects they Could Possibly Carry away, Women in Child bed being forced To Expose themselves to Coldness of ye air, whereby Their Lives are in Danger." The neighborhood had heard "That the Indians are Consulting Measures against us."

The shocked Governor immediately set out for Manatawny, expecting to find a scene of fatal carnage. Though he discovered, on his arrival, a community "under very great Terror & Surprize," the only physical victim appeared to be a man who had been "slightly wounded in the belly." Relieved, the Governor counseled his people to calm themselves, then turned toward home. He had barely begun his return trip when he learned of a second fear-inspired incident in the area. It had occurred across the Schuylkill in Tulpehocken, and there were fatalities.

Here, too, John Roberts was involved, and this was not about an Indian attack, but a white men's unprovoked murder of Indians. What had happened at Roberts' home on the Cacoosing ("Owl") Creek was later narrated by one of the perpetrators, John Winters. Convinced that a full-blown war had begun, Winters had been surprised to notice several Indians lingering at the house of his neighbor Roberts. When, later in the day, Roberts' son came rushing with an appeal for help, Winters grabbed his gun, recruited his brother Walter and father-in-law, and headed for the Roberts home. On the way they "concluded," he testified, that "if we saw any *Indians*, we would not kill them, but bind them, and carry them to Justice *Boon's* House."

As the tensed vigilantes approached the Roberts' residence they saw a young Indian sitting on the wood-pile, making arrows. As the gun-carrying Walter Winters came toward him on a log over a little run, the alarmed Native "took up his Bow," testified Walter's brother John,

> and fixing an Arrow to it, look'd steadfastly and earnestly at him; and [Walter] seeing him in that Poster, immediately shot at him. And he fell to the ground. With that [Walter] cryed out to me, *Shoot, Shoot*; and then I shot in among the *Indians* and killed an old *Indian* Woman named *Hannah*, but did not know it was she, until we had subdued the rest of them, which I thought were Enemies to us. I struck another Woman two Blows, with the Butt-end of my Gun, and knock'd her down; and then I struck down an *Indian* Girl, and pursued after more that were in the Swamp, but did take no more. Then coming back from pursuing them, I saw *John Roberts* with an Axe strike the Woman that I knock'd down, and sunk a Place in her Scull that I could have laid my Fist in it.

What was going on here? "I thought all along," John Winters later claimed, that "they were Enemy *Indians*, and that we kill'd them in Defence of our selves, our Neighbours and Country." His brother Walter testified similarly: "I thought . . . that I did my Country, my Neighbors and Family Service. . . . I did it with no other Intent, than to defend my self and save our Lives." In that patriotic mood the brothers turned up the next day across the Schuylkill at Boone's Mill, bringing two Indian girls who had survived the attack, and apparently expecting some reward for their heroic service.

Horrified by the possible Indian reaction to this white-caused violence, Governor Gordon issued a hue and cry for the capture of the Winters brothers, and gave orders that the Natives they had killed at Cacoosing be properly buried. He was relieved to hear from Shawnee Chief Kakawatchy an explanation and apology for what had happened at Manatawny, along with a request for the return of the gun dropped by one of the Shawnees.

At the same time, the Governor decided to use a parley he had recently scheduled with Indians out at Conestoga (there had been no treaties with them for five or six years) as an occasion to dispel the growing Native suspicion that William Penn's friendly policies were no longer in effect. Among the Indians to whom he quickly sent invitations with gifts were Sassoonan and his relatives at Shamokin. The Governor then took 30 officials on horseback to Conestoga, where he approached the Natives with the utmost respect and lavish gifts. Sassoonan was reported to have not been able to make the trip on such short notice. He sent his likable young nephew Shakatawlin to interpret for the Lenapes, and to bring word that Sassoonan was willing to talk. He offered to come down past Tulpehocken to meet the Governor at a former Lenape village called "Morlatton," near the Schuylkill, a few miles from the forge of the Native-friendly Rutter.

This was a moment when the severe anxiety among the general public likely reached the ears of Mennonite settlers in the peaceful Salford woods. As for James Logan, angry at rumors of the Indians distrusting him personally, he felt "more danger of a misunderstanding with our Indians than I have ever known since I came into the place almost thirty years ago." All of Philadelphia waited in suspense to hear how the Natives at Conestoga had responded to the elderly Governor's plea for peace, and when the news proved encouraging, the city collectively breathed a sigh of relief. The diplomatic party returning from Conestoga was excitedly welcomed by an impromptu set of socialites bringing a picnic-like "collation" into the woods just outside of town. The bill for this unusual celebration was paid by one of Logan's wealthy fellow Commissioners of Property, Richard Hill.

No one was more pleased than Hill and Logan with Natives at peace, which they hoped would be re-affirmed when Sassoonan arrived with relatives of the murdered Indians. In preparing for that meeting, Logan recalled the quitclaim he had induced Sassoonan to sign ten years earlier. If necessary, the document could be used to prove that there remained no land for "our Lenappys" to dispute.

In view of the "long hard Winter" that had made "Corn and Provisions very scarce," Governor Gordon had sent word for Sassoonan to come all the way down the Schuylkill past Morlatton to Philadelphia, where supplies were more plentiful. The Governor's Council tried to lighten the mood of Sassoonan's delegation by assuring the Natives that the murderous Winters brothers were "in Dungeons with Iron Chains on them." Furthermore, a major present was being prepared, with impressive "tokens of ... friendship" to reaffirm the earlier atmosphere of relations with a generous William Penn:

10 Strowd Matchcoats	2 dozen knives
5 Blankets	2 dozen Scissors
5 Duffels [cheaper cloth]	2 dozen Tobacco Boxes
10 Shirts	2 dozen Tobacco Tongs
25 pounds [Gun-]Powder	1 dozen Looking Glasses
60 pounds Lead [for bullets]	100 Flints
1 Pound Vermillion [red face-paint]	

This generosity, Sassoonan later remarked, "gladden'd his heart." And there was a special gift for the slain Indians' relatives who accompanied him: "three Strowds, three Blankets, three Duffels & three Shirts to cover the dead Bodies again, & ... six Handkerchiefs to wipe away their Tears.... that the Relations [relatives of the deceased] may be the more easy in their Minds, that they may Know we grieve with them, & they may be comforted."

The seriousness with which anxious Philadelphians took the visit of Sassoonan's delegation was evidenced by the size of the non-official crowd that showed up to hear him speak on his second day in town, June 4, 1728. Word had gotten out that the only venue spacious enough was the Quakers' "Great Meeting house" at Second and High Streets. The extent of the "vast Audience" that "filled the House & all its Galleries" was perhaps exaggerated by James Logan's estimate of "two or three thousand," but there was no mistaking the charged atmosphere. It was a unique moment when the last Lenape leader from the Neshaminy and Perkiomen watersheds could publicly express his people's feelings.

The cast of characters that day was notable. Sassoonan had brought along two nephews— Opekasset and the younger Shakatawlin (the latter able to translate)—with more than a dozen "others of the Delawares." Also present was a single Shawnee representative, as well as a more important figure with a non-Lenape name: Shikellamy. The latter had been sent by the Six Nations to live near and monitor the mix of Native tribes at Shamokin, especially the Delawares, whom the northern tribes regarded as their vassals. From this time on, Shikellamy would be Sassoonan's close observer and sometimes suspicious neighbor. On hand to interpret was the Lenapes' old friend, Wissahickon miller Farmar, long familiar with their ways and language. The Indians and interpreter now faced the imposing stares of Governor Gordon, his Council members including Commissioners Logan and Hill, and bigwigs such as lawyer Andrew Hamilton, Speaker of the Pennsylvania Assembly.

Sassoonan spoke first, "in the name of all the Indians present." Even if he had earlier meant to complain or at least explain their disturbed feelings, that impulse must have been softened by the previous day's effusive welcome and pile of "Presents." He now "rejoyces," said the interpreter, "that this great Company is to hear him." He had especially enjoyed hearing "his Great Friend & Father William Penn" (whom he had seen 45 years earlier at Perkasie) "so much spoken of." Since he and the Indians had "always lived in Love," he was hoping that even after the recent violence "all things will be made up in love," and that "there may never be any Misunderstanding between us." Noting that both the Lenapes and their "Christian" friends had "young Children," he hoped that what was here being spoken in peace would be remembered by them "for ever." He further wanted the "great numbers present" to remember William Penn's repeated expression "that the Christians & Indians ought to have but one Head, one Heart & one Body." That iconic concept had taught Sassoonan to "look on them all as one People, with the desire that they may always so continue." True, "ill people," such as might appear among both Christians and Indians, had lately caused an "Accident . . . to the Indians." Nevertheless, in the spirit of Penn, "We must unite in Love, all ill things must be done away and forgotten, for we are one People." And that, concluded the elderly sachem, was all that he had to say at the moment. When he returned in two months he would "speak more fully."

This brevity, probably disappointing to the huge and eager audience, certainly did not satisfy James Logan. Sassoonan was "then told," Logan recorded, that if his little Lenape group "had anything at all on their Minds, it was now a proper time to speak it, that it might be heard by all this Company if any." In response, the old sachem made an eyebrow-raising move, asking his likewise elderly white friend Thomas Rutter to come and sit beside him. Then, repeating his appreciation for the Governor's policy of friendship between "the Indians and Christians," Sassoonan said he would always try to "strengthen &

increase it," making the "Path" of communication between Philadelphia and Shamokin "open & plain." "He will always keep it wide," rendered the translator, "& root and cutt up every Bush & Grub that may stand in the Way." Having been kindly invited to this meeting, he was satisfied "that Justice is to be done," and when he would come again "after Harvest," he would expect to find the whole matter "buried." He himself would "Cover it deep over with Earth."

Then, in an equally telling gesture, Sassoonan turned from the Governor to address the assembly's other looming presence, James Logan, to confess what he had intended to refrain from speaking about until his next visit. It was the emotional shock of the settlements he had seen while coming down through "his Lands" in Tulpehocken. Now that he was "an old man & must soon die" (according to Farmar's translation), "his Children may wonder to see all their Father's Lands gone from them, without having received any thing for them." So many "Christians" have settled near them that soon "they shall have no place of their own left to live on." That would likely produce "Misunderstanding" between the children of the Christians and Sassoonan's people.

At this, Logan, having heard what he had had expected and was prepared for, "craved Leave" for himself "to answer the Indians." Though "unable to walk" because of the previous winter's accident, he had lost no emotional force, and now quickly changed the subject from Sassoonan's feelings to his own, as a Commissioner of Property. William Penn, he said, who had indeed treated the Indians fairly, had instructed the Commissioners to do the same, and they had strictly obeyed. But since there had lately been accusations from people whose political motivation had been "to beget an Uneasiness in the Indians," he would take this opportunity to publicly disprove their allegations. Sassoonan had leveled similar complaints a decade earlier when he and other Indians came to Philadelphia harboring the "notion that they had not been fully paid for their lands." Logan had confronted them on that occasion with a pack of deeds proving them wrong, and they, after receiving a friendly present, had been "entirely satisfied" to sign a quitclaim for all their land. To prove his point, Logan now again pulled out that very 1718 document, and had it read aloud—in entirety. Then, while the huge audience watched, the document was "fully explained to the Indians in their own language." In response, Sassoonan and his nephew Opekasset admitted that they recognized their own marks among a dozen Native "signatures," and "acknowledged that it was all true, and that they had been paid for the Lands therein mentioned." This, at least, was what Logan said had happened.

But Sassoonan countered. He asserted that the "bounds" of the land described in the 1718 quitclaim reached only as far as Oley, and did not extend west of the Schuylkill, into Tulpehocken. Logan began to disagree, only to have Farmar—a business partner of Rutter—come to Sassoonan's defense. The land in Tulpehocken, he stated, was beyond the quitclaim's purview. Thus blocked, Logan changed the subject by insisting on the innocence of the Commissioners of Property in the recent non-legal Palatine takeover. He was seizing the chance to counter publicly the skepticism regarding own machinations. The Tulpehocken displacement (by the Palatines from New York), he now asserted before the vast audience, had happened "wholly against" the "minds" of the Commissioners, "& even without their knowledge."

At this point Sassoonan became emotional, adding that he had been unable to "believe the Christians had settled" so thickly in Tulpehocken until, while coming down from Shamokin a few days earlier, he had seen "with his own Eyes . . . the Houses and Fields they had made there." But the dismay of his *cri de coeur* was answered with withering accusation as Logan pulled out his second trump card. He had gotten wind, he said, after he had left his house in the morning, that this subject would come up, and had therefore sent someone to find in his files still another crucial item. This was none other than the appeal submitted four years earlier by the Palatines of New York to the former governor, William Keith, for permission to purchase lands in Tulpehocken. Astonishingly, Logan now treated the huge audience and the Lenapes to an entire reading and translation of *this* document, too. It was indisputable proof, he pronounced, that it was by the authority not of the Commissioners of Property, but of former Governor Keith, that Tulpehocken had been lost to the Indians without remuneration. Logan "now hoped," as his own minutes put it, "that such of this Audience as had been so sollicitous to have the Indians complain of James Logan might go away satisfied. They had complained, and they were answered."

Logan's tirade had deflected the audience's attention from the pathos of the Lenape mourners to his own self-righteous vindication. Having lost his point with the Natives, he nevertheless had the gall to appeal to them not to offer any violence now to the invading Palatines, since the latter were good people. Rather, the Lenapes should "wait till such time as that matter could be adjusted" (i.e., payment could be arranged). That was a new note—an acknowledgment that there could be some future compensation for the Tulpehocken land, instead of the premeditated, document-asserted denial of their claim that Logan had first offered.

There was more to come, since a judge in attendance, Andrew Hamilton, wanted his own turn before this audience. He, too, had been greatly angered, while accompanying Governor Gordon to Manatawny, to hear comments from people believing that the Indians had been treated unfairly. Some of that opinion had come from persons in this very audience, he claimed, and "it would be most proper [for them] to declare openly [here and now] what they had to say on the subject." At that, Rutter, apparently still seated beside Sassoonan, "stood up & denied that he had said any such thing as that the Indians had not been satisfied for their Lands, &c." There again—in the secretarial record's dismissive "&c"—followed the tell-tale choice not to transcribe what may have been the most specifically revealing comment in this interchange.

Now ignoring the Indians, the unpopular Logan jumped back into the fray with passionate rhetoric intended for "the audience only." "Many" of them, he knew, "would have been glad to see me in the wrong." While it was one thing to have political arguments in Pennsylvania's government, he fumed, he had heard "numerous reports" of hints to the "poor innocent Indians . . . that they are wrong'd in their lands." That was "exceedingly wicked" enough, but something even worse was in circulation: a "shameless but malicious Story" that Logan had profited personally in his handling of "a vast Quantity of Indian Goods" that William Penn had sent over "for a present to the Indians." Anyone spreading that baseless rumor should blush for shame, if they were capable of blushing.

A final request for a turn to further exculpate the Commissioners of Property from suspicion came from Logan's friend and co-member Richard Hill. He insisted that the Commissioners, having been seriously admonished by Penn, "would never have agreed to that settlement of the Palatines in the Tulpyhocken Lands" where "the Indians were then seated." The fact, as had now been publicly documented, that it was all the former Governor Keith's fault, had proved "how groundless all the Noise is, that has been made of the Commissioners patenting the Indian Lands." It could have only come from a politically motivated "Design to beget animosities, and raise a Disaffection in the Inhabitants."

The oxygen in the meeting, officially called to "treat" sympathetically with the mourning Indians, had been largely used up by defensive politicians. Yet Governor Gordon pronounced genially, "We have now brightned the Chain & strengthened our League & we are as one People." He had ready a "Proclamation" commanding "all the English" to be "kind to the Indians." When it was read and interpreted to Sassoonan's group, they "appeared highly satisfied," wrote Logan. No explicit promise that the Indians would be finally paid for Tulpehocken appeared in the minutes. They did record, however, that the Natives "readily agreed" to inform other Indians of what had transpired in this "Treaty," and their pleased acceptance of the Governor's parting gift of "Bread, Pipes & Tobacco, with five Gallons of Rum to comfort . . . you in your return home."

It would be another five months before Sassoonan returned to Philadelphia to fully express his people's response to the recent killings. During the interim, the hot-headed Winters brothers were brought to the gallows at the town of Chester. Before "many hundreds" of witnesses, John Winters confessed, "I am sorry for the Indians Deaths, that then were so barbarously put to death by us, which if we had known at the Time, we should not have been guilty of their Blood." Apparently no or few Indians were present to hear the last words: "And here I come to an End, praying God to forgive me my Sins, which are great and many, and this great Sin, for which Cause I die. I pray God, and I hope you will pray to God, to receive my Soul."

Through the execution of the Winters brothers, Pennsylvania's government paid both a legal and a diplomatic debt to the Lenapes. But it had not assuaged their restlessness, nor did it allay the concerns of the Iroquois, who later stated, "None of our Indians saw the men die, many believe they were not hanged, but transported to some other colony." Logan, sensing the unease while waiting for Sassoonan's next appearance in Philadelphia, wrote to Penn's sons in England that many of the Lenapes (formerly of Tulpehocken) were moving west into the "Ohio" or "Allegheny" country. There was even an extreme report that almost all the Natives except Sassoonan himself had left Shamokin for Allegheny. Out there, officials knew, the "Delawares" would be exposed to the French opponents of English control. This could turn them, "into our deadly Enemies," Logan recognized, "for the Injury we have done them in robbing them of their Lands." He was all too well aware, as he wrote to the Penns, that "Indians, from one generation to another, never forget their Rights nor to revenge the Wrongs they have received."

No agreement had yet been reached on an *amount* of remuneration for Tulpehocken, but surveyors hired by speculators were already busy there and on other land still not purchased from the Natives. Serious money was changing hands in England between the debt-threatened Penn brothers and the affluent young heir William Allen. On a smaller scale in Pennsylvania, the Commissioners were quietly yielding to the repeated applications of a newly wealthy German immigrant, Caspar Wistar. Having come in the 1717 wave of Palatines, he was imitating his speculating father-in-law, Dirk Jansen of Germantown, who had bought and sold tracts of land in Lower Salford, on Indian Creek next to both Gerhart Clemens' plantation, and that of Gerhart's minister Dielman Kolb.

The continued surveying could not be hidden from Natives who, finding deer ever scarcer on either side of the Schuylkill, were losing trust in the white officials. North of Logan's ironworks at Durham, the Shawnees were suddenly reported to have disappeared with their women and children from their village at Pechoquealin, "leaving their Corn Standing." From Shamokin came a letter declaring, "People in our Parts is freed that there is som Miscif hacin by the Indians." And why had Sassoonan not quickly returned to Philadelphia as he had promised? All this, plus two more shipfuls of Palatines that had arrived with "no special license," made for what Logan called a "melancholy prospect."

On October 10, 1728, Sassoonan finally arrived in Philadelphia with a mixed cluster of Natives, excusing his delay on account of his having been "taken very ill," and asking the Governor for "a Time to hear them." The old headman said that he would now speak not only on behalf of his own Lenape people, but those of the landless Brandywines and the Shawnees on the Delaware. This was useful to the Philadelphia officials, who could deal with Sassoonan as a "king," while accepting his newer Lenape name: Alumapees. They much preferred giving presents via a single leader rather than to representatives from multiple Native clans. Alumapees himself surely knew that his people's respect had been enhanced by what he could collect from the white people and share with them. Now, coming with pleasant memory of the previous visit, where he had been respectfully heard by a mass audience and awarded with gifts, he could expect more of the same.

Having "swallowed" down all he had heard at the gathering in June, Alumapees was returning in the hope that "Every thing between us is quiet and easy." "He wishes," recorded the minutes, "that our present friendship may last as long as the Heavens & the Stars therein, & that no ill grounded jealousies may ever interrupt it, but that we may ever joyn hands together as friends & Brethren." He pointed out that his Lenapes actually had a tradition of peacefulness, endorsed and even commanded by their Native superiors. Those Five (now) Six Nations had "often told them that they were as Women only, & desired them to plant Corn & mind their own private business" while the Iroquois "would take care of what related to Peace & War."

At this point the old sachem began to wax eloquent. "He says that the Indians have had good Times ever since the Christians settled here," recorded the secretary,

> & he hopes they will still continue so as long as the Sun & the Light shall Endure, & desires there may be no Coldness between us, so as to hurt them, or any of their or our Children. That what he now says comes from his heart, & he speaks honestly and sincerely, for they are not as Words that come from the Mouth & are no more thought of; they proceed from his very heart, & hopes that what has pass'd between the [new] Governour & him has not been anywise misunderstood, & wishes a good Agreement may still subsist between us.

Such words were making clear that even after the recent Tulpehocken killings, and in the midst of the Lenapes' de facto expulsion from the last of their lands, they could entertain William Penn's original dream of peaceful relations.

Listening to Alumapees, we might wonder how Penn's dream had been so efficaciously seated in his people's imagination. Reading one of Penn's many articulations may help us feel its power. In 1701, well before Sassoonan/Alumapees had left his native woods for the Susquehanna, the Colony founder and Indians from Susquehanna to the Potomac had jointly declared: "There shall be forever hereafter a firm and lasting peace Continued between Wm. Penn, his Heirs & successors, & all the English & other Christian Inhabitants of [Pennsylvania], & the . . . Kings and Chiefs, & their successors, & all the Severall People of the nations of Indians. . . ." In fact, "They shall forever hereafter be as one Head & One Heart, & live in true friendship & Amity as one People."

Mere "words, words, words"? Alumapees would not regard them so. He "hopes," continue the minutes at Philadelphia, that "all the differences" recently evident between the Europeans and his people

> will be buried deep & covered up from the Sight, that when our & their Children in after times, observe the great Friendship that has been between us, it may rejoice & gladden their Hearts. And he hopes that all Differences are buried, & that the Earth round about is made so smooth & Even that their Children may afterwards say; This is the Place where our Fathers & our Brethren (meaning the Christians) Ended & composed all their Differences, so that now there remains no footsteps of them.

Could modern Pennsylvanians imagine a history that would have fulfilled rather than mocked this hope expressed in 1728 by Alumapees in the city of Brotherly Love, which he intended to be spread among all the Natives for whom he spoke?

The impoverished visitors confirmed their sentiments with a gift of "eight Bundles of Skins." Governor Gookin, grateful for Alumapees' accompanying words, acknowledged them as coming "from the Heart of a Friend and Brother, in true Love." Citing the "links in the Chain" of peace between William Penn and the Natives, Gookin admonished Alumapees to "repeat them over & over again to your Children," so "that you may have them at all times stamp'd on your Hearts and fixed in your View."

Finally came the expected concluding ceremony of gifts to the visiting Natives—coats, shirts and blankets, gunpowder and lead, with "Bread, Rum, Pipes & Tobacco." According to the minutes, the Indians "express'd their Satisfaction by a harmonious Sound peculiar to them." The repeated "Yo-hah" that had cheered William Penn 45 years earlier at Perkasie could still echo from the Lenape diaspora at Susquehanna.

But for how much longer?

CHAPTER TWENTY

Pain

1729–1732

Pennsylvania Dutch, rather than Lenape or even English, would be the language of Salford for two centuries following its white settlement. If Salfordians spoke of 40-mile-distant Tulpehocken in 1729, they pronounced it "Dolbehuck." Nearby Skippack had become "Schibbach," recalling the village of Schüpbach in the Bernese Emmental, ancestral home of Salford's Bergeys, Haltemans, Kratzes, and Lederachs. Perkiomen was now "Barkeyome," and the tributary above Clemens' mill on the Branch Creek was "Insching Grick" (Indian Creek). "Dutch" speakers called the Native maize *Welschkan* (literally, strange grain) and turkeys *Welschhühne* (foreign poultry).

Beyond names and labels, there were new concepts to grasp, none more important than what was granted to Gerhart Clemens in January of 1730: that of being a citizen of Pennsylvania. Along with the latest set of nearly 100 German-speaking applicants, a third of them Mennonites, Gerhart's legal status was now equal to that of any of "His Majesty's Natural born subjects of this Province." Busily at home in what had been renamed "Penn's Woods," his family would have minimal interest in the departing Native noncitizens who were now landless, placeless, and of course stateless.

Among Pennsylvania's new citizens was Salford Minister Dielman Kolb Jr., whose earlier emigrating brothers Jacob, Martin, and Johannes lived at nearby Skippack (their older brother and neighbor Henrich—the first American Mennonite bishop—died in this year). As had occurred months before on a Mennonite plantation out at Conestoga, where most of more than 200 applications for citizenship had been submitted by *wehrlos* (nonresistant or defenseless) Mennonites, their "word" or promise of loyalty had been accepted in lieu of the usual hand-raising oath taken by the *Karicheleit* ("church-people," the Mennonite term for Lutherans and Reformed neighbors). Now, as citizens, Gerhart Clemens and fellow Mennonites with names such as Bechtel, Clemmer, Detweiler, Drissel, Fried, Hunsicker, Souder, and Ziegler could legally sell or transmit to their descendants any land for which Pennsylvania's Proprietors had granted them patents (documents proving that they had paid in full). They were now owners, permanently at home on land surrendered by its "Original People."

By contrast, Lenapes and Shawnees encamped around the Forks of the Susquehanna were experiencing an unraveling of their recently regrouped community. Some of their number were disappearing across the mountains westward through "Allegheny." The town of Kittanning growing on the Ohio River reportedly had 300 Delaware and 260 Shawnee residents. Sassoonan, honored though he might be by his people as Keeper of the Wampum, was leading an abject existence at Shamokin. A year and then another had passed since he had at last been promised pay for Tulpehocken, but there was still nothing to show for it beyond the few ceremonial gifts he had brought back from Philadelphia and distributed. Meanwhile, it was known by officials that his people were "in great want." What was plentiful, Sassoonan observed, was the supply of rum from Philadelphia hauled in "horse-loads" past his door daily by rude traders who would take wampum in payment. In his despairing moments, the Wampum Keeper could not resist the temptation to use the sacred currency to pay for his own liquid respite.

Sassoonan had the local fellowship of a man considered his successor, Opekasset, and of his bright young nephew Shakatawlin. The latter, nicknamed "Sam," was of special interest to James Logan, who called him "the truest and honestest" Indian he had known. Three other nephews of Sassoonan—brothers Pisquetomen, Shingas, and Tamaqua—also exhibited leadership qualities. Beyond his inner circle, Sassoonan was in frequent contact with Shikellamy, the half-white Oneida keeping tabs on the Six Nations' Lenape "subjects" camped around the Susquehanna's Forks. Further afield, the Wampum Keeper would soon have to deal with the estimable presence in Tulpehocken of a late-coming New York Palatine named Conrad Weiser. Having been sent as a boy by his father to live with the Oneidas, Weiser was fluent in the Oneida language. His arrival in Tulpehocken in 1729, bringing the attention of the Six Nations ever closer to their Lenape "cousins," would throw a minimizing shadow over Alumapees' people. Our account of Alumapees will need to be wary of Weiser's and Shikellamy's Iroquois-favored and Delaware-belittling testimony.

Honored in his role as he might be by his own wounded people, Alumapees was also an embodiment of their overwhelming loss of place. He must have sensed, behind the persistently friendly messages and personal gifts from James Logan, the powerful Commissioner's urge for Lenape permission to buy and sell the highly vendible land back in Tulpehocken. In fact, Logan had already dipped into such dealing. In private correspondence, on the other hand, he was acknowledging that "not one acre" there had been purchased from the Indians by the Penns, and that the situation could not be changed legally without the Penn family's representation. The Natives at Tulpehocken and Lehigh would negotiate only with a Penn, and in person.

In a letter to James Steel, under date of November 18, 1729, Logan wrote: "It is now not only Sassoonan, our very good friend, and his people of our Indians, that we have to deal with, but the [Lehigh] lands also on the Delaware above Tohickon creek must be purchased of others. But the main business of all is to induce John Penn himself to come over. The Indians all expect him next spring, everybody expects him, and it is in vain for him to expect that others will do his business for him."

Hearing that Sassoonan had been blessed with a son, Logan took the opportunity to "caress" the elderly sachem. "I hope he will grow up as a young flourishing tree," wrote the Philadelphia magnate. Having two young sons and two daughters from his own late marriage, he observed that "good sons are the crown and glory to old years." And since he had heard that his "brother" at the Forks of the Susquehanna was "weak and not very healthy this winter," Logan sent a gift of "two planting hoes" which he hoped the fragile sachem would see "used in the spring." More importantly, he sent along "a bottle of the richest . . . canary wine, a great comforter to sick hearts, for so I have found it." All too prescient was an accompanying admonition that Sassoonan should "have one small dram at once when he is weakly and no more at one time."

Brooding in his spanking new mansion, Logan wrote to the Penn sons in October 1730 that the Indians had become dangerously "uneasie" over the two years since they had been promised remuneration for the lost Tulpehocken. It was this kind of distrust, Logan warned, that in other colonies had caused Indian wars.

Although Pennsylvania had been spared so far, since "no People, have a truer Notion of Justice than [Indians], nor more forcibly insist on it, it cannot be expected they will much longer take Words or Promises for any sort of Pay, especially while they see one year pass over after another without any Effect from all that has been said to them." Aware that "Indians, from one generation to another, never forget their rights nor to revenge the Wrongs they have received," Logan recommended that if one of the Penn brothers did not come over immediately, it would be good to send a substantial gift in money "particularly to Sassoonan, alias Allummapies their honest old King, and Opekasset [his intended successor], with a handsome but not costly Coat to each of them as a present . . . to themselves, and the rest to be divided amongst them and their People." Time was running out.

Concern was humorously evident in Philadelphia in the following spring (1731), when a false report that one of the Penns was on an arriving ship brought a crowd rushing to the docks. This disappointment, however, was nothing compared with the dismay at double news brought from Shamokin by Shikellamy, the Six Nations' monitor of Alumapees. The European gifts of disease and alcohol had reached Shamokin. Opekasset, Sassoonan's presumptive successor, had succumbed to the smallpox that had recently killed 288 Philadelphians. The other news was incredibly worse. Miserable old Sassoonan, in an alcoholic stupor, had stabbed to death his own beloved nephew Shakatawlin ("Sam"). Having then come to his senses, he was reportedly too remorseful to eat, and apparently prepared to die.

What rum-twisted synapse had misfired in the normally tractable old man's brain? Had he kept himself drunk against the humiliation of being unable to share with his impoverished "children" any more "presents" such as he had formerly brought back from his negotiations? Or is it fair to wonder whether any suspicion had lurked in his psyche that Logan's self-acknowledged grooming of Shakatawlin as a successor had hinted at a bypassing of his own role? In any case, all too accurate had been Penn's observation, back when Sassoonan had been "a little lad," that rum turned the Natives into "beasts." There had been frequent examples of this over the intervening years, but how could this have happened at the symbolic heart of the Lenape peoplehood? And how was it, among the Natives, that they could more pity than condemn their faltering leader?

A sympathetic Moravian missionary put it candidly: "The Indians having learned *Drunkeness* of the White People, do not reckon it among the Vices. They all, without Exception, and without Shame, practice it when they can get strong Liquor." Alumapees was regarded by his people as a victim, not a murderer. "It does not among them," wrote the missionary, "hurt the Character of the greatest Warrior, the gravest Counsellor, or the modestest Matron. It is not so much an *Offence*, as an *Excuse* for other Offences; the Injuries they do each other in their Drink being charged, not upon the *Man*, but upon the *Rum*." Indians expecting to have a drunken episode were known to charge some of their men to stay sober and keep any weapons away from those about to imbibe.

How might we answer those tempted to link Lenape loss of land with alcohol (albeit introduced by precisely the takers of the land)? Should this be the end of our narrative?

Hardly. For one thing, at its other pole the immigrant community at Salford would have its own sad inebriates, even in Mennonite families such as the Clemenses and Zieglers. And the Lenape story, though tenuous, has never died. Landless, aged, and humiliated as he might be, Alumapees would live another 16 years, and though accused by some of the westward-drifting Natives of "drinking away" the Lenape land legacy, he would never be rejected as titular head by those around him. After him, in fact, his leadership role would continue in a set of four nephews.

However shocking Pennsylvania's officials found the report of Sassoonan's act, the last thing they wanted was to lose favor with the still unpaid Lenapes. Governor Gordon, having heard that Sassoonan's "Grief for the unhappy Accident was so great that it was like to cost him his life," immediately sent a gift of two coats and a letter inviting the despairing sachem to revisit Philadelphia. While James Logan claimed this as his own initiative, his motive had little to do with offering comfort. His "design," he wrote to the Penns in England, was to "see" while Alumapees was still living "(for he is very old) if we could possibly agree with him [about the *amount* of payment] for their [Tulpehocken] Lands, and so much depends on the Success of this [that] it ought by no means to be delay'd even one month longer."

Significantly, prior to Alumapees' scheduled public appearance with the Governor on August 12, Logan met privately with the sachem and his nephew Pisquetomen. Though sensing a suspicious attitude in Pisquetomen, Logan wheedled signatures from both uncle and nephew on a strange little agreement denoting a personal "gift" of land at Tulpehocken. What was this about? The language was imaginative, to say the least, as it carefully claimed "Alummapis alias Sassoonan" to be "chief of the Schuylkill Indians and Indian Owner of the lands lying on the Branches and upper part of the said River Schuylkill." It was not in exchange for money, but "In consideration of the love and good-will that I bear to my friend James Logan" that Sassoonan was said to be willing "at this writing [to] give and grant . . . five hundred acres of land . . . southward of Tulpehocken." The land was to be conveyed not to Logan but several Palatine customers to whom Logan had already privately and illegally sold that much acreage. Sassoonan, of course, could not read. The secret document, endorsed also by monitor Shikellamy, was a ruse to cover Logan's tracks from the Penns who had never allowed Tulpehocken land to be sold in the first place. Yet the legalese employed was as official-sounding as in the indentures for David Powell's "crooked affair" at Salford 14 years earlier: "from this day for all time to come and for ever without any further Claim or Demand to be made for the same for any part thereof by me or by any other Indian whatsoever."

It had not been an issue of land, but Sassoonan's near suicidal depression that had motivated Governor Gookin to invite the sachem to Philadelphia. It was on the latter theme that Gookin, on the day following Logan's private conversation, addressed Sassoonan in a public session with the Colony's Executive Council. "When we first heard of the unhappy Death of our Friend Sam Shakatawlin," began the Governor, "we were exceedingly grieved for it."

> We heard . . . that you were so much afflicted for his loss that you forbore taking necessary food, and that after we had lost two very good Friends, Opekasset & him, we were in danger of losing you also. To prevent this you were sent for, that we might take care of you and preserve your Life, that you might still remain longer amongst us and continue to Preserve Peace, which we understood was always your inclination.

Sassoonan responded that indeed "Grief for the unhappy Accident was so great that it was like to cost him his life." As he had "lamented," he had "refused any Nourishment," but on receiving the

Governor's letter had "come hither & taken Food to keep himself alive." The Governor's kind words, he said, gave him "great Comfort." He now intended to "hold fast" to "that which is good & not depart from it." He was also "glad" that Shikellamy, representing the "Five Nations," was "now present & hears what is said, for that they, the five Nations, all his People and the English are as one."

What had happened, observed the Governor, had renewed concern for the effects of "that pernicious Liquor, Rum, which has too often occasioned mischief before." There were "many good laws" against its over-use, "but you are so fond of it . . . that you will find means to procure it." Yes, agreed Alumapees, "the Indians have made frequent complaints" about its excessive availability. But "He cannot understand," continue the minutes, "why such Quantities come" from Philadelphia to Shamokin. Even so, when asked if he wished that "an entire stop" be made to "the sending up of Rum amongst the Indians," he demurred, suggesting that rather than having liquor brought up "by the English . . . if any Indians want it, they should come to Philadelphia for it." What he feared was that "Rum Quarrels" might break out between "the English & the Indians . . . & Murder ensue," which would "loosen the Tye between" them. Well pleased with these thoughts, the Governor presented Sassoonan with two coats and a blanket, and said they would move on to "other Affairs" the following day.

What hung in the air was how low a payment the humbled old headman might be persuaded to accept for Tulpehocken. Logan was mentally preparing a "Discourse" on the subject—not for a mutually learning conversation, but as a private lecture aimed at imposing on the Lenape folk-mind a syllabus of concepts out of another narrative than their own. Its purpose was simply to intimidate their "king" (a non-Native term). From that fraught moment survives, in Logan's own secretarial hand, one of Colonial Pennsylvania's most ironic documents, preserved among his private papers at the Historical Society of Pennsylvania in Philadelphia. Seldom or perhaps never have its two pages—under the heading "To Sassoonan or Allumapies &c at Philadia 13 Aug. 1731"—been published in their entirety.

Having observed how shrewd a translator Pisquetomen was, Logan did not want his services when conversing with his uncle about the price of Tulpehocken. "I concerted measures with Sassoonan," Logan wrote, when bringing the old man to the mansion at Stenton, "to have that fellow laid aside and a better substituted in his place.

Logan had been in crutches since his fall in 1728, but had lost nothing of his mental acuity. To "discourse," as he put it, with Sassoonan "about the Lands you claim," he wished to start "from the beginning." A logic unrolls:

> The great King of England having millions of Subjects under him sends his ships abroad to most parts of the world to trade. Some of these coming long since into this Countrey, found it inhabited only by Indians, who had no Arms but bows and Arrows, no Cloathing but the skins of Beasts, no knives or Axes but sharp stones and shells to cutt with, these Indians seeing the goods that the English brought, were desirous to Trade with them, and other Nations as Dutch and Swedes came afterward. . . .

Since "the English," ran the bland narrative, had been "the first who discover'd [!] these Lands, the other nations yielded the Command to them and all joyn'd as one people." Surely Sassoonan could appreciate the concept and necessity of discovery. Only with that recognized, could real history begin.

> Above fifty years agoe the great King of England gave William Penn who was a great man at home with the King leave to bring over into this Countrey as many of his People as would accompany him and he gave him power over those people to settle a Government, to appoint Judges, to hold Courts and to punish evil doers. He then came with a great many ships full of good People, and because this would cost him a great deal of Money, many Thousands of Pounds, he agreed with his People that they should pay him something towards this great Charge, therefore every man who was to have any Land here Paid a small sum of Money for the right of taking up Wm Penn as their Governour, yet all he ever receiv'd has not been enough to pay his Debts, the Countrey has cost him more than ever he has gott from it. He has been oblig'd to sell a good part of the Estate his Father left him in England and other places for money to pay those he ow'd to.

And upon receiving this Little from his People he further promis'd them, that they should pay no more for the Lands they took under him neither to Indians nor others, and accordingly a Law has been pass'd here that none but William Penn or his Children or those they Imploy should buy any Lands of the Indians, and now no man can agree with the Indians for any Lands but they or whom they shall appoint.

When Wm Penn first arriv'd here with his People He immediately called together the Chiefs of the Indians, and told them he was come over to them with leave of the great King of England and had brought a great number of good People to live amongst them who should furnish them with what they wanted, that they should be his Brothers and his People and the Indians should be the same, they exceedingly enjoyed at this, they bid him and his People welcome, he made a strong Chain of friendship with them which has been kept bright to this day, the Indians offer'd them their Lands to settle on, but He would buy it of them and paid them for it in such goods as they had occasion for, Nor would Wm Penn ever Suffer any of the People to enter on any Land till the Indians were Honestly paid for them, he was just and true to his word, he lov'd the Indians and they lov'd and honour'd him as their Father.

When he came last over hither he had no further occasion to buy any more Lands at that time for his people, when he first came ashoar Menanget and Hetkoquean with some other Indians hastened to Philadelphia with presents to welcome him, they offer'd him their Lands, if he wanted them, but he did not. In two years or less he was oblig'd to return to England and design'd back hither in a little time and to live and die amongst his People and the Indians, but business hindered him, at length he fell sick and continued so six years after which he died and left his Children young.

While he was sick and Children not grown up to be men, they could doe nothing for this Countrey. In the mean time great numbers of People were oblig'd to leave their own Countrey, and came over hither to get bread, these went of their own heads and settled the Indians Land. This was contrary to the mind of Wm Penn and his Children and those that were under them. We never agreed that the Indians should be disturb'd, we survey'd or run lines round the settlements of the Indians that none might come in upon them, so we did in Chester County and so we did round the Indians at Conestogoe, and Tulpyhocken Lands were survey'd and were to be kept till the Indians left them for two of Penn's Children, but Gr Wm Keith when he was Governer here being false to his trust broke Wm Penn's order, he sent people to settle Tulpyhockin but as these men [i.e., the Palatines coming down from New York] were sent over by the Queen of England [in 1709] and went not there of themselves but were sent, they are now become good men, and love the Indians.

Wm Penn's Children, being now grown up one of them was coming over hither last spring, he had settled his business and left it to a good man to manage for him in his absence, as he was coming away that good man died, he was then forced to stay longer but one of them is coming.

You are told that the people now give great prices to one another for Land which may be true, the ground this House stands on was of no value before Wm Penn came over, no man would give six pence for it, but now Philadelphia is built there is shipping and Trade, and it is of great value, the English people make it so, Iron is at first a stone in the ground of no value at all where it lies, the English dig up the Stone melt it with mighty fires beat it out and then work it into knives guns axes that are very valuable, It is so with your lands they were worth nothing to you before Wm Penn and his People came, the English make it of value by using it.

But Wm Penn made it a Law that none of his people should hold any of the Indians Land till he himself or his children bought it, they get very little for them from the People, and are at very great Charges. Yet out of that Little they will pay the Indians, and none but they can buy them.

Finally, having portrayed Pennsylvania's founder as a financial victim of his own generosity, Logan appealed to the starving Lenapes to show mercy.

> You have heard how Purchases have been made of the Indians from the beginning and Wm Penn's Children will proceed in the same Manner with you, we will treat with you in their behalf, therefore we desire you to consider what Land you have to sell and set moderate reasonable price on it such as Wm Penns children can pay, and it shall be paid you.

The Indians were not to be too hard on the Europeans!

Sassoonan's simple response to this shrewdly crafted scenario was less than satisfactory to Logan, who recorded that the old sachem at least acknowledged that "when Wm Penn first came into this Countrey he himself was there a Little Lad. He remembers when Wm Penn went up to Perkasie and met the Indians there [with sachems] Menanget, Hetkoquean and Taminy... present." He also agreed that "When Wm Penn first came in he called the Indians together [and] proposed to purchase their Lands, ... they said they would give it to him."

Sassoonan, however, crushed as he was with knowledge of his drunken deed, had not come to Philadelphia to subject his people's welfare to pressure from a land-dealing Commissioner. Logan had to record that though the weary sachem "understands every word that has been said, being "here alone," he "cannot answer here. He will go home and talk with the other Indians, who are concernd in the same Lands and when they have conferr'd together they will give their Answer" (i.e., as to what amount of pay they will accept for Tulpehocken).

Though Sassoonan had traveled to Philadelphia with only four other Natives—Pisquetomen and his wife, Shikellamy, and another young Indian from Shamokin—their visit was considered important enough that their horses were pastured and fed for seven nights, and several of the animals were shod at the government's expense. In addition, Sassoonan was presented with a saddle and a hat, and both he and Pisquetomen received coats "with lining and trimmings." For all the rhetoric about rum, four three-gallon kegs filled with the liquor rode home with them, and ten bushels of meal were ordered for the Indians at Shamokin, who were said to be "then in want."

While Sassoonan received most of the attention in Philadelphia, Shikellamy had dramatically raised his own profile. It was he who had brought the news of Sassoonan's tragedy, and then Sassoonan in person, to the city. He gave access to the councils of the Six Nations, who claimed control over the Delawares, Susquehannocks, and Shawnees. Why not, thought Logan and other officials, deal directly through Shikellamy with the more powerful Iroquois, rather than with the ever-complaining "Lenappys," to promote a "treaty we must have"? So the Lenape-watching Shikellamy was quickly commissioned with wampum and "a handsome present" to invite the Six Nations leaders "to hasten down to treat with us." The purpose, Logan explained, was to help the northern Natives, if possible, to "Strengthen both themselves and us." This was coded language. Aware that as far as the Lenapes were concerned, the move was diplomatically underhanded, Logan wrote, "I must not be more particular here."

Shikellamy soon returned successfully from his northern diplomacy, bringing along a Cayuga sachem and, more importantly, the recent newcomer in Tulpehocken, Conrad Weiser. Able to speak one of the northern Native languages, Weiser was unusually trusted by the Six Nations as an adopted son, and an invaluable resource in their new conversation with Pennsylvania's officials. From this time forward, Weiser—even more than the half-Indian Shikellamy—would give Philadelphia officials an entrée to the Six Nations that allowed them to de-emphasize their older respectful relationship with the "Lenappys" and that people's aging, alcoholic headman.

In contrast with the eroding Native community at the Forks of the Susquehanna, life in the Perkiomen watershed was gaining warmth. The last "vacant land" along the lower East Branch was being bought up and sold by speculators such as Germantown's Dirk Jansen and his rising son-in-law, 1717 immigrant Caspar Wistar, or Philadelphia officials such as Nicholas Scull and James Steele. In 1732 the increasingly populated Salford Township's whole eastern half, reaching all the way to the Bucks County line, was surveyed into a new township called not "Indian Field" but "Franconia." This echoed the homeland of Germantown's leader Franz Daniel Pastorius, who as an old man had bought 800 acres from surveyor Thomas Fairman at the head of the Skippack Creek (site of present Souderton). Here the usual Philadelphia speculators were also busy, and here, too, some of the immigrant purchasers—Clemmers, Funcks, Hunsbergers, Moyers, and Reiffs—were Mennonite.

In adjacent Lower Salford, as earlier mentioned, the Clemenses' neighbors Henrich and Magdalena Ruth could compare memories of the same German community with the Allebachs who bought half of their 200-acre plantation. Settling next to the Clemens plantations had proved destiny-changing for daughter Elizabeth Allebach. Her marriage to the oldest Clemens son—miller Johannes—in May 1732 made her co-owner of the land on which this story is written 285 years later. Another of the now frequently arriving ships with Palatines brought young brothers Heinrich and Johannes Clemmer, who settled in Franconia and Lower Salford, respectively, the latter one farm away from the Ruths and Allebachs.

Unlike in Sassoonan's starving scene, human fellowship could be hopeful in the nascent Salford community. Mennonite, Lutheran, Reformed, and Dunker neighbors, freed from multiple European taxes, joined frolics for tree-clearing or *aufblocken* (raising log buildings). To be sure, there were setbacks. After a decade the community had lost the services of an excellent schoolmaster, Christopher Dock, of unknown Rhineland origin. With a family of only two daughters, he had withdrawn from his profession, perhaps to work up his own small plantation in Upper Salford. An increase in German-speaking children in the community pricked his conscience, however, and ten years after his withdrawal he reemerged to resume teaching at schools held in the Mennonite meetinghouses at Salford and Skippack, where Gerhart and Anneli Clemens' grandchildren were reaching school age.

It might have been a Clemens toddler whose death was reported in the November 27, 1731, edition of Benjamin Franklin's *Pennsylvania Gazette* as follows: "A Child about two years old, in the Township of Salford, walking on a narrow plank over a Pool, accidentally fell in and was drowned." Was this the *Marili* (little Mary) memorialized in family lore passed down on the farms created from the original Clemens tract? For two centuries local mothers would warn children to steer clear of the *Mariliploch* (little Mary's hole), a cavity in a meadow beside the Branch Creek, at the foot of a field where, after a rain or plowing, innumerable stone points ("arrowheads") would be found.

CHAPTER TWENTY-ONE

Late Payment
1732-1733

ONLY 34 OF 156 PALATINES boarding the *Love and Unity* at Rotterdam in 1731 would reach Philadelphia—a year later as passengers of the smaller *Norris*. The first ship was inadequately provisioned, so when it drifted off course and its crew mutinied, passengers were denied bread for eight weeks, and through half of that period received daily rations of only "a pint of grouts" (coarse meal) for every "Five Persons," and a "Quart of Water a Person." While casting more than 100 corpses overboard, the survivors—including at least some of Mennonite Caspar Shirk's family—were forced to purchase rats and mice to eat. The landing they finally managed was at Martha's Vineyard, where they had to endure a court trial before heading for Philadelphia.

Likewise, the last Palatine-bearing vessel to arrive in 1732, a "pink" named *John and William*, took nearly two months longer than usual to reach port. Among its weary passengers was another Mennonite family with the Emmental name of Brechbühl.

Penn had had enough respect for watery risk to have written two wills before voyages. At the age of 37 his life had been saved only by the desperate bailing of fellow sailors in a North Sea storm. Even after a calm Atlantic return from his Colony to England in 1684 he had mused philosophically: "Have a care where there is more sail than ballast." Whereas his disappointing son Billy made the Atlantic round-trip soon after his father's second return in 1701, the Proprietor himself, to his considerable regret, never again sailed westward.

Penn had been dead 14 years by the time another son—23-year-old Thomas (second son in the second Penn family)—booked passage for Pennsylvania. Tormented by family debt, Thomas had remained at home with his brothers until increasingly alarming reports out of

Philadelphia demanded his intervention. Frustrated land speculators were fuming, and the post-1727 flow of Palatine immigrants had increased to "greater Quantities," he feared, than "consistant with the welfare of the country." So Thomas set sail for his late father's Province in the late spring or early summer of 1732, during a season that saw a record 2,000 Palatines arrive in Philadelphia aboard ten ships.

The cautious young Proprietor was probably a passenger on the *Samuel*, captained by Hugh Percy through a routine crossing that concluded in Philadelphia on August 11, 1732. Aboard that ship as it had set sail from Rotterdam in May and paused at Cowes on the Isle of Wight was the latest cluster of Mennonite emigrants from the Kraichgau. It had been 22 years since the first of their relatives had set out for "Charolina," only to wind up as the pioneer Mennonite nucleus at Conestoga in future Lancaster County. That group had successfully appealed to Dutch Mennonites for help in paying for their passage. Since the resurgence of Palatine emigration in 1727, however, the Dutch had wearied of providing such aid. Aware of this, Kraichgau ministers Kindig, Landes, and Meyer had advised their departing members not to request assistance with transatlantic fares, but to focus on finding a good ship and captain.

The names on a *Lÿste der Paltzers* (list of Palatines) seeking passage to Pennsylvania compiled in Rotterdam earlier that spring were recognizably Kraichgauan: Hans Behr, Michael Dährstein, Christian Geman and his brother Benedict, Christian Frantz (with 14 children), Oswald Hochstetter (with the most equity), Christian and Hans Huber, Christian Marty, Martin and Samuel Meyer, Hans Moselman, Jacob Oberholz, Hans Scherer, Hans Scherer's widow and sons-in-law Ulrich Burckhalter and Jacob Gutt, and Hans Wittmer. At least some of those émigrés managed to book passage on the *Samuel* in May; a list of 106 adult males aboard the ship (compiled upon its arrival in Philadelphia) included men with such surnames as Burkholder, Frantz, Gehman, Good, Hostetter, Mosiman, and Oberholtzer. (Other typically Mennonite names on the list were Brechbühl, Eby, Eberly, Freed, Gochnauer, Kreiter, and Stauffer. A 12-year-old Valendine Hunceker was also recorded.)

Most of the *Samuel*'s Mennonites were able to pay for their own passage. Several, like 21-year-old Michael Dährstein from Hasselbach, had promises of help from friends already in Pennsylvania. This transoceanic Mennonist trust would prove dependable. Redeemed from the *Samuel* in Philadelphia, Michael would marry a niece of Salford minister Dielman Kolb, and eventually establish a mill a few miles farther up the East Branch than those of Gerhart Clemens and Bishop Henrich Funck.

While nine more shiploads of Palatines arrived that fall, the experience of the people who had given the Perkiomen its name was one of departure. There would be no Lenape counterparts to lists like the *Samuel*'s passenger manifest, identifying 269 newcomers to Pennsylvania (including 84 children). While those refugees from crowded Palatine hofs found space in the Perkiomen woods, it was the hungry Lenapes' lot to be waiting with their wampum bearer Alumapees, 90 miles west at the Forks of the Susquehanna, for the overdue payment for the last of their land at Tulpehocken.

In Philadelphia, reports of nearly a dozen shiploads of Palatines headed for the city were eclipsed by the thrilling rumor that a vessel bearing a son of William Penn was sailing up the Delaware. To pregreet him, elderly Governor Patrick Gordon set off immediately for Chester, and was joined en route by so many locals that "they made a body of 800 horse." Upon the entourage's arrival in Philadelphia, cannon boomed from ship and shore, bells rang, and bonfires flared. Fire-engines "played all afternoon," fascinating a party of visiting Indian "Chieftains" from the Six Nations. The sachems' colorful presence (in response to the Governor's recent invitation) was uncannily serendipitous, making possible, within a week, a full-scale treaty with the 23-year-old bearer of the mythic Penn name.

Over the course of nine days beginning on August 23, 1732, some 20 Iroquois "chiefs" consulted with the newly arrived Proprietor through Conrad Weiser, who had grown up knowing one of their languages. The northern Natives used the same punning name for young Penn that they had applied to his father: *Onas* (their word for feather or quill, used as a pen). In fact, they would address all succeeding governors of the Colony by that name. (The Lenape word for "feather," also applied to Penn, is *Miquën*.)

Appealing to the visiting Natives' memories, a visibly nervous Thomas Penn asserted "that the Friendship & strict Union which my Father began with all our Friends, the Indians, and his Governors after him have cultivated, I shall take care to improve and strengthen." The Six Nations sachems were no doubt reminded of the wampum belt the senior Penn had left with the Lenapes in 1701 for delivery to the Iroquois, to which Philadelphia officials had added five fine coats—one for each of the northern "chiefs." Now they heard Thomas Penn, who was eager for Lenapes to part with their land inexpensively, say, "My father made a Chain and Covenants for himself and his Children, and I his Son, will to the best of my Power make that Chain yet stronger and brighter on our Parts, that it may continue so to all Generations."

Undeclared during the celebratory week-long conference was the Pennsylvania officials' hope that a good relationship with the Six Nations might help ease the last of the Lenapes and their land claims out of the Lehigh or Delaware "Forks" region. The officials were more transparent in urging the northern Natives to encourage those Lenapes and Shawnees drifting westward into French-influenced "Allegheny" country to return to the Susquehanna watershed. Here the name of "old Chief" Sassoonan was invoked, with the approving comment that he had only recently "sent Messengers" from Shamokin "to his people at Ohio, requiring them to return."

After days of private sessions at the Governor's house, the culminating proceedings with the Six Nations were moved into the Philadelphia Quakers' "Great Meeting House" which, four years earlier, had been filled to hear the Lenape headman testify. This time, too, mounting public concern and the exciting Penn presence had drawn a "very great Audience" to pack the house to its galleries. Along with another call to bring back the western-drifting Delawares, there was "advice" to the Six Nations to avoid "needless wars." A special request was for their hunters to take any runaway "Negroes" they found to the nearest sheriff, since their Quaker and Lutheran "Masters" needed the slaves to "get their bread."

Finally, the Six Nations were promised that they would always be welcome in Philadelphia, where "We will constantly keep a Fire for you." The closing language soared in the spirit of the legendary original Proprietor:

> This League and Chain of Friendship & Brotherhood, we now make with all the Six Nations . . . for us and all our People, and for our Children and Children's Children, with you for all your Nations, and for your Children and Children's Children to all Generations, to continue so long as the Heavens, Sun, Moon, Stars & the Earth shall Endure.

This address was not directed at the Lenapes. Had their Sassoonan, still waiting out at the Susquehanna for his own people's recognition, been present, he would have heard in it a drift of attention from his people—Penn's original Native friends—to the more powerful northern coalition that often talked down to their weaker Lenape "cousins."

The array of ritual gifts to solemnize the Six Nations treaty was impressive: coats, blankets, 300 pounds of gunpowder, bullets, guns, shoes, buckles, stockings, kettles, knives, scissors, combs, 100 pounds of tobacco and a gross of pipes. A special "highly pleased" cheer rose from the Indians when the young Proprietor added to the present "Six fine japanned & gilt guns" that he had specially "brought over . . . to be delivered one to the Chief of Each of the Six Nations." The large pile, expressive of the Proprietor's desire to weaken the Indians' French-ward drift, was heavy enough for the Natives to request horses to carry their bounty home.

That was all well and good, but what about the upstaged Lenapes who had now been waiting four years not for diplomatic *gifts* but for *payment* they had been promised for their lost land? They and their nearly suicidal headman Sassoonan were already so "in want" that they had recently been sent ten bushels of meal from a mill at Tulpehocken. Yet the aging sachem still had to wait a week after the conclusion of the Six Nations' treaty for his chance to represent his people to the newly-arrived Proprietor. And when the meeting finally occurred, it took place not at the Governor's residence nor in Philadelphia's "Great Meeting House," but under Logan's nose at his new brick mansion six miles north of the city.

For the long-awaited consummation, "Allumapis of the Schuylkill Indians" had again brought along his astute nephew Pisquetomen and four other men. That the nine officials meeting them, including Logan and Conrad Weiser, were well aware of how highly the old Lenape sachem estimated the worth of Tulpehocken, showed in the size of the collection of goods they now listed as payment. This was in ironic contrast with Logan's deliberate attempt a year earlier to persuade Sassoonan not to be expensive to the poor Penn family. Though the total of goods and money now offered at Stenton was actually larger than the worth of the "present" given to the Six Nations a week earlier, it did not seem excessive to Sassoonan, who carried the 47-year-old memory of a generous William Penn in peaceful parley at Perkasie.

There, as he had told Logan, the spirit had been so free that the Lenape sachems had offered to give land to their gracious guest.

The impressive payment Sassoonan (who had never before negotiated a treaty) now agreed to receive for his people's last land will be remembered here just as listed in the document he receipted on September 6, 1732:

> 20 brass Kettles, 100 stroudwater matchcoats of two yards each, 100 Duffels Ditto, 100 blankets, 100 yards of half tick, 60 linen shirts, 20 hats, 6 made coats, 12 pair of shoes and buckles, 30 pair of stockings, 300 lb. of gunpowder, 600 lb. of lead, 20 fine guns, 12 gun locks, 50 tomahawk or hatchets, 50 planting houghs [hoes], 120 knives, 60 pair of Scissars, 100 tobacco tongs, 24 looking glasses, 40 tobacco boxes, 1000 flints, 5 lb. of paint, 24 dozen of gartering, 6 dozen of ribbon, 12 dozen rings, 200 awl blades, 100 lb. of tabacco, 400 tabacco pipes, 20 gallons of rum, and fifty pounds of money, to us in hand paid or secured to be paid by Thomas Penn, Esqr.

Though this was remuneration specifically for Tulpehocken, that name was not even mentioned in the deed, which simply stipulated all "Lands lying in or near the River Schuylkill . . . or any of the branches streams fountains or springs thereof, Eastward or Westward."

This final signing marked a profound threshold for the last Lenapes to inhabit land along the East Branch of the Perkiomen Creek now owned and occupied by German-speaking farmers (who were no doubt oblivious to the dealing at Stenton). From that moment on, no land "between the branches of the Delaware River and the branches running into the River Susquehanna" could be regarded as Lenape land. And now they were alarmed to notice trader John Harris of Paxtang (future Harrisburg) expanding his operation on the Susquehanna. He had "built a House," came the report, and was "clearing fields" at "the Mouth of Choniata" (eastward-flowing Juniata River), a mere 35 miles downriver from the Susquehanna Forks. Sassoonan, who lived there, quickly joined with his Six Nations mentor Shikellamy asking Harris "to desist from making a Plantation." The concern was enough for Shikellamy to carry all the way to Thomas Penn in Philadelphia, where it was not reassuring to be told that Harris' new house was only for trade, with just enough land cleared around it "to raise corn for his horses."

In the careful quitclaim language of the long-delayed Tulpehocken deed, Sassoonan acknowledged that some of the payment in goods and money was "to us in hand paid" on the day of the signing, while the balance was "secured to be paid by Thomas Penn." Indeed, nearly a year would pass before any of the "secured" goods were delivered to the Lenapes—fully five years after Logan's admission that the Indians were owed remuneration for their Tulpehocken land.

In the meantime, Logan continued his private land dealing. As noted earlier, he had induced Sassoonan to sign a document conveying to the speculator 500 acres that he had already secretly sold to settlers. As a main partner of the iron furnace at Durham, Logan was working to eliminate remaining Lenape claims to that area. More importantly, he was a principal owner of land along the Lehigh River near its confluence with the Delaware. The main "chief" in that area, Nutimus, a non-Unami Lenape born just east of the Delaware, had privately accepted £60 from Logan to free up land for the iron works. But six years later, when Thomas Penn came to deal with Nutimus, the latter was in a firmly resistant mood.

Penn's arrival also brought a moment of financial reckoning for Mennonite farmers at Salford. Driven by his own family's debt, the young Proprietor now demanded immediate payment of the annual quitrents Pennsylvania settlers had ignored since their original purchases, as well as any amount they still owed on their land. As Skippack and Salford settlers tried to meet those demands, some discovered significant discrepancies in their patents. Gerhart Clemens, for instance, learned through a resurvey of his property in 1734 that it contained 102 acres more than the 588 acres surveyor-seller David Powell had hastily calculated 16 years earlier. Now an elderly weaver in the process of transferring most of his land to his three sons and son-in-law Valentine Kratz, Gerhart was forced to pay an extra £25, 10 shillings to cover the additional acreage. Fortunately for him, he had the wherewithal to do so, and, unlike in Sassoonan's case, to confirm rather than be denied a home on the earth for the seven succeeding generations until his and Sassoonan's stories would be remembered together.

A major part of the wealth visible at Logan's Stenton had come via its owner's cornering of the Colony's fur trade. In 1717, when multiple shipfuls of Palatines had expanded the Mennonite communities at Conestoga, Logan had immediately ordered a large covered wagon to shuttle furs and trade goods between the Susquehanna and Delaware Rivers. Two such vehicles, dubbed "Conestoga wagons," were driven for Logan by Mennonite settlers Johannes Miller from the Pequea and Hans Graff of "Groffdale."

Crippled by his fall, Logan slept on the first floor of his Palladian mansion, from which he looked out on August 16, 1733, to see someone else's "Dutchman's Wagon." It was Sassoonan, surrounded by a party of Lenapes arriving to haul away the long-promised Tulpehocken payment. The resulting conversation had to be interpreted by Sassoonan's suspicious nephew Pisquetomen ("whom," Logan complained, "we too well know, yet he seems well enough inclined to interpret faithfully, the contrary of which is a very great crime with them"). Understanding that the old sachem was saying that "we have got all his land, that it is good Land, and he ought to have good Goods for it," Logan thought he had better tamp down the expectation of a payment supposed to be worth £700 by conveying "a righter notion of the bargain." That attempt produced "a good deal of Consultation" among the Natives, who seemed "not to be in the best of humours." Sassoonan "has no more to sell," Logan recorded, "& when these goods are gone, of which he [personally] is to have no great share, he shall have nothing." The difficult discussion continued until the Lenapes consented to proceed six miles down the Germantown Road into Philadelphia, where they could at least "view" the goods they had come for. "Treat them kindly," Logan tipped off the Philadelphia officials, "and leave them no manner of room to complain."

Entering Philadelphia, Sassoonan's party may have observed another docking of the *Samuel*, the ship that had brought Thomas Penn, Michael Dährstein, and 267 others to Pennsylvania on its previous voyage. Now, almost exactly a year later, it delivered 291 more Palatines onto Philadelphia's wharf, including more "redemptioners." Among the latter was 18-year-old Friedrich Altdörfer, a Kraichgauer from the village of Steinsfurt, five miles west of Michael Dährstein's former home at the hamlet of Hasselbach. Lutheran by baptism, Friedrich lacked the Mennonite connections of his Dierstein and Ruth neighbors. But he apparently made a good impression on young Hans and Anna Clemmer who, with a baby Susanna, needed hands to clear their 100 acres just south of the horizon from the Clemens, Allebach, and Ruth plantations. On the same day Sassoonan was finally reimbursed for the last of his people's land in Tulpehocken, Hans Clemmer agreed to pay Friedrich's passage in exchange for his indentured service. Their conversation had the exact same accents the Altdörfers, Allebachs, and Ruths had used when living a few miles from each other in the Kraichgau. The penniless Lutheran's family name—newly spelled "Alderfer"—would eventually become the most common Mennonite surname on the land bought by Gerhart and Anneli Clemens. Three centuries later Friedrich's descendants would jealously preserve his Lutheran *Gebetbuch* (prayerbook) published at Marburg in the year before he had been taken in by the Salford Mennonite community.

CHAPTER TWENTY-TWO

Honored and Bypassed

1734–1736

As our story enters its tenth decade, William Penn and Hans Stauffer have been replaced by their children. Our third character, the "little lad" of the Perkasie woods in 1683, is now about 60. Living in a wigwam at the Forks of the Susquehanna, he is still honored by his Lenapes as Keeper of the Wampum. Sadly, though, the rum he has often accepted for cooperation with the European immigrants has left him a partial victim, accused by some of his own west-retreating folk. Logan can refer to him as both the "honest old king" of the Delawares and a "poor creature."

The 59-year-old magnate of Stenton, with brown hair unsilvered and eyes needing no spectacles, was unable to mount his bench as Chief Justice without crutches. His astonishing intellectual vigor, though, was undiminished. Even before moving up from Philadelphia to the 525-acre "plantation" he named for his father's Irish estate, Logan's affluence had given him time to experiment with the reproduction of Indian corn, and send the results to scholarly approval in Europe. He had ordered, read, and understood Isaac Newton's revolutionary *Principia Mathematica*, and translated—in poetic form—a Latin classic on the theme of old age. The second floor of his woods-embraced mansion held one of the western world's largest personal libraries.

As for the children of the deceased Hannah Penn, they had grown into their 20s at Ruscombe expecting to be very rich from the overseas sale of their father's lands. Instead, his debt to the ten Quakers who had bailed him out with a huge mortgage, and whose families were now demanding repayment, had them increasingly frightened. Their anxiety in England thus paralleled that of Alumapees living abjectly where the woods no longer held enough deer for his people to thrive. Philadelphia officials worried about that situation, but were relieved to hear that the loyal old sachem was trying to call his westward-drifting Lenapes back from Allegheny, where the riverside village of Kittanning was said to be accruing 300 Delawares and almost as many Shawnees.

In contrast to Native dissolution, 29 miles northwest of Philadelphia the family of Hans and Kinget Stauffer's daughter Anneli Clemens was rooting firmly along the East Branch. Life's challenges here were less economic than natural. And what a social difference there was between Gerhart Clemens' present and former Rhineland scene at the village of Niederflörsheim, where only one of the other 17 families had been Mennonite. Here the four Clemens offspring were birthing three dozen grandchildren on adjacent farms at the border of which they could worship in their own free little *Fassammlinghaus*. And in the surrounding woods the majority of families helping each other raise log barns and houses had Mennonite names: Bergey, Clemmer, Halteman, Kolb, Lederach, Meyer, Reiff, and Ruth.

A half-mile up the Branch from the Clemenses a lingering Indian family brought, in exchange for bread, game for the table of the Dunker Preisses. Their descendants would talk of Natives playfully rolling off their round loaves like hoops. Next up the tributary called "Indian Creek" families with the Zurichian names of Funck, Landis, and Oberholtzer were continuing, not losing, their people's identity. Rosenbergers had a New Testament printed in Zurich only seven years after the Anabaptist movement had been born there in 1525. A folio Bible from the same print shop in the same decade, carried up to the Palatinate, had come over from the Ibersheimerhof with a Bachman family. Inserted in the massive heirloom was a lovingly calligraphed bookplate dated in 1708, just before the Clemenses had left the Palatinate. Now the Bachman owners, settled 20 miles north of Lower Salford on land uncleared of Indian claim, had a daughter Catharine to provide a wife for the American-born Abraham Clemens. As in his Salford community, the Bachmans had a little meetinghouse near the head of the Lehigh-feeding Saucon Creek. Undocumented later claims that Indians "regularly" visited the services in the Saucon meetinghouse are reminders that land all around there and northwards, which Lenape sachems other than Sassoonan were stubbornly withholding from Thomas Penn, was nevertheless being quietly bought and retailed by Philadelphia's William Allen.

Unlike with Lenapes, the story of immigrant Mennonites in Philadelphia, Bucks, and Lancaster Counties was about gaining an optimistic foothold on ground others had fled. The Salford Clemenses and their minister-neighbor Dielman Kolb were actually adding—and selling—acreage in land beyond the Branch Valley. Dielman, later accused of amassing property, even deeded land to his wife Elizabeth Schnebele's son back in Mannheim on the Rhine. Gerhart's deals included selling 52 acres next to his daughter Anna Kratz's plantation to a new Reformed immigrant, Willem Kerkes (Garges). Gerhart also leased another section from his nearly 700-acre Branch purchase to Lutheran Georg Wägele who had moved down from the unsuccessful Palatine settlement on the Hudson River.

When the young newcomer Wägele (whose father joined the Ephrata Cloister) had corn to be ground, he could simply haul it across the creek to the tail race of Johannes Clemens' mill. The economics of that business was another contrast with what had been necessary in the Palatinate. Back there Dielman Kolb's brother-in-law on the *Geistermühle* on the Wiesbach near the Clemens' home had to submit 40 malters (150 bushels) of grain annually "to the castle at Erbensbüdesheim," and provide a similar amount gratis to its aristocratic owners. In fact, all of the castle's grinding had to be done by miller Peter Galle, and in feudal tradition he had to submit, every three years, a symbolic half malter of white meal along with a fat pig. Small wonder that a son of Peter would shortly follow his Kolb uncles to their transoceanic scene.

There was, of course, the annual quitrent from which Pennsylvania's Founder had vainly hoped to receive necessary income. On this topic the arrival of Thomas Penn had been a wake-up call for "Receiver" James Steele. When the latter checked his records, he could find no evidence of quitrent payments from Salford's neighboring "Bebbers Town" since farms had begun there 30 years earlier. Having himself joined the speculators in Salford and Indianfield (Franconia) land, he was personally acquainted with Mennonites there, and could ask Skippack's tanner Michael Ziegler and deacon Jacob Kolb to do the unpopular work of collection for him—"forthwith." The best way to proceed, he wrote, was for Ziegler's "people to meet and pay" either Ziegler or "any other that they may think fit what is due from each of them, so that the [Proprietors] may be paid what has been so long due to them."

As 30-year-old Thomas Penn had at last sailed for the colony of which he and his younger brother Richard were quarter-owners, he had been pursued by desperate letters. "We are now at the Mercy of our Creditors," warned older brother (and half-owner) John, "without anything to Maintain us." The father's wealthy Quaker rescuers were running out of patience. "To be continually dun'd for Debts that are due," as John put it, while having "nothing to Live upon but what Comes from [Pennsylvania] . . . is Certainly the most uneasy Life a Person Can live under." In their alarm, the brothers had already accepted cash for a questionable sale of 10,000 unsurveyed, unlocated, unpurchased, and still Indian-occupied acres in Pennsylvania. The buyer was an immensely wealthy young Philadelphian who had been living in London while getting an education. This William Allen, after returning to Pennsylvania in 1725, had continually kept the Penns afloat by buying allotments of land never yet agreed on by the Indians, from the Forks of the Delaware to Tulpehocken. Within a few years he would have acquired over 20,000 acres, including land he sold to Mennonites in the Saucon Creek watershed.

Among the Penns dealing with Allen was the unscrupulous junior William of the first family, who, having long before cashed out of his "manor" that had become Norriton, was now past 50. His son Billy sold his own grant of 10,000 acres, yet unlocated, to Allen. Equally demanding was Billy's aunt Laetitia Penn Aubrey, who wrote to her half-brother Thomas to find a buyer for her legacy of 5,000 acres, which was then also handily sold to Allen. Likewise, Billy's sister Gulielma Fell urged the sale of the 10,000 acres promised in her grandfather's optimistic will. In her case, another cash-loaded buyer eager to invest—Philadelphia's rising button-maker Caspar Wistar—was allowed to buy the sales rights for Tulpehocken land that had not yet been paid for by the invading Palatines of 1723. Allen's and Wistar's markups, when computed, are astonishing in their ratio to the investments.

The Penns' maneuverings were a creeping, then galloping, departure from the original "prudent Measures" their father and grandfather had taken to "cultivate a perfect good understanding with the Natives." "The Peace of this Province," commented James Logan, had "happily enough continued" for half a century; "the foundation of this was Justice and Assurance [that the Natives] should never be depriv'd of one foot of their land but by their own Consent on fair Purchases from them." Now, after what had happened a few years earlier in the Brandywine and Tulpehocken watersheds, it was the turn of Lenapes in villages at Lehigh, around the Forks of the Delaware, to notice unannounced surveyors chaining their way through the woods, and feel a hollowing of the wampum-endorsed original Penn promises.

Logan had reason for making the point that Alumapees, however humiliated and landless, was still "considered and respected as the Chief" of not only his own grouping originating south of the Lehigh, but of "all our Delaware Indians." Now that the "Forks" Delawares, or Munsees, were proving more stubborn than Sassoonan, Logan wanted to keep whatever advantage the old man's easier friendship—even from out at Shamokin—might provide in dealings with the Lenape population as a whole. It was thus initially reassuring, two summers after the final Tulpehocken payment, to see Sassoonan showing up unexpectedly with ten other Lenapes at Stenton. But the visit proved abortive, leaving Logan nervous. Dinner had already been served when the visitors appeared, and because of the "excessive heat" Deborah Logan had no more "fresh meat in the house." Wanting to continue former hospitality, she had quickly sent out for "a joint to make them a good breakfast in the morning," only to find that they had "packt up and were gone before sunrise." This meant that they had "fared very poorly with us," observed Logan, "comparatively with their former entertainment here." Sassoonan, before being finally paid for Tulpehocken, had "always been well entertained and with markes of respect while he had anything." It would not be good that he "should now think as others must also notice of it, that having parted with all his land, and also with all the Pay for it, tho' he holds the same rank with his people, he is slighted and disregarded when there is no further advantage to be made of him." Clearly, Sassoonan's friendliness still had strategic value.

There was a double sensation at the Philadelphia docks on September 22, 1734, when the *St. Andrew* from Rotterdam landed with 261 passengers. Included were 181 "Schwenkfelders" whose passage had been paid by wealthy Dutch Mennonites taking pity on their flight from persecution in Silesia (in present-day Poland). Logan was intrigued that, having been bountifully gifted by Mennonites for their voyage with bread, butter, cheese, meat, and beer, the newcomers had enough hard money left to buy a large tract. For them, too, the Perkiomen watershed left by the Lenapes would turn out to be a welcome home, though not, as they had hoped, all in one tract.

More surprising than this is to find that on the same date (on the same ship?) had come, at last, none other than Thomas Penn's older brother, 34-year-old John. Returning as Pennsylvania's half-owner to the city of his birth, he was nursing a strange scheme: a land-selling lottery aimed at making a quick £7,000 to £12,000 that would eliminate the family debt. He must or should have known that this was certain to be opposed in principle by Quakers, and it would indeed soon fizzle among hoped-for purchasers. In any case, John was quickly taken by his brother to visit the southernmost Lehigh sachem, Nutimus, the Jersey-born Munsee Delaware who had moved across the Delaware to his grandfather's home on the Durham Creek, just north of the Haycock Mountain. The Penns now came to confer with him about gaining a release of the last Lenape land above and below the Forks of the Delaware.

It was eight years since investors Logan and Allen, in pursuit of their iron-making venture, had extra-legally paid Nutimus the good price of £60 for land on the Durham Creek (south of the Lehigh River). Later, the Penns had allowed Allen to survey farther north, and now their goal was to free from Munsee claim all the sweep of land across the Forks up to and beyond the Blue Mountain. Whereas Logan could observe that "no People have a truer Notion of Justice than [the Lenapes], nor more forcibly insist on it," he now advised the Penn brothers to offer the Natives a very minimal rate of pay. When he heard that some Munsees in the Minisink north of the Water Gap in the Blue Mountain range had already sold land on their own, at a rate many times the one he was suggesting, he called the purchasers "vile" and the process "wicked."

Unsurprisingly, the meeting at Durham in October 1734 between the cheap-talking Penn brothers and a well-aware Nutimus was a mutual disappointment. The sachem, like Sassoonan old enough to have remembered when his guests' famous father had first come to the Delaware, compared them unfavorably. He would not forget how Thomas, as he put it, persisted in "begging and plagueing us to Give him some Land, and never gives us leave to treat upon any thing till he Wearies us Out of Our Lives."

Indeed, the Proprietary brothers, not giving up their demands at Durham, would only change their tactics. They decided to summon other Munsee sachems from north of the Lehigh (where Allen had been extra-legally surveying and selling for three years) to a larger gathering at another location. This was at Pennsbury, the original (though ruinously decaying) estate on the west bank of the Delaware 40 miles, as the crow flies, southeast of Durham. Peacefully bought from the Indians in the year of the first Penn arrival, this location would evoke favorable memories. It would also make possible the presence of James Logan, whose injured leg would not have allowed a jolting ride to Durham, but could tolerate, if barely, a barge trip up the Delaware to the Falls at Pennsbury.

Perhaps, thought the Penns, new arguments could shove the Munsees determined to stay living in the Forks into a proper understanding of their situation. But the Jersey-born sachems were no pushovers. Nutimus, known as a blacksmith and "Indian doctor," lived south of the Lehigh, while three others resided above it. Lappowinzo, living where the Hokendauqua Creek emptied into the Lehigh (in future Northampton, northwest of Allentown), would prove capable of forceful speech. Three miles eastward from him lived Tishekunk, sometimes called *Weheland* or "Captain John," at a village called *Welagamika* (site of future Nazareth), where with his cleared land he had "a fine large peach orchard." Ten miles still farther toward the Delaware was the "improved ... piece of land" belonging to Tunda Tatamy, whose service in translating had won him the unusual right from the Penns to call 300 acres his legally owned property.

Eventually, in response to missionaries, four Munsee sachems (except Lappowinzo) would accept conversion to the Christian faith. What would be their motives? Certainly, preachers, baptisms, and churches had been appearing all the way to the "end of the wilderness" where, according to Lower Salford's unordained Reformed pastor John Philip Boehm, German-speaking immigrants (he called them "poor sheep") in "Saucon, Macungie, Maxatawny, and Great Swamp" were as thirsty "for the hearing of God's Word as dry land for water." By comparison, what Natives might have observed in the fractious infant congregations could hardly have seemed inviting. Boehm, for instance, accused fellow Reformed pastor George Michael Weiss of baptizing several Indian children whose parents were "still heathen." In Tulpehocken there was a noisy ecclesiological "Confusion" as Lutheran and Reformed members sorted out church loyalties. There, in the very months of the Penn-Lenape conference at Pennsbury, a spectacular break saw a group including Tulpehocken's Conrad Weiser burn the Heidelberg and Augsburg Confessions, and, immersed in new baptisms proposed by a charismatic Dunker monk named Conrad Beissel, follow him to wear biblical beards at a unique new monastery called "Ephrata" in Lancaster County.

The Mennonites east of the Schuylkill, now numbering perhaps a thousand souls, also had their churchly issues. That they were not forgetting their own story was evident from the complaint of a poor widow immigrating in 1735. While her aspiring son was immediately trying to unseat Salford's Reformed Pastor Boehm, she could hardly find shelter other than among local Mennonites. But they, to her "heart's grief," kept telling her stories of how their Anabaptist forebears had been tormented by hers in Zurich. That had been in punishment for their non-standard Christian practices which, especially in regard to the use of force, could be freely practiced in Pennsylvania.

A few months before the Penn-Munsee meeting at Pennsbury, the ordained Mennonite men of "Skippack, Schuylkill, Germantown, Great Swamp [and] Goschenhoppen" had conferred on whether *wehrlos* (defenseless) Christians, in this unusual country, could serve as constables. Further, was it consistent with defenselessness to demand payment of obligations under the threat of law? And church-wise, what about the practice of footwashing? Such an agenda would mean little to the Native population, and there is no documentation of Mennonites exchanging spiritual conversation with the people they were replacing on the land. What would make more sense to some Natives in approaching years would be the colorful piety of Moravian missionaries.

The Penn brothers had announced the date of May 5, 1735, for the Pennsbury meeting, with a new strategy in mind. It was to confront the reluctant Lenapes with a document (possibly just brought over by Thomas) that would prove that the land stretching far north of Pennsbury along the Delaware River had actually been ceded to Founder Penn by the Natives' ancestors in 1686. Historians vary as to the authenticity of the draft of a treaty which Thomas claimed to have recently discovered. It had blanks and was not signed or sealed, but in the text was a most important indication as to how the land involved was to be measured. The northern extent, leading up from a spot on a branch of the Neshaminy Creek, was to be determined by how far walkers would travel in a day and a half. Personal testimony was obtained from elderly Bucks Countians William Biles and Joseph Wood, who declared they remembered a treaty being held, but did not know whether a deed had been executed. The place where the treaty had been made was not mentioned anywhere in the document.

Anticipating a favorable outcome of such negotiation, Philadelphia's speculating William Allen was steadily pursuing new purchases in the Forks region. One agreement, dated April 10, 1735, was for land immediately encircling Tishekunk's village. Meanwhile the Penns, seizing on the "day and a half" motif in the old document, commissioned Bucks County's Sheriff Timothy Smith and surveyor John Chapman to test how far north that much traveling time would take them. The seriousness of this showed not only in the considerable expense required for horses and supplies, but in repeated urgent demands by the Penns, as the day of the Pennsbury meeting approached, for exact reports on the trial run even while it was transpiring. Having taken the sheriff and surveyor from the northern border of the Pennsbury plantation up across the very head of the East Branch of the Perkiomen Creek, and just west of the Haycock, the trek had proceeded 48 miles, across the Lehigh River and all the way to the Blue Mountain. This was information the Penns needed before dealing with the cautious Lenapes.

To the meeting at Pennsbury, of critical importance to land-savvy James Logan, had come not the Alumapees whose origins were in what was now Philadelphia County, but the Lehigh Munsees Nutimus, Lappowinzo, and Tishekunk. The latter dubiously confessed remembering some of the Lenape sachems' names they were told were on yet another old document shown to them, but countered that whatever land was described on it reached only as far north as the Tohickon Creek where it entered the Delaware River. Lenapes living south of that confluence were not, said the sachems, part of the Forks Indians (Munsee/Unalimi) people.

Fortunately for posterity, John Penn, with whatever motives, seems to have wished to compliment the Indians, since during the Pennsbury meeting he and his brother summoned the Colony's well-known Swedish artist Gustav Hesselius to paint portraits of Tishekunk and Lappowinzo. Long familiar with both "savage" and admirable traits in the Native population, Hesselius was considered too likely to paint "what he sees" to do a portrait of Logan's wife Deborah. But that realism produced our iconic and only photograph-like images of Lenapes as they had nobly appeared to William Penn. Both sachems wear shoulder-draped blue blankets or strouds, and each has a chipmunk- or squirrel-skin tobacco pouch on his chest. While Tishekunk, whose pouch contains a white clay pipe, has an unmarked countenance, Lappowinzo's is daubed with signs. Both faces evince confident dignity. If only Sassoonan, "the honest old king of the Delawares," had been there to receive this honor!

On May 8, Logan made a major speech, the color of which would not be totally lost to posterity because it was still emotionally quoted two decades later by Tishekunk's younger brother or nephew Teedyuscung. Once again, in phrasing that Logan had used in earlier reference to Brandywine and Tulpehocken, he argued that the Penns were "not a little surprised and concerned that [the Indians] should now . . . make Objections to or entertain any Doubts about" the "Purchase" indicated on the newly recovered documents. According to William Allen, Logan said he "hoped" that the Indians would "not raise any Disputes about that Purchase . . . or Words to that Effect." The Indian memory was more graphic. In their pictographical idiom, Logan had warned Nutimus that if he continued to resist the Penns' wishes he would "make the big Trees and Logs, and great Rocks and Stones tumble down into our Road." That meant danger, and the Indian impression was of downright intimidation. Logan "did not value Newtymas," went their quote 20 years later, "but look'd upon Him as the little Finger of his left Hand." In contrast, while "Stretching out his arms," Logan called himself "a great big man."

When Nutimus seemed to assert his own authority as a chief of the "up River Indians," Logan asked how that could be, since, as everybody knew, Nutimus, Lappowinzo, and Tishekunk were all born east of the Delaware River. Nutimus' answer was that his mother's origin on the west side gave him his "Right" there. Further, as far as the Indians were concerned, the River did not make a boundary between their people living on both sides of it. For that matter, scoffed Nutimus, why did Logan claim a right here when he himself was born across a greater water? We would surely have more of such flavor if the text of a speech by Lappowinzo, though originally recorded, had not been suspiciously removed from later archives. This is a loss to our understanding of his people's sense of foreboding. It was certainly not forgotten by the Delawares, who, living in Ohio lands in 1762, would mention it to the governor in Philadelphia. As it was, the Munsee chiefs said that before they could conclude their response to the newly proffered documents they would have to consult with other sachems who were not then present.

Conclusive or not, the Pennsbury meeting did nothing to slow the process of land purchases already underway. Within a month, William

Allen's surveyors were laying out the 5,000 acres that were to become Nazareth, and a 500-acre "Tract No. 1" of another 5,000 acres where the town of Bethlehem would appear. The Penns themselves ordered 6,500 less salable acres to be "Surveyed for the use of the Indians" along a branch of the Hokendauqua Creek, home of Lappowinzo. On this "Indian Tract Manor," stipulated the Penns, any Indians of the region would be expected to relocate. But this early American "Indian reservation," designed for the Penns' advantage, would prove a total failure.

Meanwhile, as Indian resentment became increasingly evident, Logan recommended that gifts be sent to Sassoonan, "the Chief of all our Delaware Indians."

John Penn seems to have remained for a while at Pennsbury, being "indisposed." While launching his ill-fated lottery, he managed to sell to a Philadelphia speculator a 12,000-acre legacy designated for him from his father in the Pennsylvania-written will of 1684, before John had reached his second birthday. Now, a survey just east of the Schuylkill near future Pottstown showed that the size of the tract was 14,000 acres, and it brought John "2000 guineas." Even this, however, and other sales were hardly enough to pay the Penns' back interest, and John was already planning for his return to England in September.

As the year 1736 had begun, Thomas Penn was continuing informally to grant lands above the Lehigh to William Allen, and by midsummer the two men, joined by Logan, were planning a major move. It was to enhance the long-sought relationship with the Iroquois Indians who, among other things, as now realized, could help dislodge the Forks Lenapes from their claim. In order for us to understand the new move, it would be helpful to watch the process unfold in the private papers of Thomas Penn. While these are archivally preserved up to this point, those for the two and a half years after July 1736 are suspiciously missing. What was it that someone did not want the world to know?

We do have Logan's correspondence, which in July reported confused rumors of the approach from Shamokin of a mixed bunch of western "Mingo [chiefs] with Allumapis, Lapawinsse, and 30 more men, besides a great number of women." These Natives, supposed to arrive a day later, were said to be bringing "a large Present, & . . . they are to sell land." Clearly, something was stirring, and two weeks later Alumapees did indeed arrive. To keep warm an affection he genuinely felt for officials he hoped would still be generous in return, he brought, in accordance with his chiefly name, some of his people's wampum.

The "very old chief" had been surprised after crossing the Schuylkill to hear at Squire Boone's mill at Oley that old Governor Patrick Gordon, whom he had hoped to greet, had suddenly died. His journey, he reported to the Governor's Council, had not been "to treat about any thing of Importance, but only to pay a friendly visit" to the well-known authorities the Lenapes had dealt with for years. His people considered them to be "Brethren whose Welfare they think themselves obliged to enquire after, as they & the Indians are one People." They had come trusting that these powerful "Friends" (Logan was now head of the Governor's Council) would "still continue their Regard towards the Indians, & their Care & Concern for preserving the same Friendship that has hitherto subsisted between us and them."

Presenting "two small strings of Wampum" (as recorded in the meeting minutes), Alumapees "desired that our Tears on account of [the Governor's death] may be wiped away, & that we may not longer be sorrowfull, but that the Sun may again shine out to dispell the Clouds & our Hearts grow cheerful." Further "presenting a Belt of Wampum of ten Rows," the old chief "said that as the Minds of Men were apt to be discomposed by Sorrow, he now gave this Belt with their earnest desire that our Minds should return to the same Frame & Composure as formerly, and that by eating & drinking we should endeavour to forget our Grief." And that was all, concluded Sassoonan, "of what they have to say." (There was no mention of the unspoken expectation of a diplomatic "present.")

To this touching brotherly address the Logan-headed Council's reply was that as "an old Man, [Alumapees/Sassoonan] must remember that there have been many Treaties between this Government and the Indians [and] that the Chain of Friendship has often been brightened & strengthened." These officials, including Thomas Penn, who were eager to erase the Lenapes' last hold, now asserted that "Our Treaties have been faithfully kept on our part, [and] have likewise been carefully observed on the part of the Indians, and we hope they will always continue firm and lasting." Although the latest Governor had died, "the Indians are still to consider that it is with William Penn's family that they are to treat, & one of his Sons is now here present."

This friendliness was welcome enough, but what the officials were more eager to hear was what Alumapees could tell them about the Six Nations. "Nothing particularly," he replied, though he did expect them to "be with us next Spring." And with that the meeting was dismissed until the following day, when the Council made clear their disappointment. They "requested" Alumapees to let the northerners know of his own visit to Philadelphia, and to keep agent Conrad Weiser aware of "any word he might hear from the Six Nations."

Then it was time to affirm the unexpected Lenape visit, with gifts "valued at 20 pounds," symbolizing the continuing of Alumapees' influence: "Four strowds, four blankets, four duffels, four shirts, 20 pounds of powder, fifty pounds of lead, one dozen tobacco tongs, one dozen knives, tobacco & pipes, one hundred weight of bread, five gallions of rum." Even that was not enough. "The proprietor [Thomas Penn]," it was announced, "with whom you are now going to dine, will take some further Care of our old friend Allummapees." Why this generosity? Clearly, Penn and Logan, who had heard that the Lenapes at Shamokin were themselves hoping for help from the Six Nations, wanted to nudge their old chief in another direction. All they wanted from him was to serve (against his own people's interest) as a conduit of any information regarding the *Haudenosaunee* (Six Nations) that might aid in dislodging the last of the Lehigh Indians.

Having come to Philadelphia on August 20, Alumapees could hardly have gotten back to Shamokin by September 1, when 110 Indians carrying a white flag arrived on the Susquehanna in 18 canoes. It was the long-awaited Six Nations follow-up to their treaty with Thomas Penn of 1732—some 40 men and 70 women and children heading at last for Philadelphia. Alertly present to give the northerners a diplomatic greeting was Conrad Weiser, who must have called the "council" that met "in Alumapees's house." Did the host have any qualms about the intentions of these Senecas, Onondagas, Cayugas, Oneidas, Mohawks, and Tuscaroras on their way to Philadelphia? Probably not, since he himself had just been feted there at Thomas Penn's table. Yet the vectors of life in this city were multiple beyond the imagination of a trusting Native. While Shamokin bulged with the Iroquoian guests, Philadelphia's docks received America's first three Amish couples. The 100-foot-long "Gallery" of its new State House echoed with a retirement party for Mayor Allen, whose own wealth made this "the most grand, the most elegant entertainment that has been made in these parts of America." And with the talk of an arriving Indian delegation, the town went newly abuzz. "For these many Years," as James Logan put it, "there has not been so great an Appearance here of Chiefs of these Nations as at this time." He was extremely eager to complete a land deal with the Iroquois.

There were multiple venues for the treaty process—at Stenton, in the Governor's Executive Council, and at the opening public celebration on October 3, when the city's great Quaker hall drew "a very large Audience that filled the House and its Galleries." For the next week and a half Logan, President of the Council, with Thomas Penn observing, had charge of every session. It was expensive to have the Indians feasting and lodging at Stenton itself, but worth it, because there things could be discussed that would not be reported in the proceedings soon to be published by Benjamin Franklin.

The Six Nations began with hearty appreciation for the offer of "Onas . . . to provide and keep for us a Fire in this great City." Continuing the sacred metaphor, they had "now come to warm ourselves thereat, and we desire and hope it will ever continue bright and burning to the End of the World." As Sassoonan had repeatedly done for his Lenapes, their more powerful "uncles" had brought meaningful gifts. One was a bearskin laid down in support of what the Six Nations considered a "great Article": they wanted to expand the new relationship "between all the English and all our Nations" to take in "likewise the Delawares, Canays, and the Indians living on Sasquehannah, and all the other Indians who now are in League and Friendship with the Six Nations." These were words, strategically welcome to the ears of James Logan, which would have been heard differently by the absent leader of the Lenapes, who had been repeatedly told by the Six Nations to stay out of power relations. Something basic was developing here.

On October 11, after long discussions with Thomas Penn on territory and price, the northerners signed "Releases" to him for "all the Lands lying between the Mouth of *Sasquehannah*, and *Kekachtaninius* Hills [Blue Mountain]." On the following day Logan reminded the Indians of what they had agreed to "at our great House in Town, in the presence and hearing of some Thousands of our People." This had been done, he stressed, "not only in Behalf of us ourselves and yourselves, but for our Children and Children's Children, to all Generations, as long as the Sun, Moon, and Earth, endure." Interpreter Conrad Weiser rendered the thought as, "We are to become as one People, and one Body," in an understanding "never to be changed, but to be kept in everlasting Remembrance." The language that in previous years had been shared with "our Lenappys," was now directed to a different audience, with the intention of gaining its influence in dislodging the last of the smaller nation.

Anticipating their homeward journey with the goods for payment of their land-release, the Indians asked and received promise for "Horses and Carriages to make their Journey home as easy as possible." As they viewed the size of the actual "present," they responded "with great Thankfulness, those of each Nation alternately by themselves, and then all of them together, joining in their usual solemn Sound, when they express their Satisfaction."

After the northerners had left town, Logan kept thinking of something he and Thomas Penn had not yet gotten in the treaty, or even in the more private discussions at Stenton. Nothing specific about the Forks Indian issue had been made clear in the public discussions. As in his demand for quitclaims from the Lenapes in 1718 and 1732, Logan wanted explicit, documented statements. So after the northern guests had left Stenton, accompanied on their homeward journey by Conrad Weiser, Logan sent after him a letter and money from the Proprietors, with careful instructions to get the departing Six Nations delegates "to Declare that they may release all their Claim and Pretensions whatsoever to all the Lands between Delaware and Sasquehannah from their mouths as far northward as to that Ridge or Chain of mountains called the Endless . . . mountains." Acknowledging that, though the northerners really had no claims along the Delaware, Logan prevaricated that it might be "proper" to get a written "release" from them for all their claims (they had none!) or "Pretensions whatsoever to all the Lands between Delaware and Sasquehannah."

With these instructions, Weiser, traveling with the homeward-bound Iroquois, received two Logan-written documents he was to induce the Six Nations sachems to sign, along with coaching as to how to proceed. Weiser was to remind the Iroquois that, since the "Solemn Leagues" they had just agreed to had made them and the English "Brethren" and "one people," they must "constantly remember that they must not assign transfer release nor any way . . . make over their Right or Claim to any of the Lands within ye Bounds of the Government of the Province of Pensilvania to any Persons whatsoever whether white people or Indians." That would take care of Lenapes Nutimus and Alumapees who, as we have noted, Logan had heard intended to make their own appeal to the Six Nations. Only with the "Proprietors" themselves" or "the Children of Wm Penn or . . . those who act under them in their behalf and by their order" were there to be any land dealings. And to his supplied documents, instructed

Logan, "they are Desired to put their hands before their Return from this Province into their own Countrey."

Weiser was to proceed with flattery. "The reason to be given them," advised Logan, is that while the Six Nations are considered "honest, wise, discreet, and understanding men—and we can treat with them with pleasure," the Lenapes "Pesqueetomen, Nootamis, and the like" are "weak and too often knavish." Of course "we are always very kind and take great care of them as of ourselves—that they may in no point be abused—yet we are not willing to enter upon Treaties with them as with our Brethren of the five Nations for whom we keep our fire." Henceforth, it was only with the Iroquois, "for whom we keep our fire," that Pennsylvania would "treat . . . in behalf of all or any of the others."

Actually, the Iroquois returnees, though drunk with gifts of rum and extra money, were skeptical of the Logan-urged signing. "It went very hart," reported Weiser, "about syning over their right upon delaware because they Sayd they had nothing to doe there about the land. They war afaired they shoud doe any thing a mis to their cousins, the delawars." The persuasive devices to which Weiser had to resort had just barely succeeded. "I must goe," he wrote, "to Carry up some of their goods with about ten Horses. There is no help for it. They are disabled to Carry for sicknes and strong liquors sake. The Charges will be some what larger than you most Expect." But the shrewd agent had inveigled 15 signatures for the larger of the two "deeds." Logan had what he wanted: an Indian recognition that the Delawares were now "a people of no virtue, and have no where a fire burning. . . . They have no land remaining to them."

This, drunkenly expressed at the Forks of the Susquehanna under the very nose of the Lenape wampum keeper, meant that the die had been cast for the dismissal of the last Lenapes from the Lehigh, or anywhere.

John Penn in England welcomed the post-treaty news. What gave him "particular pleasure," he wrote back to Logan, was the concluding Six Nations "message" regarding the Lehigh Indians: "that they had no land to sell." As for the Lenapes at Shamokin, they would be shortly reported as starving again. In the language of the far-ranging new treaty between their "Brethren" in Philadelphia and their northern "uncles," Alumapees and his people had been betrayed.

CHAPTER TWENTY-THREE

The Crookedest Affair

1737

A PARTICULAR YEAR, recalled by different persons, can evoke decidedly various emotions. For the long-term reputation of Pennsylvania, 1737 would not be a good year.

For Alumapees on the Susquehanna, the early spring was dismal. There was so little to eat at Shamokin that Conrad Weiser, stopping there for provisions on a journey to the Six Nations, found almost nothing to purchase. "I saw a blanket," he reported, "given for about one-third of a bushel of corn." All he could buy for himself was a little corn meal "and a few beans."

For the Conestoga Indians on the "Manor" that James Logan had staked off for them beside the Susquehanna a generation earlier, April 1737 brought significant change. Cash-hungry Proprietor Thomas Penn had abruptly decided to accept payment for roughly 10,000 of the tract's original 16,500 acres on which Mennonite immigrants had informally settled and since prospered. Approved by Logan as "ready to pay," those settlers could now apply for warrants to have their tracts surveyed, the first step in the process by which a landowner could eventually receive a patent for his property. (Logan viewed neighboring Scotch-Irish squatters in a different light; at his direction, 29 of their log houses were razed.) Before long, even the 400+ acres originally set aside for the Conestogas would be eyed by a Mennonite farmer believing he could induce the Indians to leave so he could "purchase the whole vacancy."

For Philadelphia's immigrant button-maker Caspar Wistar, May 1737 was another profit season, as he sold land for a farm and mill on the Lehigh-feeding Saucon Creek to Mennonite George Sevitz, at a markup of 500%.

For Thomas Penn the end of May brought the pleasure of recognizing one of the Lehigh Forks Indians appearing in Philadelphia.

Having heard Lappowinzo speak impressively a year earlier, Penn took the opportunity to groom him now for a full confirmation of the old documents presented to the Indians at Pennsbury. As he had done for Alumapees, the Proprietor took Lappowinzo home to dine, and then surprised the Lehigh sachem with a present worth £30. This had Lappowinzo in a mood to agree that there ought now to be a walk "to fix the bounds" indicated in the old deeds Penn had "found."

For Pisquetomen, the trusted nephew of Alumapees, early August meant a journey to Philadelphia, where he mentioned that his uncle was presently at Tulpehocken.

For Palatine-born miller Johannes Clemens and his wife Elizabeth on the East Branch of the Perkiomen, the end of August marked the birth of a first son. "We called him Gerhart," runs the inscription in their Bible, "after his grandfather, with the good hope that he would learn to fear God, in the sign of Pisces."

Lappowinzo was soon back in Philadelphia, this time with "a great number of Indians." Included were Tishekunk, Nutimus, and Manawkyhickon, the latter a sachem from farther north at Wyoming on the North Branch of the Susquehanna. Though he had not been with the other Delawares at the bargaining at Pennsbury, he was now serving as their speaker.

Ready to greet the Natives at Stenton were Proprietor Thomas Penn and "ten Gentlemen," mostly from what had been the deceased Governor's executive "Council." Its currently acting President, James Logan, explained that they were gathered to finish discussion of the "Lands" to which, "tho' formerly fully and absolutely released by the Indians, then inhabiting those Parts" to Penn's father, those Natives' successors "had of late made some claim." To keep everything clear, the speech Logan had given at Pennsbury was read and interpreted to the audience that now included older Natives who had not attended the earlier occasion.

In response, speaker Manawkyhickon gave Thomas Penn "a belt of Wampum with four Rows," saying that he would "be sorry if after this mutual Love and Friendship anything should arise that might create the least misunderstanding." However, said Manawkyhickon, while the Proprietor himself knew well "how the Lines mentioned in the deeds" were "to run," the Indians did not. No problem, replied the gentlemen, promptly drawing up a little map of the proposed day-and-a-half walk. Shown to the trusting Lenapes, the simple sketch brought them to agree that, considering what they had now heard and seen, they were "sufficiently convinced" of its "truth," and were therefore willing to join in "a full and absolute Confirmation" of the cession of the land as apparently depicted in the 1680s. They did have an important request: that once they had signed, they might still "be permitted to remain on their present settlements and Plantations," should these be located "within that purchase, without being molested." Certainly yes, responded the officials, repeating assurances they had given at Pennsbury.

Unable to read, the Indians of course got the impression from the hastily made draft that it showed land extending northward along the Delaware from the top of the old Pennsbury purchase to as far as what they understood to be the mouth of the Tohickon Creek. What was actually drawn was the Lehigh River at the Forks. And the quitclaim James Logan had once again written up was for all the land

> from a Corner Spruce Tree by the River Delaware . . . and from thence running along the ledge or foot of the Mountains . . . West North West to a corner white Oak marked with the Letter P, Standing by the Indian Path that Leadeth to an Indian town called Playwickey, and from thence extending Westward to Neshameney Creek, from which said line the said Tract . . . doth extend itself back into the Woods as far as a Man can goe in one day and a half . . . and from thence to the aforesaid River Delaware.

The Indians were asked to certify willingness, "for ourselves and all other the Delaware Indians," to "fully, clearly and Absolutely Remise, Release, and forever Quit claim unto . . . John Penn, Thomas Penn, and Richard Penn, All our Right Title, Interest, and pretentions whatsoever of, in, or to the said Tract or Tracts of Land, and every Part and Parcel thereof." To make everything legally air-tight, they were also acknowledging

> that neither We, or any of us, or our Children, shall or may at any time hereafter, have Challenge, Claim, or Demand [to] any Right, Title or Interest, or any pretentions whatsoever of, in, or to the said Tract or Tracts of Land, or any Part thereof, but of and from the same shall be excluded, and forever Debarred.

Signed on August 25, 1737, at Philadelphia: "And We do hereby further Agree, that the extent of the said Tract or Tracts of Land shall be forthwith Walked, Travelled, or gone over by proper Persons to be appointed for that Purpose."

Logan had all he wanted, and on the next day issued careful instructions to Bucks County's Sheriff Timothy Smith. He was to find and enlist "that man of the three which traveled and held out best when they [had earlier] walked over the land." This would prove to be young Edward Marshall, a recently married hunter and occasional chain carrier for the county's Surveyor General Benjamin Eastburn. A second walker was to be James Yeates, who had also been on the earlier team. The third was Solomon Jennings, a settler on land recently bought from William Allen on the south bank of the Lehigh. The Sheriff was requested to go along himself, and oversee horse-borne liquor and bedding "for those men as may be needfull." Eastburn's assistant surveyors Nicholas Scull (son-in-law of Jennings) and John Chapman (who remembered being treated kindly by Indians as a boy) were also on the team. To ensure fairness, three young Indians had been deputized by their people to accompany the walk: John Combush, Joe Tuneam, who could speak English well, and his brother-in-law Tom. The group thus amounted to about 20 men. They had been charged by Logan to "be sure to choose the best ground and shortest way that can be found."

There was a show of legality in the early morning of September 19, 1737, as the Sheriff and surveyor Scull checked their watches at a tree between John Chapman's land and the Wrightstown Quaker Meetinghouse. A nephew of the Sheriff had already been sent ahead with provision-loaded horses, as the walking crew set off at 6 a.m. sharp. Heading northward, they kept parallel, according to the old document, with the Delaware River on their right. Before noon they had crossed the little Deep Run and Tohickon Creeks, when the oldest runner, Jennings, gave out and quit. Toward sunset, the other walkers, now well north of the Tohickon Creek, crossed the east-running Lehigh, on whose southern bank Jennings lived. By then the three young Indians, Combush, Joe, and Tom (probably unaware that the lead walker was stoked by a promise from Thomas Penn of a 500-acre reward for the fastest walker), were calling on Marshall "not to run." The Native expectation, after all, had been that the walk would reach only up to the Tohickon. Nearing the Lehigh crossing, the Indians said that since they were now past "all the good land," "they did not care how far or where" the walkers "went to." Marshall, it turned out, was going straight ahead by compass, which led away from the river.

After the two walkers had been on their feet for 12 hours, Sheriff Smith, with watch in hand, encouraged them to charge up a hill just ahead. When he called time, Marshall grabbed a sapling, saying he was done. But he and competitor James Yeates had already beaten the record of the entire preliminary walk and, shocking the Indians, were nearing the Blue Mountain range. From their night camp beside a creek near the villages of Lappowinzo and Tishekunk, the audible beat of a dance at Hokendaukwa (on the site of future Northampton) drew off Combush, the last of the three Indian walkers.

By morning, which brought rain and mist, several horses had strayed, and there were no Indians ready to accompany the walkers. Delayed for two hours, Surveyor Eastburn and his deputy went to talk to Lappowinzo at his nearby village, asking for Indian replacements. The annoyed sachem accused the walkers of having already traversed "all of the best land, and they might go to the devil for the bad." In response, "he would send no Indians with them." Nevertheless, Combush rejoined the group, and stuck with them for another ten miles until quitting again.

The two surviving walkers, Marshall and Yeates, followed an Indian path running from present-day Northampton to *Pokopoghcunk* (now Parryville). They had four hours left—until 2 p.m. Still carrying a compass, Marshall and Yeates were followed by Enoch Pearson and Alexander Brown, the latter with watch in hand. Suddenly, while heading into the Pocono Mountains near Pokopoghcunk, an exhausted Yeates (who had finished the earlier test run) fell face-down into the rushing Pohopoco Creek. Lead runner Marshall was forced to turn back for the rescue. Badly shaken and at first unable to see, Yeates died, according to some accounts, three days later.

Though likewise spent, Marshall continued on alone to scale a 1,700-foot mountain at a 45-degree incline. Finally, nearly five miles later, at two o'clock, he struck his hatchet into a tree. He had reached the Tobyhanna Creek some 20 miles north of the Blue Mountain (near present-day Jim Thorpe and the Route 209 exit on the Northeast Extension of the Pennsylvania Turnpike).

It remained to run the document-prescribed line eastward to the Delaware. While the Indians had expected a direct turn to the river's nearest point, Surveyor Eastburn and his deputies chose instead a right angle to their previous, compass-oriented path. This took the line to the Delaware River at the Lackawaxen Creek (across from future Port Jervis), thus embracing not only the celebrated Minisink flats, but all the salable land south of the Blue Mountain range—territory belonging to the Munsee tribe, which other Delawares had no right to convey. The northern line, whose direction had not been defined by treaty, actually assured the acquisition by Thomas Penn of 1,200 square miles, comprising 780,000 acres.

There was tension as the returning party of walkers passed Lappowinzo's village. An Indian quietly pointed a gun at Sheriff Smith and an aide, who were not surprised at what they felt was the reason. "Indeed," remembered the aide, "the unfairness practiced in the walk, both in the way, where, and the manner how it was performed, and the dissatisfaction of the Indians concerning it, were common subjects of conversation in our neighborhood for some considerable time after it was done." Two months later, as walker Marshall met Lappowinzo and Tishekunk again at Hokendauqua, the sachems argued that the walk had not been "fairly performed nor the courses run as should have been." It should have been kept on "the course agreed on between the Indians and the Proprietors," which was to run either along the Delaware "or the next Indian path." In response, the Indians expected to "go down to Philadelphia next May with every one a buckskin, to repay the Proprietor what they had received from him and to take their land again." They were not planning to leave the Forks because of what Tunda Tatamy, uneasy now on his special grant from Thomas Penn, called "the hurry walk."

In contrast, the Proprietor himself was gratified, writing home a few weeks later to brothers John and Richard of how he had "at no very great expense concluded with the Delaware Indians." It had been "with their consent [that] the lands in the upper part of Bucks County" had been "measured by walking a day and a half's journey." "Tho' done to their satisfaction" (!), this had taken in "as much ground as any person here ever expected." There was no document of the agreement to send along with the letter, since, Penn prevaricated, asking for a new one "would have lessened the validity of the former [1686] deed." All Thomas had to show was the Logan-written quitclaim which included "an acknowledgment of their ancestors' [1686] sale." Nor were there any minutes of the proceedings yet to enclose, "but I will send you a copy of them with one of the deeds by the next ship to London." Even more, there had been no "regular" report as usually would have been filed by surveyor Eastburn. All this, in addition to what we have already noted: the Proprietor's own papers for these months would permanently disappear. Even after the Delawares, two decades later, blaming the injustice of 1737, would turn and attack, a no-longer-Quaker Thomas Penn would write that while he supposed the walkers chosen had been "proper persons used to walk," he hoped "that nothing unfair" had been done. "If there was," he observed, "it was contrary to my knowledge or desire." After all, those Forks Indians "had been very troublesome . . . being quite ignorant of former sales."

Possibly nothing of these frontier moves of 1737 came to the ears of the Mennonites along the East Branch of the Perkiomen, 24 miles south of the Lehigh as the bird flies. Life there, unlike in Lappowinzo's and Tishekunk's villages, was increasingly organized. Johannes Clemens, with new first son Gerhart, was doubtless pleased to see a road proposed to connect his mill with one on the Perkiomen Creek (at future Salford Station). This would improve the "large beaten path" that had been "much used" by "Some scores of families—Higher up in the Country . . . for twenty years past (tho' upon Sufferance)."

The same threshold year, in its last month, would be marked as sad in the Salford neighborhood. Hans Clemmer, young settler between the farms of Jacob Clemens and Andreas Lederach, was killed when his horse—it would be claimed—ran against a post. It was a tragedy that would have long Branch Valley resonance, since widow Barbara (Detweiler) Clemmer would marry her Lutheran indentured servant Friedrich Altdörfer. Embracing Barbara's faith, Friedrich would become a leader in her Mennonite clan. Centuries after the Alderfers would take over the Clemens Mill, descendants living along the Branch would preserve not only Friedrich's Lutheran prayer book, but his employer's Mennonite devotional *Güldene Apfel*, in which was scrawled, "This book belongs to me Friedrich Alltörfor, and whoever steals me is a thief."

CHAPTER TWENTY-FOUR

Brethren? Uncles? Friends?

1738–1741

In 30 minutes, a cloud of passenger pigeons winging southward from the villages of Lappowinzo, Tishekunk, and Tunda Tatamy in the Lehigh countryside could reach and cross the East Branch of the Perkiomen in Lower Salford Township. "The noise they made," remembered a man from near Shamokin, "though yet distant, reminded one of a hard gale at sea, passing through the rigging of a close-reefed vessel." A quieter domestic sound along the Branch was the swish of miller Johannes Clemens' waterwheel. Both he and his brother Jacob were getting deeds in the summer of 1738: one for Johannes' 151 creek-straddling acres, and the other for Jacob's 136 acres on the adjacent gentler slope. Both farms shared the western border of Henrich and Magdalena Ruth's level homestead on Salford Heights, surveyed by David Powell when the Clemens brothers were little boys. The family of Christian Allebach, who had bought the southern half of the Ruths' original 200 acres, had given miller Johannes his wife Elizabeth.

Lappowinzo, Tishekunk, and Tatamy, who had scoffed in the fall of 1737 at the "Walking Purchase," noticed surveyors in the woods. Tatamy had "applied," four years earlier, for legal ownership of the "piece of land of about 300 acres" on which he lived. This, he maintained, was in "consideration of services he had rendered as interpreter and messenger to the Indians." It is intriguing to learn that, seven months after the walk, Thomas Penn *gave* Tatamy a patent for his plot. Even that, though, did not satisfy the Munsee sachem's concern. Three years later he would outright *pay* Penn £48, 16 shillings and 5 pence for the ground he had been living on, making him the first native-born person to formally purchase land in Pennsylvania.

Out at famishing Shamokin, Alumapees also had concerns, as many of his people were continuing the drift toward Allegheny. When he heard that a new governor—George Thomas—had arrived from England, remembering that Thomas Penn had asked him to visit once a year, he led a ragged delegation of hungry Delawares, old and young, to Philadelphia. Presenting the Governor with strings of wampum and a few furs, the old sachem was a picture of pathos, to be described by future historians as manipulatable by officials. His word this time was that he had been noticing "some little rubs" in the path between his people and the English—but that now, face to face with the Governor, the way seemed "clear and plain." He hoped that the traditional "perfect Friendship and good understanding between the Indians and this Government" would grow "Stronger and Stronger," and that no one would ever be able "to interrupt and break it." While it had often been said that the Indians and the English should be "as one Body," he preferred a stronger image: they should be "all as one Heart . . . without any Distinction." The relationship should be "clear without spot, like the Sun in a fair Day without a Cloud from rising to Setting." And thus, still functioning as his people's diplomat, Alumapees laid down three bundles of "DeerSkins in the hair" from which, he suggested, gloves could be made for the Governor. They were "but a trifle . . . but he had no more," and that was all he had "at this time to say to the Governour."

Finding the more than 30 pelts in the bundles worth £8, the officials realized that a "present [was] of course to be made . . . in return." Since "the Old man [had] now become very weak, and the other Old people with him as well as himself [were] poor and necessitous," the return present should be worth no less than £30. For Alumapees, who had obviously expected his visit to be profitable, the present was enough to confirm the old feeling of mutual respect, conveyed in coats, blankets, hats, shirts, powder and lead, knives, and a gross of pipes with tobacco. Crowning it all was an impressive personal gift from Governor Thomas, recognizing the old sachem's role on behalf of his people: "a matchcoat laced with silver and a silver-laced hat." Thomas Penn was clearly not yet ready to alienate the Delawares whom, whether at the Susquehanna or Lehigh, he was scheming to bypass. When, a month later, Nutimus also brought gifts from the Forks, he was returned a present worth twice as much as the one for Alumapees.

In the following summer (1739) a delegation of Shawnees on their way to Philadelphia stopped at Shamokin to meet with Alumapees.

Calling them "My Grandchildren," the sachem wished them well on their long-expected visit, and as their head, sent along a string of wampum for his English-speaking "Brethren." Though the Shawnees reported upon arriving in Philadelphia that their "Grandfather" would follow them "when the Moon is at the full," the Council minutes do not record Alumapees' subsequent arrival.

Making news that fall, in the columns of printer Ben Franklin's *Pennsylvania Gazette*, was the fatal accident at Skippack of Dielman Kolb's older brother, deacon Jacob, struck in the head by the massive beam of his cider press. Another "Palatine" at Skippack, crossing a creek "with his Waggon, wherein was his Wife, Children and Goods, was carry'd away with the Stream, but with much Difficulty their lives were saved, and most of their goods." Yet another Skippack "Palatine" drowned in a swollen creek, and there would be an account of a Lancaster County farmer, Ulrich Brechbühl, son of the well-known Benedicht, killed when he fell in front of the wheels of his Conestoga wagon.

There was a sensation that November with the arrival in Philadelphia of a spellbinding itinerant preacher, 25-year-old George Whitefield, a "Calvinist" priest of the Church of England. Holding forth from the Courthouse Gallery four evenings in a row, he drew crowds estimated to number 6,000, who listened "in awful silence." Printer Franklin, thoroughly secular as he was, could not help admiring, befriending, and promoting the mesmerizing orator whose "every Accent, every Emphasis," in Franklin's description, and "every Modulation of Voice, was so perfectly well turn'd and well plac'd, that without being interested in the Subject, one could not help being pleas'd with the Discourse, a Pleasure of much the same kind with that receiv'd from an excellent Piece of Music." It would be joked that Whitefield could convert a sinner simply by pronouncing the word "Mesopotamia."

Eighteen miles out at Neshaminy, where the devout minister Gilbert Tennent lived, Whitefield preached to 3,000 souls gathered in a churchyard, bringing many of them to tears. "There might be a thousand Horses," he recorded, "which the people do not sit on to hear the Sermon as in England, but tie them to the Hedges; and thereby much Disorder is prevented." Ten miles on at Abington, having "preached to 2000 from a porch-window of the meetinghouse," Whitefield marveled at "how such Bodies of People so scattered abroad, can be gathered at so short a Warning." Then, as quickly as he had appeared, the preacher was off to Georgia, to join Moravian missionaries who, he had heard, were ministering to African American orphans.

The evangelist's absence from Pennsylvania would prove brief but eventful. In his mansion at Stenton, the 66-year-old Logan suffered a stroke, leaving his right side partially paralyzed and his one good leg disabled. Though for a time his memory was affected, and for months he could not write, he recovered all of his intense interest in public affairs as news arrived that the King of England had declared war on Spain. Then Whitefield was back, flush with a plan for a school for Black boys, for which he asked collections from his ever-larger audiences. Franklin, who helplessly emptied his own pockets when the offering was taken, reported that one sermon had triggered an intake of "Seventy Pounds Sterling, for the Benefit of the Orphan House in Georgia."

The sensational evangelistic campaign would become linked to our story on April 22, 1740. On that date Whitefield, his dream having shifted from Georgia to Pennsylvania, promised to pay £2,200 from his new funds to speculator William Allen for 5,000 acres at the Forks of the Delaware. "Mr. Whitefield," ran a report, "proposes to give orders for building the negroe school on the purchased land, before he leaves the province."

Two days after his deal with Allen, Whitefield rode out to Skippack, "a very wilderness part of the country [where] many Dutch people are settled." His main point of contact there was a devout Schwenkfelder farmer, Christopher Wiegner, who with his spiritualistic convictions was acquainted with Whitefield's friend Peter Böhler, a German Moravian friend of John Wesley. Here the preachers Whitefield and Böhler—educated at Oxford and Jena, respectively—were at the edge of Mennonite country, where most of the "2000 Hearers" spoke only German. "It was surprizing to see such a multitude of people gathered together," wrote a participant, "in such a wilderness country, thirty miles distant from Philadelphia." "I never saw more simplicity," remarked Böhler. Whether or not the audience (possibly including curious Alderfers, Clemenses, and Ruths from adjacent Salford Township) knew what the evangelist was saying, he himself was reportedly "exceedingly carried out in his sermon," exhorting "poor sinners to come to Christ by faith, and claim all their privileges." Afterward, Böhler, a deacon in the Moravian Church, preached in German.

That evening in the house of miller Henry Antes, recently converted from a Reformed Church affiliation to the intensely pious Moravians, Whitefield asked Böhler to find the location for the "school for negroes" he planned to build on his just-purchased tract. Responding enthusiastically, Böhler and aides set off within 24 hours for the Lehigh Forks. Ten miles above the river they arrived at an "Indian village," where they spent the night in the woods. This was where the future Moravian town of Nazareth would appear. But when Böhler arrived it was called *Welagamika*, the home of Tishekunk, with cleared fields, a graveyard, and peach trees that had just finished blossoming.

Tishekunk, also called "Captain John," certainly had no plans to have his home taken over by strangers. What he thought when, at the end of May, a dozen Moravians arrived and began to dig a foundation for a large schoolhouse-dormitory, is not recorded. Then came a second surprise, as news arrived from Philadelphia. Peter Böhler, while describing the operation to Calvinist owner Whitefield, had found the evangelist so angered by the Pietist Moravian language that he called off the project, ordering the missionary builders to abandon it. Of course nothing of this would have made sense to Tishekunk, any more than shortly finding that a calmed-down Whitefield had peacefully sold his 5,000 acres to the Moravians, who could now plan to return and complete the project under their own auspices. First, though, in the following spring, they would begin another settlement a few miles south on the northern bank of the Lehigh, to be called "Bethlehem."

As for Alumapees, 80 miles west at a greater Forks, he seemed undaunted by any talk about the recent eastern "Walk." In August 1740 he showed up as usual in Philadelphia, this time with a group including not only Delawares who had drifted toward Allegheny, but also some Mingoes. (Never using the term "Five" or "Six Nations," the Delawares rather referred to their Iroquois "Uncles" as "Mengwes" or "Mingos.") Logan, mending from his stroke, was curious, doubting whether these latest-arriving "Delawares" had anything particular on their minds "beside brightening the chain." The citizens of Philadelphia in general, especially the pacifist Quakers in the Assembly, were on edge, roiled by Governor Thomas' calling up of several companies of volunteer soldiers for Britain's current "War of Jenkin's Ear."

Once again Alumapees appeared before a large audience in the great Quaker Meetinghouse. His speech this time became passionate as he declared that his Delawares, their Mingo friends, and the white officials were all good *Brethren*. Ironically, this friendly rhetoric was innocent of the Logan-advised Six Nations' conspiring with the white "Brethren" at Philadelphia to get rid of the very last (Munsee) Delawares remaining on their Lehigh homeland. It was music to the ears of officials worried about possible Indian resentment to hear from Alumapees, "My Children, the Delaware, and my Uncles, the Mingoes . . . are glad to see their Brethren here. . . . We are Pleased when we meet you, our Brethren, to have none but good Tidings to speak of, and that there is nothing amiss between us." "I tell you again," translated Conrad Weiser,

> that our Friends, the Mingoes . . . are come into your House, which we look upon as our own home. We . . . are very careful to maintain Peace and Friendship with you as you are with Us. We are very sensible of the Fruits of Peace. We feel its benign Influences, comfortable as the Sun Beams; when we or our Friends speak to you, you may depend on our veracity, for we speak from our very Hearts; we and all our neighbor Indians . . . are all of one Mind and one Spirit towards you.

The frail old sachem, though in a begging mood, was still the voice of the Delawares.

A true leader, however, could not omit representing his people's dissatisfactions. "We are great hunters," Alumapees complained, "but your young men have driven off the game. We want you to keep your young men away." And there was more. "We want our guns and axes mended free." Still more: "I hear that . . . the Mingoes get a better price for their Skins at Albany or Raritan than we do from you, and that for one Buckskin they can get from those Traders a large bag of Powder" (gesturing the size). "The Mingoes tell me that they get so great a price for their Skins that I am ashamed to tell them how small a price the Delawares get from you who are our Brethren."

> Deer are now become very scarce and we hope you will Allow Us something of a better price for the future. Your young men have killed so many Deer, Beavers, Bears, and Game of all sorts, that we can hardly find any for our selves. Therefore, we desire that your people would abstain from

Hunting, that we may have the benefit of it to support ourselves, for God has made us Hunters, and the white people have other Ways of living without that.

This was on behalf of the Shawnees and Delawares living farther west than the Susquehanna home of their titular head and speaker.

Alumapees also spoke more than hintingly for himself: "I have brought down my Gun and my Ax Broken, as we have no Smith living amongst us and I hope you will get them mended for me." Finally, with Conrad Weiser translating, the speech became specific. "Brothers Thomas Penn and Governor, We have brought you 160 good Buck Skins, and not one Doe Skin among them. Brethren I have said a Great Deal; I am now grown Old, so that I could hardly come down to you for want of a Horse, and I have been sometimes obliged to borrow one."

The intensely concerned Governor requested that "presents to the value of 150 pounds be made to the Indians and that sums of money be appropriated for their entertainment." As for Alumapees, he was clearly still the spokesman for the Delawares. Though his people had received pay for their last land five years earlier, his new plea brought him the significant diplomatic gift of a horse, saddle, and bridle.

If, in the summer of 1740, the Unami children and Shawnee "grandchildren" were pacified, their Munsee Delaware cousins at the Delaware Forks were not. Neither was the general white populace, sharply polarized over the Governor's demand for military recruitment. The election in October attracted, according to Quaker merchant Israel Pemberton Jr., "the greatest appearance of People that Ever was known in this Province." William Allen estimated that the electioneering had "brought down upon us about 400 Germans who hardly ever came to elections formerly, perhaps never 40 of them having voted at any other election." He was getting to know more of "the Dutch," as he called them, to whom he was retailing land that he had bought a decade earlier along the Deep Run in Bucks County. In his opinion they seemed "a sordid people," in that they were "very loth to part with any money."

The Forks Indians, it was becoming clear, were also very loth to part with the patrimony that William Allen was selling around them. A bitter letter, dated November 21, 1741, came to Jeremiah Langhorne of Neshaminy, 18 miles north of Philadelphia. A co-owner with

Logan and Allen of the Durham forge land purchased 15 years earlier from Tishekunk and Nutimus, Langhorne had succeeded Logan as Chief Justice. Now the Munsees above Durham, appealing to him and "all Magistrates of Pennsylvania," demanded "that You would take Notice of the Great Wrong We Receive in Our Lands." Some 100 white families had appeared around them, claiming that "Thomas Penn has sold them the Land." It seemed "Very Strange," went the letter, "that T. Penn Should Sell . . . that which was never his for We never Sold him this land."

There had never been "anything," went the letter of complaint, "but honest Dealings & Civility" with the father William Penn. But the aggrieved Munsees wanted no more maneuvers from the son. "If he lets us alone," they wrote, "We will let him alone." Claiming that they had sold only three special tracts (including Durham) north of the Tohickon Creek, the Forks Indians now demanded that "Thomas Penn Would take these People off from their Land in Peace that we May not be at the trouble to drive them off." They were dead serious. "We Will hold fast With both Our hands not in privately but in Open View of all the Countrey & all Our Friends & Relations [including] the Eastern Indians & Our Uncles the five Nations. . . . We Shall Stand at Our Uncles Breast When We Shall Speak." Little suspecting that their Iroquois "Uncles" had four years earlier agreed with the white "Brethren" to sell them out, the Munsees were imagining that mutual respect could be re-established. "Now Gentlemen & all others," they concluded, "We have lived in Brotherly Friend Ship So We Desire to Continue the same if So be We can be Righted any Manner of Ways So We Remain Your Friends."

As if this were not offensive enough to the Philadelphia officials, two months later came a similar complaint from Indians still farther north. "We cannot injoy our Birth-Right in Peace and Quietness," they stated, without being "abused as if we were Enemies, and not Friends." If they spoke up for their rights, there would be "an Uprore" putting them "in Danger of being cut in Pieces and destroyed." It was all supposed to "scare us to be easy and let them alone in their wicked Ways to take our Land and never give us any thing for it." The Governor, hearing that these Munsee Delawares (as well as Alumapees) were thinking of sending a message requesting aid from the Six Nations, was correctly suspicious that the unwelcome recent letters had been drawn up for the Indians by Quakers who opposed him politically. His advice to the complainers was to consult the document that James Logan had contrived for Six Nations leaders to sign five years earlier, in secret support of the expulsion of the easternmost Indians. What the Forks Lenapes could do now, observed the Governor, if they wanted further information, was to attend (at their own expense) the forthcoming meeting when the Six Nations would come for the completion of their payments of the treaty of 1736.

When, once again, on August 7, 1741, an increasingly frail Alumapees showed up in Philadelphia, he had three topics in mind. One was to say farewell to Thomas Penn, who was about to return to England. A second was to make clear, in the midst of the simmering Native-English tensions, that he wished to be friends with all. Living "in the middle," as he put it, "between the [Six] Nations and his [white] Brothers," he was minded to cooperate with both. "He loves his Unckles and he loves his Brothers," noted Logan, "and desires to have the paths that lead to both places [clear] and open."

Alumapees was a peaceful man. His third desire, though, was less pleasing, actually downright unacceptable to Logan. It was that, after the old sachem's death, the Delaware leadership would pass to his intelligent accompanying nephew. As far as James Logan was concerned, Pisquetomen was a Lenape who knew too much, and who, unlike his uncle, could not be easily manipulated.

CHAPTER TWENTY-FIVE

"What Ground You Stand On"
1742–1743

Historian John Heckewelder wrote that when the Delawares would "speak with the Europeans about their ancestors," they would "boast" and "delight in describing their genealogies," being "so well versed in them" that they could "mark every branch of the family, with the greatest precision." Doubtless that was the case with sachems Tishekunk and Tatamy, born east of the Delaware, but living across the river on their ancestors' homeland in future Northampton County. Tishekunk had cleared land for his peach orchard, and Tatamy, a few miles eastward where a future town would take his name, was "farming in a small way" on his 300-plus acres. The concern of both sachems as to whether they could keep their Lehigh homes was not lessened by a visit in June 1742 from a unique German-speaking Lutheran: Count Nicholas von Zinzendorf, of Saxony.

With the double aim of uniting Pennsylvania's Protestant fellowships and winning the Natives to Christianity, Zinzendorf had already traversed the Perkiomen watershed. His second stop on that tour had been in the home of Dielman Kolb's minister brother Martin at Skippack, where the sensational English minister George Whitefield had recently preached. The widely known Count, who had earlier organized the sending of Moravian missionaries from Germany to a worldwide range of destinations, was not only personally acquainted with Whitefield, but had also made strong contacts with Mennonites in Holland.

Zinzendorf moved quickly and aggressively. On the Christmas Eve after his arrival in Pennsylvania in 1741, he had been at the infant Moravian settlement where the Monocacy Creek flowed into the Lehigh, eight miles south of Tishekunk's village, and christened it "Bethlehem." Three weeks later he set out from Germantown on his tour aimed at gathering Pennsylvania's German-speaking sects into a "Unity of Brethren." His first stop was at the Pietist Christopher Wiegner farm where Whitefield had preached 20 months earlier. Next came his visit at Skippack with Martin Kolb and "heads of the Mennonites," as he called them, where he "discussed with them their doctrine and practice."

Quite likely present that day was Kolb's friend, Bishop Henrich Funck of neighboring Franconia Township. The astute miller on the Indian Creek had been sharing with the influential Kolb brothers a growing sense of insecurity for their people, a feeling deep-woven from the start of their two-century-old spiritual family story. The namesake descendant of the man expelled from Bern with its symbol branded on his back, Funck had come to Pennsylvania 46 years later with the immigrants led by Bishop Benedicht Brechbühl. While passing through Holland, they had been promised Dutch counsel and diplomatic support if they ran into unforeseen trouble in the New Land. Twenty-five years later Funck and Kolb were remembering that pledge, and sending an appeal for spiritual help to Amsterdam. Up to now, they reported, their nonresistant community in Pennsylvania had thrived, enjoying the Province's unusual freedom of conscience for their *wehrlos* (defenseless) convictions. Their communities were expanding over the landscape (Martin Kolb's son Isaac had acquired land up the East Branch in Rockhill, and Kolb cousins were buying land from William Allen on the Deep Run, a tributary of the Delaware-feeding Tohickon Creek). Yet, alarmed by political polarization and talk of war, the signers of the letter to Amsterdam were wondering if they had made a mistake by coming to Pennsylvania without inquiring more carefully into possible civil problems.

Concerned to preserve memory and spiritual identity, Bishop Funck had welcomed the recent immigration of a German printer named Christopher Sauer. This Dunker-favoring Pietist had set up a shop in Germantown, and in 1742 announced plans for a quarto Bible, the first in a European language to be printed in America. Funck got from him a new printing of the *Ausbund*, the Anabaptist songbook that in Europe had to be issued secretly, but could here be identified as published in Germantown. Some of its homely texts were of uncannily contemporary resonance, as in "Song 71":

Christe, thu dich erbarmen   Christ, show to us your mercy
Verleih uns dein Genad   Vouchsafe to us your grace

> *Gedrengt werden wir Armen* We poor are shoved together
> *Man laßt uns hie kein Statt* We are allowed no place,
> *Kein Fried noch Ruh auf Erd* No peace on earth nor rest,
> *Es wird verjagt dein ... Herd* Away your flock is chased.

Appended to this first American edition of the songbook appeared "A True Account of the Brethren in Switzerland in the District of Zurich, Regarding the Troubles They Experienced for the Sake of the Gospel." The family names mentioned, such as Frick, Hege, Kolb, and Landis, were reminders of faith of the grandchildren now on farms from Skippack to Deep Run. But Henrich Funck and Dielman Kolb wanted even more story. Having come to Pennsylvania in the 1717 wave led by Benedicht Brechbühl, they had shared his "special love" for the Dutch *Martyrs' Mirror*. Now they were writing back to Amsterdam, wondering whether they could get it translated into the language that their oncoming generation could read. How much, they wondered, would it cost to have it translated and published, with or without the pictures?

Considerably broader than the Mennonite view was the ecumenical dream of the visiting Moravian Zinzendorf. Hoping for Lutheran, Reformed, Mennonite, and Schwenkfelder cooperation, he moved on from Martin Kolb's home in Skippack to Falkner's Swamp and then Oley. At his invitation, the Skippack Mennonites, who hardly knew what to do with this challenge to their denominational separateness, were still represented in the attendance of Martin Kolb's elderly ministerial colleague, Yellis (Julius) Cassel. Zinzendorf challenged him: "I'll wager as much as you will that within a year half of the Mennonites will join the Moravians." Cassel, it would be claimed, humbly declined to engage. "And why not?" asked the ebullient Count. "Wagering," came the reply, clearly in confusion as to what such imperious ecumenical rhetoric was all about, "is for idle fellows and light-minded folks."

If Yellis Cassel had stayed a day or two longer at this unique Oley conference, he would have been more astounded, as Moravian missionaries brought to Oley three Indian converts from New York, had them "baptized into the wounds of Jesus," and renamed them "Abraham," "Isaac," and "Jacob." Had Funcks, Kolbs, or Cassels even thought of such a thing? But over the next 15 years Zinzendorf's Moravian associates at Bethlehem on the Lehigh River would baptize nearly 150 Delaware Natives (including Tishekunk). Hoping for even larger results than this, the Count continued to visit with Lenapes from both the Lehigh Forks and the Susquehanna (Shamokin) diasporas. In June 1742, coming with his teenage daughter Benigna to view the building up of future Nazareth, he became aware that this location just north of Bethlehem had been a little Lenape farm. Its owner, Tishekunk ("Captain John"), was refusing to leave with his family. Zinzendorf and the Moravians building the new Christian village did not want to order the "Captain" off the property, though they had purchased it from George Whitefield (who had bought it from William Allen). By some accounts, Zinzendorf then paid out of his own pocket the price Tishekunk demanded. The settlers said that if the Native "Captain," who had planted "a little field of winter wheat," could be persuaded that the land was no longer legally his property, "he would be permitted to return at will for his crop of Indian corn, which was stored in a sod-covered crib." A month later the community said they would be willing to consider Tishekunk a kind of tenant, still allowed to work on "the land he has cleared."

Moving on a few miles eastward to visit Tatamy's 300-acre plantation, the missionaries had an interesting conversation. Tatamy (who would later be baptized by Presbyterian missionary David Brainerd), had so little intention of leaving the land granted to him by the recently departed Thomas Penn that he was now paying hard money to own it like a white person. He gave the Moravians an account of his Delaware people's spiritual views (would that this had been written down!), and the visitors in turn explained their concept of Christ's sacrificial death for the forgiveness of sin.

From there, Zinzendorf's party found other Lenape villages, and, continuing through the fall, had remarkably persistent, even dangerous encounters with Natives farther northwest at Wyoming, on the North Branch of the Susquehanna. There he explained his mission to a group of Shawnees ominously "painted red and white, each with a large knife in his hand." Although their chief evinced no interest in the Christian gospel, the aristocratic Count persisted over a week in the village, passing out little gifts from his party's stock of provisions. When there was almost nothing left to give, remembered a participant, "The very clothes on his back were not spared. One shirt button after another was given away, until all were gone, and likewise his shoe-buckles, so that we were obliged to fasten his underclothes with strings."

The approach of fall 1742—the season when Shamokin's aging Alumapees was likely to appear in Philadelphia—brought growing expectation of a much larger delegation. Six years after the Six Nations chiefs had received half-payment for their lands on both sides of the Susquehanna, they were returning to collect the other half. Logan, bodily limited and well aware that the grounds of his Stenton estate might be overrun by the visitors, was at first annoyed that any group led by the Lenape Alumapees (who was not involved in the Six Nations' dealings) might be thoughtless enough to add more mouths to the hungry crowd. "I think all proper measures should be used to prevent their coming," ordered Logan, "for they . . . will be most unwelcome." But then the thought occurred that it might be a good idea, after all, for the Delaware wampum keeper to witness firsthand what was going to be settled regarding land at this significant occasion.

The arriving crowd of Six Nations Indians quadrupled expectations. Pouring onto the Stenton grounds, they were nevertheless welcomed with food, "wine and other liquors," and informed that the goods of their half-payment were ready for them at the house of the recently departed Thomas Penn. Here, where the chiefs were given a "handsome dinner," could be heard a repeated "solemn cry of thanks" from the Iroquois as greetings and concerns were exchanged. The subsequent proceedings, lasting a week (July 5-12, 1742), moved between the Penn house and the great Quaker Meetinghouse where 14 years earlier Alumapees had spoken before the city's populace. Now, though he and nephew Pisquetomen had come to town, their presence was not noted by the secretary in the first week.

"Upwards of 200" Indians were included in the audience gathered on Tuesday in the Meetinghouse where, with Conrad Weiser interpreting, the list of goods for payment of their land west of the Susquehanna was read off. Beginning with 500 pounds of powder, 600 pounds of lead and 45 guns, and proceeding through coats, shirts, hats, shoes, hatchets, knives, hoes, needles, flints, and "looking glasses," the list concluded with 200 pounds of tobacco and 25 gallons of rum. All of this had now been moved to the Meetinghouse, announced Governor George Thomas, as he laid down a string of wampum to emphasize how "particularly fortunate" he found the timing of the occasion. Since "We are in Daily Expectation of a War being declared" between England and France, he observed, it was important to reinforce the sense of the English and the Six Nations as "one flesh and one people." Continuing with the Indian idiom, he then laid down a belt of wampum to promise that "we on our part shall enlarge our fire that burns between Us."

The Iroquois response in the following day's session, again in the Meetinghouse, came from the mouth of the Onondago Nation's Canassetigo, described as "a tall, well-made man" of about 60, with a "very full chest and brawny limbs" and "a manly countenance." His "good-natured smile" and the "surprising liveliness in his speech" gave him an "awesome presence," according to the secretary at a later occasion, that "turned heads whenever he walked into a room." Now in a good mood, he was "pleased to hear" that the English wished to "enlarge the fire" with his people, and "make it burn brighter." But he was less than satisfied with the value of the goods just described. Acknowledging that it matched the worth stipulated on the agreement written back in 1736, he suggested that had Thomas Penn not just left for England he would now, in a fresh view of the Indians' current extreme poverty, "have made an Addition." After all, when these goods would be divided, each person would receive only a small portion. "We therefore desire," orated the Speaker, that "if you have the keys of the Proprietor's chest, you will open it and take out a little more for us."

The Governor parried that the departed Proprietaries John and Thomas Penn had "taken the Keys of their Chest with them." Recognizing the serious gambit that he and his Council would need to consider, he reminded the listening Indians that "Had not [the white people] come amongst You these Lands would have been of no Use to you any further than to maintain You." But he could not sidestep the "particular" Six Nations complaint against settlers squatting along the Juniata River, just west of the Susquehanna. Canassetigo had roundly demanded that "they may be forthwith made to go off the Land, for they do great Damage to our cousins the Delawares." If Alumapees was present to hear of this sympathy for Lenape "cousins," he might have understood the Iroquois to be supportive of his people's rights. (How trustingly wrong he would have been!) As for the Iroquois themselves, they were not to be fooled by the Governor's statement that he had sent magistrates to improve the Juniata situation. That was too much for the listeners, who interrupted the speech with an unusual outburst. "So far from removing the people," they protested, those officers had "made surveys for themselves, and they are in League with the Tresspassers."

Logan had been present every day so far (by Six Nations request), and was there again for a smaller gathering in the Penn house on Friday, July 9. This was the first session to record the presence of Alumapees (listed as "Sassoonan," with his nephew Pisquetomen), and Nutimus from the Lehigh Forks. Both of the headmen were there because the officials wanted them to hear the Six Nations' response to the Forks (Munsee) Lenapes' unwillingness to leave their homes. Logan, true to his long-time strategies, had brought legal documents. "Now lying on the Table" were (1) the half-century-old "deed" by which William Penn had supposedly bought the land extending north of his manor of Pennsbury; (2) the hand-drawn map which had fooled the Forks Indians in 1737 into agreeing to the day-and-a-half Walk; (3) the Lenape-criticizing letter written by Logan and endorsed by rum-encouraged Iroquois signers on their way home from their treaty in 1736; and (4) the two (white-written) letters of complaint recently sent down from the Forks Lenapes.

Governor Thomas spoke carefully, reminding the Six Nations chiefs that "the last time [they] were here" (in 1736), interpreter Conrad Weiser had brought back from their homeward journey "Your Letter, wherein You request of him & James Logan that [Delawares of the Forks] would not buy land." That letter, of course, had actually been written by Logan, and had only been signed by reluctant Iroquois yielding to Weiser's persuasion. As for the two recent Lenape letters of complaint, they had abused "your good Brethren our worthy Proprietaries" John and Thomas Penn with "the utmost Rudeness & ill Manners," the Governor admonished Nutimus. That was why he had sent "messengers" to alert Nutimus that the Iroquois, when they came to Philadelphia, would be informed of this. Then came a pitch to the listening Iroquois, openly requesting a quid pro quo:

> As you on all occasions apply to Us to remove all White People that are settled on Lands before they are purchased from You, and we do our endeavours to turn such People Off, We now expect from You that you will cause these Indians to remove from the Lands in the forks of the Delaware, and not give any further Disturbance to the Persons who are now in Possession. To enforce this we lay down a String of Wampum.

At this point the documents Logan had laid on the table were read in English, and given to Conrad Weiser for interpretation to the Six Nations chiefs. There would of course be no record of what Nutimus or Alumapees and his astute nephew Pisquetomen thought, if, after listening to the translations, they fully understood what was happening.

The helpfully cooperative mood of Canassetigo could well have been enhanced by the realization that there was going to be an addition to the payment his people had come to collect. And indeed the agenda of the next session, on Saturday afternoon once again in the "Great Meeting House," was to make the Six Nations visitors an extra "present from the Governor, the Council, the Assembly and all our people." The itemized list of items, worth £300, was read off impressively, after which "the Chiefs and all the Indians returned their solemn thanks." Finally, Canassetigo promised he would have some further interesting response (which Alumapees and Nutimus, who were not recorded at the presentation, would need to hear).

The concluding treaty session, taking place in the Penn house on the following Monday, July 12, though small in attendance, would turn out to be one of the most often-evoked moments of Colonial Pennsylvania history. Canassetigo, speaking for the "sundry Chiefs of the Six Nations" present, and certainly stoked by the substantially increased present of the previous Saturday, was in top form. "The other Day," he addressed his white "Brethren, the Governor and Council,"

> you informed us of our Cousins, the Delawares with respect to their continuing to Claim and refusing to remove from some land on the River Delaware, notwithstanding their Ancestors had sold it by Deed . . . to the Proprietaries . . . upwards of fifty years ago . . . and then you requested Us to remove them, enforcing your Request with a String of Wampum.

"Afterwards," continued the narration, the Governor had shown the Iroquois their own "letters" (actually composed by Logan!) and the other documents on the table. Canassetigo, though he could not read himself, had bought into the spirit of anti-Delaware logic. "We see with our own Eyes," he declared, "that [the Delawares] have been a very unruly People, and are altogether in the wrong in their Dealings with you." As a result, the Six Nations had now agreed to require the Forks Indians "to go over the River Delaware and to quit all claims to any Lands on this side."

Then, laying down a string of wampum in response to the one from the Governor, Canassetigo picked up a larger belt and turned toward Nutimus' group of Forks Delawares. "Cousins," he orated, "You ought to be taken by the Hair of the Head and shak'd severely till you recover your Senses and become Sober; you don't know what Ground you stand on, nor what you are doing." Incredibly, the speech was accusing the "cousins," whom the Six Nations claimed to have been protecting, of being "maliciously bent to break the Chain of friendship with our Brother [Thomas Penn]." Echoing ambiguous old themes of intertribal defeat and subjugation, Canassetigo called the Forks Lenapes "Children" whose behavior was unlike that of their protectors, the "wise United [Six] Nations." In fact, "We find you are none of our Blood." To the satisfaction of the listening Governor and Logan, the orator now ordered Nutimus and his group "to remove instantly." They could cross the Delaware eastward to their native New Jersey, or move up to Wyoming or Shamokin at the Forks of the Susquehanna. "Don't deliberate," came the insulting command, "but remove away and take this Belt of Wampum."

After the speech had been translated into English and the Delaware language, Canassetigo had a further thought, and another string of wampum to enforce it. The Delawares, he said, and their descendants, were never again, to "the latest Posterity," to be involved in land affairs of any kind. Taking their string, the Forks and Susquehanna Delawares were to "depart the Council and consider what has been said to you."

That was the end of the meeting for Nutimus. As for Alumapees and Pisquetomen from Shamokin, who probably also left at this juncture, the dismissal was less than ultimate (as later events would show). We should also observe that neither Tishekunk nor Tatamy, who expected to stay living at the Forks, were recorded as mentioned at this meeting.

Canassetigo had a few concluding and important thoughts for the white "brethren." One was a hope that the watching James Logan, whom the Indians had "press'd . . . to leave his Retirement, and prevailed [on] to assist once More," would be assured of their thanks. "He is a wise Man & a fast friend to the Indians,"

> and we desire when his Soul goes to God you may choose in his room just such another Person of the same Prudence and Ability in Counselling, and of the same tender Disposition and Affection for the Indians. In Testimony of our Gratitude for all his services, and because he was so good as to leave his Country Home and follow Us to Town, And be at the Trouble in his advanced Age to attend this Council, We present him with this Bundle of Skins.

To this Canassetigo added three closing requests: that "Traders" be required to pay higher prices for deerskins; that "the Rum Bottle" be opened "in greater Abundance" for the trip homeward; and that "Waggons" be supplied to carry the goods of the present "to the Place where they are to be Conveyed by Water" (on the Susquehanna).

Gratified, the Governor responded,

> The Judgment you have just now pass'd on your Cousins the Delawares confirms the high Opinion We have ever entertained of the Justice of the six Nations. . . . These unhappy [Lenape] People might have always liv'd easy, having never received the least Injury from Us; but we believe some of our own [Quaker!] People were bad enough to impose on their Credulity, and engage them into these wrong Measures [i.e., their written appeals to the Six Nations, the Chief Justice, and the Governor], which We wish for their Sakes they had avoided.

There would indeed now be "Rum to serve you on your Journey, since you desire it" and the "Waggons" had been ordered.

Was it any wonder that old Logan, reporting the same day that "The Six Nations . . . have ordered the Delaware Indians to remove immediately off the land in the Forks . . . and they are preparing to leave," could conclude, "This has been, throughout, an excellent treaty"? Or that Thomas Penn, when he read the news in England, would be "glad the Treaty with the Indians is so well ended and everybody pleased with it, which is somewhat very extraordinary at this juncture"? Or that Nutimus, like Brandywine's Checochinican before him, would now sense that his family had no more country at all? Or that Alumapees and his nephew Pisquetomen, returning to

Shamokin after having heard Canassetigo's insulting tirade, would feel a deepening change in their relation to the Six Nations?

Whereas Nutimus clearly had no future at the Forks, his fellow sachems Tishekunk and Tatamy (who had not been at the Philadelphia meeting) had no intention of leaving their Lehigh homes. Tishekunk was being influenced spiritually by the Moravians and their Count Zinzendorf, who had negotiated to buy off his land claim at what was now being called "Nazareth." In these same months the missionizing Count traveled out to Shamokin to preach to the Delaware-Shawnee-Mingo grouping at the Susquehanna's Forks. No evidence exists as to whether he talked to Alumapees there; what was recorded was that he asked the Natives to stop their "prodigious noise, with drums and singing" while he attempted a devotional session. Told by Conrad Weiser that the Indians did not understand abstract ideas, Zinzendorf found them, in Weiser's words, wishing to "hold to that God who allows deer and maize to grow for them." In contrast, Tatamy of the Lehigh Forks would be coached through a conversion experience by the young Calvinist missionary David Brainerd, and would expect to own land as a Christian.

The region's Mennonite settlers, in the fall of 1742, had their own issues. For reasons unknown, ten of their "leaders" stopped in with the young Moravian community at Nazareth, but after they had "merely looked around the place . . . left again after a stay of two hours." At around the same time a "single Br[other] Jacob Detweiler [shared] the sacrament with us for the first time," and a year or two later an Abraham Groff from Goschenhoppen would also join. In Lancaster County, as well, after Zinzendorf had preached there, the Moravian fellowship gained a few Mennonites. Most of the latter, though, were less concerned about the state of their souls than about their future on the land they had paid to live on. Some, like the now aged Gerhart Clemens of Salford, had been legally "naturalized," but most were not, the main reason being that, like Quakers, they could not in conscience swear an oath, whether for citizenship or any other reason. Sympathetic Quakers in the governing Assembly in Philadelphia helped them repeatedly to apply for naturalization to the Governor (himself an Anglican under the British Crown), but there had been no success.

Now that there was a British war with Spain, tension mounted between the pacifist Quaker majority controlling the Assembly and the Governor, who was allowing indentured servants to leave their contracts to enlist in military service. Whereas the Quakers refused to advance funds to use in raising recruits for "the King's service," the non-pacifist Penn "Proprietary party," to which the Governor and wealthy William Allen adhered, feared that the upcoming election of October 1 would be unfairly manipulated. As Allen put it, Quakers had recently "brought down upon us about 400 Germans who hardly ever came to elections formerly." Not more than a tenth of them, he estimated, had voted before. There were rumors that this time there would appear hundreds more "Germans" than ever. We may guess that these would include Mennonites from the Salford-Franconia area, since, when naturalization without oath would be allowed a few months later, many men from that area would be enrolled.

To ensure fairness, Allen proposed that "inspectors" or judges of the authenticity of submitted ballots should be equally chosen from both parties. When the Quakers rejected this as a ploy by the anti-Quaker minority, anger rose in members of the Proprietary party. Some who agreed with the latter alerted a gang of sailors from ships at the wharf a few blocks from the voting station, telling them to prevent Quakers and "Germans" from crowding others from the voting proceedings. Stoked with an early morning draft of rum, the sailors were immediately denounced (and thus enraged) by an elderly Quaker. With Allen standing smiling nearby, they set out to intimidate any "broad brims" (Quakers) that would act unfairly. A ship captain was heard calling, "Damn you, go and knock those Dutch Sons of Bitches off the Steps." Soon after the sheriff's horn signaled that voting could begin, the sailors, as if at a given signal, descended flailing into the Quakers and Germans, blocking the stairway up to the election balcony. Heads were cracked and glass was shattered before the sailors were driven back to their boats and arrested.

There had not been a scene like this in William Penn's Philadelphia before. It took lengthy hearings and months-long mutual accusations for tempers to cool, and William Allen would remain out of political power for years thereafter.

Following the election, the non-swearing Germans, including dozens of Mennonites, earnestly renewed their application for naturalization—to be legitimate on the land they occupied. In a striking parallel, representatives of the supposedly dismissed Lenapes came to Philadelphia to press their own claim. "Those rascals the Delaware Fork Indians," reported Secretary Richard Peters to Thomas Penn, had written "a letter to the Governor wherein they pray that as they are become Christians and of the same religion with the white people they may be permitted to stay on their Lands and not to remove to live with Heathens, though of their own nation." Having had the "impudence," in Peters' opinion, "to subscribe themselves, 'Your Honour's brethren in the Lord Jesus,'" they had come to town "to prosecute their petition" with the Governor himself.

The Executive Council was bemused by Tatamy's and Tishekunk's claim that, having embraced the Christian religion, they had "grown into considerable knowledge thereof." It was on this basis that they "begged permission to remain where they were near the English, and under the same laws," and "that a portion of land might be set apart for their use." Skeptically, the Governor summoned the two sachems into his Council for some questioning "regarding their knowledge of Christianity," which, after the interview, he described as "very little, if any at all." And did they know, he asked, "the nature of last summer's treaty with the Six Nations?" To be sure that they did, he had Canassetigo's fiery expulsive speech read to them, and asked if they understood it. It was "the bad behavior of the Delawares" who had protested, the Governor explained, that "had brought all this upon them." Tatamy responded simply that since he had been granted his 300 acres by the Penn brothers, he wished to stay there "in peace and friendship with the English." Tishekunk (who was dealing with Count Zinzendorf for compensation of his land) said that while he "did not at present own any land," he would like "to buy some if he might be allowed to live among the English."

Sent outside the room, the Indians waited while the Council decided against granting their petition. Not only might it be "resented by the Six Nations," they argued, but it could reawaken the recent "troubles with the Delawares." Thus Tatamy and Tishekunk could only remain living in the Forks with "the consent of the chiefs of the Six Nations." Tishekunk would have to move, because his former home was now "the property of persons [Moravians] who bought it from the Proprietors." Further—and this was stated over and over by the Governor—no other Indians were included in this partial permission except Tishekunk's and Tatamy's "own families dwelling in the same house with them."

Within weeks a parallel small delegation arrived at the door of the Quaker-dominated Assembly. It represented the non-swearing "Germans" so rudely reminded in the recent election of their own non-legitimacy. After they asked to testify, "Some of the Petitioners . . . were called in and heard accordingly." Pleased to learn that the Assembly had "already [repeatedly] sent up a general Bill to the Governor, in Favour of all in their Circumstances, they withdrew." Unlike with the Indians, of course, there was no suggestion of the petitioners being non-Christian. The Anglican Governor's response to them was that, while being badgered by Quaker obstinacy over military preparations, he had been too busy to solve the naturalization issue all along. And by February 3, 1743, he did indeed see passed into law "An Act for naturallizing such foreign Protestants as are settled or shall settle in this Province, who, not being of the People called Quakers, do conscientiously refuse the taking of any oath."

At that time Governor Thomas was considerably more concerned about Indians than Germans. On the very day of his signing the new naturalization law at Philadelphia, out at Shamokin a message he had sent by Conrad Weiser was being delivered to Alumapees. Bespeaking the Governor's concern for continuing good relations with the Delawares, it described Alumapees as one who "had always been a good ffriend and observer of treaties." In appreciation, the Governor had sent wampum and a "matchcoat" for Alumapees "to cover his old body." In that moment Alumapees was troubled by a murder of an Indian who had traveled through Shamokin to Virginia, and was actually so poor that he had to apologize for not being able to "do as he would have done if he had been able"—he had no wampum to give in return. By the following April, however, he could send a "Belt consisting of nine Rows of Wampum" to convey "his Joy" that recent ominous "Differences between the Inhabitants of Virginia and the Six Nations [were] likely . . . to come to a good Conclusion." Since, at Shamokin, "He lives midway between the one and the other, and as [travelers] must pass thro' the place of his residence, a State of War would be very disagreeable to him."

Even happier with their situation that month were some 80 Mennonite men among those who at last "took and subscribed the Qualifications" allowing them to become naturalized citizens of Pennsylvania. The signers from the community where Gerhart Clemens and his children had lived for 25 years were Palatines whose American-born children were intermarrying in a community as stable as the Delaware one was eroding. Included were signers Christian Allebach, Friedrich Altdörfer, Hans Ulrich Bergey, Christian Halteman, Nicholas Halteman Sr. and Jr., Gerhart Clemens' son-in-law Valentine Kratz, three Jacob Landises, Christian and Hans Meier, Hans Reiff, Henrich Ruth, Hans Andreas Swartz, and Hans Wyerman Sr. and Jr. The fact that the list does not include any Kolbs (including minister Dielman), or Funcks (including Bishop Henrich) was probably due to their being, as ordained Mennonite leaders, less ready to complicate their identity. After all, the Kolbs and Funcks were still writing to the Netherlands for spiritual advice.

Gerhart and Ann Clemens, now old like Alumapees on the Susquehanna, had children on adjacent farms. The two oldest, Jacob and Johannes, had just been certified as citizens, while their brother Abraham and sister Anna (wife of Valentine Kratz), having been born there by the Branch, needed no naturalization. They could now, unlike the indigenous folk who had left stone markers in their soil, own the land they lived on. Their people's songs had been published in Germantown, with a set of their Swiss grandparents' stories, and their worried Salford minister Dielman Kolb was appealing to Amsterdam for a Mennonite storybook, which would become the biggest volume published so far in America. In contrast, there would be no memory of Lenape song or story by the Branch.

CHAPTER TWENTY-SIX

Publication, Pathos, Profit
1744–1747

WHEN IMMIGRANT WEAVER Gerhart Clemens died in 1744, his plantation was embraced by multiple Branch Creek-divided farms of his posterity. At least 20 surviving grandchildren ensured that the family name had a future on this ground. We know less about the descendants of sachem Alumapees, who would pass on three years later amidst the Lenapes at the Forks of the Susquehanna River. We do read that a granddaughter married to Andrew Montour had children John and Madeline. The four impressive nephews—Shingas, Pisquetomen, Tamaqua, and Delaware George—were among the hundreds of Delawares moving westward to Allegheny and the Ohio River.

Whereas Sassoonan's hut is only a picture-less memory, the solid brown stone dwellings of miller Johannes Clemens and his minister Dielman Kolb remain literally in the Perkiomen watershed. Worshipers in the present Salford Mennonite Meetinghouse face a wall of stones re-mortared from the Clemens mill. Scanning a Bible archived at Mt. Clemens, Michigan, we are charmed to read Johannes and Elizabeth Clemens' notation, made there along the Branch, at the birth in 1750 of their second son: "We call him Jacob, who will be our comfort in our old age, in the sign of the Pisces."

Imagining, by comparison, what comfort Alumapees might expect among his starving relatives at Shamokin, we muse that, though he couldn't write, we have greater entrée into his personal story than into that of the Mennonite immigrants by the Branch. After all, words he exchanged with Thomas Penn, the Colony's governors, or agent Conrad Weiser are not only on record but, after three centuries, ready to glow on screens anywhere in the world. So are, to be sure, German words read in the Branch Valley during the old chief's last years. In a monthly *Geschicht Schreiber* from the shop of printer Christopher Sauer, the Clemenses, Kolbs, Lederachs, and Ruths could advertise the straying of their heifers, horses, and sheep, or be urgently reminded in 1743 that there was currently "no place or people," whether in church, nature, or academia, "without talk or cry of war." Meanwhile, as the Franconia and Salford Mennonites waited in vain for a reply from Amsterdam, Sauer astonishingly issued from tiny Germantown a quarto-size Bible in the German language. Except for one prepared for New England's Indians, it was the first Bible published in America.

Sauer's subsidized low price must have underscored for printer Benjamin Franklin that he was not attracting the trade of the German-speaking populace. What Bishop Henrich Funck found important about Sauer was his printing not only the Mennonites' songbook in 1742, but Henrich's *Mirror of Baptism* two years later. Sauer, a Pietist of strong Dunker leaning, had not put his name on the title page of Funck's book. But that title echoed a larger project in which he *did* have interest: the monumental Dutch *Martyrs' Mirror* of 1660 that Henrich Funck and Dielman Kolb had been hoping to see translated into the language of their rising generation. Although in Sauer they now had access to a printer capable of such a project, they were cautious. Could a man of such passionate Dunker preference be trusted with a non-immersionist, Mennonite-based project? There was another, less worrisome Dunker option in Lancaster County's Seventh-Day Baptist commune at Ephrata, with its printing press and highly educated prior who knew seven languages. A graduate of the University of Heidelberg, Peter Miller had served as a young Reformed pastor in the Skippack community before joining the Cloister. He accepted the task of translation, and was able to sleep only four hours nightly over the course of the next three years, he would later claim. His work was so scrupulous that Henrich Funck and Dielman Kolb, reading every page as it first fell from the press, could find no errors.

Not hearing of the sacred project until it was nearly finished, a Lancaster County Kropf family brought in an old paper for consideration. What must translator Miller have felt as he read a list of Anabaptists executed in Bern, copied by two brothers from the record book of a Bernese prison tower where they were held? This, too, was part of the martyr story. Even though the last pages of the great *Mirror* had been set in type, the newly found list of names was inserted in the margins of two pages. And at the book's very end a page of commentary called attention to the *besondere Liebe* (special love) for the book evident in the Franconia-Salford mentors Funck and Kolb.

What about the forest people of Alumapees? Would their folk memory become a mere blank? Not according to Conrad Weiser, who had spent several years as a member at Ephrata, and was now a frequent visitor at Shamokin. "Their histories of times of war and peace, covenants and treaties," he explained to his Lutheran son-in-law, "are transmitted by certain wise old people who are no longer able to support themselves. The young people occasionally come together to have the history sung to them by one of these old professors of history. They bring something from the hunt and for it receive the tradition. . . . There are certain tones and positions of the body according to whether the subject manner is joyful, sad, or indifferent."

Weiser's already deep knowledge of Indian mentality was enhanced by personal experience of a final crisis in the life of old Alumapees. In 1744 the land around Shamokin, into which at least 15 fur-traders had followed the Delawares, was convulsed by the murder of trader John Armstrong and two associates. The Delaware attacker, Mushmeelin, felt he had not been dealt with fairly. The Native response to his arrest dangerously divided Mushmeelin's relatives among the 150 Delawares living around the island in the Forks of the Susquehanna (present Packers Island). Alumapees, disparaged by Weiser as having been intermittently drunk "for the past two or three years," was frightened by the "great noise" among his polarized people. After trying to discern who was guilty by employing what Weiser called a "conjurer," the old sachem fled temporarily into the bushes, appealed to neighboring Shikellamy (the Six Nations' eye on the Shamokin Indians), and sent for Weiser to come. Only after a tense procedure in which Alumapees deliberately confessed to Weiser that his people had "transgressed" and were "ashamed to look up," and an unrepentant Mushmeelin was hauled bound to Philadelphia (where he was later hanged), did the Shamokin community regain its calm.

An account written by Weiser two years later takes us into the solemn presence of our now aged character Alumapees. His people had invited about a hundred persons, including messengers from the Governor, to a "feast" recognizing the seriousness of the recent events. "After we had in great silence devoured a fat bear," Weiser remembered, the oldest of the chiefs (whom Weiser does not name) "made a speech," calling it a "great misfortune" that one of his people had killed the three white "brethren." But the sun, not completely set, "had only been darkened by a small cloud, which was now done away." The murderer was "like to be punished, and the land remains in peace." In conclusion, wrote Weiser, the old speaker

> exhorted his people to thankfulness to God; and therefore, he began to sing with an awful solemnity but without expressing any words; the others accompanied him with great earnestness of fervor, spoke these words, "Thanks, thanks be to thee, thou great Lord of the world, in that thou hast again caused the sun to shine, and hast dispersed the dark cloud; the Indians are thine."

Surely the unnamed speaker was Alumapees. Frail and fecklessly inebriated as he might persistently be, it was in his voice that the transgenerational voice of his people was heard. Their acknowledgement of him as their ceremonial head was not something that could be defined or dismissed by white mentality.

Weiser, who could feel the emotion in the old chief's song, had been given by boyhood contacts among the Iroquois a different initial insight into Indian consciousness than that of the Moravian and Presbyterian missionaries who appeared repeatedly at Shamokin in 1744-45. He himself "occasionally [had] endeavored to tell [the Indians] something out of the books of Moses," his son-in-law recorded. But even if one were able to quote and express the historical truths in some fashion in their language, Weiser commented, the Lenapes would reply, "What your God has revealed to you on the other side of the ocean may all be true, but that has nothing to do with us; our God has revealed other things to us on this side. You abide by your affairs and we will abide by ours."

We have now heard almost our last words from Alumapees. Too weak in 1744 to make his traditional yearly journey to Philadelphia, he sent a delegation to the Governor with "a bundle of skins," acknowledging (regarding Mushmeelin's attack) that "something worse than any thing that ever happen'd before, and which we are very Sorry for," had indeed occurred. But while freely confessing the "Blood [that] has been spilt by us contrary to the Chain of Friendship," the emissaries emphasized that their people continued to "remember all our Treaties, and that by them we became one Body and one People with our Brethren; We remember every part of them." These were not arrangements made by the Six Nations for the Lenapes, but covenants the Lenapes had agreed to on their own. Pleased by this tone, the Governor accepted the apology and promised a gift in return for the proffered furs. "I do not impute the murders that have been committed to the whole Delaware Nation," he assured the emissaries. He followed that statement with a request: that they send to Philadelphia the two young Delawares who had been (wrongly) accused of conspiring with Mushmeelin. The delegates' response to this showed the traditional respect the Delawares had for their own declining sachem: "They could not undertake" such an important move, they said, "without the Consent of their Chief"; they would first need to "Communicate the Governor's Request to Alimopas."

The Governor had a further concern. Having been informed (apparently by Weiser, who was in contact with Shikellamy) that Alumapees was "growing very old" and was now "at the point of Death," he wondered who the Delawares "intended to Choose for their Chief when that should happen." The emissaries' reply—that there was no decision on "that matter," but that as soon as there was the Governor would be given "Notice of it"—was a clear message. Weak as the landless Delaware diaspora had become, they had kept their identity, something of which they, not the white government, were in charge. Thus corrected, the Governor warned the delegates to be "very careful in their Choice [of a successor to Alumapees], and especially with regard to the Sobriety of the Person," since a man "greedy of Strong Liquor would neither be able to Advise nor to Act for the Interest of their Nation." To this "Advice" the rum-soaked Alumapees' delegates could only respectfully agree before heading back to the Susquehanna.

The veteran wampum keeper did not have political power. That was in the hands of Shikellamy, the Six Nations' "viceroy" living watchfully on the other side of the Susquehanna. Thus it was to Shikellamy that Conrad Weiser brought eight men that fall to build a 50-foot-long log house. On the other hand, it was with Alumapees that missionary David Brainerd wanted to talk in the spring of 1745. Intrigued by the Indian community of some "fifty houses," he described it in his journal as spreading "partly on the east side of the [Susquehanna] river partly on the west and partly on a large island" in the river fork. "About half" of the "near three hundred persons of three tribes speaking three languages wholly unintelligible to each other" were Delawares. Brainerd found that their frail chief—naked, nearly blind, and lying on a bearskin—was considered near death. Yet in those same weeks when Weiser and a Moravian missionary also stopped in, they reported having had "the honor to smoke a pipe" with the ailing sachem. Calling him "the hereditary king of the Indians," the missionary remarked that "it is not known on whom the Kingdom will descend." Though "very old, almost blind, and very poor," Alumapees still obviously had "power over, and is beloved by his people; and is a friend of the English." Negatively, someone gave the missionary a completely wrong impression that Alumapees' "sister's sons" were "either dead or worthless." The adjectives are revealing of contempt. Such an impression could only have arisen from the Shikellamy-Weiser mentality. Shikellamy's loyalties had been given clear expression in his giving one of his own sons the name of the Iroquois-favoring James Logan.

That fall Brainerd was back at Shamokin, with an assistant he had recently baptized, none other than Tatamy of the Lehigh Forks. When Alumapees, appearing somewhat "recovered," turned out to be "kindly disposed and willing to be instructed," the evangelist spent a Saturday afternoon "discours[ing] with him and others respecting Christianity." That evening he wrote in his journal: "I could not but hope, that God would bring in these miserable, wicked Indians; though there appeared little human probability of it; for they were . . . *dancing* and *revelling*, as if possessed by the *devil*. But yet I *hoped*, though *against hope*." On the following day, Alumapees again "kindly received" the visitor, who was nevertheless disappointed to find "many of them in the place . . . so drunk from day to day, that I could get no opportunity to speak to them." As night approached, once again with Alumapees' "cheerful consent," Brainerd finally managed to assemble nearly 50 sober listeners showing a surprising attention and "considerable desire of being further instructed." All in all, the young missionary's favorable impression of the Lenape chief needs to be considered against the disparaging opinions of Weiser and Shikellamy, neither of whom had any love for the Lenape dream.

These were hard times indeed at Shamokin. There had been an extra bitter winter, freezing the Delaware River solid at Philadelphia. The peripatetic translator Andrew Montour, who had married a granddaughter of Alumapees, called it the worst famine season in memory. And once again in the summer of 1746 Delawares sent to Philadelphia reported that their chief was too ill to come himself. There was another visit by David Brainerd, who this time brought along his young family. As in the previous year, the fading headman "seemed disposed to hear" as his guest "discoursed . . . upon divine things." But the summer of 1747 would be the old sachem's last.

With Conrad Weiser reporting Alumapees as no longer "able to stir," there was still no obvious successor among his "relations." This annoyed both Shikellamy and Weiser, who wrote, "Yet he will hear of none so long as he is alive." Nor did any of the Delaware people "care to meddle in the affair" (i.e., dismiss their leader because he was weak or disrespected by others). Their land having been sold, he and their veneration of him were most of what they had left. Shikellamy's impatient advice—that since the old man had "lost his senses, and [was] uncapable of doing anything," it was the government's responsibility to name a successor"—did not make Lenape sense. After all, friendly though he might be, Shikellamy (who did not appreciate the favor that the Delawares gave Alumapees over what he himself would have liked to have as a representative of Iroquois authority) wasn't part of the Lenapes' own story. He was a Haudenosee, sent down to monitor the Delawares by the Six Nations who five years earlier had ordered the last eastern Delawares out of their traditional homeland. The long boast of the northerners that the Delawares were their subjects had never convinced the Lenapes that anyone but they themselves had custody of their own identity.

In July Weiser had a terminally bleak report: "Olumapies would have resigned his crown before now" if it were not for his "keeping of the public treasure (that is to say, the council bag), consisting of belts of wampum." Unfortunately, he was using the wampum to buy "liquor, and has been drunk for this two or three years almost constantly, and it is thought he won't die so long as there is a single wampum left in the bag." Again, the negative view is Shikellamy's. Could there have been a more squalid picture? Yet, in spite of all that their chief and they had abjectly lost, the Lenapes were not about to disrespect their sachem. He was theirs. Indians, in any case, were "remarkable," in the words of historian John Heckewelder, "for the particular respect which they [paid] to old age." They would never try to contradict those who, as they would say, "have lived through the whole period of our lives, and long before we were born." The old ones had "not only all the knowledge we possess, but a great deal more."

Nor were the starving Delawares around Shamokin interested in an invitation by the Six Nations to move closer to them, farther up the Susquehanna's North Branch. The Governor at Philadelphia said he had no objection if they went. What was more important to him was what they might think and do after Alumapees' death.

From their point of view, reported Weiser, the Natives at Shamokin "would like to have a blacksmith sent to them." Watching all this carefully was Logan at Stenton, now past 70. Though crippled and feeling the effects of his stroke, he made a point of urging Weiser to do whatever possible to keep Alumapees' intelligent nephew Pisquetomen from succeeding to his uncle's office. Logan felt that dealings should bypass the old Delaware sachem in favor of the Six Nations' Shikellamy. The Moravian missionaries, too, recognized the Iroquois agent's greater importance as they built a blacksmith shop near his house while Alumapees lay dying.

As this account is less "history" than musing, let us compare the bleak scenario at Shamokin in 1747 with growing domestication elsewhere in Pennsylvania. In the place where, 64 years earlier, Sassoonan had watched his elders discuss land, a brother-in-law of Penn's son Richard was advertising in Franklin's *Gazette* the auction of "13 tracts of 100 to 260 acres in the manor of Perkasie." Or, turning to Tulpehocken, where Sassoonan had been shocked by the sight of houses in 1728, we witness 600 persons attending a Reformed communion service led by the recently arrived Michael Schlatter of St. Gallen, Switzerland. Along the Lehigh River, just above the Blue Mountain, some 500 Natives gather to help launch a mission town named "Gnadenhütten" (Huts of Grace), as Moravian missionaries share a bear-meat and Indian corn lovefeast with newly baptized Natives. One of them, Teedyuscung, seems particularly promising, as he receives the biblical name "Gideon." Whereas his half-brother Tishekunk had cultivated a peach orchard south of the Blue Mountain, now "Indian brethren" celebrated, north of the Lehigh gap, a "completion of plowing," and were "ready to do seeding." Even Nutimus, having been recently expelled from the Lehigh Forks, was doing surprisingly well in a new settlement up the Susquehanna's North Branch at Nescopeck, where visiting Moravians found him with five sons and their wives, as well as a family of five black slaves.

And what about the Mennonites, whose great translating, paper-making, and printing project was piling up over a million pages along Lancaster County's Cocalico Creek? Salford and Franconia families were spreading up the Perkiomen's East Branch, with new mills erected by Jacob Landis and, across the Bucks County line, Michael Derstine. Michael and his brother-in-law Isaac Kolb were being ordained deacon and minister, respectively, at Rockhill. Isaac's elderly uncle Dielman Kolb had the encouragement of seeing his son-in-law Andreas Ziegler ordained to follow him as minister at Salford. Farther eastward in Bucks County, too, children of Salford and Skippack Mennonites were buying land from William Allen along the Tohickon-feeding Deep Run. (Though Allen had called "the Dutch" a "sordid" or money-loving people, he could appreciate well-paying customers.) Feeling especially welcomed by the rich speculator, the Deep Run Mennonites would tell their children that he had not only given them cheaply 50 acres for a meetinghouse, but donated a silver cup for their communion. In fact, whether by the Perkiomen or Saucon or Tohickon Creeks, the Mennonite community, in contrast to that of Alumapees, was strengthening and expanding. Even the Welsh-settled Neshaminy area caught the attention of Salford's Henrich Ruth, who, after 30 years, was looking for land better drained than where he farmed beside the meetinghouse on Salford's heights.

Also unlike hungry Shamokin, Salford was a community with resources and mutual aid. When the Ruths' near neighbor Christian Allebach died in 1746, there were relatives to care for his wife and children. Meal was ground along the neighboring Branch Creek by Christian's son-in-law Johannes Clemens. Bills paid after the funeral showed the availability of doctor, carpenter, miller, shoemaker, schoolmaster, storekeeper, tailor, tanner, weaver, and auctioneer—all German-speaking immigrants from Europe. It betokened the establishment of a set of intermarrying Alderfers, Bergeys, Clemenses, Kulps, Lederachs, Landises, Moyers, Ruths, and Zieglers that, keeping the Palatine dialect as the children of their Lenape predecessors faded ever farther westward, would root ever deeper, for two and a half centuries, into this land.

To be sure, Perkioma's horizon in 1747 was dark with talk of war. The letter to Amsterdam in 1742 having never been answered, a follow-up missive had been sent *"in eyl"* (in haste). Non-pacifists like Benjamin Franklin and Logan were increasingly angry with the Quaker-dominated Assembly that would consent only to non-military expenses. Franklin, though a deist non-believer in church doctrine, was about to recommend a New England-type fast-day "to promote Reformation, and implore the Blessing of Heaven on our Undertaking."

Several months after the death of Alumapees, government business sent Weiser once again from his Tulpehocken home to Shamokin. There several Lenape spokesmen gave him a string of wampum, saying that they would come to Philadelphia in the spring "to consult with their Brethren over some affairs of Moment." Now that they were chiefless, "like Orphan Children," they were hoping that their white "Brethren" would give them "good Advice and Assistance, as the People of Pennsylvania & the Delawares were like one Family." Weiser welcomed such language. Calling this "the first time we had publick Notice given us of the Death of our good Friend & Brother Olomipies" (privately he had been hearing disrespectful words from Shikellamy), he told the mourners to dismiss what was left of their worries. They would be welcome as ever to conversations in Philadelphia. "I assure you," he concluded, "that the President & Council of Pennsylvania condoles with You over the loss of your King our good Friend & Brother." With this he gave the familiar gift of five strouds (body-length blankets).

Weiser was candid with his son-in-law, the Lutheran pastor Henry Melchior Muhlenberg, regarding the Indians' outlook. "They say," he explained, "that the white people should have remained on their own ground and lived there and not bothered them. We came over here with no other purpose than to take their land away from them, to decrease their catch of game, fish, and birds, to drive them farther into the wilderness, and to make their life difficult." And there was almost no hope of their truly understanding the missionaries' message, since "their language lacks the essential phrases and expression with which to convey the spiritual and heavenly truths and make them understandable." Nor were Indians anxious to join one side or the other in an English and French war. They had "to be bribed," wrote Weiser, "and won over with enormous gifts." Fortunately, "they would much rather see the English victorious ... because they get their goods more cheaply from them than from the French."

Neither Weiser nor the Philadelphia officials (nor the Six Nations with whom they consulted) wanted to see Alumapees' choice—canny nephew Pisquetomen—become the head of the troubled Delawares. Fully aware of these dynamics, Pisquetomen was leaving the Susquehanna for Allegheny territory. Weiser promoted the choice of a friendly Delaware named *Lapapitton* for the head sachem role, recommending him as "an Honest, true-hearted man with very good

Natural Sence." But the Lenapes were not to be imposed on from outside their own initiative. Lapapitton understood the situation all too well, being afraid, reported Weiser, of being "Envyd and consequently bewitched by some of the Indians." Weak as the Lenapes had become, they made it clear that they, not the Six Nations or their henchman Shikellamy, would say who their leader was. In fact, it would be five years before the Six Nations would try again to give the Delawares a leader more to their preference, and their new choice, Pisquetomen's brother Shingas, would turn out to be just as dangerously resentful as his older sibling.

For our story, the passing of Alumapees is as nodal as the turn of a century. For the six decades of his positive relationship between his people and their Europe-born replacement population, its key slogan had been the word "Brethren." Such had been the flavor, in August 1745, of the huckleberries brought by Indians to Moravians making pies for their harvest love feast. But woe to the outermost settlers on Susquehanna, Tulpehocken, or Lehigh lands of the Lenapes' interest when, eight years after their last chief's death, his nephews would return to that very ground, not bearing wampum, pipes, and deerskins, but wielding hatchets.

CHAPTER TWENTY-SEVEN

Still "Brethren"?

1748-1755

WERE OUR NARRATIVE to veer southward into Virginia shortly after Alumapees' death, it could link in imagination a pair of young surveyor assistants in the Potomac and Shenandoah watersheds. Both men were destined to experience Indian attacks. The younger fellow, as a military officer, would have two horses shot from under him but survive unscathed, nine years before Hans Roet (John Ruth), Mennonite minister and father of 13 children, would lose six of them and his own life to the tomahawk. His celebrated compatriot, though childless, would become owner of 65,000 acres, and be called the "Father of His Country." Along the way, he would converse with the nephews of Alumapees.

In a treaty of 1744, the Six Nations had given up claims to all land south of the Ohio River. Encouraged by this, within three years wealthy Virginia planters, including two brothers of George Washington, formed the Ohio Land Company, to invest in lands west of the Allegheny Mountain range. They hoped to purchase a large tract, subdivide and sell it to settlers, and possibly take over the formerly French-controlled fur trade. In 1750, expecting to build a fort and retail 300,000 acres, they sent out advance man Christopher Gist to select an area for the first settlement.

Any knowledge of this would have gravely disturbed Lenapes and Shawnees who, having been crowded out of earlier landscapes, had been finding another home where they could again hunt successfully in the formerly thinly populated Ohio River watershed. We can only imagine what it would have been like for them to understand that their new home had been specifically promoted in England as a lap of abundance for potential Mennonite migrants. The trans-Appalachian soil had actually been eyed for two decades as potentially good for

> wheat, barley, rye, Indian corn, hemp, and flax, as well as silk and many other useful things, delivering up a greater harvest than a plot of land in Germany does, since it can be cultivated for ten to twenty years without needing fertilization. . . . Many horses, cattle, and sheep can be kept and raised, seeing there is a lot of good grass. . . . There is abundant cattle, called buffalo, and elk. Sometimes there are twenty to thirty buffaloes in a herd. There are also many harmless bears. . . . Deer, too, are found in great abundance, and Indian [turkey] cocks and hens, each weighing twenty to thirty pounds.—If people can provide themselves only with bread and some cows for milk and butter, and with garden produce such as potatoes, peas, beans, etc. in the first year, they will have enough to eat, with all the meat and many kinds of wild animals and fowl, and live better than the richest nobleman.

The very scene that had benefitted the recently dispossessed Delawares was already attracting another population.

Traversing the Allegheny range had certainly not erased from the Delawares' memory the Brandywine, Lehigh, or Tulpehocken valleys they had abandoned. A chief named *Nemacolin*, now living 30 miles south of the junction of the Monongahela and Ohio Rivers, put it bitterly to Gist in December 1751. "You was sent to us last year from the Great Men in Virginia," he complained, "to inform Us of a present from the Great King over the Water, and if you can bring news from the King to us, why can't you tell him something from me?" Gist, who hid his compass to avoid revealing his Virginian employers' speculative interest, found himself "obliged" to include in his report to them this protest about the Brandywine lands taken over from Nemacolin's father Checochinican several decades earlier. "The White People" who now lived on those lands, said Nemacolin, "will neither let me have them nor pay me anything for them. I desire that you will let the Governor and great men in Virginia know this—It may be that they will tell the great King of it, and he will make Mr. [Thomas] Penn or his people give me the Land or pay me for it." Little or nothing did Nemacolin know of the Ohio Company's royal grant for the land to which he had moved.

Just as apprehensive were the people of now-deceased Alumapees, whose nephews would be, for the next 15 years, the most notable

Delaware leaders moving west of the Alleghenies. One of them, Tamaqua, challenged Gist pointedly. Where, he asked, with newly arriving French claiming "all the land on one Side the River Ohio, and the English on the other Side," did "the Indians' land lay?"

Nemacolin had established a trail running 30 miles northward from his residence (near future Brownsville, Pennsylvania) to the important junction of the Monongahela and Ohio Rivers (site of future Pittsburgh). Whereas to Virginian investors that path promised a route for land-purchasing settlers' freight wagons, its destination held a more sacred place in Native memory. Just downstream from the well-known confluence rose a 16-foot-high burial mound in which, before being diminished by later industrial operations, archaeologists would find artifacts dating to about 500 BC. This was the vicinity where the nephews of Alumapees had made their new home, joining with various southern Iroquois called Mingoes. Though Mingo chief *Tanacharison* had pronounced Alumapees' nephew Shingas headman of the western-arriving Delawares, Gist also heard that Shingas' more genial younger brother Tamaqua was considered "king." In any case, it would be these two brothers, both short of stature while of differing temperaments, who would leave the largest Lenape imprint on the communal memory of the next tumultuous years.

It was at Shingas' riverside village, in October 1753, that he was found by George Washington, a 21-year-old surveyor/major sent up by the Ohio Land Company to find out what French personnel were doing in the region, and demand that they leave. Having heard that Shingas was the Delawares' "king," Washington included him in a planning meeting at the Indian village of Logstown. The topic was how to suppress the increasing French presence that had left lead plates planted to indicate first claims. For Shingas, the arrival of an officer from Virginia could hardly have been a pleasant experience. Only two months earlier he had traveled east with his brothers Pisquetomen, Tamaqua, and Delaware George to Carlisle in order to complain to Pennsylvania's governor about the incoming French. How far west did the Lenapes have to go to find freedom from settlers? Having known what it was to leave Perkioma and Tulpehocken, had they moved on again from Shamokin only to be caught between two foreign empires making their new Ohio home the cockpit of foreign-born rivalries? Would the Delawares have to choose a side in the global English-French struggle?

Tanacharison informed Washington that he had recently told the French how things looked from the Native point of view. "Both you and the English are White," he had declared. "We [Indians] live in a country between [France and England], therefore the land does not belong either to one or the other [of you]; but the GREAT BEING above allow'd it to be a place of residence for us; so Fathers, I desire you to withdraw, as I have done our brothers the English." Washington, though glad to hear that the French were told to back off this land, had every intention of seeing it taken over by his own Ohio Company investors (of which his two older brothers were members), and he himself would eventually own over 60,000 acres between the Potomac and Ohio Rivers. Returning to Virginia, he reported that he had "spent some Time in viewing the Rivers, and the Land in the Fork, which I think extremely well situated for a Fort." His surveyor's eye had also enjoyed the "considerable Bottom of flat, well-timbered Land all around it." Pleased, the Ohio Land Company immediately sent men to widen Nemacolin's trail to the Monongahela and build a blockhouse there.

What was darkly building in the subconsciousness of Lenapes scattered from the Susquehanna to the Ohio was still hardly thinkable. Tamaqua was friendlier than his brothers, but all four men were acutely aware that even the Susquehanna land they had left was newly threatened by settlement. Back at Shamokin, prospering agent Conrad Weiser, who had recently built the first house at the Forks of the Schuylkill (Reading), was in on a spree of land acquisition. "Our people," he wrote in February 1754, "Should be let loose to Set upon any part of the Indian lands," as long as the Natives agreed to the government's "terms." Of course "the Indians would Come in and demand Consideration. . . . But what Can they Say" to people they had acknowledged, in the treaties they had signed, as "Brethren"?

The wave of German-speaking immigrants following 1748 had more than doubled the Province's population. Settlers now spilling out from filled-up Philadelphia, Bucks, and Chester Counties had included what the Colony's Secretary Richard Peters, himself one of the speculators, called "vile People." Not all, of course, were considered unscrupulous. In 1751 Abraham Bauer from Hereford, on the northern edge of the main Mennonite community at the head of the Perkiomen, had found land west of the Susquehanna in future Huntington County. In the same year a northward migration came from

Franconia, a geographic Mennonite center, from the family of immigrant Christian Meyer. Three of his six children (including a helpless Jacob) were part of the main local Mennonite leadership. Christian Jr. was an influential deacon, Barbara was married to deacon Abraham Reiff (who would later move to Lancaster County), and Anna was the wife of Bishop Henrich Funck. But there was also a discordant family note: in 1734 their sister Elizabeth had married a neighboring Dunker, Nicholas Opplinger Jr., whose 154 acres on the border with Lower Salford lay on unwatered high ground a mile south of the Funck mill on the Indian Creek. Bishop Funck's concern about the issue of baptism had been evident in the little book he published on the subject in 1744, a decade after his sister-in-law Elizabeth's marriage. Now the Opplingers, like the Bauers of Hereford, wanting something better than their first purchase, sold it and got a warrant for land far up "Behind the Blue Mountain" ("*Hinder dem Blauen Berg*," as Nicholas put it), at the Lehigh Water Gap. Here on the lonely site of future Palmerton, ten miles downstream from a remarkable new Moravian/Indian mission town named "Gnadenhütten," the Opplingers were the only other white people beside the European-born missionaries.

In her parents' last days, Elizabeth Meyer Opplinger had asked them about a rumor that her father might have "wanted to disinherit" her (for marrying an immersionist Dunker?). They declared that was not the case, she claimed after their deaths. With her mother exhorting "from her own deathbed," her aged father had promised Elizabeth "that she should [have] her inheritance like another child." Yet when Christian died just after his daughter moved northward, she learned that the only part of the family inheritance to be shared equally by the children was an initial £3 each, and that the rest was designated only for the three siblings either ordained or married to ordained men. Shocked, Elizabeth and Nicholas seem to have returned from the funeral to their lonely cabin facing the Lehigh without conferring with her deacon brother Christian Jr. or brother-in-law Bishop Funck. Instead, after enduring the harsh winter of 1751-52 with the loss of £40 equity in his horses, Nicholas wrote a passionate appeal back to Franconia. Surely, he proposed, there had been some kind of mistake. Or could his father-in-law possibly have been prompted, while dying, into revoking the deathbed promise to a daughter? If so, wrote Nicholas, "we are certainly sure that you are convinced in your hearts that this was not rightly done." About to be appointed Northampton

County's first constable (and thus perhaps not an ordinarily devout Dunker), Nicholas begged his Mennonite brothers-in-law to imagine what he called the "downcast countenance" of their sister and her son Christel on the remote Lehigh.

Cruel as a settler family's hurts and grievances might be, could they run as deep as the gradual, numbing loss felt by the Original People for not only their timeless homeland but a newly adopted one? The realization was dawning more slowly in Lenape-occupied land than in New York or Virginia, but eventually it would be overwhelming. Even a person such as Weiser, able to speak an Iroquois language, could be recognized by a son of his closest Native friend as "one of the greatest thieves in the World for Lands." And surely one of his greatest single land-affecting moves was what he achieved at a major treaty with the Six Nations in the summer of 1754. Just as George Washington was returning to the Ohio territory (this time with soldiers to force out the French), representatives from seven of the 13 American colonies were meeting at Albany, New York, to consider a proposal by the rising Benjamin Franklin. Its main purpose was to make a defensive "Union" against both French maneuvering and the unease among the Six Nations whose land was being non-legally settled. While the union plan failed, there was success on another topic. Pennsylvania's delegates had been told "to try," while at the unprecedented meeting, "by all the means in their power to make a Purchase" of land from the Six Nations, "and the Larger the better." To their pleasant surprise, they not only found the Iroquois willing to discuss this over two belts of wampum, but the large assembly then allowed them to negotiate the deal in private session.

Weiser, though feeling rusty in the tongue he had learned when living as a boy with the Mohawks, was recommended as the interpreter. At first he found the 70 attending Iroquois resentful about paths and houses appearing without their permission. But soon his familiar accents had them agreeing that the "Road to Ohio" (used by advancing settlers) was actually "no new Road," and in a mere day or two willing to accept £400, in addition to the £500 they were receiving as a gift for attending, as remuneration for a vast cession of land. South of their New York concentration, it ran from the Susquehanna to the Ohio watershed, and from where the West Branch of the Susquehanna passed through the Blue Mountain to as far west as Pennsylvania extended. One of only two exceptions in this "Albany

Purchase" was the land right around Alumapees' home at Shamokin, a few miles down the Susquehanna to just above where Penns Creek flowed into its west bank. "Our Bones are scattered there," explained the Iroquois, "and on this Land there has always been a great Council Fire." This, and land up the Susquehanna's North Branch at Nescopeck and Wyoming, could still serve as home for "such of our Nations ... as shall come [back] to us from the Ohio [to which Alumapees' nephews had moved], or any others who shall deserve to be in our Alliance." In fact, just then a group of the converted Indians of Gnadenhütten, led by their headman Gideon (Teedyuscung), was moving 30 miles northward to Wyoming.

Lenapes living by the Susquehanna and westward in Allegheny knew nothing of the secret treaty at Albany. It was another case of Pennsylvania officials dealing over their heads with their would-be Iroquois dominators. Before long there would be hell to pay.

In the weeks of the Albany conference there was ominous violence along the Monongahela. There George Washington and his band of 400 men ambushed a group of French soldiers they suspected might be observing them, killing the captain and four of his soldiers. Outraged, the French called the surprise an act of simple war, and used their superior military force to drive the Virginians into retreat. Washington's men could only drag their supplies and ammunition 12 miles back past the Alleghenys before reaching a place known as "Great Meadows," where they threw up and took refuge in a log stockade they dubbed "Fort Necessity." Here they were quickly besieged by 1,500 French and Indians. After resisting from ten o'clock in the morning until nightfall, with 30 men killed and 70 wounded, Washington had nearly run out of ammunition. Luckily for him, the French somewhat chivalrously asked the young American for a parley and offered terms: if he signed a surrender document (whose French he did not fully understand) he would be allowed to leave and even keep his arms. He consented, and on the following morning marched his defeated troops homeward with beating drums and waving flags. Having felt "something charming in the sound" of bullets whistling, he could have no idea that he had incited a seven-years-long transoceanic war.

Only on the laborious 350-mile journey back to the Potomac was there time for Washington's troops to reflect that among their deadly French attackers had been some of *"our own* Indians, Shawnesses,

Delawares and Mingos." A red line had been crossed, prompting Virginia's Governor Robert Dinwiddie to call for a more professional military force. The new seriousness was just as clear to the Delawares living in the Ohio watershed, such as peaceful Tamaqua and the more temperamental half-white Andrew Montour of Juniata, father of Alumapees' 10-year-old great-grandson John. Within weeks following Washington's defeat we hear the disturbed voices of both men.

In a follow-up to Washington's defeat, Weiser met with 200 Indians at the home of the prospering Irish trader George Croghan at Aughwick in the Juniata watershed. Here Tamaqua, functioning like his uncle before him, but unaware of the terms of the secret Albany agreement, presented wampum to signify to the Lenape-dominating Iroquois that the atmosphere in their relationship had changed. Addressing them as his "Oncle," he evoked the joint memory of how the Six Nations, having (supposedly) "defeated" the Lenapes in a previous generation, had repeatedly told them "that we must not Mettle with Wars, but stay in the House and not mind Counsel affair[s]." Whether or not that had reflected reality, the situation now at hand was new: "We have hitherto followed your directions, and Lived very easy under your Protection . . . but now . . . a high Wind is arising." This was a clear suggestion that the Lenapes, who had been peaceful all along with their white "Brethren" (and the supposedly superior Six Nations or Haudenosee), might now be in a different phase. Not knowing that his Delaware people had just been betrayed at Albany by the Iroquois he was addressing, Tamaqua urged them "to have your eyes open, and be Watchful over us your Cousins." No longer would these cousins allow their Six Nations dominators to define them by metaphorically ordering them to stay in the house, in a feminine role, wearing "petticoats." Delawares, too, though peaceful since the day of William Penn, could wield the hatchet.

Tamaqua, the generally reasonable Lenape chief also known by the English name "Beaver," had his own concerns about Pennsylvania's government. Turning to face its representative in the person of Conrad Weiser, the short-statured Delaware headman spoke in the Indian manner as if addressing the Governor himself. "I must now go into the Depth," he orated, "and put you in Mind of old Histories and our first Acquaintance with you." Certainly, while growing up at Shamokin, Tamaqua would have heard from his uncle Alumapees about his storied moment as "a little lad" all the way back at Perkasie.

Seven decades later that memory was vividly alive in Tamaqua's timeless imagination. "When William Penn first appeared in his Ship on our Lands," as he now put it, "we looked in his Face and judged him to be our Brother, and gave him a fast hold to tie his ship to, and we told him . . . that he . . . and his People shall be one of us, and in the same union." When this was "agreed" to by "Penn and his People," the Delawares had conceived or "erected an everlasting Friendship" with them. This, Tamaqua remarked, was the foundational historic reality which, in the midst of jostling English-French rivalries, was to be kept in mind. "We desire [that] you [the white government] will . . . let that Treaty of Friendship made by our forefathers on both sides . . . be in force from Generation to Generation." The very future of "our wife and Children's Life and those yet unborn depends on it." Then, in the traditional manner of his wampum-bearing uncle, Tamaqua presented the absent Governor with "a large belt." Recognizing Tamaqua's seriousness, Weiser promised to "take up the matter with the governor himself once he returned to Philadelphia."

Tamaqua's brotherly words had barely been spoken, however, when the Delawares and Shawnees learned about the Albany agreement. Weiser had to report that on his way home from the conference in Juniata he had found his normally "extremely good-natured" half-Indian friend and translator Andrew Montour seriously "vexed at the new purchase." When drunk, Weiser wrote, Montour "Cursed & swore" and "damned me more than a hundred times," pouring out the same invective toward the Governor and the Secretary who had negotiated the Albany deal. He "told me I cheated the Indians," wrote Weiser, and that "he will now kill any white men that will pretend to settle on his Creek." When again sober, Montour "begged pardon, desired me not to mention it to you [Secretary Richard Peters], but did the same again at another drunken frolick." Such anger, from an admired indigenous friend who, Weiser said, would 'allways . . . act according to my advise," was an ominous sign.

The newly arrived Governor Robert Hunter Morris in Philadelphia tried to mollify the "western" or "Ohio" Delawares with their own kind of language. "Notwithstanding you now live at a great distance from us," he wrote, "we look upon you to be one People with us, and that you sprung up out of the same Spot of Earth where some of us did, and now live upon it." The land issue should not be divisive. "We look upon the Place you now live on as a place of Sport and good Hunting; this never makes any Odds between Brethren. You are within Call, and we desire that a good correspondence may be kept between us and you from time to time, especially in time of Danger. Consider always that here is your home, and your Council Fire has been burning [at Philadelphia] for many years."

America's indigenous people would learn that such diplomatic rhetoric nearly always bore only ironic relevance to what actually happened with their land. At that very moment, even agent Weiser and his sons were freely joining a crush of speculators descending on the crumbling Indian community at Shamokin. After all, there was money to be made here. Men sent out by Weiser "to look for land for [Secretary] Peters & myself" found they had been preceded by "3 or 4" other claimants who had already made marks on trees. A German from Philadelphia, asserting that "the proprietor" (Thomas Penn) himself had assigned him "all Shamokin," had promised to bring 40 families of settlers within a year. All others were therefore "forewarned" from the properties he had marked. Aware of that situation, Weiser sons marked for their father and Secretary Peters several thousand acres and an island at the mouth of John Penn's (Big Mahoney) Creek, seven miles south of Shamokin. Indians immediately complained about these actions, saying that "the proprietor" could not "give away their land which he never as yet had purchased." But as Weiser himself had asked, what could they say to accuse people they had acknowledged by treaty as "Brethren"? And what was he to say to them in the harsh winter, as they were "continually plaguing" him? They "have almost nothing to Eat," he wrote to Peters, "Because the Deers are Scarce." They have sent a "Petition to the Governor for some Provision, and the Fencing in of a Corn Field," for which they "should have an answer."

Speculators jumping in after the Albany Purchase included Lancaster County's affluent Mennonite miller Abraham Herr of Manor Township, who bought and retailed land at Penns Creek to the recently arrived Bernese immigrant family of Jacob King (Jean-Jacques LeRoi). While the King children stayed with the Herrs, the parents worked vigorously to "improve" the acreage near the boundary of the Albany Purchase. This was land that Shingas, Pisquetomen, and Tamaqua knew well. Why, asked observant Indians, were these settlers working so hard? To pay for the land, was the answer. And how much was the price? persisted the Natives. When they were told, according to local lore, they were outraged at the difference in rate between what Indians and the speculators were paid. The King family thus occupied a sensitive space.

England and France had not yet declared war when Virginia Governor Robert Dinwiddie engaged a professional soldier for the assignment at which the amateur Washington had failed—removing French threat from the Ohio lands. Sixty-year-old British officer Edward Braddock had never commanded troops in combat. With his promotion to major general, he was given more power than any previous held by a military officer in America. Two Irish regiments sailed from Cork, and, after the short, stout, and quick-tempered general followed them across the Atlantic in February 1755, recruitment in the Colonies increased his forces to 2,200 "regulars."

Braddock's arrogance would cost him. He did accept the application of 23-year-old George Washington, whose knowledge of the Ohio was invaluable. Helpful, too, was postmaster Benjamin Franklin, who, while consulting about forthcoming military dispatches, was startled by Braddock's boast that taking the French fort on the Ohio could "hardly detain me above three or four days." To Franklin's caution about an Indian ambush, the major general replied, "These savages may, indeed, be a formidable enemy to your raw American militia, but upon the King's regular and disciplined troops, sir, it is impossible they should make any impression."

Braddock wanted to march to the Monongahela with not only packhorses but cannon and 150 big-wheeled four-horse wagons. Moving the latter would require widening the Nemacolin trail. When the general angrily found only a few wagons available, Franklin, knowing that every farm in Lancaster and York Counties had a wagon of the kind needed, announced payment of the King's gold for the rental of horses, wagons, and teams (with drivers). He not only spoke to a crowd of "Dutch" at Lancaster but personally paid out advances at three locations. Impressive as this project's instant success was to Braddock, it was possibly more so in a negative sense to the "nonresistant" ministers of the community watching their members quickly supply about a quarter of the demanded wagons. In any case, a few weeks later, on May 15, 1755, an unusually ecumenical combination of nonresistant Mennonite, Amish, and Dunker leaders signed an appeal to the Colony's Assembly in Philadelphia, explaining their convictions. Gold accepted for rental of wagons was one thing, but there were limits on related issues. "Some," they wrote, "may be ready to Say that the Menunists, now hearing that an invasion is threatend by the French on this Colony . . . endeavor to Screen our Selves from lending our Assistance against the Invader." Rather, "it is only a Sense of the command of God upon us forbidding us to take up Arms against any." It is actually "our fixed principle," they declared, "rather than take up Arms in Order to defend our King, our Country, or our Selves, to Suffer all that is dear to us to be rend from us, even Life it Self." It was thus a matter, they protested, not of "Contempt to Authority," but of acknowledging what they believed to be "the mind and will of our Lord Jesus Christ as Lord."

Indians, too, were carefully considering the situation as Braddock's unprecedented army gathered and trained at Will's Creek (Cumberland, Maryland). Cherokees, though invited to join the expedition, declined, but others, including Shingas of the Delawares, considered the possibility. After his people had lost Perkioma, Tulpehocken, and Shamokin, would a French-cleared Ohio territory be their hope of living and hunting in peace? By his own later account, Shingas, "with 5 other Chiefs of the Delaware Shawnee & Mingo Nations," approached Braddock to ask "what he intended to do with the Land if he Could drive the French and their Indians away." The general, doubtless impatient to get on with his anticipated victory, replied that it would be the English who would "Inhabit & Inherit the Land." Shingas then persisted, questioning "whether the Indians that were Friends to the English might not be Permitted to Live and Trade Among the English and have Hunting Ground sufficient to Support themselves and Familys." After all, "they had no where [else] to Flee To But into the Hands of the French and their Indians" (who were also Shingas' Indian enemies). At that, Shingas remembered, Braddock became clearer, stating: "No Savage Should Inherit the Land." Disappointed, Shingas and his fellow sachems took this answer to their people, but tried again the following morning "in hopes [that Braddock] might have Changed his Sentiments." When the general made "the same reply as Formerly," Shingas told him "That if they might not have Liberty To Live on the Land, they would not Fight for it." That, Braddock replied, didn't matter, because "he did not need their Help and had No doubt of driveing the French and their Indians away." This, when Shingas and the other chiefs reported it to their people, left them "very much Enraged." Some of them, recalled Shingas, "Immediately Join'd the

French. But the Greater Part remained neuter till they saw How Things wou'd go Between Braddock and the French in their Engagement."

Only eight Indian scouts and warriors remained with the 1,400 British and nearly 700 American regulars marching northwest from Will's Creek on June 10, 1755. To gain time, Braddock sent a "flying column" ahead. He marched behind, leading a force of 400 men and two companies of Virginia rangers, with two howitzers, cutting a road. As they arrived at the Monongahela, the reinforced French troops awaiting him sent out from their new Fort Duquesne 855 soldiers and 637 Indians, including some Delawares. Watching from the bushes on either side of the narrow newly-cut road, they heard and saw marching a formation of red-coated, flag-carrying soldiers playing their "Grenadiers' March." What Braddock had imagined would be an intimidating royal spectacle was a shooter's target to the hidden Indians. As the Natives began firing, the helmeted British officers, obvious on horseback, "fell very fast" (62 of 83 being killed or wounded). Firing grapeshot into the trees did nothing to stop the invisible Indians, who could brace their guns to pick off targets. George Washington, twice unhorsed but remaining unscathed while his clothes were pierced by bullets, would recall how Braddock's forces "were so disconcerted and confused by the unusual hallooing and whooping of the enemy whom they could not see" that "a general panic took place ... from which no exertions of the officers could recover them."

The fighting lasted three hours, during which Braddock had several horses shot from under him. As he tried to remount yet again, he was brought down by a bullet to the lung, and was carried to the rear. After that, Washington wrote, the troops "broke and [ran] as sheep before the hounds." Indians closed in to scalp and plunder the dead and wounded—and to drink gallons of captured British rum. The British had lost 878 men out of the flying column's 1,466 soldiers, while French and Indian casualties were about 30 killed and 60 wounded. The mortally wounded Braddock was heard to remark "Who would have thought? We shall better know how to deal with them another time." Those proved to be his final words. His body was buried in the middle of the road that his men had cut a week earlier. Indians dragged prisoners naked from the battlefield to the French fort, where they were tortured, and some were roasted to death.

Back at Cumberland, George Washington wrote prophetically, "I tremble at the consequences that this defeat may have upon our back settlers, who I suppose will all leave their habitations unless there are proper measures taken." Meanwhile, the new French commander at Fort Duquesne was seizing the moment to exhort the Indians who had helped defeat the British, as well as those who had had sat back and watched. History was about to turn. Having just seen how easy it was for the French to triumph, the Indians should now spread out and chase the British not only from the Ohio land, but "back to the sea-cities," where French armies would "come and finish the destruction." It was time to take scalps in revenge for losing their land.

CHAPTER TWENTY-EIGHT

Vengeance

1755–1758

SEVENTY-TWO YEARS after the boy Sassoonan had watched William Penn celebrate brotherhood with the Lenape sachem Tamany at Perkasie, that dream had turned into a nightmare. Sassoonan's resentment-stoked nephews Pisquetomen and Shingas led warriors from Kittanning on the Ohio River to descend with bloody clubs on isolated families all across the interface between Native and white dwelling. Why did that have to be, when a kinder dream could persist, such as nine miles downstream from Penn's 1683 rendezvous with Tamany? There on the Perkiomen's East Branch a second Clemens generation, many of whose cousins had remained on Palatine hofs, was sinking permanently peaceful roots into their tree-cleared plantations. Grown-up Jacob Clemens, already a grandfather, was a prospering distiller, with the largest family among his siblings, while his adjacent miller brother Johannes had the fewest offspring. The Clemens children, with neighboring Allebachs, Altdörfers, and Ruths, had only yards to walk to the meetinghouse where for seven years school had been taught three days a week by the memorable Christopher Dock, and every other Sunday Dielman Kolb preached using a new German Bible published by Christopher Sauer in Germantown, only 20 miles to the southeast.

Was it in the uncleared acreage (where these words are now being written) across the creek from Johannes Clemens' millrace that in the fall of 1755 he noticed someone else's red cow with white spots mingling with his cattle? Such strays, local families would recall, were sometimes brought home by an elderly Lenape woman who, remaining behind while her clan migrated westward, was taken in by a local family. She ate turtles, they said, and told children when it thundered that the Great Spirit was angry. In fact, for decades small Lenape groups lingered by the Indian, Neshaminy, and Perkiomen Creeks.

Though deacon Jacob Kolb's accidental death at Skippack had been untimely, his progeny was ensured. He had conveyed land up the Branch at Rockhill to his son "Strong Isaac," who was soon called to ministry there. Jacob had conveyed adjoining land to Isaac's brother-in-law Michael Derstein, now prospering with a mill of his own. Having had his ship fare paid by locals a quarter-century earlier, Michael now welcomed his brother Johannes, arriving on the *St. Andrew* with a stock of textiles and tools to sell. Sadly, Johannes disembarked so ill that he soon died, and his goods had to be auctioned off. There was trouble in Lower Salford in 1755, with a quarrel between settlers Frederich Goetz and Christian Stauffer, namesake descendant of the aged Bernese refugee recalled earlier. According to his neighbors, Goetz objected so strenuously to the widening of the Maxatawny Trail (Lower Salford's future main road) across his land that "bloody blows" resulted.

No one in the young Skippack-Salford-Franconia community recorded a docket of joyful or sad domestic incidents that might have given subsequent generations glimpses into the settlers' daily lives. Unlike the thick colorful journals of neighboring immigrant Lutheran minister Henry Melchior Muhlenberg (son-in-law of Conrad Weiser), Salford's story must be searched out from deeds, wills, or simple business records—Jacob Clemens providing his son-in-law, storekeeper Michael Ziegler, with 30 barrels of whiskey, or Christopher Dock with a barrel of cider. Though conscientious schoolmaster Dock, after consulting with minister Dielman Kolb, had recently written America's first essay on pedagogy (1750), neither in that humbly pious manuscript, nor in a doctrinal work that elderly Bishop Henrich Funck was writing, nor in hymns by his Dunker neighbor Johannes Preiss (claimed by descendants to be the grandson of a Lenape woman on the Indian Creek), was there a hymn of local reference. These people were too busy transforming a formerly "vacant" landscape to think about describing their encounter with it for their *Nachkommenschaft* (posterity). Minister Dielman Kolb, who could read both the Dutch and German languages, and who carefully noted the dates of his birth and immigration on the flyleaf of a Bible, could certainly have done more. There would have been family narrative enough, with his son-in-law Andreas Ziegler ordained to assist him in 1745, or his wife Elizabeth's son Isaac Schnebele arriving from Germany in 1749, and settling just south of the Blue Mountain in northern Lancaster County.

No, we have to construct our own narrative. And what a story it becomes, beginning on October 16, 1755, the day when Johannes Clemens' advertisement regarding a wandering cow was published in Christopher Sauer's monthly *Bericht*. Just south of Shamokin, at Penns Creek, where the line of the Albany Purchase passed through newly established plantations, came a stunning Indian assault. According to one source, the Swiss-born immigrant victims recognized eight local Delawares among the attackers, while other accounts attributed the leadership to Sassoonan's nephew Pisquetomen, who, encouraged by the French at Fort Duquesne, had come east from Kittanning with his brother Shingas to exact vengeance for the loss of their land. Among the settlers killed at Penns Creek was the recent immigrant Jacob King, found at the door of his cabin with "his back barbarously burnt and two Tomahawks sticking in his forehead." Part way through the attack, the Indians had stopped to smoke a pipe with neighbors who were still alive. Speaking in "High Dutch," they declared, "We are Allegany Indians, your enemies. You must all die!" They then proceeded to kill the men in the household, and took two young women prisoners. The bloody procedure was thick with symbolism, with a chain left on one corpse mocking the work of surveyors of this land never ceded by the Delawares or Shawnees. The captive girls were taken on horseback west, and eventually to Kittanning on the Allegheny River.

Shingas, who had grown up at nearby Shamokin before moving with his brothers across the Alleghenys to Kittanning, quickly sent two scalps up the North Branch of the Susquehanna, encouraging Delaware Natives at Wyoming, with their leader Teedyuscung, to join the western (Allegheny) Indians' campaign. This frightened the watching Iroquois, who considered the Delawares their "nephews," and whose sympathies were with the British rather than the French, into sending a man named Scarouady from Allegheny to Philadelphia with a request that Pennsylvania's government supply weapons to the Delawares to be turned against the French. Scarouady was sympathetically dined by Quaker leader Israel Pemberton Jr., and the pacifist Quaker-dominated Assembly listened to the Indian's plea. But there was no interest in the military support he begged for, and, after days of waiting, he left in tears. How, he wondered, were the murderous French-supported western Delawares to be stopped?

This was now a "French and Indian War" that would torment Pennsylvania for seven years. The reports of Indian atrocities, coming thick and fast, included one at Cumberland, then two awful assaults led by Shingas, in both Great and Little Coves. To the east, a Kobel family was massacred in Tulpehocken. Even more alarming was an attack, still farther east, on the Christian village of Gnadenhütten on November 24, carried out by two dozen Natives led by Captain Jacobs of Kittanning. Jealous of Moravian influence, the Natives destroyed the peaceful village on the Lehigh where Teedyuscung had been christened "Gideon." A day or two later Philadelphia was shocked when some "*Dutch*," as one spectator wrote, "brought down . . . in a Waggon, the Bodies of some of their neighbors, who had been just scalped by the *Indians*, and threw them at the *Stadt-House* Door, cursing the *Quakers* Principles, and bidding the Committee of Assembly behold the Fruits of their Obstinacy."

By the end of December there had been so many attacks (with over 200 killed and many more kidnapped) and appeals for help that the Pennsylvania Assembly reluctantly set aside funds for defense. The response of Salford and Skippack Mennonites was to send seven wagons loaded with food and clothing for the 800 frightened refugees crowding into Bethlehem on the Lehigh. Benjamin Franklin was sent north with a company of men to construct a string of forts from the Delaware to the Susquehanna. On his 50th birthday, as they neared the Lehigh Gap, they came to "the house of a German," wrote Franklin, "and in his barn we were all huddled together as wet as water could make us." The barn's owner was constable and tavern keeper Nicholas Opplinger, who had moved up from Franconia Township two decades earlier.

There was even an attack, on New Year's Day 1756, led by the man the Moravians had named "Gideon." Teedyuscung had been living with the flock of 70 he had led out of Gnadenhütten 30 miles northward to Wyoming on the Susquehanna's North Branch. Before long, however, with his people barely avoiding starvation, the colorful sachem would regret and try to reverse his hostile course. In contrast, the western or "Allegheny" Delawares only ramped up their assaults, with Shingas killing members of a Studebaker family and sending more captives to Kittanning. He went on to smash a private family fort (McCord) near future Chambersburg, killing or kidnapping 27 victims there. Though short of stature like his less belligerent brother Tamaqua, Shingas was becoming known as "Shingas the Terrible," and earning the distinction of a $700 bounty placed on his head. Things had gotten so bad that on April 8 Governor Robert Morris pushed through a law promising graded payments for both adult and underage male or female Native scalps. Though few were ever turned in, the Scalp Act of 1756 solidified the enmity of the western Delawares. On April 14, Penn's colony declared war on them.

This was too much for the outraged Quakers, six of whom resigned from the Assembly, soon to be joined by four more. To some degree this signaled the end of Penn's "peaceable kingdom" dream. On the other hand, it triggered Quaker initiative. Israel Pemberton Jr. argued vehemently that a new approach was needed when dealing with Natives. It was through meetings and gifts (following William Penn's tradition), and finding what was in each other's thoughts, not threats with weapons, that meaning and reconciliation could happen. This in turn was an insult to the Proprietary party of the formerly Quaker Thomas Penn, who deeply resented the long-standing political opposition of the Quaker-dominated Assembly.

To this day historians are divided in their assessments of the Quaker response to recriminatory Indian assaults. To be clear, the present writer's instincts hew mostly to the side of the pacifist Quakers. Their response in April 1756 was to invite Natives to a series of dinners at Pemberton's sumptuous brick mansion, surrounded by formal gardens at Chestnut and Third Streets at the heart of Philadelphia's most fashionable district. That fall, they formed a non-governmental Friendly Association for Regaining and Preserving Peace with the Indians by Pacific Measures. The idea was to provide or at least offer to the government a service of mediation with the Indians.

Publisher Christopher Sauer, claiming "many friends among the Germans," commended the Quaker venture, with the suggestion that other groups "who are against bearing arms" would also be likely to "contribute [funds] towards a Peaceable way." If a voluntary subscription plan could be set up, Sauer would "write to them to conclude about it in their meetings, especially . . . the menonists wich are most able and willing to contribute to such a purpose." More money might be collected that way, he wrote, "than what many will think." Events would prove him right. Within a few months Dielman Kolb's son-in-law Andreas Ziegler wrote to Pemberton that the Mennonites had had a meeting "about the affairs of the Indians for gathering some money," and that "more of our meeting [would] do the same." If possible, Andreas would like to talk to the new Governor William Denny about it. Similarly, 43 Schwenkfelder men of Salford and Towamencin joined to promise contribution to the Friendly Association.

Even as horrendous attacks by the "western" or Allegheny Delawares continued—with one of the worst occurring at Fort Granville (future Lewistown)—the Governor invited Teedyuscung's "Susquehanna" Delawares now gathered at Wyoming to a preliminary peace talk at Easton. The location was a concession, requiring the Philadelphia officials to come up to meet the Natives at the Lehigh Forks. The town that Thomas Penn had envisaged there (as he had done for the town of Reading where the Tulpehocken joins the Schuylkill) was still a rudimentary village. Pleased, Teedyuscung sent word desiring some Quakers to be there beside the government officials. Hearing this, members of the Friendly Association quickly raised £1,200 (four times the amount contributed by the Assembly), filled a wagon with presents, and appeared at the treaty in a group of 20 led by Israel Pemberton. The purpose of the meeting was to see if a more basic treaty could be held in the fall.

Leading the Indians was their towering, mercurial, and self-appointed "King" Teedyuscung, described by the government's secretary as "a lusty rawboned Man, haughty and very desirous of respect and Command. He can drink three Quarts or a Gallon of Rum a day without being drunk." Just before leaving Wyoming, Teedyuscung had been surprised by a visit of some Allegheny Delawares, imploring him to join their attacks. Flattered by the authority this implied, he had told them to wait for a decision until his return from Easton. He was of course wondering how, having recently led an attack of his own in the Lehigh country, he would be received by officials at the upcoming meeting.

The surprisingly friendly reception Teedyuscung received at Easton so touched him that he "shed tears in abundance." This figured to be a turning point for him and his Susquehanna Delawares. Of course things were still tentative, with the jealous government officials demanding that "no Person should speak [unofficially] with the Indians," and setting "a guard . . . near their lodgings to prevent it." Though this was clearly nothing other than protection against Quaker meddling, Teedyuscung, for his part, would not speak with Governor Morris "unless the Quakers were present." He also demanded, probably on Quaker advice, that "all that I have said . . . may be taken down aright." Speaking in what the Secretary called "a very pathetic

Tone," the lapsed Gideon used a Native term that intrigued his English-speaking audience. What he meant, said a translator, was that "The times are dangerous, they will not admit of delay, *Which Shiksy*, [meaning] do it Effectually, and do it with all possible Dispatch." So a treaty was planned for November, and Teedyuscung wept with joy again as the Quakers boarded a departing "ferry." The government officials, annoyed by how they had been outshone in the Indians' view by the Quakers' liberal gifts, nevertheless agreed privately that those presents had been what had made their peace deal successful.

Before the negotiations could be resumed, there was stunning news from the west. An army under General John Armstrong had smashed Kittanning, the key river-divided town of the Allegheny Delawares, 45 miles up the Allegheny River from Fort Duquesne. The part of the town on the eastern shore, where the fearsome Indian leader Captain Jacobs had a home, had gone up in flames. The Captain had cursed and sung defiantly before receiving a fatal wound. The news set off church bells in Philadelphia, and the chief's scalp was shipped across the Atlantic to an appreciative Thomas Penn. On the other hand, Pisquetomen's brothers Shingas and Tamaqua, living on the western shore of the town, had escaped with many of the recently taken prisoners kept there. They found new lodging 30 miles northwest of Fort Duquesne, in a set of villages by the Beaver Creek called "the Kuskuskies," not far from the future border of the state of Ohio. This place—80 miles southeast of future Cleveland—now became the center of the westward-moving Lenape-Shawnee community.

Two months after the fall of Kittanning there was optimism at Easton as some 40 Susquehanna Delawares regathered to attempt a treaty. The new Governor, temperamental William Denny, concerned to signal that he, rather than the overly-helpful Quakers, was in charge, marched a troop of flag-waving and drumming soldiers up to the shed of meeting. Yet the Indians could not be kept from consulting with their Quaker friend Pemberton. Before long, to the dismay of Conrad Weiser and official secretary Richard Peters, there was a sensation. The inexperienced Governor, in dialogue with Teedyuscung, allowed him to change the expected subject of discussion to the reason for the eastern Delawares' recent attack. What, Denny deliberately interposed, was the more fundamental grievance that could have undermined the long-celebrated relationship between English and Native brethren?

The effect of the Governor's question on the listening Indians was electric: they were actually being asked for their opinion! It could be laid out by a formidable spokesman who could never forget having been rhetorically intimidated in the lead-up to the Walking Purchase of 1737. He had heard Logan tell his uncle Nutimus, "It wou'd not be worth his while to trouble himself about the Land." If Indians did resist, it would only "make the big Trees and Logs, and great Rocks and Stones tumble down into our Road." That had been at Durham in 1734. Now, at Easton in 1756, it was the Native voice that was given the floor.

Animated with obvious vainglory, Teedyuscung rose to the Governor's bait with a speech that has ever since been quoted both favorably and otherwise. "I do not need to go very far," he began, stamping his foot. "This very Ground that is under me was my Land and Inheritance, and is taken from me by Fraud." At least that was the wording one transcriber noted. The official secretary Richard Peters, representing the Penns, was upset, and dropped his pen as Teedyuscung went on: "When I say this Ground, I mean all the Land lying between Tohiccon Creek and Wioming, on the [north branch of the] River *Sasquehannah*." The Governor responded by asking "what he meant by fraud [the key word] and forgery"? Teedyuscung answered in Indian manner, allowing him to speak in the first person as representative of his people, "When I agreed to sell the land by the way the River runs," he explained, "the young Proprietaries [Thomas and John Penn] came and ran the line by a straight course of the compass. And by that means they took in twice the quantity of land that was intended to be sold."

At least four hastily transcribed versions of this speech remain for historians to analyze. All agree that its subject had been recommended to Teedyuscung by his Quaker advisors, for strategic purpose. The present treaty had, after all, not been called to rehash the issue of the Walking Purchase. And since, before long, Teedyuscung himself would give up his thesis of fraud, what value could the phrase "this very ground" have as part of a book title? The answer is in the passion bursting reflexively in the Native voice. One observer, Benjamin Franklin, after reading the official record of the meeting, noted that "The warmth and earnestness" of the Delawares' insisting "on the wrongs that had been done" them were "much too faintly expressed." Historically correct or not, out of order or not, maintained or not,

Teedyuscung's phrase throbs in American memory—not only for the intensity of Native feeling but also for the frightened official animosity it triggered. Simply put, the anger of the Indian rebellion beginning in 1755 was about losing their place on the land. And as to whether resentment for the notorious 1737 Purchase was or was not still a live issue 19 years later, events only six months after Teedyuscung's speech would make that clear, as, a day's walk south of Easton, Indians still seeking vengeance on Edward Marshall, the chief walker of 1737, searched out and killed his wife and children.

Knowing he had touched a nerve, Teedyuscung nevertheless acknowledged that he had not particularly "come to make this Complaint, nor had I intended to speak this now." He had spoken at the Governor's pointed "request," and was not demanding anything but "that you may know the Grounds of our uneasiness and look into your hearts and consider what is right, and do it." To the Indian audience's delight, Governor Denny evinced no offense, and the realization that their complaints would be considered left them almost beside themselves. "The Joy which appear'd in the Countenances of the Indians," noted Pemberton, "canot be express'd." There were "full & repeated Expressions of Approbation by their hearty united Yeho at ye End of every Sentence." When the interchange ended they "hurry'd across the Benches to offer [the Governor] their hands," one of them crying out, "Oh! he is a good man there is no Evil in his heart." Now they could expect a treaty that would address their basic concern: land. Their boisterous chief could not refrain from weeping again as he bade an appreciative goodbye to the helpful Quakers boarding their Philadelphia-bound boat on the Delaware.

Encouraging as was this move toward peace with the eastern Delawares, it did nothing to stop the western maraudings from "Allegheny," led by warriors such as Shingas and Pisquetomen. News of ten more horrifying massacres taking place from April to August 1757 must certainly have reached the ears of Salford and Skippack Mennonites. Among them, Andreas Ziegler, taking up the role of his dying father-in-law Dielman Kolb, would have been especially concerned. There was shocking news from northern Lancaster County, where Andreas' wife Elizabeth's half-brother Isaac Schnebele was farming near the Blue Mountain. On May 30, 1757, Schnebele's barn was torched and 18 cattle killed by Scotch-Irish neighbors angry that, as a Mennonite, he would not help with militaristic defense. Andreas

Ziegler and his brother Michael went to talk to Israel Pemberton, to get an update on the negotiations with the Indians. Around this time, Pemberton, seeking more contributions, looked up the Lancaster Mennonites' influential bishop Benjamin Hershey.

With the approach of yet another and more formal treaty session at Easton, Pemberton wrote out his thoughts to "esteemed Friends Michael Ziegler & Dielman Kolb" (he had apparently not learned of Dielman's death). His language about "a lasting peace . . . with those Poor People [who] from our Bitter enemys . . . may be brought to become our Good friends, and . . . be a Hedge to us to prevent the incursions of the French Indians" was Quaker talk. But it was not without practicality and realism. The Indians would not be convinced "of the Sincerity of our Intentions," went the letter, "without granting them such Assistance as may oblige us to be at a considerable expense." Since Andreas had promised that his people would "be willing to assist us in this good work," Pemberton was hoping that their "not having done any thing" so far had only been due to their being "at a Loss how to proceed." Andreas should now "think of the most proper methods for raising Money amongst you for carrying on so good & necessary a work, and so well becoming both you [Mennonites] and us [Quakers] who cannot for conscience sake be assisting in carrying on of war." In response, Andreas, whose farm lay only a mile from those of the Clemens members in his Salford congregation, called for substantial contributions.

Again in June 1757 Easton was the scene for the treaty agreed on in November. And again, this time with 300 Indians attending, Teedyuscung insisted on a clerk of his own. The Quakers, annoyingly to the Governor, supported this request, saying that if it were not granted they would take their gifts and go home without giving the Indians as much as a shirt. Teedyuscung just as firmly reminded the Governor that "In the Complaints I made last [November], I yet continue. I think some Lands have been bought by the [Penn government] from *Indians* who had not a Right to sell, and to whom the Lands did not belong." The violence of the previous year had to be understood as proceeding "from the Earth, as well as [from] our Differences and Grievances." Of course the attack he himself had led had been French-inspired, but if the land issue "was not the principle Cause that made us strike our Brethren, the English, yet it has caused the Stroke to come harder than it otherwise would have come." Having listened to these thoughts, challenged Teedyuscung, it should be possible for the officials "to look strictly into your Heart," remembering that after all, the Indians "always . . . acknowledge you above us in Abilities, Strength and Knowledge." And there was a further persistent request. Drawing a rough map on the table before him, Teedyuscung asked that a substantial grant of land, containing the Lenape community of Wyoming, be permanently set aside for them. Once that was done, the complaint of being turned out of the land would be gone.

Since there was no particular objection by Governor Denny to Teedyuscung's demand (though it would never be satisfied), there could now be another joyous conclusion. "A handsome Entertainment" was provided for everyone, from the officials to the Indian children. There was a formal "proclamation," after which the Governor "expressed his Satisfaction at being one of the happy Instruments of bringing about this Peace." "Great Chearfulness" reigned as troops fired three volleys, and the Indians danced to the light of a "large Bonfire."

Following the latest meeting at Easton, Israel Pemberton, needing significant funds to pay for the Indian gifts he was proposing, stayed in continuous contact with Mennonites of both the Skippack-Salford and Lancaster communities (Bishop Hershey said his flock now had money available). He also kept requesting permission to help in governmental dealings with the Indians. He did not yet know that the Governor's Council was supplying to Thomas Penn in London a very unflattering view of the Quaker involvements at the treaties. It was impossible, went a letter, not to think that Teedyuscung's complaint of fraud had come from any source other than the "malicious suggestions and management of some wicked people, enemies to the Proprietaries . . . those busy, forward people" who had the nerve to "appear in such crowds at the late Indian treaties, and there show themselves so busy and active, in the management and support of the Indians, in those complaints against the Proprietaries."

In return, the Penn brothers begged their American sympathizers to refute any charges of fraud, "so that our innocence may appear to the world." It was the typical political way of making not themselves but the opposing party the cause of a crisis they both deplored. There was an unpleasant conversation with Benjamin Franklin, who had been sent to London to negotiate other matters. He was so shocked, he wrote home, with Thomas Penn's cavalier objections to criticism, that he had "conceived at that moment a more cordial and thorough contempt for him than I ever felt for any man living." In his secular opinion, the famous family name was destined "to rot and stink in the nostrils of posterity." Thomas Penn was just as polarized, writing to Philadelphia that nobody in London thought much of Franklin, or had heard about his electrical experiments.

Transatlantic verbal blows were one thing, but in Pennsylvania physical hatchets and clubs were steadily breaking the heads of the outermost settlers. Among the victims were members of the Amish Nicholas Hostetter family in Tulpehocken. Five children of Lebanon Township's Dunker Peter Wampler were kidnapped. Mennonite John Snavely, another of Andreas and Elizabeth Ziegler's relatives, was among those killed. Would there be no letup in murderous assaults by Allegheny Delawares, such as had occurred with their Susquehanna counterparts?

Teedyuscung sent his son west with wampum to Allegheny, where his news of peace-talk at Easton stirred incredulity, but also hope. A change of heart was glimmering among the western Delawares, who were wearying of French control. A nascent "peace faction," headed by Tamaqua, was not opposed by his brother, "Terrible" Shingas. In the early months of 1758 a 47-day journey on horseback brought several Allegheny Indians to Teedyuscung's Wyoming, where before long none other than elderly Pisquetomen arrived with another sachem. Was it factual, they wondered, that the government, even after more than two years of Indian terror, would consider reconciliation? Teedyuscung, it was said, was so delighted to hear that Shingas now favored peace that he leaped high in joy. He would have loved to take credit for the change.

CHAPTER TWENTY-NINE

Peace Lost and Re-Attempted

1758

From the Susquehanna to the Juniata and Conodoguinet, the bloody toll kept mounting. By the beginning of 1758 Cumberland County alone, with its mixture of Scotch-Irish and German settlers, counted 928 farms abandoned. The following May, terror struck in Virginia's Shenandoah Valley. "We were 39 Mennonite families living in Virginia," declared an anguished report. "One family was murdered and the remaining of us and many other families were obliged to flee for our lives, leaving all and going empty handed." Across Virginia there had been 50 killings and more than 200 families driven homeless. Many of them straggled northeastward into Pennsylvania's Lancaster County.

On either side of the horror, it was almost impossible to understand the opposite view. What for the Indians was a bottomless visceral reaction to loss of living space, was felt on the other side as simple demonic bloodlust. Was there anyone who could bridge such a chasm? Certainly not the self-proclaimed "King" of the eastern Delawares, Teedyuscung, who, for all his swagger, was not respected by many of his own people. Nor did Governor William Denny, Brigadier General John Forbes, Conrad Weiser, or even rich Quaker Israel Pemberton have the necessary dual bona fides.

There was, however, a devout if failed Moravian missionary preacher, Christian Frederick Post, whose swordless attitude placed him in a unique position. In 17 years of ministry he had married two indigenous women: a Wampanoag Native named Rachel, and a Delaware named Agnes, whose sister had married a son of Teedyuscung. Both wives, as well as all of their four children, had died, but the widowed and now single father was still vigorous in his mid-40s. Known to be familiar with the Delawares' language, food, and concerns, he found himself called on, in June 1758, as a natural diplomat.

Governor Denny was about to see General Forbes off to the Ohio with a large army to succeed where General Braddock had failed. Forbes shrewdly observed that Israel Pemberton's Quaker initiatives at Easton had had enough impact on the Indians to suggest that through such measures the western Delawares might be peacefully led to change their loyalty from the French to the English, and thus make it easy to capture Fort Duquesne. With this in mind, Denny commissioned Christian Post to speak with Teedyuscung at Wyoming, and invite him to a meeting in Philadelphia.

It turned out that the self-proclaimed "King" of 13 Native "nations" had a scheme of his own to mollify the murderous western Delawares. He had recently received unexpected visitors from western Pennsylvania, including none other than Pisquetomen, the elder brother of Shingas, Tamaqua, and Delaware George. When Post met Pisquetomen at Wyoming (where volunteer Quakers were engaged in a house-building project), the odd missionary-and-warrior pair immediately hit it off. Perhaps Post had not heard much of Pisquetomen's reputation for anger, his violent, sometimes alcoholic rages, or his cruel killing of attempted runaways. But when the western headman, who had been sent east by his more peace-inclined brothers Tamaqua and Shingas, invited Post to a breakfast of turkey and bear meat, a respectful conversation ensued. Pisquetomen revealed that his people on the Ohio were not finding the French at Fort Duquesne, who had incited them to attack the British, satisfactory permanent neighbors. The store at Fort Duquesne, at which the Indians could trade, lacked goods, and the French soldiers themselves were almost starving. So the Ohio Delawares had sent east a large pipe and wampum to test whether the British authorities in Philadelphia would respond favorably to a gesture of reconciliation.

Post told Pisquetomen and a companion Delaware headman that he was glad to see them, and that, as he "had been twice married among them,"

> I had a great Love towards their Nation, and would speak very free with them, and they might believe me. After we had discoursed a while together they shook Hands with me, and told me, "Brother: we . . . have long time wished to see some of the Inhabitants of Pennsylvania with whom we could speak ourselves, For we cannot believe all that we hear, and know not what is true and what is false.

For their part, the western Delawares were now "sorry," said Pisquetomen, that they "had gone to War against the English," and had been wishing "often to have seen some Messengers from the Government [other than Teedyuscung] with whom they could have spoken." They in fact preferred the English, but "never hearing from them . . . and the French telling them a parcel of Lies . . . they could not tell what to do." In fact, had they definitely known what had happened at the treaty at Easton in the previous fall (1757), they would have already "chang'd Sides." They had meant now to take their plea to Philadelphia, but "idle Reports" they had heard as they traveled had made them "suspicious and afraid."

A gratified Post assured Pisquetomen that "the English" had actually been trying to send him "Messages, Belts and Invitations." In less than two weeks the two had gathered a 50-member peace delegation to take to Philadelphia. This was, of course, a place that ran deep in Pisquetomen's own family memory. Forty years earlier his maternal uncle Sassoonan, who had wanted Pisquetomen to be his successor, had negotiated peacefully there, and there he himself had translated the scornful rhetoric of the Iroquois orator ordering the last Lenapes from the Delaware Valley. Unlike his mild uncle, of course, Pisquetomen had earned a reputation as a leader of the fiercest Indian anger. But he had come peacefully now, he said, to see and listen for himself, "for we cannot believe all we hear, and know what is true and what is false."

In Philadelphia, Secretary Richard Peters questioned Pisquetomen suspiciously, but Governor Denny—about to send off Brigadier General John Forbes (also then in town) with a huge army to dislodge the French from Fort Duquesne—was delighted. Anxious lest the Allegheny Delawares impede his campaign, the general urged Pisquetomen to return home to them as quickly as possible, to advise them to remain quietly uninvolved. Taking along missionary Post, the returning party was to wear yellow ribbons and carry English flags, try to get prisoners released, and, most of all, gather strategic information for Forbes. If the Indians at Allegheny wanted peace, the government was ready to let the recent awful bygones be bygones.

Post left with the message for Ohio "in the bosom" (under the protection) of Pisquetomen. The latter, though totally loyal to Post, was far from convinced that once the French would be expelled the English would withdraw and let the Indians have the Ohio land. But by August 13 Pisquetomen, Captain Bull (son of Teedyuscung), and another Delaware named Isaac Still had delivered Post safely to the Kuskuskies. There they were welcomed by Pisquetomen's brother Tamaqua, who declared to Post, "Brother, I am very glad to see you, I never thought we should have had the opportunity to see one another more." Delaware George, the youngest of the four nephews of Alumapees, told Post that he had not been able to sleep the night before for joy of the expected visit from the east. And in the evening, recorded Post, "they danced at my Fire, first the Men and then the Women, till after Midnight."

Though the Governor's offer of peace brought Tamaqua "great satisfaction," he was not ready to discuss the return of prisoners, among whom were two girls captured at Penns Creek nearly three years earlier. What Post needed to do, said Tamaqua, was describe the Governor's peace offer to some 300 Natives of the eight "nations" clustered near the French fort (manned by 1,400 soldiers) at the Forks of the Ohio. When Post did this, presenting eight wampum belts at a meeting just across the river from the fort, French-sympathizing Natives tried to lure him into the fort itself. He declined, sensing "great peril," which was confirmed when he heard from the recently freed Penns Creek girls that if the "French Indians" had gotten him in their control, he might have been "roasted for five days." Instead, as guns boomed warningly from the fort on a Sunday, he slipped away.

On the way back to the Kuskuskies, Post had a conversation with Shingas. Speaking "in a very soft and easy manner," Shingas asked Post if he didn't think the English would still hang him if they could. No, responded the Moravian minister; that *had* been true, but the past would be forgotten. Still, Shingas said he could only wish "he could be certain of the English being in earnest." Post himself, fortunately, was trusted: "Brother, your heart is good, you speak always sincerely." But the land issue made the Indians otherwise suspicious. "We know," they said, that "there are always a great number of people that want to get rich; they never have enough. [We ourselves] do not want to be rich, and take away what others have."

Seriously exasperated by the slow discussion, Post nevertheless recorded all such comments, including some from the less trustful Pisquetomen:

> Brother, we have thought a great deal since God has brought you to us, and this is a Matter of great Consequence which

we can't readily answer; we think on it, and will answer you as soon as we can. . . . All our young Men, Women and Children are glad to see you: before you came they all agreed together to go and join the French, but since they have seen you they all draw back.

Even so, insisted the aging Lenape headman, "We have great reason to believe [the English] intend to drive us away, and settle the country, or else, why do [they] come to fight in the land that God has given us?" Or, as Shingas put it, "The English and the French fight for lands that belong to neither, but to the Indians, and this fighting is taking place in the land the Great Spirit has given us."

Here was a historically significant moment: a native of Danzig was dialoging earnestly with grandsons of people from the Perkiomen where he himself had briefly worked 16 years earlier; a tri-lingual missionary who needed no interpreter was asking Indians to listen to God, while beginning to wonder whether his two roles—political and spiritual—could be authentically combined. On and on went the discussion. "We love you more than you love us," argued Shingas, "for when we take any prisoners from you, we treat them as our own children. We are poor, and we cloathe them as well as we can, though you see our [own] children are as naked as at the first. By this you may see that our hearts are better than yours." And why didn't the French and English do their war "in the old country and on the sea? Why do you come to fight on our land?" Did the white people "think we have no brains in our heads"?

And so it went for a week as Post begged to be released so he could return to Philadelphia with the Natives' acceptance of Governor Denny's offer. The Indians were not to be rushed. Not until there had been "a great feast lasting several days," and the four nephews of Alumapees had stressed over and over their suspicions—impatiently but punctiliously recorded by Post—was he finally trusted to write down a positive answer from the Ohio Delawares and Shawnees to Governor Denny. The first to sign it, after Tamaqua, was Shingas.

Perhaps only in a story as unconventionally organized as this narrative would it be noted that in this same week another letter, also war-related, was being written 200 miles to the east in Lancaster County. It was penned by Mennonite Bishop Benjamin Hershey, who had been overseeing his people's recent donation of £680 for the peace initiatives of Quaker Pemberton. The letter, to be carried by Martin Funck, a recent victim of Indian raids in Virginia, to Amsterdam, was an appeal for financial aid, to which the affluent Dutch Doopsgezinden responded with a gift of £50.

The September 1758 agreement Post got from the recently hostile Delawares to seek peace would be extravagantly hailed by nineteenth-century historian Francis Parkman as a turning point in American history. From his point of view, the Allegheny Indians' change of friendship made the difference between a future in which English rather than French would be the language of North America. This would be disputed by twentieth-century scholars, especially Francis Jennings, who thought that whatever credit should be given belonged less to missionary Post than to Pisquetomen. It was certainly not just Post's gentle diplomacy that was prompting acceptance of the Governor's invitation. The Indians had their own motivations. They had seen that the French were no longer getting enough supplies for their store at their fort, and were very much aware of the approach of a great English army that was going to change their story.

The hesitation of Alumapees' nephews to accept Governor Denny's offer had left Post weary. Nearing home after "Thirty-two Nights . . . in the Woods" when "the Heavens were my Covering," he recorded his feelings.

> The Indians are a People full of Jealousy, and will not easily trust any Body, and they are very easily affronted and brought into Jealousy; then afterwards they will have nothing at all to do with those they suspect; and it is not brought so easy out of their Minds; they keep it to their Graves, and leave the Seed of it in their Children and Grand-Children's Minds; so if they can they will revenge themselves for every imagined Injury. They are a very distrustful People.

Even so, the missionary-diplomat would prove willing to take a second western journey, and later make his home with the Delawares.

Pisquetomen, suspicious as he was of English motives, also headed east, back to the State House in Philadelphia. Telling Governor Denny it had been "Twenty-Five days since we left Cuskushki [where] the Indians had met and sat in Council," he said he was carrying a written acceptance of peace. Pleased, Denny directed him on to Easton and the greatest treaty meeting to date. High expectations attracted a crowd of 500 Indians to the riverside town, where a multiple agenda of issues kept Pisquetomen from his ambassadorial moment for a week. But, when finally addressing the main officials at the "table," he recounted how he had carried Post "in my Bosom" to the Ohio, introduced him to the Indians there, "and . . . brought him back safe again." Then he laid on the table the Post-written document signed by 15 western chiefs, captains, and councilors. Its message was stunning: "We long for that Peace and Friendship we had Formerly."

Pisquetomen particularly faced three figures at the table: Teedyuscung, sachem of the eastern Delawares; Governor Denny, head of the civil authority; and (annoyingly to Denny), the unofficial but Indian-appreciated Quaker Israel Pemberton. Taking "each by the hand," the recently feared warrior "delivered a belt and three strings" of wampum. Apparently, protocol required that the string sent "by the Ohio Indians [for] Israel Pemberton" had to be officially handed to him "at the Table . . . by the Governor." The latter was heard to wisecrack "jocosely to those who sat next to him," regarding Pemberton, "I hope he will soon be favored with another string [rope], which he richly merits."

The fierce Lenape fighter now spoke words of peace: "Since I see you have digged up and revived that Friendship, which was buried in the Ground, now you have it, hold it fast." It was pleasing to him that, at this treaty, the land where he lived west of the Alleghenys was being withdrawn from the hated four-year-old Albany Purchase. But peace, he stressed, would not be fully confirmed until the English proclaimed it publicly, and sent more unmistakable, wampum-certified evidence of it to the Ohio community. That done, he promised, he would see that the news was "sent to the Ohio to assure an end to hostilities."

"I am glad," responded the Governor, "that you look friendly, and that there still remains some Sparks of Love toward us. It is what we believed before-hand, and therefore we never let slip the Chain of Friendship, but held it fast on our Side, and it has never dropped out of our Hands." He would indeed be sending a great belt of wampum to the Ohio Delawares as both a request to "dig up your end of the Chain of Friendship" that had been buried "by the Subtilty of the French," and an invitation "to come to Philadelphia, to your first old Council Fire, which was kindled when we first saw one another." That fire, at which Pisquetomen's uncle Sassoonan had sat in the children's half-moon before William Penn at Perkasie, and which had then not been under any overview from the Six Nations, would now be the place to "remove old Disputes, and renew the old and first Treaties of Friendship."

Heading quickly back to Allegheny with this offer, Post found the accompanying Pisquetomen, though faithful, still not sure that things were turning out all right. After all, their little embassy of peace was being paralleled by the westward march of more than 5,000 armed soldiers. Their General Forbes seemed to consider Post to be his agent to deflect the Allegheny Delawares from involvement in the upcoming assault on Fort Duquesne. They should "be kept at a Distance," Forbes wrote to them, so that they would "not be hurt by our Warriors, who are sent by our King to chastize the French, and not to hurt you." This message was put in the hands of Teedyuscung's son Captain Bull, who was traveling back west with the party of Post and Pisquetomen, which included another respected and moderate Delaware sachem named Isaac Still.

Along the way "Pesquitomen began to argue about lands again," journaled Post. It was, indeed, a singular expedition. Fearful because traveling to consult with the Forbes army took them through regions where he was remembered with horror, Pisquetomen, in his reversed position, was now begging Post to protect him "in his bosom." When they caught up with the main military forces rumbling westward, they found its officers amazed that Post could so successfully "bring the Indians to reason, using neither sword nor gun." General Forbes, now calling former enemy Pisquetomen "our brother," told him and Post to take greetings on ahead to Shingas and Tamaqua from "your assured brother, John Forbes." The irony of a general hoping for help from the diplomacy of a nonresistant Christian missionary could hardly have been lost on Post's little party, as, nearing the Kuskuskies, they were nightly serenaded by guns at Fort Duquesne, along with the "terrible music" of "the wolves."

What was the delegation's surprise when, arriving at the Kuskuskies, they found Tamaqua's village deserted, its warriors having gone out to fight against the approaching English. When those men returned and found Post there, most were angry over a (false) report that the missive he had carried east was really a secret request to General Forbes that after he had expelled the French he should call the Indians "to a treaty and then massacre them." Beyond this worry, noted Post, the Delawares, hearing that Forbes was now within 20 miles, "were afraid the English would come over the river Ohio" into their recently gained living space.

Isaac Still then sternly admonished the gathered Indians to understand that a firm peace had been established at Easton by 13 Indian "nations." But the listeners seemed "rebellious in heart" to Post, who wrote, "They concern themselves very much about the affair of land ... and are continually ... afraid the English will take their land." Only grudgingly, as the news of the peace offer from the east sank in, did the tide of opinion turn. Even as it did, the French sent over from Fort Duquesne a seductive string of wampum. But the mood having changed, the string was "kicked ... from one to another, as if it were a snake." Finally, on November 22, 1758, in anticipation "of their brethren, the English coming," the Indians "danced around the fire until midnight." When they heard the explosion by which the French blew up their fort, Post hung out the English flag, recognizing, with tears of his own, the reaction of the prisoners, folding their hands in sudden hope of deliverance.

Excitement or not, more patient process was needed. On the day General Forbes took over the abandoned, smoking ruins of Fort Duquesne, Shingas and Tamaqua came to Post with some 50 Natives to discuss further the momentous offer from Easton. Taking up the first of four strings of wampum he had brought, Post spoke in the idiom he had learned so well. "I by this string," he began,

> take a soft feather, and with that good oil, our grandfathers used, open and clear your ears, so that you may both hear and understand what your [English] brethren have to say to you. And by these strings, I clear your throat from the dust, and take all the bitterness out of your heart, and clear the passage from the heart to the throat, that you may speak freely with your brethren, the English, from the heart.

This was only the opening. Next, Isaac Still produced a calumet that had been sent along by Philadelphia Quakers (whom the Delawares trusted more than the government) out of concern that the conversation would succeed. This was the pipe, said Still, that "their grandfathers used to smoke when they met together in councils of peace." Only after this deliberate procedure by which "all had been duly prepared to hear and understand," did Post read off the Governor's answer to the letter brought to him by Pisquetomen. It was the official promise that the ancient chain of friendship was to be restored, confirmed by an accompanying "large white belt . . . having at each end the figure of a man, with streaks of black, representing the road from the Ohio to Philadelphia."

Post had to wait all day for the Indians' cautious answer. Though Tamaqua made a long speech, "nothing decisive was determined." Finally the latter simply told Post that he could go home, while he and Shingas would spread the offer of peace. While this was disappointingly underwhelming, other signs were favorable. As Post left he was pleasantly greeted by some Delaware "captains." Surprisingly, he recorded, "since I had taken so much pains in bringing a peace about between them and the English," they invited him to come and live among them. But while they wanted to "hear" from him "the word of God," they were at the same time "always afraid the English would take that opportunity to bring them into bondage."

Stopping at the ruined French fort, now dubbed "Fort Pittsburgh," Post learned that "a council with the Indians" had come to an agreement limiting to 200 the number of British soldiers they would permit to stay there. Even when this demand was angrily denied by a British official, the Indians told Post that it remained definitive. The English must now "speedily retire," insisted Pisquetomen, "to the other side of the mountains." Tamaqua's kinder words were, "Be pleased to hear me, and I would tell you, in a most soft, loving and friendly manner, to go back over the [Allegheny] mountain [range] and stay there." The Lenapes and Shawnees wanted no white settlement in the region.

Certainly an important peace had been negotiated, but it was a tentative one, containing seeds of future trouble. As Tamaqua and Shingas tried to stay positive, their older brother remained suspicious, and would soon fade out of the records. Pisquetomen's fears had not been trivial. Fort Pittsburgh was soon ten times larger than its French predecessor; within three years its Forbes-replacing Commandant Henri Bouquet would receive a tally of 162 houses, 221 men, 73 women, and 38 children in the fortified settlement. Soon there would be 50,000 white settlers west of the Alleghenys. Having left the Neshaminy and Perkiomen for the Schuylkill, then the Forks of the Susquehanna, and now the Allegheny, the Delawares were perforce starting again still farther west along the Muskingum River, a northern tributary of the Ohio. But even there—unlike German-

speaking plowboys picking up arrowheads along the Perkiomen—
they would find no abiding home.

CHAPTER THIRTY

Competing Narratives
1759–1762

Israel Pemberton's Quaker protégé Charles Thomson had been outraged by what he saw while clerking at the Easton treaty attempts. "Pains seem to have been taken," he observed, "to make Teedyuscung drunk every night since the business began" in order to render him "unfit to say anything worthy of being minuted by his own secretary." It was to place on record a fair account of the proceedings that the 30-year-old schoolmaster had written up an "Enquiry Into the Causes of the Alienation of the Delaware and Shawanese Indians from the British Interest." Much like the present book, this was a quotation-filled attempt to "collect into one view what relates to ... Lands" in order to show "whether there be any just Grounds" for the Delawares' complaints of "being cheated."

A copy of Thomson's manuscript sent quickly to London was read approvingly by Benjamin Franklin. Back in Philadelphia, however, the Penn brothers' secretary Richard Peters, who had refused to record Teedyuscung's most dramatic words, took an opposite view. His Penn clients in London predicted that Quakers would "publish in England" their opinion "that the Delawares wou'd never have taken up the hatchet ... if the Proprietors had done them justice." Those meddlesome do-gooders had "put arguments into [the Indians'] mouths," wrote Peters, and would be sure to edit the resulting Native's "speeches with their own corrupt glosses."

When dealing with competing narratives, "it may not be improper," as Thomson put it, to consider the sources drawn on. "The *Indians*," after all, had "no Writings, nor Records among them save their Memories and Belts of Wampum." Thus we "only have Recourse to the Minutes taken, and records kept, by one party." If there had been unfairness, those doing the recording would obviously not have been motivated "by minuting every Thing truly, to perpetuate their own disgrace."

Thomson claimed his own credentials as special. Once the Indians at Easton had sensed his sympathy, he had found himself "admitted into their council" and "deep into their politics," where he could "investigate their claims." In fact, he wrote, his "being by a solemn act adopted into their nation and called to assist in their councils" had given him authentic "knowledge of their internal policy, customs, and manners." In response, they had awarded him the name *Wegh-wu-law-mo-end* ("The man who tells the truth").

Franklin, finding the "Enquiry" well drawn up, called the "shocking" story "a Mixture of Madness, Folly and Knavery!" For him too, "obtaining Justice for the Indians" was "a Matter of the utmost Importance," which he believed could be obtained even while the Penn brothers in England were making "loud Declarations of their Innocence." Whereas they, in contrast to Thomson, blamed "all the Indian Complaints . . . on the Malice of the Quakers," Franklin was ready to have the "Enquiry" published immediately. This would be delayed, however, for a year, with readers proving generally divided according to their prior opinions.

Pemberton, who had by now been clerk of both the Philadelphia and New Jersey Quaker Yearly Meetings for a decade, continues at the center of our story. His sympathies were a continuation of those of his grandfather Phineas Pemberton, who had been a close friend and neighbor of William Penn at Pennsbury. Thoughts Phineas had expressed could relate equally to the historic mistreatment of Anabaptists and Quakers and what was now happening to the Lenapes. After all, as Phineas had put it, to have been "a despised people, in our native land, accounted by the world scarce worth to have a name or place therein" was the Quakers' own story. In fact, "We had not been a people at this day had not the Lord stood by us." Who, if not the Friends, would now stand by the land-losing Lenapes?

Phineas' grandson Israel was head of Philadelphia's Quaker school system, and the most influential representative of the majority Quaker presence in Pennsylvania's legislative Assembly, where he would be mocked by political enemies as "King of the Quakers." Though having withdrawn his actual membership from the Assembly, he still "took a great share," as Peters saw it, "in the conduct of all [its] matters, being much more hearkened to than he ought to be." While a strict pacifist, he could be overbearing in manner, and was anecdotally recalled as not averse to physically intimidating unruly persons. His tendency was to give Indians the benefit of the doubt, claiming that many of them had a clear sense of right and wrong, and when "treated with that Truth and friendship, which the principles of Christianity dictates," were "faithful and steady" friends and allies. If Quakers had charge of Indian affairs, he reasoned, the frontiers would stay peaceful.

Pemberton knew personally most of our story's main characters. The wampum brought specifically to him by Pisquetomen at Easton had been a clear reminder of his special standing with the Delawares. A few months later, Salford minister Andreas Ziegler's coming to see him in Philadelphia had begun a relationship that he called "well becoming both you [Mennonites] and us [Quakers] who cannot for conscience sake be assisting in carrying on of war." He was in conversation with missionary Christian Post, and likewise, in a commercial venture, in touch with General Forbes of the successful western military campaign. No sooner had he learned of the triumph at Fort Duquesne than he fired off a detailed order to London for a substantial shipment of goods for trade with the western Delawares, as well as for treaty gifts. They must be of good quality, he stipulated, and shipped immediately on two separate boats. He then hired and sent out to Fort Pittsburgh—increasingly known as "Fort Pitt"—a Quaker storekeeper with trade goods purchased with £1,500 donated by the Mennonites and Schwenkfelders, and £500 of his own money. As to the "present" such as expected by the Indians at any treaty, Pemberton wrote that he would leave it to General Forbes whether to identify it as coming officially "from the Government or from us as Trustees for the Menonists and Swingfelders." This was all moving too briskly for the Friendly Association, who demanded that he return to them the Mennonite-Schwenkfelder money, and run the Indian trade as a business with his own funds.

Pemberton sent wagons and pack horses rushing saddles, kettles, gridirons, hatchets, pipes, blankets, tobacco, and lead toward Fort Pitt, even using a sleigh to cross the frozen Susquehanna River. The point of both trade and presents was to get the Indians to return their prisoners, including the surprising minority of those whom the military had already rescued but were slipping back to their captors. It was taking considerable time to unify Indian opinion. In March 1759 it was reported that more than 1,500 Indians of various western regions had visited the Kuskuskies to hear the peace-advocating counsel of Tamaqua, Shingas, and Pisquetomen. Could these Turtle-tribe nephews of Alumapees, so soon after going violent in 1755-58, win the hearts of multiple Native "nations" back to their deceased uncle's peace-pipe tradition? Tamaqua's leadership indeed seemed to thrive initially with this proposal, but it was undermined by Indian suspicion and resentment toward the British refusal to withdraw from the scene of their victory.

Again, in July 1759, 500 Indians, well aware of Pemberton's wagon-loads of goods, attended a hoped-for treaty at Fort Pitt. Storekeeper James Kenny, dealing with Tamaqua, noted in his journal a very favorable impression of the headman. Older brother Pisquetomen, though, remained edgy. Two escaped young women prisoners reported their impression that he was "not hearty for the English." He himself asked Kenny pointedly why so many British soldiers were continuing around the fort that was being rebuilt on a scale well beyond that of the departed French. Quakers, of all people, he said, should tell the truth. When Kenny said he had heard nothing about the British staying, Pisquetomen could only hope he was right.

Tamaqua was growing in stature as a unifying voice for all three Delaware groups (Turtle, Turkey, and Wolf), and was trying to stay hopeful. "Ever since the Treaty at Easton," he told the Governor's delegation at Fort Pitt, "we have looked on the Peace to be Confirmed between you and us; And it gives us great Pleasure to see it now in a manner confirmed between you and all . . . the several [Indian] Nations to the sun-setting." In the friendly manner of his deceased uncle, Tamaqua spoke with Delaware authority, telling the officials, "I have brought with me some of your flesh and blood." While this amounted to only two prisoners, he made it as impressive as possible. "There they set," he pointed, evoking the emotional bond Indians made with captives by whom they replaced lost family members. "One is my Mother, the other my Sister. I deliver them up to you, in the presence of all here." But, "Do not think I am tired of them; no, I love them as well as I do my own Mother and Sister." And this relation was to endure after the women would be taken home by their white relatives. "Do not hide them," Tamaqua insisted; "When I go down, I shall Call and see them."

An added request was less endearing. Now that peace was being affirmed, stated Tamaqua, it was only appropriate that the Indians be given rum to celebrate. This was such a sensitive subject to the gathered Indians that when their young men heard Tamaqua's words translated, they burst into laughter that they could hardly stop. When the request was granted, the result was a predictable communal weeklong spree. Tamaqua's own son was now continually carrying rum from Fort Pitt to the Delawares' new village on the Muskingum.

For all the promising oratory, the prisoner-return had been only token-sized, and Indian satisfaction was minimal. At a smaller gathering at Fort Pitt in October 1759 Tamaqua reminded the officials of a promise that "the Indians of all Nations, should have Goods here as cheap as they were sold in Philadelphia." "Perform your Promises," he begged; "don't make me ashamed. At present Goods are dear here, on account of the great number of White Men; but I hope Goods will be sold at such Rates as will encourage all [the various Indian] Nations to come here and Trade."

While negotiating, Tamaqua admonished his Christian interlocutors, "God above has heard all; and I hope . . . that we will be able to convince each other of our sincerity." But could there be authentic interchange of thought between a people losing their land and another who were in the process of taking it? Haven't humans often recognized the phoniness of such an expectation? In this very week the oracular Samuel Johnson of London was reflecting, in his 81st weekly "Idler" essay, on the interwoven ironies of his English nation's protracted military struggle with the French to take over another people's homeland, and expecting those Natives to accept the logic of the scenario. "Some there are," Johnson had an imaginary Indian saying, "who boast their humanity, and content themselves to seize our [hunting grounds] and fisheries, who drive us from every tract of ground where fertility and pleasantness invite them to settle."

> Others pretend to have purchased a right of residence. Their treaties are only to deceive, and . . . defraud us. They have a written law among them, of which they boast, as derived from Him who made the earth and sea, and by which they profess to believe that man will be made happy when life shall forsake him. Why is not this law communicated to us? It is concealed because it is violated. For how can they preach it to an Indian nation, when I am told that one of its first precepts forbids them to do to others what they would not that others should do to them?

As to the English and French who "have now drawn their swords upon each other, and referred their claims to the decision of war," what more, wondered the London sage, is the claim of either nation than that "of the vulture to the [rabbit], of the tiger to the fawn?"

As no momentum grew toward a conclusive treaty, messenger Post wrote back from the Kuskuskies to Governor James Hamilton: "The [Natives] are more afraid of loosing their hunting ground than their lives." They suspected (correctly) that the diplomatic overtures were a "scheme to incroge [encroach] upon them." Another treaty attempt at Fort Pitt in April 1760, though again largely attended, included hardly any mention of the burning issue of prisoners. Tamaqua, showing up at every conference, kept hoping that "the ancient friendship" remembered by his family could be renewed, and "last to our latest generation," but he himself was not ready for a serious deal. Alluding to the persisting "French and Indian War," he observed that the Indians could still "see the bloody Hatchet in one of your Hands." Now that "we have buried ours," he continued, he was offering a belt to "take that Hatchet out of your Hand." If the English wanted to "turn the edge of it against [their] common enemy" (the French), they could "use it but I desire you may let us live in peace."

Israel Pemberton, following every turn, bristled with nongovernmental initiatives, vainly urging Pennsylvania's officials to set a boundary for the English settlements so that the Indians would "have a country left them sufficient for their support in their wandering way of living." He wrote to Bishop Benjamin Hershey in Lancaster County that Tamaqua's people would not negotiate "with men who were employ'd in war," and would enter into no serious discussion until they would meet "their old Brethren at their old Council fire at Philadelphia." Hearing from Kenny that now might "be a likely time to prevail" upon the western Delawares to accept schools, Pemberton used Friendly Association funds to encourage schoolteacher Post to make his home among the Delawares who, led by Tamaqua and his brothers, had moved west to the Muskingum watershed in Ohio. Following in their tracks, Post built a creekside cabin a mile upstream from Thomas Calhoun's trading post and the Lenape village of 40 wigwams. Optimistically traveling back to Bethlehem to look for help, Post hired a 19-year-old English Moravian cooper's apprentice named John Heckewelder. This devoutly imaginative man, who would eventually interpret the Lenapes' mindset to the reading public, was destined to become one of the Delawares' best white friends.

In early 1761 Pemberton was excited by a personal message (bypassing the Governor) from Tamaqua, promising to come to Philadelphia in the spring or summer with captives who would there be granted their release. Hardly able to wait, Pemberton suggested that if in the meantime any Indians were already willing to free their prisoners, "the full value" of their traveling expenses would be "immediately" paid by "the trustees of the fund raised by the Menonists."

Disappointingly, as fall arrived Tamaqua did not fulfil his promise. Instead, he led a party of Lenapes and Shawnees to Detroit for a meeting called by British Indian agent Sir William Johnson. Here Tamaqua's leadership of the Delawares flourished, as he called a council of his own, explaining to a variety of "nations" his preference for cooperating with the English rather than the French. Johnson, pleased at hearing of Tamaqua and Shingas spreading the peaceful news from Easton, presented them with an impressive wampum belt that depicted Delawares "holding fast the Chain of Friendship" by linking hands with western Indians to their left and "English" officials on the right. The compliment left Tamaqua feeling confident "that if we held this Chain of Friendship fast, our Children & Grandchildren should grow up and live to great Ages." He was in fact "so pleased" with the belt that he said, "We put it into our Hearts," and were ready at last to carry it east for a full treaty at his uncle Sassoonan's "Old Council Fire."

After the Detroit assembly, Tamaqua made a diplomatic visit to Fort Pitt. When his approaching company fired several rounds from across the river, he was "saluted with 5 cannon" from the fort. Here, too, he spoke powerfully to attentive Indians. "He seems," journaled Kenny, "like a steady, quiet middle-aged man of a cheerfull disposition, but low statu[r]e." Among the listeners was Teedyuscung, who, though too drunk to participate, told Tamaqua "that Pittsburgh was no place to hold Council [and] that the Old Fire was [at Philadelphia]. Pittsburgh was only a place for Warriors to speak in."

Finally, Tamaqua sent two men to talk to officials at Philadelphia "who have our Friendship"—the surest sign yet that there might be reconciliation. One of the messengers, laying down a wampum belt of ten rows, said that they had come east specifically to view the place of your Council Fire, where our old men and yours used to meet, and formerly sat and agreed together as brothers. I am very glad to find those Council Seats very clean, and the Fire burning clear; They look as they formerly did; Our old men [Shingas and Tamaqua] are now preparing to come again to visit you, and take their Seats with you at this Council Fire as they used to do.

Delighted, the Governor invited the Assembly to join him in celebrating the long-delayed treaty, but the following summer, as noted, brought no Allegheny delegation.

Tamaqua was also dealing with intra-Delaware issues. His influence among the Lenapes was being challenged by a leader named *Netawatwees*, called "Newcomer" by the English. The challenger was part of the Turkey clan, while Tamaqua belonged to the Turtle group. Tamaqua's leadership was also being questioned by *Custaloga*, a member of the third Lenape group: the Wolf clan of Munsees. And there was an even more influential Munsee figure, a seer named *Neolin*. In 1761 the latter experienced a powerful dream commanding him to draw the Delawares back from their fraternization with white people. Mixed with some values learned from the Moravians, such as sexual purity, Neolin's vision called for giving up not only the white culture's rum, but its selfish economy and technology (guns and gunpowder). In fact, he urged that the Europeans should be expelled from the Indians' homelands. If this were done, the dream promised a return to a life with game replenished in the woods and indigenous ways restored. Hundreds of Natives of various tribes, though not including Sassoonan's nephews, responded favorably to the "path to happiness" sketched by Neolin on a deer hide. In 1763 his vision would stoke a violent, treaty-ignoring, pan-Indian uprising from the Mississippi to the Great Lakes. This was in contrast to the pacifist vision of another Moravian-influenced Munsee, *Papunhank*, whose significance would be recognized in twenty-first century scholarship.

As both Governor Hamilton and merchant Pemberton were expecting a treaty at last, the Governor alerted the Assembly that there would need to be substantial "Provision" for both the expense of hosting the Indians and the traditional "present ... which, upon this Occasion, and after so long an Intermission, [will] undoubtedly be expected to be a liberal one." This was important to Pemberton, whose

Friendly Association had just received another contribution of £200 from "Menonists residing in the Counties of Philadelphia & Berks."

On March 11, 1762, the Governor noted that, since Philadelphia had a current fear of smallpox, he was inviting the Allegheny Delawares to meet him instead 70 miles westward in Lancaster. At this point Frederick Post, who had not yet returned to his Ohio cabin, was in touch with all of the principals in our story. On the evening of March 14 he showed up unexpectedly at the home of Henry Melchior Muhlenberg, son-in-law of the recently deceased Conrad Weiser, and pastor of the Lutheran church at Trap (later spelled "Trappe"), 20 miles north of Philadelphia. There was "a long discussion," recorded Muhlenberg, with this "honest Zinzendorfian agent, who is trying [to negotiate a treaty] with the Indians between Fort Pittsburg and Fort de Trois." Just as significant was Post's departing promise to Governor Hamilton that he would facilitate the western Delawares in their coming to Lancaster, and serve as their interpreter.

When Post and his assistant Heckewelder arrived at the Muskingum, Tamaqua engaged them in a lengthy discussion concerning the three-acre plot Post was clearing for a garden. The Indians were particularly sensitive on the topic, as they had observed that where English settlers planted extensively, forts and towns eventually followed. French priests from Detroit had needed only a little area to plant flowers, Tamaqua pointed out. Post should similarly limit his clearing to a half-acre. Warned by Post to keep his reading and writing hidden from the Indians, Heckewelder went into a steep learning curve. It was sharply clear that the Lenapes had their own divisions, especially as to which of three figures—Tamaqua, Delaware George, or Netawatwees—should lead a party to the upcoming treaty palaver at Lancaster. Even old Nemacolin, still smarting over his clan's loss of their Brandywine homes, wanted to go. But it was Tamaqua who, coached by Post, set out with a group of 25 "warriors" for the conference.

In these same weeks Teedyuscung came to Philadelphia in a puzzlingly expectant mood. While expecting to see Tamaqua and Shingas at Lancaster, he had received an invitation to yet another treaty at Easton, by Indian agent Johnson, for the specific purpose of finally clearing up the eastern Delawares' reiterated complaints of land fraud. Continuously in touch with Pemberton, the flamboyant chief had decided to turn down the Easton invitation, and brought his son Amos to tell this to a surprised Governor Hamilton. All in all, the boisterous eastern Delaware "king" had become less confident in his long-reiterated demands. Neither Pennsylvania officials, nor the powerful Six Nations controlling the territory north of the Lehigh Forks, were giving him what, with Pemberton's steady encouragement, he had been requesting for years: a permanent, guaranteed place for his people at Wyoming on the Susquehanna's North Branch. And now there was a new threat: settlers from Connecticut were appearing. "I sit here as a bird on a bough," lamented Teedyuscung, with no ground on which to safely alight with his people. Ten new houses built for his village by Quaker volunteers were no acceptable substitute for actual ownership of the land beneath them. Now Governor Hamilton, questioning Teedyuscung curiously in Philadelphia, elicited the surprising information that for a gift worth £400 the veteran complainer might be willing to close out his long-reiterated campaign.

A hundred Delawares were present at Easton in June 1762 when royal agent Johnson opened what would be a final and momentous treaty inquiry. Deeply suspicious of Israel Pemberton, who was once again in attendance, Johnson had been told by Peters of an Indian comment that "Governor Pemberton gives us everything, but Governor Denny has it not in his power to comply with any of our Demands." As the treaty began, Johnson noticed that Teedyuscung was "constantly nurs'd and Entertain'd at Pemberton's" lodging, and he knew that the Quakers had "a handsome sum" ready for presents which would "greatly influence the Indians in [their] favour."

Once again Teedyuscung (who had been drunk until Pemberton's arrival) demanded his own clerk, and asserted his original complaint of his people's loss of their land. Johnson replied that the only testimony necessary was a reading of his own official records of the disputed Walking Purchase deal—in untranslated English. At first Teedyuscung seemed to submit to the ensuing four-hour reading, but a day later, having consulted with Pemberton, he said he had understood nothing. At this a participant challenged Teedyuscung's honesty, which, in turn, made the watching Pemberton furious. Rising, Pemberton engaged in a face-off with Johnson, during which, it would be gossiped, the latter drew his sword, then closed the meeting.

The next day's parlay also proved abortive, but the session a day later was game changing. A clearly wearying Teedyuscung, sensing the weakening of Pemberton's pacifist vision in the face of the insistent Proprietary version of reality, and aware that a major gift would follow if he surrendered, suddenly withdrew his half-decade-old accusations of fraud. Concluding a long rambling speech, he put it baldly: "I did not come to put my hand in your purse or to get clothing. I give up the land to you and the white people." His resistance was broken. Though stiffly rehearsing his own people's grievance, he acknowledged that there might not have been conscious chicanery on the part of the Proprietors. They might simply have viewed matters in another light.

As the subdued Delaware "king" left Easton with gifts reportedly purchased with £1,200 from the Province and £300 from the Friendly Association, he could expect another set of rewards, along with those to be given to the western Delawares, at the forthcoming treaty conference at Lancaster. As for his Quaker advisors, they were mocked in Philadelphia as having been made fools of at Easton. But Israel Pemberton, who had not yet spent all the Mennonite money, was gearing up for another try.

CHAPTER THIRTY-ONE

"Our Hearts Are Good"
1762–1768

REMARKABLY FEW MEMORIES of Indians survived in Perkioma. There were reports of a lone Native repeatedly marking a grave in Franconia Township with a leaf of tobacco (subsequently smoked by a hired man on a Clemmer homestead). Descendants of the Prices on the Indian Creek continued to claim a Native grandmother whose people had brought them game in exchange for bread. Schwenkfelders recalled an Indian begging at a cider-making bee, showing with his fingers a desire for "only so much!" It would be claimed that Skippack's Henry Hunsicker, successor bishop to Andreas Ziegler, preached a funeral sermon for an Indian woman in Lower Salford as late as the year 1800. But only at the edges of the Mennonite diaspora—at Saucon, or even farther north where late-arriving Showalters and Basslers lived beside the Lehigh—would there be allusions to Natives visiting Mennonites as they met for worship. It would be from Moravians, not Mennonites, that future generations learned of Lenape contacts.

Trying to recover memories of the people our forebears supplanted on Perkiomen land reminds us that we have only bargain basement access to our own story, begun in Europe. Recent 300th anniversary celebrations of Lower and Upper Salford Townships produced only vague generalities regarding our Native predecessors, and there was no mention of where they had gone when they left this area. What, after all, is there to tell? That by 1760 the three-decades-old log meetinghouse on the Salford Heights of the Ruth homestead had been replaced by one built of stone? That half of the expense was contributed by farmer Peter Freed, doubtless a near relative of Jacob Clemens on the adjacent distillery farm? Deacon Jacob at least kept a ledger, recording payment for the new building's shingles and the congregation's contributions for the poor. It also shows that his wife Barbara bore an astonishing 19 children, greatly outpacing her sister-in-law at Johannes Clemens' neighboring mill on the Branch Creek. Of Barbara's and Jacob's three sons named for their father, only one lived beyond infancy, and not he but a brother, Gerhart, named for his immigrant grandfather, would inherit the homestead. Should our story note that the surviving namesake son reportedly suffered—like Sassoonan—from alcoholism?

This was a peaceful scene, where there had been no Indian attacks. In the improved schoolhouse a short walk from their father Jacob's distillery, the Clemens children were being taught three days a week by the aging Christopher Dock. By his own preference, the book-length manuscript for his *Schul-Ordnung* (School-Management), which Salford minister Dielman Kolb had encouraged him to write, remained unpublished pending his death—in fact it had been misplaced somewhere in Christopher Sauer's shop in Germantown. Meanwhile, Dock allowed the printer to publish his "Golden A.B.C." as a broadside, and, in Sauer's periodical *Geistliches Magazien*, "A Hundred Necessary Rules of Conduct for Children." Also in the *Magazien* appeared two "spiritually rich" hymns and an *Abschiedslied* (farewell song):

> My thread of life runs to its ending;
> My pilgrimage is nearly done.
> O God, a guide to me be sending,
> To guide my footsteps safely home,
> To help me hold the rudder sure,
> When life's last storm I must endure.

More distinctly than any memory of the departed Lenapes, the pietist Dockian resonance left an impression in communal lore. It would be gossiped that the old schoolmaster could not be provoked to anger. He had told printer Sauer not to worry about his missing Schul-Ordnung manuscript. He had declined to wear linsey-woolsey because such mixing was forbidden in the Old Testament books of Leviticus and Deuteronomy. In his final will, witnessed by "Both Honest Mans" Andreas Ziegler and prospering Friedrich Altdörfer, Dock had requested that there be no "Publick Vandue" of the 100-acre Upper Salford property, "blessed with water, good Meddowe and other good opportunity," for which he had paid the family of William Penn. His sons-in-law were to have "no power to spoil any green Woods, Except to Reform the Fence." It would be claimed that the devout preceptor died on his knees in prayer for his pupils in the meetinghouse-schoolhouse at Skippack.

Another will and testament ruling out the traditional "vendu" was composed by the equally spiritual but more economically prosperous Bishop Henrich Funck, whose family had now flourished for decades along the Indian Creek. Unlike his ancestors in Zurich, Henrich had been able to labor peacefully in his mill upstream from the Prices, with three of his sons (one also a bishop) succeeding in mills of their own. He had authored two books and sponsored two more: a reprinting of his people's hymnal, and a translation of their vast martyr story. Now, as a widower confessing "that we have no abiding place in this sorrowful world," he wrote with Anabaptist scrupulosity that it fell "heavily" on him "to see how to order all things rightly." He devoted twice as much language in his will to daughter Esther ("lame in all her limbs") than he did addressing bequests to his other eight children. Supported with a larger allocation of funds than bequeathed to her siblings, Esther was to be cared for "in sickness and in health, with meat and drink, and lodging, and . . . kept clean in washing and mending her clothing and bedding, and . . . kept clean of lice and other vermin, as also of all other uncleanliness." This responsibility was not to be taken lightly. "I do fully authorize [the deacons] to call my executors to account," wrote Henrich, to ensure that his daughter had "a good place" and her bills were paid. Finally, though scruples had deterred him from seeking citizenship in his adopted Pennsylvania, and he was now trusting that everything might be "made and finished in accordance with brotherly love, Christian forbearance and righteousness," the ailing bishop acknowledged a role for secular order: if anyone accountable to the conditions set forth in the will proved "disobedient," it would "be well to make use of the instituted law against them."

It is from such scattered threads, devoid of Indian references, that we attempt to weave a realistic narrative of Perkioma's first half-century of the post-Lenape era. A little texture is offered by Sauer's renamed periodical, the *Pennsylvanische Berichte*. Where but in its homely columns would Georg Wägele, purchaser of some of the Clemens acreage, announce that, as he and his wife had separated, he would no longer pay bills that she incurred? Where else would fence-disputing Friedrich Götz advertise that someone's bag of feathers had been mistakenly deposited in his market wagon? Or where else could we read that a local indentured servant named Christian Denk had disappeared with his family without paying his debts? Where else could miller Johannes Clemens and his brother-in-law Valentine Kratz post notices of unaccountable additions to their cattle herds—in Valentine's case a black cow, and in John's, a little horse with "a white star on the front of its head and a bell on, with a mark like IDM and also an IR in a heart"? And who but a righteous Sauer would notify readers that a "neger" (slave) in Germantown—despondent over having been stolen from his home country, and saying he would rejoin his wife and children—had been found hanged with his pockets stuffed with apples?

How unscripturally rare are any memory-haunting details in the picture left behind by Salford's Mennonite pioneers! Could there not have been one pen to describe for their descendants the genial hubbub of an *Uffblucka* (raising of a log building) along the Indian Creek, or of a communal field-grubbing, a hay-mowing, a fall apple-schnitzing or cider-making? Is it a spiritual virtue to have left behind only a washed-out picture of one's generation? Why was there no diary entry to evoke the twang of miller Clemens' zither, or his neighbor Henrich Ruth's "dulcimar"? And why are we left with no evocation of the atmosphere of even so important a *fasammling* as when, in May 1762, Salford's minister Andreas Ziegler was made bishop in the place of the deceased Henrich Funck? What irony, when compared with how we can be taken intimately into the ambience of a Lenape funeral!

In the spring of 1762, with tensions still delaying a return of prisoners held captive by the Indians, there was worrisome talk in Pittsburgh (the burgeoning settlement including Fort Pitt) from a trader named Thomas Kinton. He had known the Indians at nearby Kittanning before the town's destruction in 1756, and recalled that when they had "found a Rat and Kill'd it," the rodent foreign to their culture had prompted the old men to predict that they were about to lose their land to either the French or the English. They reasoned thus because such a fate had been foreseen by "their Grandfathers on finding a Rat on Delaware before the White People came there." Similar persistence of Native memory was impressing missionary Christian Post's assistant John Heckewelder, living 60 miles to the west among Lenapes on the Muskingum. One of the Indians there claimed to have lived as a boy "where the first house in Philadelphia was being built," and had "assisted in furnishing the workmen with fish, and caught rabbits for them."

Heckewelder sensed that the Lenapes along the Muskingum tributary known as *Tuscarawas* liked him better than they did his employer Post, who had directed the teenager to work among the Indians. The Lenapes honored Heckewelder with the name *Piselatulpe*, the Unami word for "turtle," the very symbol of their tribe. The young missionary grew especially close to Shingas, the diminutive old chief with wire-distended ears and nose disfigured from a drunken brawl. Though notorious for savagery in warfare, Shingas had another side, and was now reportedly showing white people "the Most Kindness & generosity of all the Indians thereabouts." He had prevented the standard torture of a prisoner from the Great Cove by recalling that the man had always treated passing Indians with hospitality. Once, when Shingas noticed Heckewelder watching two young prisoners "amusing themselves" with two of the old man's native-born sons, he asked what the young white man was thinking. Simply "Looking at his prisoners," answered Heckewelder. To this Shingas responded, "When I first took them, they were such; but now they and my children eat their food from the same bowl or dish." This was "equivalent," in Heckewelder's understanding, to saying that the white prisoner boys "were in all respects on an equal footing with his own children or alike dear to him."

Such cordial conversation was not enough to keep Heckewelder from feeling a mounting resentment in other Delawares toward his presence. He made a canoe to haul game and bring cedar wood down the river to make tubs for the Indians, but it was soon stolen. In April 1762 he was left alone on the Tuscarawas as Post accompanied Tamaqua and two dozen Delawares to the forthcoming treaty at Lancaster. Shingas had been expected there, too, but declined to go out of fear of revenge. He was thus at home when his wife caught a sudden fever and died. What followed was a memorable experience for Heckewelder, proving to him that, though the Delawares had moved five times in the previous half-century, their culture was still intact.

With women crying all day long, "She is no more!" the young missionary assistant found himself asked to serve as a pallbearer with trader Thomas Calhoun. He took careful notes, describing the body, laid out in a coffin provided by Calhoun, dressed in new clothes covered with rows of silver ornaments and wampum.

Her scarlet leggings were decorated with different coloured ribbands sewed on, the outer edges being finished off with small beads also of various colours. Her mocksens were ornamented with the most striking figures, wrought on the leather with coloured porcupine quills, on the borders of which, round the ankles, were fastened a number of small round silver bells, of about the size of a musket ball.

Together with vermillion face paint, it all struck the young white observer as an attempt to "set her off in the highest style . . . in such a manner, that perhaps nothing of the kind could exceed it."

Gifts were placed around the body: "a new shirt, a dressed deer skin for shoes, a pair of scissors, needles, thread, a knife, pewter basin and spoon," and other trinkets. Then a lid with a hole for the spirit's egress was fastened, and the pallbearers summoned. "Mr. Calhoun and myself were placed at the foremost pole, two women at the middle, and two men . . . in the rear," Heckewelder recorded. With women still wailing, Shingas walked near the coffin, followed by his warriors, and then everyone else. Last came two strong men carrying loads of European-made goods from Calhoun's store. When the procession reached the place of burial 200 yards distant, the coffin lid was lifted and the large crowd seated itself in a half-moon configuration, with Heckewelder and Calhoun given a place of honor. Shingas sat by himself, "weeping with his head bowed to the ground."

For more than two hours, only occasional sighs and sobs broke the silence. Finally, about an hour after noon, six men stepped forward to lower the coffin into the ground. Several women suddenly rushed between the men and the casket, grabbed the corpse by its limbs, and began calling to their deceased friend, "Don't leave us! Come with us!" After 15 minutes they sat down again, still crying and plucking distractedly at the grass, as the men lowered the coffin, laid two poles over it lengthwise, and stepped away. Shingas then approached slowly, stepped onto the poles, walked over the grave, and continued far enough onward that he could not hear what was happening as the grave was closed and marked with a post.

By now it was about two o'clock, and, with a thunderstorm brewing, Heckewelder wanted to leave. But the Indians fashioned a little shelter for him and Calhoun, and after the rain stopped, the gathering was served with food that had been cooked nearby. Finally the mood turned festive, as everyone—from the oldest to the youngest—received a gift. The little girls got small items such as gartering, tape, needles, or beads;

> the older ones received a pair of scissors, needles and thread, and a yard or two of riband. The boys had a knife, Jews-harp, awl blades, or something of similar value. Some of the grown persons received a new suit of clothes, consisting of a blanket, shirt, breech-cloth and leggings, of the value in the whole of about eight dollars; and the women, (I mean those who had rendered essential services) a blanket, ruffled shirts, stroud and leggings, the whole worth from ten to twelve dollars.

Calhoun, from whom most of the goods had been purchased, estimated their total worth at $200 (equivalent to $4,800 in 2021). Heckewelder himself received a silk cravat or handkerchief and a pair of leggings. Deeply touched by the six-hour ceremony, he recorded that the Indians placed a kettle of food on the grave every evening for the next three weeks.

Thus, in the thick of the currently swirling suspicions, the young Moravian missionary assistant had begun to build a personal, lifelong bridge of interracial understanding all too rare in the story of America. Looking back as an old man, he would recall often observing "with emotion" a "remarkable delicacy" in Native attitudes, which, as he put it, "does honour to their hearts, and shews that they are naturally accessible to the tenderest feelings of humanity."

While Shingas had stayed behind, his brother Tamaqua and missionary Post were on their way east with a set of prisoners to be returned. Headmen Netawatwees of the Turtle tribe and Custaloga of the Wolf tribe, having disagreed with Tamaqua over too easy a surrendering of the prisoners, had sent delegates, but did not go themselves. The journey itself was troubled. The two dozen Delaware men accompanying the prisoners, unhappy to see Post at the head of their party, were hoping to "deliver" him "to the Governor & tell him to keep him at home." Post "had much ado to keep them from Liquor, because they would absolutely have it." There were delays when horses strayed. At Carlisle, people crowding around to gaze at the prisoners gave the Indians enough liquor to make them "very drunk" and, much to Tamaqua's displeasure, "carried one of the prisoners off in the night."

When the group stopped at Harrisburg on the Susquehanna, they were surprised to meet several Senecas bringing wampum from the Six Nations to what the Delawares had expected to be their own conference. Waiting at Lancaster were not only Governor James Hamilton, but Israel Pemberton, whose ability to give more "presents" to the Indians from the Friendly Association had been strengthened by recent Mennonite contributions. Not until August 9, four months after the Delawares' departure from the Tuscarawas, was the Governor notified that Tamaqua and his delegation of half a dozen "nations," encamped outside of town, were ready to talk. Tamaqua was requesting that, since the Delawares had been the "first invited" to the treaty session, they were now to be addressed "without waiting any longer for the *Six Nations*." In response, the Governor came out and "took them by the Hand"—a war-cancelling gesture to stir echoes of William Penn and Tamany at Perkasie. The old dream of shared peace was not dead! Returning after a few days with wampum, Hamilton spoke in the familiar Native mode: "With this String I clean your Bodies from the Dust and Sweat, and open your Eyes and Ears, that you may see your Brethren with Chearfulness, and hear distinctly what I have to say.... I open the Passage to your Hearts, that you may speak freely . . . as Brethren ought to do."

Tamaqua's responding speech was equally friendly. We can hear in it the persistent dream of a longed-for alternative to the breakdown of human relationship. "When our Grandfathers used to meet our Brethren," said this peaceful nephew of Sassoonan, "they cleansed each other's Hearts & took away all Grief & Sorrow out of them." He knew, of course, that what was chiefly on the Governor's mind was anxiety for the return of prisoners. He admitted that though 17 of them had been brought, there were "some behind yet," who "chuse to stay with us" because they "meet with good Usage, and live as we do." In any case, Tamaqua had come to make peace. "Now, Brother," he urged, "let us join heartily & put our hands together to put away the Cloud"

> so that our Children and Grand Children when they meet may rejoice to see one another, and live to great Ages in

peace. We see plainly that good Road which our Grandfathers used when they travelled to your Council Fire [at Philadelphia], to consult about our Affairs when we lived in Friendship. We will join with you to keep that Road open and good. I assure you it was never yet quite Stopt up; We find our old Council Fire, which our Grandfathers made, is still burning; Now, by this Belt, I collect dry Wood to put to the Fire and make it bigger, so that the smoke may rise to the Skies; when other [Indian] Nations see it they will know by the light that I have been in Council with my Brethren.

Further, Tamaqua hoped for mutual respect. "When any of our Brothers, the English, come amongst us," he said, "we always take pity on them, and give them Victuals, to make their Bodies Strong, and we desire that you will do the same to such of us as come amongst you, or live with you."

When Tamaqua concluded his speech, the Governor approached the seated prisoners "and received them, one by one, from the hands of King Beaver" (Tamaqua). Among the released captives listed on this occasion were a "Holtemen" and a "Studebecker."

Several days later, this time with Teedyuscung present, the Governor wanted a specific response from Tamaqua's delegation. Calling them "Brethren of *Allegheny*," he said, "As we are Face to Face, be plain and tell whether you are satisfied with, and approve of, what was done at the last Treaty at *Easton*, and whether you lay any Claim to those lands." Tamaqua was crisp: "I know nothing about the Lands upon the Delaware, & I have no concern with Lands upon that river." Whatever the Governor and Teedyuscung had agreed to at Easton was acceptable. In fact, Tamaqua wanted to "say nothing about Land Affairs." What he had "at heart," and had come to the meeting for, was "to confirm our Friendship, & make a lasting peace, so that our Children & Grandchildren may live together in everlasting peace after we are dead." Gratified, the Governor responded, "You speak like an honest Man, and I hope that the Friendship that has been made between us ... will remain firm, as long as the Sun shines, and the Rivers run."

On the day set for ceremonial gift giving, the Delawares came into town to see the presents laid out in the brewery of John Hambright. Governor Hamilton began by telling Tamaqua of his "Orders" from the Penn brothers "to make a Present of considerable Value to the *Delaware Indians*" as soon as the Walking Purchase dispute "could be ended, and the Proprietaries Characters cleared." With Israel Pemberton looking on, Hamilton continued, "The good People of the Province have been pleased to make an Addition, of Equal Value." It was all "to be equally divided between you, as a Proof of the Regard, both of the Proprietaries and People, for their old Friends, the *Delaware* Nation." And with that, the Governor meant to close by wishing that "the Peace and Friendship, which have been renewed betwixt us at the Treaty, may continue and grow stronger, as long as the Sun shall shine, or the Rivers run." But the session proved not quite over, as Teedyuscung stood up to state that since he had deliberately given up "all claim to the Lands on the River Delaware" at Easton, it was now Tamaqua's responsibility to make this very clear to the western Lenapes. Then, turning to the Governor, the long-complaining eastern sachem was equally explicit: "Our Children and Grandchildren shall never be able to say hereafter, that they have any Right or Claim to the Lands that have been in Dispute upon that River."

The deal was done. The Governor delivered to Tamaqua and Teedyuscung "respectively *Two Hundred Pounds*, in milled Dollars, and the Value of Four Hundred Pounds in Goods, to be equally divided between them." And there was more, apparently from the Friendly Association: for "*Beaver*, and those who came with him from the *Ohio*, the Value of *Four Hundred Pounds in Goods*," and for "*Teedyuscung*, and his Friends and People . . . the Value of *Two Hundred Pounds in Goods*." This bounty was to be distributed, admonished the Governor, "in the most just and equitable Manner." Giving too much "to their young Men" might tempt them, "instead of laying it out in Things necessary and useful, . . . to debauch themselves with strong Liquors." Such an endangering of the Chain of Friendship "would be a very ungrateful Return for all the Kindness we had shewn them." Finally, the Governor took both Tamaqua and Teedyuscung "by the hand" and the conference was over.

It would be gratifying to record that this long-sought reconciling at Lancaster was an important turning point in our story. But, disappointingly, as the Delawares returned toward Ohio, Pittsburgh's storekeeper James Kenny found them generally dissatisfied, their unequally distributed treaty gifts already "mostly lost." Trader George Croghan reported that they had been "Robd of almost all their horses and other things." The returning Post, too, after having been away for

15 weeks, was disappointed to meet his assistant Heckewelder fleeing eastward with the report that he had been warned by friendly Indians on the Tuscarawas that it was too dangerous for him to remain there. Post himself, arriving at his lonely cabin, found his garden ruined and the Natives giving him "small hope of being Alowed to Plant anything next Spring." By mid-December he also gave up and headed back east.

Eight decades had passed since Penn, bringing presents to Perkasie, had been offered land as a gift. The "canticos" the Proprietor heard appreciatively on that occasion celebrated a promise of Natives and English being "brethren." By comparison, the gift-based prisoner interchange at Lancaster came off as a swan song. The technology of the European immigrants' diplomatic gifts would only serve to further separate the Indians from their indigenous relation to the land. What had happened at Lancaster was not the renewing, but a last flickering of the old council fire.

Despite Tamaqua's continued attempts to inspire his people with his deceased uncle's dream of peace, Lenape leadership shifted from the Turtle tribe to the Turkey tribe and to the Wolf tribe's Custaloga and Neolin. Tamaqua invited Teedyuscung and the now aged Nutimus to move west to the Muskingum, but received no response. The resentment among starving Delawares and Shawnees was rising toward Sir Jeffery Amherst, the British officer now in charge of Fort Pitt. Unwisely confident that he controlled a defeated people, and dead set against the idea of presents (which he considered "bribery"), Amherst raised the prices of trade goods, and denied the sale of guns and gunpowder. In response, as traders cheated, the increasingly sullen Indians stole. The concept of "trade" being the medium of coexistence between white and indigenous people did not account for the instinctive generosity that had charmed William Penn at Perkasie. And Tamaqua, unlike his predecessors Sassoonan and Tamany, lacked sufficient respect from some of his own people to restore a working relationship with the British authorities.

The Natives were shocked to learn that a treaty concluded in Paris on February 10, 1763, ended the Seven Years' War and ceded all of North America to Great Britain. Netawatwees, it was said, was rendered speechless for a time. Now that the Indians could no longer play off the claims of one European nation against the other, their fear of advancing English settlement spiked. In April a Neolin-inspired leader named *Pontiac* called a war council, and by fall Native raids similar to those of 1755-57 had killed or taken prisoner more than 600 settlers.

Tamaqua did not favor the renewal of conflict, and kindly warned traders to move out from the Muskingum. Perplexed as he might be over the aggressively continuous white settlement, he could not forget what he called "the Friendship that formerly Subsisted between our Grandfathers and the English." Only months earlier, when his people had been offered "Peace" by the English King, they had "Joined it heartily and Desired to hold it always good." But diplomatic talk was losing its appeal, as was his leadership. Storekeeper Kenny heard Indians complain that Tamaqua had really been made king more by the Virginia speculators than by his own Lenape people. His peace initiative was flagging.

Our 120-year, four-generation-long story will not close on a cheerful note. Eight months after the Lancaster treaty, as "Pontiac's War" was getting underway, the Quakers' Friendly Association was dissolved in Philadelphia. A reckoning drawn up on April 19, 1763, noted that all but £30 of the last £260 collected had been "Contributed by the Menonists." Might this mean that money from Salford, Franconia, and Skippack had helped to pay off Teedyuscung? Incredibly, the latter died on the day that reckoning was completed. He was lying in a drunken sleep at Wyoming when his home and the other Quaker-built houses in the village were torched, presumably by land-hungry Connecticut settlers. The 1758 Easton treaty had not, after all, quieted all land issues. Before the year was out, the arsonist "Yankees" would themselves be murdered by Teedyuscung's avenging son.

Out in Ohio, Lenapes and Shawnees sent Pontiac a supportive war belt, asking for help to avenge their loss of Kittanning and the recent death of Teedyuscung. Within weeks the violence increased from the Great Lakes to Virginia. All the recently built forts except those at Pittsburgh, Ligonier, and Bedford fell to the Indian attackers. By June 1763 Pittsburgh was jammed with over 500 safety-seeking settlers, some of whom showed symptoms of smallpox. "Every hour," wrote a terrified inhabitant, "we hear of scalping." General Amherst, in charge of Fort Pitt, wrote that it was necessary to use "every strategy in our power" to "reduce" the attacking Indians. Colonel Henri Bouquet agreed: "I wish we could . . . hunt them with English Dogs . . . who would I think effectively extirpate or remove that Vermine."

Tamaqua and Shingas approached the settlement with offers of a cease-fire, but were turned away, and when two more Delawares came to discuss a possible peace, they were given a gift of "Blankets and a Handkerchief out of the Small Pox hospital," with the "hope" it would "have the desired effect." We may wonder whether this had anything to do with the death of Shingas shortly thereafter.

The remaining months of 1763 were tumultuous and frightening. In Lancaster, where Bouquet was planning a campaign to subdue the "Allegheny" Natives, fear arose among the area's last 20 resident Conestoga Indians in their village beside wealthy Abraham Herr's farm. "Michael" and "Mary," a Lenape couple living with the Conestogas, were so alarmed that they moved to a hut on the farm of Mennonite Christian Hershey near Manheim. That summer Bouquet led a force that defeated Indians at Bushy Run near Pittsburgh. At Wyoming, a son of Teedyuscung avenged his father's death, torturing, killing, and roasting ten New England settlers. As consternation mounted in Lancaster County, Michael and Mary were allowed to hide in the Hersheys' large arched cellar. The impoverished and frightened Conestogas, hearing that a new Governor, John Penn (son of Richard), had arrived in Philadelphia, sent off to him a quick welcome and appeal for clothing. But before it could be read in Council, a gang of irate "Paxton Boys" rode into the Conestogas' village and clubbed to death the six Natives they were able to find. Foragers would later discover in the victims' huts cherished documents that included one signed by William Penn in 1701. The 14 Conestogas who happened to be away selling basketry when the attack occurred were quickly rounded up and placed in the Lancaster jail for their own protection. But the Scotch-Irish patriots got to them, nonetheless, and smashed their skulls. The corpses, taken to the nearby farm of Mennonite Valentine Metzler, were "thrown on top of one another in a hole, without a blanket or cover, like a dog."

This was Pennsylvania? This was chaos, and it would continue. Even if the Natives had heard that the King of England, victorious over the French, had proclaimed a dividing line to "reserve" for "the Use of the . . . *Indians*, all the Lands and Territories" west of the Appalachians, it would have made no difference in their future. For though the "Proclamation" ordered any settlers already in the west to relocate, the surge could not be stopped. In less than a decade there would be 50,000 white settlers west of the Appalachians.

Tamaqua continued to hope for a restoration of peace, but Pontiac's War worsened to the point that Governor Penn offered rewards for Indian scalps. Hundreds of settlers had been captured and never heard from again. Tamaqua's tribe had returned only some of their prisoners. In order to rescue the others, and subdue the still rebellious western Indians, recently successful Colonel Bouquet set out for the Muskingum in October 1764 with a force of nearly 1,500 men. Though preferring to avoid battle, the Colonel had every intention of destroying the Indian villages—especially those of the Lenapes and Senecas—unless they surrendered and agreed to all of his demands.

The Indians quickly saw that their only option was cooperation. Tamaqua, who retained enough leadership to claim that he spoke "in behalf of the chiefs, warriors, women and children of our tribes," told Bouquet that they were "all glad to embrace peace once more with their brethren." Presenting 13 prisoners who, he claimed, were "the last we have remaining in our tribes," the sachem also known as "King Beaver" thanked God for "the opportunity to take [Bouquet] by the hand in peace, which shall never more be broken on our side. Our young men shall now think of nothing but hunting, to exchange their Skins and Furs with their brethren for Cloathing." When Bouquet then allowed 12 days for the return of all captives, over 200 were brought in, most of them welcoming their release, though a few did everything they could to escape Bouquet's grasp.

Aged and reportedly soon to be baptized by the Moravian missionaries, Tamaqua could now imagine an era of peace restored. But bloody incidents persisted, with blame for both sides. A murder committed by several white men prompted Governor Penn to send two apologizing "commissioners" to Pittsburgh in the spring of 1768. Among the more than 1,100 Natives who showed up were 13 Delaware "chiefs," led by Tamaqua. Speaking for "the old men of the different nations present," King Beaver could still say, "We the Delawares, Shawanese, Munsies, Mohickons, Wyandotts and our uncles, the Six Nations, will keep fast hold of the chain of friendship." Presenting a belt of wampum, he declared, "We . . . desire the Governor will take hold of the end of this belt, which we stretch along the road between him and us, in order to clear it of the briars and brush that have grown up in it, that we may all travel it in peace and safety." His rhetoric grew earnest: "When you consider our speeches, you will find that our hearts are good, and that we are determined to preserve the road of peace free from any interruption on our parts. We desire that you will take the same care on your parts."

The very last words of Tamaqua available for our story, recorded at a small "private Conference" following the larger assembly, touched on three topics of increasing weight. "We have laid to our hearts," he acknowledged, the Governor's complaints about "the folly of our young people in stealing your horses." At the same time, it was only right for him to be reminded that white "young people" were "frequently" guilty of the same behavior. More serious was the topic of trade prices—a matter Sassoonan had politely brought to Philadelphia in his first years as a headman. Now, 56 years later, his nephew Tamaqua was still both concerned and courteous. While the Lenapes would not suspiciously inquire how much "the traders who supply us with goods" had paid for them wholesale, it was worryingly evident "that they do not allow us the same price for our skins and furs as they did formerly." The Governor should therefore "speak to them to allow us a sufficient price for our peltry."

The third topic, though given the fewest words, was the weightiest. Tamaqua's words on it link our story's final chapter with the moment in its first when his uncle, as a "little lad," had observed his predecessor Tamany negotiating at Perkasie with William Penn. "Brethren," came Tamaqua's concluding plea, "The country lying between this river and the Allegheny mountains has always been our hunting ground." But just as by the Perkiomen and Neshaminy, then at Brandywine, Tulpehocken, Shamokin, Kittanning, and the Beaver Creek, and now along the Tuscarawas, "the white people who have scattered themselves over it, have, by their hunting, deprived us of the game, which we look upon ourselves to have the only right to." Governor Penn, grandson of the great William, should "prevent" this "for the future." The fundamental question of the Lenape story was still, and would continue to be: having given up their homeland, on what other land could the Original People live?

Tamaqua is believed to have been baptized by the Moravians before he died in 1770. As the Lenape story continued, the three phratries—Turtle, Turkey, and Wolf—would experience a coalescing of their "Delaware" peoplehood. Nearly a century of sequential displacements would take them to Indiana, Missouri, Kansas, and many of them, in the 1860s, to "Indian Territory." In the twenty-first century, some 11,000 descendants of Pennsylvania Delawares would be living in eastern Oklahoma. By then, though they had forgotten many of the Lenape place names in the Delaware Valley, the people living there were still pronouncing them. Several, spelled *Bergosen*, *Matetchen*, *Sackem*, and *Skiepak* in a 1773 bishops' report, had become the names of Mennonite congregations. *Lehay* (Lehigh), where Lappowinzo had lived, was on the list. Even the phonetically spelled "Term" (Durham) showed that there was a Mennonite cluster (Springfield) where Nutimus had sold land to James Logan. Of course, until the English language would take over daily discourse in the 1930s, the familiar indigenous names would be colored by Palatine accents: Bargeyoma, Domencin, Guschehuppa, Madetchty, Schibbach, Sacona.

Whether among the "Dutch" of Perkioma or the Welsh of Neshaminy, memory of the departed Lenapes faded early. In 1831 the language of Baptist minister Joseph Mathias, born in Hilltown in 1778, was unspecific, describing the Lenapes as having been "generally peaceable, obliging and kind as neighbours." As the land was cleared, "these sons of the forest [had] peaceably migrated to seek new hunting grounds." Sometimes returning to visit their native scene, they had resided "with little molestation on large tracts of timberland, and along the streams of water, in wigwams, employing themselves in hunting, in fishing, in cultivating small lots with Indian corn, and in making and selling baskets and brooms."

In the late twentieth century, the region's remaining farmers could still point out slopes yielding "arrowheads." But only a few local residents had stories to tell. Raconteur Isaac Clarence Kulp had heard of an Indian appearing in this community around the time of the Civil War, asking about a "white grandfather" along the Indian Creek. Someone showed him the Price homestead, but no other hospitality was offered before the visitor turned to walk back home. At Gratersford on the Perkiomen the name "Abraham Trees" was still legible on a gravestone dated 1866. In 1975 Isaac Clarence Kulp's neighbor Titus Derstine remembered that when he had plowed along Hackman Run in Franconia Township, one of the horses' front legs plunged into the ground up to the shoulder. That, Titus was reminded, was just where neighbor Henry Hagey had marked on a map: "Indian Grave."

EPILOGUE

This Has Been a Musing

THE ORDER in which we receive the stories by which we make sense of life is neither chronological nor rational. I was 82 before my thinking about my predecessors on this land was refocused by an angry Indigenous recollection of the Walking Purchase of 1737.

I had told my first tale publicly at the age of ten. After wandering away from fourth grade classmates on a visit to the Philadelphia Zoo, I was being protectively held in a house on the grounds. I did not know that this was a retreat named "Solitude," built on the banks of the Schuylkill River by a grandson of William Penn, and the story I told was not true. As a bat, fluttering about the ceiling, awakened among good-humored attendants a lively banter, I made a baseless folk-style claim that the creature had gotten into my hair. I was only trying to contribute to the fun, and immediately felt an exaggerator's remorse. Persisting over the years, it has kept me wary against any fiction creeping into my present three-stranded story.

At a family reunion in my 30s I stood beside the Indian Creek—in a field from which a neighbor had harvested many "Indian" stone artifacts—to offer a story of our departed grandfather Abram Landis. A wonderfully kind, humble farmer, he deserved commendation, and I did my storytelling best. To illustrate his patience, I recounted his taking me along in a truck to fetch a calf from a neighboring farm. When the poor slaughter-destined creature, lurching behind the driver's seat, deposited the contents of its bowels down the back of my grandfather's neck, he had been so . . . And all of a sudden I realized that the story I was telling to illustrate the old man's patient character was false. It was surely not his patience but his vehement disgust that had seated the incident in my memory! I looked at my audience with horror. I was lying to them, even when I had only meant well. Should I stop in midstory and say, "Sorry, this was all an illusion," leaving my listeners confused? Hardly. After all, our grandfather *was* a genuinely patient man. And while the facts of my story were false, the point I was making was true!

In 1980 a film project took me from Philadelphia to Paraguay. There I watched "Indians" clearing fields near the town of Filadelfia, founded in 1930 by Mennonite refugees from communist Russia. Desperately poor Paraguay was the only country that would then accept such resourceless immigrants. They must not have seemed like a threat to the indigenous people living there in abject poverty, since, instead of moving away from their infiltrated homeland (as had "our Lenappys" of 1709), they clustered permanently around the white newcomers.

Fifty years later, I observed Paraguayan Natives clearing acreage that Mennonites had only recently "given" them in the colony of Fernheim. After a group of smiling schoolboys sang "Juanita" for us foreign visitors, I talked with a few of their fathers who were grubbing out saplings to make fields, and asked one of them what he was thinking. He replied soberly that it was about having a place on the land for his *hijos* (sons).

Thousands of these indigenous people, like hundreds of eighteenth-century Lenapes from the Lehigh to the Ohio, had accepted the Christian faith of the newcomers on their homeland. "*Me llamo Juan Giesbrecht*," one man told me, by which I understood that he had been renamed for the Mennonite who had baptized him. Unlike the Moravian-baptized Natives butchered in Ohio by American soldiers during our Revolution, thousands from what has been called "one of the most intact indigenous cultures in South America" have not only survived, but against all historical precedents are presently exempted by the Paraguayan government from military service because of nonresistant beliefs they have adopted from Mennonite settlers. By now, with academics clucking over white domination, it has been 90 years that the two peoples have lived together without an eruption of hostilities such as occurred in North America in 1755, 1763, and 1782.

I have wondered why a parallel scenario could not have emerged here in Perkioma. Only in my 70s, as I began to listen, did I learn that my Salford congregation had participated in the story of the 1930 resettlement of Mennonites in Paraguay by sending down used farm equipment, and that one of our devout sisters had been corresponding for nearly five decades with a Mennonite woman in Fernheim. Then I met an elderly griot, Fernheim's Peter Klassen, who had written not only a two-volume history of his people in Paraguay, but five books of short stories illustrating his topic—as no one had done for our Pennsylvania communities, though they were two centuries older. This was puzzling and shaming. Why had we, with much better economic advantages, not made such an effort? Instead of having a story to tell about our own people's encounter with their predecessors on the land we regarded as God's gift, we had only sentimental generalities. The stories that could have been told!

In January 1985, on a short-term teaching assignment in Kansas, I realized I was near a northeastern Oklahoma community of some 10,000 Lenapes. I had heard about and seen locally photographed slides of their Nora Thompson Dean (Touching Leaves), a widely known woman of wisdom who could still think in the Lenape language. Following her mother, who, in her own adolescent vision had heard the trees singing to her, Nora had profoundly absorbed Lenape lore. I knew she had visited our community in Perkioma, but I had been so preoccupied at the time that I took no notice. Now, when I asked after her, I learned (to my life-long regret) that she had died only a few weeks earlier.

My wife and I were at least able to visit Nora's home in Dewey, east of Bartlesville, Oklahoma, and talk with her husband Charley (who gave me two ears of black and white corn), their daughter Louise, and their friend Jim Rementer. Born and reared in the Wissahickon watershed just south of my Perkioma, Jim only learned as an adult that he had an ancestor who was killed by vengeful Lenapes in 1756. He had found himself drawn to probe beyond a youthful fascination with "Indians" into an acquaintance with and eventual adoption into the Lenape family in eastern Oklahoma. Having been close to Nora Dean and what she knew, he was in the early stages of creating a "Talking Dictionary" which, with the development of the Internet, has made it possible for the world to learn the Lenape language.

Thirty-five years after Nora Dean's death, Jim remembers a moment from a conversation she had while visiting a Quaker meetinghouse in Philadelphia. In the presence of a man dressed to represent William Penn, Nora was asked what she thought of Pennsylvania's founder. When she replied that she had long gotten the impression from her people that he was a scoundrel, the costumed actor walked away. Had he remained, Jim observes, he could have heard her explain that with fuller information she had learned that it was Thomas Penn, rather than his father, who had engineered the loss of her people's homeland.

In 1989 I was invited to speak at a conference on the topic of Native-White relations in the Lehigh region. Listeners were polite, but I knew my speech displayed ignorance. This was the year when our Mennonite community was creating a "Heritage Center," to be built a mile west of the Indian Creek, on the border shared by Lower Salford and Franconia Townships. The Center's entrance was designed to welcome visitors via a "Wall of Memory" composed of stones from historical sources. Blessed with an expert local mason, we gave him a colorful pile of donated stones, including a piece of granite from a local quarry carved into miniature-brick shape by African American Al White of Sumneytown, and a piece of petrified wood shaped like the African continent, brought from there by a missionary's relative. I contributed a stone pestle I had found on our homestead by the Branch. But when proudly shown the mason's finished work, I could find none of the three stones just mentioned. Why, I asked, had Al White's granite block not been used? "There it is," the mason pointed. Alas, he had knocked off a large corner of the stone to fill a nonrectangular space, so that Al's artifact was unrecognizable. And what about the pestle? I inquired. "It's there," said the mason, pointing to a small circular end of the pestle which had been inserted lengthwise into another small space. And the petrified piece shaped like Africa? It had been rotated to fit a space shaped like South America. We had the data, but, in the pattern we had imposed, no particular story.

Walking in Bartlesville, I asked the first person I encountered how I could meet some Delawares, and was given the name of Dee Ketchum, a well-known varsity basketball star and coach of the region. Dee and his wife Annette proved to be a refined, full-blooded Lenape couple who answered my questions candidly, while correcting my ignorance. When I used the phrase, "the Cherokee Trail of Tears," Annette commented, "We all had our trail of tears"—a correction that ensuing reading proved all too true. It impacted me to the point that, as the 500th anniversary of Columbus' "discovery" of America approached, I felt we who had lived on Lenape land for nearly three centuries should take notice. Dee and Annette accepted an invitation from our Mennonite historical society to visit us on Columbus Day weekend in 1992, and we hired a bus to take them with a group of interested local people on a tour of Lenape-related sites in Montgomery and Bucks Counties. I arranged for the Ketchums to speak in four local churches, and we held a banquet in our Salford meetinghouse, with a menu including turkey, venison, potatoes, succotash, cranberry sauce, and pumpkin pie. Dee performed a dance in costume, then fielded our questions. I was left nearly speechless when, in thanks for our invitation, he gave me a beaded eagle feather. Only years later would the PBS documentary *Long Journey Home* take us deeper into the Ketchums' own story.

The following Monday we took our guests to the Washington Cathedral where some 3,000 Native Americans representing 35 tribes celebrated 500 years of survival since the landing of Columbus. To the thunder of the loudest drums I had ever heard, a spectacularly costumed caravan of Natives flowed up the center aisle. Annette Ketchum and my wife Roma, looking for somewhere to sit, were inadvertently swept into the advancing pageant, then deposited on the front seats, where they looked at each other with surprise. Among the voices from the platform we heard that of Lawrence Hart, Cheyenne Peace Chief and Mennonite minister in Oklahoma. A Choctaw bishop exhorted, "The power to remember and pass on the story of the people is at the heart of what it means to be a tribe or the people of God."

After giving yet another shallow discourse on the Lenapes of Eastern Pennsylvania, I felt an obligation to do better, and thus began this book. What should be its tone? Anger? Sorrow? Amazement? Sympathy? Amusement? The latter option was the flavor of an anecdote shared with me by a sympathetic Mennonite historian of relations between Mennonite missionaries and Comanches in Oklahoma. From the annals of the great Cherokee Outlet Land Rush of 1893 came the tale of a Mennonite couple who took off at the crack of the starter's gun, the husband driving, and his wife, seated behind him in the wagon, holding a stake to mark their claim. After a furiously rough ride brought them to a choice spot, the husband turned to confer with his wife, only to find that she had been thrown from the bouncing wagon. Retracing his route, he found that she had planted the stake where she had landed, and that was now the site of their homestead. How, I wondered, would such a story, retold as a joke at, say, an Oklahoma Mennonite quilting, sound to Lenapes whose ancestors had followed a Trail of Tears through Ohio, Indiana, Illinois, Missouri, and Kansas into "Indian Territory"?

In 2006 I spent several days at a memorial gathering in western Oklahoma called by Lawrence Hart and his family and friends. We walked to the banks of the Washita River, last home of Lawrence's memorable Peace Chief predecessor, Black Kettle. In contrast to other Natives who were responding to the incursions of white settlers with savage attacks and kidnappings, Black Kettle had persisted in offers of friendship. Nevertheless, in 1868 the Civil War veteran General Phil Sheridan issued orders "to destroy [Indian] villages and ponies, to kill or hang all warriors, and to bring back all women and children." Soldiers under the command of General George Armstrong Custer, guided by Osage Indians, galloped into Black Kettle's village, firing randomly at men and women alike until most were killed. Then the troops slaughtered 875 ponies and horses along the creek. The village "ceased to exist." Listening to a park ranger laconically recount those horrifying events along the Washita, we were numbed. Of course, as heir to eight peaceful generations along my own (Branch) creek, I felt no personal connection to that bloody extermination. Later, though, after hearing that Custer could speak "Pennsylvania Dutch," I was startled to recognize his descent from Germantown's immigrant Kosters, of Mennonite-turned-Quaker stock from Kaldenkirchen, Germany.

"Tears," wrote poet Alfred, Lord Tennyson, "I know not what they mean." Erica Littlewolf of Montana, Mennonite descendant of Cheyennes killed at both the Washita in 1868 and Fort Robinson, Nebraska, in 1879, knows what her tears mean. They are of a kind, she writes, "that leave me thinking I could not possibly cry more, only to stop and begin crying again . . ., tears that remember the past, think about the future and demand to be felt in the present."

A tear glistened on the cheek of an Alsatian Mennonite farmer in response to my remarking on his visible love of the land. Decades later I saw land-related tears in a Presbyterian Church in Lancaster, Pennsylvania, hosting a collection of Indians at a remembrance of the 1763 Conestoga massacre. Banners waving under a cross at the front of the sanctuary visualized the anguish of a timelessly plangent wailing. Yet the same meeting, we later learned, had triggered another kind of tears. There was an announcement that a memorial longhouse like those used by Pennsylvania Natives for worship would be built in Lancaster County. A Native in the audience, who had no expectation that the idea would be fulfilled any more than all the broken promises his people had heard, was still so moved by the mere proposal that he wept until two in the morning. (And the longhouse was indeed built, next to the 1719 Mennonite "Herr House.")

Epilogue

There is a special note in the grief of the Lenapes' memory. After all, they were recognized among other Indian nations as "the Original People," the "Grandfathers." The powerful Six Nations—who called Lenapes their "cousins," told them to wear figurative petticoats, and conspired with Thomas Penn to cheat them of their land—acknowledged this tradition. This irony became complex for me at a meeting of historians in 2011 at Stenton, the colonial mansion of James Logan, as a representative of the Senecas spoke on how his people had been officially mistreated over the years. Having only recently read about the Walking Purchase of 1737, I was wondering what the listening Sassoonan might have thought of the contemptuous Senecan oratory in 1742 by which the last of the Lehigh Lenapes were commanded to leave their homes? When I asked the speaker's opinion of this, he replied that he had not heard anything about it.

The real inflection point in my thinking came in the following summer, in the year when the World Council of Churches, in cooperation with the United Nations Permanent Forum on Indigenous Issues, called for a repudiation of the medieval "Doctrine of Discovery." A miscellaneous group of Lenape-oriented persons, planning to retravel the route of the notorious Walking Purchase, invited me to join them. Knowing no Lenapes myself (Pennsylvania's percentage of indigenous persons being the lowest in the United States!), and with only a preliminary knowledge of the Purchase, I was intrigued to accept.

Of three moments in our tour that stand out in memory, the first came as I conversed with a Lenape man who lived 20 miles northwest of my home. We were waiting for the rest of the traveling group to arrive at the Wrightstown Quaker Meetinghouse in Bucks County, where the original Walk had begun. As we approached a tall cedar tree, he casually pulled out a knife to scrape from the trunk a handful of its shaggy bark, and stowed the shavings in a pouch reminiscent of the little tobacco sacks on the chests of Lappowinzo and Tishcohan in the famous Hesselius portraits of 1735. The act seemed instinctive. Later I learned how significant the cedar fragrance is in Lenape imagination and ceremony.

The second startling moment came just before the actual tour began, when, from our circle of 16 persons in ordinary dress, came spontaneous gestures of worship. A woman declaiming "The stones cry out for justice" invoked the name of Jesus to defeat the powers that had historically mistreated the Lenapes. A smoldering passion, punctuated with the quiet beat of a tambourine-like hand drum, was unmistakable.

The third moment—when our group, having crossed the Tohickon Creek, stopped near the village of Ottsville some 17 miles from Wrightstown—left the boldest signpost on my inner landscape. With traffic roaring on the Easton Road behind us, the group gathered around a narrow seven-foot-high red stone marker inscribed:

> EDWARD
> MARSHALL
> WALKER OF
> PA.
> SEPT. 20.
> 1737.
> GOV.
> WM. PENN.

Just beneath, someone had scratched the celebratory outline of an arrow. Again, there seemed to be an instinctive response. Starting to walk around the weather-beaten stylus, each person picked up a rattle, while a man began beating his tambourine and yelling "Hey!" A woman spit at the monument, and a man slapped it, loosening a fragment from the top and handing it to one of the other men, who hurled it against the main trunk, then stood with his back toward it. On and on went the performance, with no apparent objection to my video camera. I was then, and have remained, transfixed by the experience. Time between 1737 and 2012 had collapsed. We were in an unfinished story.

Our northward retracing of the infamous Walk ran a mile or two east of where in 1683 William Penn had discussed land with Tamany. In the present town of Perkasie, the East Branch of the Perkiomen fills a small but beautiful Lake Lenape, while in adjacent Hilltown Township the North Branch of the Neshaminy has been dammed to create Lake Galena. Close by, one of our last Mennonite dairying families, the Hockmans, call their place "Penn View Farm," not with reference to Penn and Tamany's nearby rendezvous, but because, when the barn was built in 1916, someone standing on its peak and peering through binoculars discerned the statue of "Billy Penn" 22 miles to the south, atop Philadelphia's City Hall. The 26-ton monument, designed by Alexander Milne Calder and installed in 1894, is the world's largest roof-mounted statue. For nine decades, as its lithe, unvarying profile evoked our region's legendary peaceful history, an unspoken "gentleman's agreement" allowed no building to challenge the 548-foot height. But our world and its myths are changing. After 1985 two skyscrapers quickly rose well above the broad brim of the Quaker hat, and since then ten more increasingly tall buildings have obscured the familiar silhouette.

In 1995 a smaller but still-impressive 20-foot sculpture of Tamany was erected at Front and Market Streets, halfway between City Hall and the Penn Treaty Park on the site of historic Shackamaxon. With a wampum-bearing eagle on his shoulder, the famous chief stands on a turtle embodying his people's creation story. He gestures welcomingly toward the towering Penn, to whom the turtle would probably have seemed less strange an image than a Christmas tree or Easter bunny.

By a milestone 29 miles northwest of downtown Philadelphia, and some 400 feet from the Branch Creek, I write in the house in which I was born. Only after returning to my birthplace at the age of 57 did I calculate that it had stood here since 1806. The interval between that year and my homecoming seemed like a dreamily long time, until one spring day a turtle waddled up from the creek to deposit her eggs. To the confusion of her inner GPS, the location she sought had been covered by a house for 180 years. Joking as we carried the turtle wriggling back down the meadow, we were not consciously mocking the token of creation held in veneration by our Unami predecessors.

We had brought symbols of our own. Inside the house, my wife was crafting, in medieval fraktur characters, the words *Die erd is des HERRN* (the earth is the Lord's), to ornament our living room. I had found the obsolete spelling in a Bible printed in Zurich in 1536 and carried to Pennsylvania in the immigration of 1717. The opening verse of its Psalm 24 had been repeatedly quoted by my ancestors in both Zurich and Bern, when threatened with expulsion from their fatherland. Indeed, some of the *Täufer* expelled from the Bernese Emmental—homeland of Bergeys, Derstines, Kratzes, Gehmans, Lederachs, Ruths, and Yoders destined to live in Perkioma—had been accused of an almost *abgotisch* (idolatrous) attachment to their natal landscape.

Feeling that same kind of love, I assembled, across from the text in our living room, a panel of preindustrial artifacts symbolizing the quarter-millennium of our people's farming this ground. A two-handled crosscut saw recalls the woods, while a sickle and a cradle tooth evoke the grain. Beside them hangs a flail with oak head joined to a limber hickory handle by eel skin from the Branch. A reproduced zither reminds us of miller Johannes Clemens' instrument: the earliest "dulcimer" documented in America. The rustic bricolage warms my heart with such love that in a recent dream I saw a series of golden wheat fields framed by green woods, and woke with an oneiric glow in the memories of living from and with this land.

Suspended just below a stone hand-hoe I found along our creek sways the beaded eagle quill I received at the 500th anniversary of the *Santa Maria*'s landing on an island in the Bahamas which its captain named *San Salvador*. It reminds me, beyond the Lenapes' punning name Miquën (feather) for William Penn, of the musing of the Oklahoman who gave me this symbol, on how he could hold in his heart the Christian story that had come along with the unimaginable genocide brought by Columbus.

Is there a reciprocal generosity, I wonder, in the dream-narrative I have tried to weave here? Though the reach of my Anabaptist story is not as ancient as that of the Lenapes, I consider it prefigured as far back as when they were first glimpsed by a European. Giovanni da Verrazano, probing northward along the American seacoast in search of a passage to Cathay, missed the opening of the Chesapeake Bay, and ultimately landed near Manhattan. Information from his report of July 24, 1524 to his sponsoring King Francois included an admiring account of Natives giving him a friendly welcome. While this could hardly have echoed all across Europe within two years, a quip in Zurich, Switzerland, in March 1526, makes me wonder. Almost two centuries before Zurich-born Ann Reiff Clemens came to live here along the Branch, a cluster of her spiritual ancestors were speaking of America. They had become homeless in the land of their birth, sentenced to life imprisonment for the crime of baptizing each other. In giving up all killing and oaths, they anticipated William Penn's convictions a century and a half later. But such a break with convention had frightened Zurich's officials into consigning them to a tower-dungeon on the city wall, only a few rods from the tall mansion in which their patrician leader Conrad Grebel had been born, and which he had until recently stood to inherit. Three weeks after their jailing they all crawled out through a helpfully unlocked window, and were found shivering in the adjacent moat. According to court testimony, they were asking each other, Where to? "One said he would go here, and another there." Some said they would go to Horgen (home of my ancestral Landis family) to find work. "But the others joked among themselves and said they would go to the red Indians across the sea."

It is no joke that in the two centuries before Gerhart and Ann Clemens came here most of their and my people were not considered to be citizens who could own land. Nor was it a joke for them to find home and citizenship in Penn's Woods. It was rather the seriousness of what they and William Penn believed that had led to my being born and seeing grandchildren grow up on this ground. But it is also no joke for me to have lived most of a century knowing almost nothing about "the red Indians" my people replaced. Certainly, had I been among those arriving here in 1709, 1710, and 1717, my outlook would have been no broader than that of those Palatines. But their progeny are at a threshold of conscience, asking: Shouldn't the descendants of a people who, having fled their own homelessness, supplanted others on the earth that is the Lord's, hear more of the story of those they replaced? My own musing is only part of the broader awakening. Twenty-nine miles south of my desk, newly sculpted images—of Turtle, Turkey, and Wolf—have been appearing on the streets of Fishtown, once called "Shackamaxon." A tap of a key or a verbal cue lets us hear Lenape language and music. We should not neglect to listen.

Even the devout Isaac Watts, whose hymn of 1719, quoted in the Preface, had seen "nothing" in the American woods "but beasts of prey, / Or men as fierce and wild as they," could intuit a kinder wisdom:

> Seize upon truth where'er 'tis found,
> On Christian or on heathen ground. . . .
> Amongst your friends, amongst your foes,
> The flower's divine where'er it grows.
> Neglect the prickles and assume the rose.

About the Author

WITH FAMILY ROOTS in Switzerland, **John Landis Ruth** was born in 1930 on a farm 29 miles northwest of Philadelphia, Pennsylvania, and was ordained a minister in the Mennonite Church at the age of 20. His Ph.D. thesis at Harvard University was titled *English Hymn-Writing in America, 1640-1800*. After teaching English and American literature at Eastern University and Universität Hamburg, he turned to film documentaries on the Amish and Hutterites, and narratives of eastern Pennsylvania Mennonite life, including *Maintaining the Right Fellowship* (1984) and *The Earth is the Lord's* (2001). In 1971 he and his fraktur-artist wife Roma Jeanette Jacobs returned with their family to his birth community and homestead, from where he served as associate pastor of the Salford Mennonite Church from 1972 to 1994, and led historical tours in Europe for 45 years.

A LIFELONG KANSAN, **Raylene Hinz-Penner** (*Foreword*) is retired from a career teaching contemporary American literature and creative writing, first at Bethel College in North Newton, Kansas, and later at Washburn University, Topeka, Kansas. She writes poetry and creative non-fiction, especially related to place. In 2007 she published *Searching for Sacred Ground: The Journey of Chief Lawrence Hart, Mennonite*, a story of intertwining peace traditions, Cheyenne and Anabaptist Mennonite. Her current writing project grapples with how Mennonite settlers tell their stories of life on the land, how they acknowledge the land that was homeland to generations of Native peoples. Her 17th-century Mennonite farmer ancestors migrated and settled land from the Netherlands to Moravia, Prussia, eventually Russia, and then the U.S. There her parents settled on Dust Bowl land in southwest Kansas bordering the Oklahoma Panhandle in 1950.

Kathryn Katz Photography

ACKNOWLEDGEMENTS

THIS BOOK and others preceding it were made possible or enlarged by support from friends in my local Mennonite community. From 1975, with a group headed by R. Wayne Clemens of Souderton, until 25 years after my retiring from the ministry at the Salford Mennonite congregation, I have been given "Freedom to Write." My move into a field other than what I was trained for had more to do with the community's readiness to listen to its own story than with professional promise. Already, while I had been teaching literature in the 1960s, Charles Hartzel Price, owner of a hatchery in nearby Telford, was publishing careful research on his family's Reformed Church roots in Europe. Untrained like me, he recognized and encouraged my undertaking. Also well prior to my late-breaking interest was the quest of Lower Salford-born Lee Hallman, who at the age of eight had picked up his first "arrowhead" beside his home built on the soil of a Mennonite Moyer homestead. By the time I learned to know Lee, his houseful of finds ranged from a jasper point dating to the Paleoindian Period 15 millennia before our time, picked up 700 feet from the edge of my own homestead, to a trader's Dutch coin he had found a few miles up the East Branch of the Perkiomen Creek. The latter had been minted in 1643, a year before the events recounted in this narrative began to unfold.

My childhood friend Leon Moyer, having grown up on the next farm to ours, had listened to his Dunker grandfather, Waldo Emerson Ziegler, relate how, after every rainfall on our little valley's newly plowed ground, he would find stone tokens of our Branch Creek predecessors. Even in our 80s, as Leon and I stood musing in those fields, he stooped, surprised, and picked up another stone point. His fellowship in local story was substantial.

I owe thanks to the Indian Valley Public Library in Telford for access to Charles Price's collection there, and to Joel Alderfer and Forrest Moyer for many favors at the Mennonite Heritage Center at Harleysville. At the Pennsylvania Historical Society in Philadelphia, with its unique portraits of Lenape headmen Tishekunk and Lappowinzo, I was repeatedly served by staff patiently bringing up from their million-fold trove documents providing texture for my story.

I am also grateful for the insightful Foreword written by Raylene Hinz-Penner, bringing to my story her perspective on cognate spiritual heritage and sense of living on Native ground.

By 1987, when I and my wife Roma Jacobs returned to live in my birthplace, she had become a sought-after practitioner of our region's

Pennsylvania German fraktur art. To the old homestead, so unexpectedly our destination, she brought a restoring energy that has made living here by the Branch Creek a varicolored poem. In 1992 she visualized my themes in a fraktur poster greeting the 500th anniversary of the arrival of Columbus with motifs and names the Lenapes had given to our creeks.

Finally, and most appreciated, my son Philip Gerhart Ruth, whose name we meant to echo that of the ancestral purchaser of our homestead's ground, has lent his multiple gifts to this book. His maturing insight into our geographic, cultural, and spiritual heritage has borne adult fruit in more than a dozen books of his own. Through an agreement with Cascadia Publishing House publisher Michael King, Phil has served as both editor and designer of this book.

SELECTED SOURCES AND READINGS

Alderfer, E. Gordon. "James Logan: Patron and Natural Philosopher," *Pennsylvania History*, 24 (April 1957), 101-120.

_____. "James Logan: The Political Career of a Colonial Scholar," *Pennsylvania History*, 24 (January 1957), 34-54.

Allen, William. Letter Book. Historical Society of Pennsylvania, Philadelphia, PA.

Anderson, Fred. *Crucible of War: The Seven Years' War and the Fate of Empire in British North America, 1754-1788*. New York: Alfred A. Knopf, 2000.

Banner, Stuart. *How the Indians Lost Their Land: Law and Power on the Frontier*. Cambridge, Mass.: Harvard University Press, 2005.

Battle, J. H., ed., *History of Bucks County, Pennsylvania*. Philadelphia: A. Warner & Company, 1887.

Becker, Marshall. "The Lenape Bands Prior to 1740: The Identification of Boundaries and the Processes of Change Leading to the Formation of the Delawares," in Herbert Kraft, ed., *The Lenape Indian: A Symposium*. Seton Hall Archeological Research Center, No. 7 (South Orange, N.J., 1984), 19-32.

_____. "Lenape Land Sales, Treaties and Wampum Belts," *Pennsylvania Magazine of History and Biography*, 108 (July 1984), 351-356.

_____. "The Swedes and Dutch In the Land of the Lenape," *Pennsylvania Heritage*, 1984, 20-23.

Beiler, Rosalind. *Immigrant and Entrepreneur: The Atlantic World of Caspar Wistar, 1650-1750*. University Park, Pa.: The Pennsylvania State University Press, 2008.

Bierhorst, John. *Mythology of the Lenape*. Tucson, Ariz.: University of Arizona Press, 1995.

Boehm, Johann Philip. *Life and Letters of Reverend John Philip Boehm: Founder of the Reformed Church in Pennsylvania, 1683-1749*. Ed. William J. Hinke. Philadelphia: Reformed Church of the United States, 1916.

Bond, Beverly W., Jr. "The Captivity of Charles Stuart, 1755-57," *Mississippi Valley Historical Review*, 13, No. 1 (June 1926), 58-81.

Bowes, John P. *Northern Indian Removal*. Norman, Okla.: University of Oklahoma Press, 2016.

Bradley, A. Day. "Penn's Settlement on the River of Conestoga," *Journal of the Lancaster County Historical Society*, 75 (1971), 125-128.

Brock, Peter. *Pioneers of the Peaceable Kingdom*. Princeton, N.J.: Princeton University Press, 1968.

Bronner, Edwin B. "Indian Deed for Petty's Island, 1678," *Pennsylvania Magazine of History and Biography*, 89 (1965), 111-114.

_____. *William Penn's "Holy Experiment": The Founding of Pennsylvania 1681-1701*. New York: Temple University Publications, 1962.

Brown, James W. & Elita T. Kohn, eds. *Long Journey Home. Oral Histories of Contemporary Delaware Indians*. Bloomington, Ind.: Indiana University Press, 2008.

Browning, Charles H. *The Welsh Settlement of Pennsylvania*. Philadelphia: W. J. Campbell, 1912.

Bruner, D. B. *The Indians of Berks County, PA*, 2nd rev. ed. Reading, Pa.: Engle Book Print, 1897.

Buck, William J. "Lappawinzo and Tishcohan," *Pennsylvania Magazine of History and Biography*, 7 (1883), 215-218.

_____. *History of the Indian Walk Performed for the Proprietaries of Pennsylvania in 1737: To Which is Appended a Life of Edward Marshall*. Philadelphia: Edwin S. Stuart, 1886.

_____. *William Penn in America: or an account of his life from the time he received the grant of Pennsylvania in 1681, until his final return to England. Giving, as far as possible, his every-day occurrences while in the province*. Philadelphia: Friends Book Association, 1888.

Buell, Augustus C. *William Penn as the Founder of Two Commonwealths*. New York: D. Appleton and Company, 1904.

Campbell, William Bucke. "Old Towns and Districts of Philadelphia. An Address delivered before the City History Society of Philadelphia February 26, 1941," in *Philadelphia History*, 4 (1942), 1-20.

Carpenter, Roger M. "From Indian Women to English Children: The Lenni-Lenape and the Attempt to Create a New Diplomatic Identity," *Pennsylvania History*, 74, No. 1 (Winter 2007), 1-20.

Carter, Edward C. and Clifford Lewis. "Sir Edmund Plowden and the New Albion Charter, 1632-1785," *Pennsylvania Magazine of History and Biography*, 83, Issue 2 (April 1959), 150-179.

Cassel, Abraham H., comp., Helen Bell, tr. "Notes on the Iroquois and Delaware Indians. Communications from Conrad Weiser to Christopher Saur, Which appeared in the Years 1746-1749 in His Newspaper Printed at Germantown, Entitled 'The High German Pennsylvania Historical Writer, Or a Collection of Important Events from the Kingdom of Nature and the Church And from His (Saur's) Almanac," *Pennsylvania Magazine of History and Biography*, 1 (1877), 163-167, 319-323; 2 (1878), 407-410.

_____. "Recollections of Indians in Lower Salford Township," as recorded by Samuel W. Pennypacker, in Jay Ruth, *Looking at Lower Salford* (Harleysville, Pa.: Harleysville National Bank, 1984), 4.

Clarkson, Thomas. *Memoirs of the Private and Public Life of William Penn*. "Two Volumes in One." Dover, N.H.: Samuel C. Stevens, 1827.

Clausen, W. E. *Pioneers Along the Manatawny*. Boyertown, Pa.: W. E. Clausen, 1968.

Clemens, Jacob, Gerhart Clemens, and Heinrich Clemens. *The Account Book of the Clemens Family of Lower Salford Township, Montgomery County, Pennsylvania, 1749–1857*. Translated by Raymond E. Hollenbach and edited by Alan G. Keyser. Sources and Documents of the Pennsylvania Germans 1, 1975.

Clemens, Jacob Cassel, comp. *Genealogical History of the Clemens Family and Descendants of The Pioneer, Gerhart Clemens*. [Lansdale, Pa.]: The Clemens Family, [1948].

Cohen, Norman S. "The Philadelphia Election Riot of 1742," *Pennsylvania Magazine of History and Biography*, 92 (July 1968), 306-319.

Corcoran, Irma. *Thomas Holme: 1624-1695: Surveyor General of Pennsylvania*. Philadelphia: American Philosophical Society, 1992.

Cumings, Hubertis M. "An Account of Goods at Pennsbury Manor," *Pennsylvania Magazine of History and Biography*, 86 (October 1962), 397-416.

SELECTED SOURCES AND READINGS

Craig, Isaac. "Allummapees, King of the Delawares," in William Henry Egle, *Notes and Queries Historical and Genealogical*, 2 (Baltimore: Genealogical Publishing Company, 1970), 439.

Craig, Peter Stebbins, ed. *Colonial Records of the Swedish Churches in Pennsylvania, Volume 2: The Rudman Years, 1697-1702.* Philadelphia: Swedish Colonial Society, 2006.

Davis, Richard Warren. *The Stauffer Families of Switzerland, Germany and America.* Provo, Utah: Richard Warren Davis, 1992.

_____. "The Stauffer Families of the 1671 Migration to the Palatinate," *Mennonite Family History*, 12 (January 1993), 4-9.

Davis, William Watts Hart. *History of Bucks County, Pennsylvania: From the Discovery of the Delaware to the Present Time.* Doylestown, Pa.: "Democrat Book and Job Office," 1876.

Day, Sherman. *Historical Collections of the State of Pennsylvania.* Philadelphia: George W. Gorton, 1843.

Dean, Nora Thompson. *Lenape Cooking With Touching Leaves Woman*, "Second edition prepared by Jim Rementer." Bartlesville, Okla.: Touching Leaves Company, 2016.

Dilg, L. Paul. "The Man Who Set Our Boundaries," *Old York Road Historical Society Bulletin*, 37 (1977), 3-15.

Donehoo, George P. *A History of the Indian Villages and Place Names in Pennsylvania.* "Originally published, Harrisburg, PA, 1928." Lewisburg, Pa.: Wennawoods Publishing, 1998.

Duffin, J. M., ed. *Acta Germanapolis: Records of the Corporation of Germantown Pennsylvania 1691-1707.* Philadelphia: Colonial Society of Pennsylvania, 2008.

Dunbar-Ortiz, Roxanne. *An Indigenous Peoples' History of the United States.* Boston: Beacon Press, 2014.

Dunn, Mary and Martha Reamy, comp. *Index to Pennsylvania's Colonial Records Series.* Baltimore: Genealogical Publishing Co., 1992.

Dunn, Richard S., and Mary Maples Dunn, eds. *The World of William Penn.* Philadelphia: University of Pennsylvania Press, 1986.

Dunn, Richard S. et al., eds. *The Papers of William Penn*, 5 vols. Philadelphia: University of Pennsylvania Press, 1981-1986.

Egle, William Henry. *History of the Counties of Dauphin and Lebanon.* Philadelphia: Everts & Peck, 1883.

Erben, Patrick M. *A Harmony of the Spirits: Translation and the Language of Community in Early Pennsylvania.* Chapel Hill, N.C.: University of North Carolina Press, 2012.

Eshelman, Henry Frank. *Lancaster County Indians: Annals of the Susquehannocks and Other Indian tribes of the Susquehanna Territory....* Lancaster, Pa.: Express Print Co., 1909.

Fischer, David Hackett. *Albion's Seed: Four British Folkways in America.* New York: Oxford University Press, 1989.

Fogleman, Aaron Spencer. *Hopeful Journeys: German Immigration, Settlement, and Political Culture in Colonial America, 1717-1775.* Philadelphia: University of Pennsylvania Press, 1996.

_____. *Jesus is Female: Moravians and Radical Religion in Early America*. Philadelphia: University of Pennsylvania Press, 2007.

Frost, J. William. "William Penn's Experiment in the Wilderness: Promise and Legend," *Pennsylvania Magazine of History and Biography*, 107 (1983), 577-605.

Geiter, Mary K. *William Penn*. Essex, U.K.: Pearson Education Limited, 2000.

Gillingham, Harold E. "Indian Silver Ornaments," *Pennsylvania Magazine of History and Biography*, 68 (1934), 97-126.

Gordon, Thomas F. *The History of New Jersey: From its Discovery by Europeans, to the Adoption of the Federal Constitution*. Trenton, N.J.: Daniel Fenton, 1834.

Graham, Dan. "Establishing Thomas Rutter's Role in Building Pennsylvania's First Ironwork: A Literature Search," *Bulletin of the Historical Society of Montgomery County Pennsylvania*, 4 (2004, No. 1), 66-77.

Grey, Elizabeth Janet. *Penn*. Philadelphia: Philadelphia Yearly Meeting of the Religious Society of Friends, 1986. (Originally published 1938.)

Grigg, John A. *The Lives of David Brainerd: The Making of an American Evangelical Icon*. New York: Oxford University Press, 2009.

Grubb, N. B., comp. *A genealogical history of the Gottshall family: descendents of Rev. Jacob Gottshall with the complete record of the descendents of William Ziegler Gottshall*. [Philadelphia:] Gottshall Family Association, 1924.

Grumet, Robert S. *Northeastern Indian Lives, 1632-1816*. Amherst, Mass.: University of Massachusetts Press, 1996.

_____. *The Lenapes*. New York: Chelsea House Publishers, 1989.

Hanna, Charles Augustus. *The Wilderness Trail. Or, The Ventures and Adventures of the Pennsylvania Traders on the Allegheny Path*, Vol. 1. New York and London: G. P. Putnam's Sons, The Knickerbocker Press, 1911.

Harper, Steven Craig. *Promised Land: Penn's Holy Experiment, The Walking Purchase, and the Dispossession of Delawares, 1600-1763*. Bethlehem, Pa.: Lehigh University Press, 2006.

Heckewelder, John. *History, Manners, and Customs of the Indian Nations Who Once Inhabited Pennsylvania and the Neighboring States*. Philadelphia: Publication Fund of the Historical Society of Pennsylvania, 1876. (Reprint Arno Press & *The New York Times*, 1971.)

_____. "Heckewelder's Indian Names of Streams, Rivers, Places, etc.," *Pennsylvania German Folklore Society*, 5 (1940), 1-41.

_____. *Words, Phrases and Short Dialogues in the Language of the Lenni Lenape or Delaware Indians* (reprint). London: Forgotten Books, 2018.

Heckler, James Y[ocum]. *History of Lower Salford*. Harleysville, Pa.: author, 1888.

Heinrichs, Steven. *Buffalo Shout, Salmon Cry: Conversations on Creation, Land, Justice, and Life Together*. Kitchener, Ontario, and Harrisonburg, Va.: Herald Press, 2013.

Heller, W. J. "The Disappearance of the Lenni Lenape from the Delaware and Their Subsequent Migrations," *The Penn Germania*, 13 (1912), 711-17.

Hershberger, Guy Franklin. "Quaker Pacifism and the State in the Provincial Government of Pennsylvania," Ph.D. diss., University of Iowa, 1935.

SELECTED SOURCES AND READINGS 371

Hershey, Larry Brent. "Peace through conversation: William Penn, Israel Pemberton and the shaping of Quaker-Indian Relations, 1681-1757." M.A. thesis, University of Iowa, 2008.

Hinke, William J. *Life and Letters of the Rev. John Philip Boehm.* Philadelphia: Publication and Sunday School Board of the Reformed Church in the United States, 1916.

Hoffman, Daniel. *Brotherly Love. A Poem.* New York: Random House, 1981.

Horley, Craig W., Marianne S. Wokeck, et al. *Lawmaking and Legislators in Pennsylvania: A Biographical Dictionary. Vol. I: 1682-1709.* Philadelphia: University of Pennsylvania Press, 1991.

Hull, William I. *William Penn: A Topical Biography.* New York: Oxford University Press, 1937.

Illick, Joseph. *Colonial Pennsylvania: A History.* New York: Scribners, 1976.

Indian Treaties Printed by Benjamin Franklin 1736-1762. Philadelphia: Historical Society of Pennsylvania, 1938.

Jenkins, Charles F. "James Logan and Stenton," *Byways in Quaker History*, ed. Howard H. Brinton. Wallingford, Pa.: Pendle Hill, 1944).

Jenkins, Howard M. "The Family of William Penn," *Pennsylvania Magazine of History and Biography*, 21 (1897), 151-153.

Jennings, Francis P. *Benjamin Franklin, Politician: The Mask and the Man.* New York: W. W. Norton & Company, 1996.

_____. "Incident at Tulpehocken," *Pennsylvania History*, 35 (1968), 335-355.

_____. *The Ambiguous Iroquois Empire: The Covenant Chain Confederation of Indian Tribes with English Colonies from its Beginnings to the Lancaster Treaty of 1744.* New York: W. W. Norton & Company, 1984.

_____. "The Delaware Interregnum," *Pennsylvania Magazine of History and Biography*, 39 (April 1965), 174-198.

_____. *The Creation of America: Through Revolution to Empire.* New York: Cambridge University Press, 2000.

_____. *The Invasion of America: Indians, Colonialism, and the Cant of Conquest.* New York: W. W. Norton, Inc., 1975.

_____. "The Scandalous Indian Policy of William Penn's Sons: Deeds and Documents of the Walking Purchase," *Pennsylvania History*, 37 (January 1970), 19-39.

Johnson, Laura E. "'Goods to clothe themselves': Native Consumers and Native Images on the Pennsylvania Trading Frontier, 1712-1760," *Winterthur Portfolio*, 43, No. 1 (Spring 2009), 115-140.

Johnson, Ralph L. and David H. Bergey. "Genealogical Landmarks and Milestones of the Lower Perkiomen Country," *The Perkiomen Region*, 13 (October 1934), 97-279.

Juhnke, James C. and Carol M. Hunter. *The Missing Peace: The Search for Nonviolent Alternatives in United States History.* Kitchener, Ontario: Pandora Press, 2001.

Kashatus, William C. III. "Explaining William Penn: An Interview with Richard S. Dunn," *Pennsylvania Heritage*, 20 (Fall 1994), 26-32.

Keith, Charles P. *Chronicles of Pennsylvania From the English Revolution to the Peace of Aix-La-Chapelle 1688-1748.* Port Washington, NY: Ira J. Friedman, Inc., 1969.

Selected Sources and Readings

Kelley, Joseph J., Jr. *Pennsylvania: The Colonial Years 1681-1776*. Garden City, N.Y.: Doubleday & Company, Inc., 1980.

Kenny, Kevin. *Peaceable Kingdom Lost: The Paxton Boys and the Destruction of William Penn's Holy Experiment*. New York: Oxford University Press, 2009.

Kent, Barry C. *Susquehanna's Indians*. Harrisburg, Pa.: Pennsylvania Historical and Museum Commission, 1984.

Klinefelter, Walter. "Surveyor General Thomas Holme's 'Map of the Improved Part of the Province of Pennsylvania,'" *Winterthur Portfolio*, 6, (1970), 41-74.

Kistler, Ruth Moser. "William Allen, Provincial Man of Affairs," *Pennsylvania History*, 1 (1934), 165-174.

Kraft, Herbert C. *The Lenape: Archaeology, History and Ethnography*. Newark, N.J.: New Jersey Historical Society, 1986.

_____. *The Lenape-Delaware Indian Heritage: 10,000 B.C.-A.D. 2000*. N.p.: Lenape Books, 2001.

Kratz, Bernd. "Hans Stauffer of Germany and Pennsylvania," *The Genealogist*, 22 (Fall 2008), 131-169.

Landis, James G. *Lenape Homeland*. Petersburg, W.V.: author, 2005.

_____. *The Homeland in my Heart*. Petersburg, W.V.: author, 2005.

_____. *Tomahawks to Peace*. Petersburg, W.V.: author, 2009.

Lloyd, Mark Frazier. "The Johnson (Jansen) Family and Their Houses in 18th Century Germantown," *Germantown Crier*, 33, (Spring 1981), No. 2, 36-43.

Loskiel, George Henry. *History of the Mission of the United Brethren Among the Indians in North America. In Three Parts*. Tr. from the German by Christian Ignatius Latrobe. London: Brethren's Society for the Furtherance of the Gospel, 1794.

Love, J. Barry. *The Colonial Surveyor in Pennsylvania*. Harrisburg, Pa.: Pennsylvania Society of Land Surveyors, 2000.

Lowry, James W. *Documents of Brotherly Love: Dutch Mennonite Aid to Swiss Anabaptists*. Vol. I, 1635-1709. Millersburg, Ohio: Ohio Amish Library, 2007. Vol. II, 1710-1711, 2015.

McReynolds, George. *Place Names in Bucks County Pennsylvania*. Doylestown, Pa.: Bucks County Historical Society, 1942.

Mark, Beth Yoder, comp. & ed. *Our Flesh and Blood: A Documentary History of the Jacob Hochstetler Family During the French and Indian War Period 1757-1765*. "Second Edition." Elkhart, Ind.: The Jacob Hochstetler Family Association, Inc., 2003.

Marking the Historic Sites of Early Pennsylvania. "Fourth Report of the Pennsylvania Historical Commission." Harrisburg, Pa.: "Created by Authority of the General Assembly of The Commonwealth of Pennsylvania," 1926.

Marsh, Dawn G. *Hannah Freeman: A Lenape Among the Quakers: The Life of Hannah Freeman*. Lincoln, Neb.: University of Nebraska Press, 2014.

McConnell, Michael N. *A Country Between: The Upper Ohio Valley and Its Peoples, 1724-1774*. Lincoln, Neb.: University of Nebraska Press, 1992.

McLuhan, T. C. *Touch the Earth: A Self-Portrait of Indian Existence*. New York: Simon & Schuster, 1971.

McNealy, Terry A. "Recollections of Bucks' Past: Indians, William Penn, and George Washington Viewed Fifty years after the Revolution," *Bucks County Historical Society Journal*, 1 (Spring 1976), 1-21.

"Memorandum to the Commissioners for Indian Affairs, 1760," *Mennonite Historical Bulletin*, 35 (April 1974), 1.

Merrell, James H. *Into the American Woods: Negotiators on the Pennsylvania Frontier*. New York: W. W. Norton & Company, 1999.

_____. "Some Thoughts on Colonial Historians and American Indians," *William and Mary Quarterly*, 46 (1989), 94-119.

Merritt, Jane T. *At the Crossroads: Indians and Empires on a Mid-Atlantic Frontier, 1700-1763*. Chapel Hill, N.C.: University of North Carolina Press, 2003.

Michel, Paul. "Täufer, Mennoniten und Quäker in Kriegsheim bei Worms," *Der Wormsgau*, 7 (1965-66), 41-52.

Mielke, Andreas Mielke, "Michel's 1703 and 1704 Reports to Johann Rudolph Ochs in Bern," *Pennsylvania Mennonite Heritage*, 34 (April 2011), 14-17.

Milano, Kenneth W. *The History of Penn Treaty Park*. Charleston, S.C.: History Press, 2009.

Miller, J. Virgil. *Both Sides of the Ocean: Amish-Mennonites from Switzerland to America*. Morgantown, Pa.: Masthof Press, 2002.

Minutes of the Provincial Council of Pennsylvania, from the Organization to the Termination of the Proprietary Government, 10 vols. Philadelphia: Printed by J. Severns, 1851-1853.

Moretta, John A. *William Penn and the Quaker Legacy*. New York: Pearson Education Inc., 2007.

Munger, Donna Bingham. *Pennsylvania Land Records. A History and Guide for Research*. "Published in cooperation with the Pennsylvania Historical and Museum Commission." Wilmington, Del.: Scholarly Resources Inc., 1991.

Murphy, Andrew R. *The Political Writings of William Penn*. Indianapolis: Liberty Fund, Incorporated, 2002.

_____. *William Penn: A Life*. New York: Oxford University Press, 2019.

Myers, Albert Cook, ed. *William Penn's Own Account of the Lenni Lenape or Delaware Indians* (rev. ed.). Wilmington, DE: The Middle Atlantic Press, 1970.

"Narrative of Marie Leroy and Barbara Leininger, for Three Years Captives Among the Indians, The," *Pennsylvania Magazine of History and Biography*, 29 (1905), 404-420.

Nash, Gary B. "City Planning and Political Tension in the Seventeenth Century: The Case of Philadelphia," *Proceedings of the American Philosophical Society* 112 (1968), 54-73.

_____. Ed., "The First Decade in Pennsylvania: Letters of William Markham and Thomas Holme to William Penn, Part I." *Pennsylvania Magazine of History and Biography*, 90 (July 1966), 314-352; "Part II" (October 1966), 492-516.

Neff, Larry and Frederick S. Weiser, tr. & ed. *The Account Book of Conrad Weiser Berks County, Pennsylvania 1746-1760*. Breinigsville, Pa.: The Pennsylvania German Society, 1981.

Nerburn, Kent, ed. *The Wisdom of the Native Americans*. Novato, Calif.: New World Library, 1999.

Newman, Andrew. *On Records: Delaware Indians, Colonists, and the Media of History and Memory*. Lincoln, Neb.: University of Nebraska Press, 2013.

Oestreicher, David M. "Unmasking the Walam Olum: A 19th Century Hoax," *Bulletin of the Archaeological Society of New Jersey*, 49 (1994), 1-44.

Original Letters and Documents Relating to the History of Pennsylvania Hitherto Unpublished, II. Philadelphia: McCarty and Davis, 1864.

Otterness, Philip. *Becoming German: The 1709 Palatine Migration to New York*. Ithaca, N.Y.: Cornell University Press, 2004.

Owen, B. F. "The Welsh of Cumru Township: An Address Delivered Before the Historical Society of Berks County, Pa., September 12, 1899," *Transactions of the Historical Society of Berks County*, 1 (1904), xx-xxviii.

Papers Relating to the Friendly Association, Department of Records, Philadelphia Yearly Meeting of Friends, 302 Arch Street, Philadelphia (multiple volumes).

Pencack, William and Daniel K. Richter, eds. *Friends and Enemies in Penn's Woods: Indians and Colonists and the Racial Construction of Pennsylvania*. University Park, Pa.: The Pennsylvania State University Press, 2004.

Pennsylvanische Berichte. Germantown: Christopher Saur, 1746-1754.

Pennypacker, Samuel Whitaker. "Bebber's Township and the Dutch Patrons of Pennsylvania," *Pennsylvania Magazine of History and Biography*, 31 (1907), 1-18.

Pointer, Richard. "An Almost Friend: Papunhank, Quakers and the Search for Security Amid Pennsylvania's Wars, 1754-65," *Pennsylvania Magazine of History and Biography*, 138 (2014), 237-68.

_____. *Pacifist Prophet: Papunhank and the Quest for Peace in Early America*, Lincoln, Neb.: University of Nebraska Press, 2020.

Preston, David L. *The Texture of Contact: European and Indian Settler Communities on the Frontiers of Iroquoia, 1667-1783*. Lincoln, Neb.: University of Nebraska Press, 2009.

Price, Charles H., Jr. *A Hartzell-Price Family History and Genealogy*. Telford, Pa.: author, 1971.

Price, Edward T. *Dividing the Land*. Chicago: University of Chicago Press, 1995.

Pritchard, Evan T. *Native New Yorkers: The Legacy of the Algonquin People of New York* (Revised Edition). Tulsa, Okla.: Council Oak Books, LLC, 2007.

Richter, Daniel K. "A Framework for Pennsylvania Indian History," *Pennsylvania History*, 57 (1990), 236-261.

_____. *Facing East from Indian Country: A Native History of Early America*. Cambridge, Mass.: Harvard University Press, 2001.

_____. *Trade, Land, Power: The Struggle for Eastern North America*. Philadelphia: University of Pennsylvania Press, 2013.

Riedweil, Johann. *Ein Beitrag zum Täuferjahr. Spuren einer Täuferfamilie vom Gürbetal ins Emmental; Mit Gotthelf Exempeln*. Liebefeld, Canton Bern, Switzerland: Hans Riedwyl [2007].

Roach, Hannah Benner. "The Planting of Philadelphia. A Seventeenth-Century Real Estate Development," *Pennsylvania Magazine of History and Biography*, 92 (April 1962), 3-47.

Roeber, A. G., ed. *Ethnographies and Exchanges: Native Americans, Moravians, and Catholics in Early North America*. University Park, Pa.: The Pennsylvania State University Press, 2008.

Rubin, Julius H. *Tears of Repentance: Christian Indian Identity and Community in Colonial Southern New England*. Lincoln, Neb.: University of Nebraska Press, 2013.

Ruth, John L. "English Hymn-Writing in America, 1640-1800," Ph.D. thesis, Harvard University, Cambridge, Mass., 1967.

_____. "William Rittenhouse as Minister: A Steady Presence in an Unsteady Context," *Rittenhouse Town: A Journal of History*, 3 (2006), 20-58.

Schutt, Amy C. *Peoples of the River Valleys: The Odyssey of the Delaware Indians*. Philadelphia: University of Pennsylvania Press, 2007.

Schwartz, Sally. *"A Mixed Multitude": The Struggle for Toleration in Colonial Pennsylvania*. New York: New York University Press, 1987.

Shannon, Timothy J. *Iroquois Diplomacy on the Early American Frontier*. New York: Viking, 2008.

Shurley, Daniel. "How Pennsylvania Erased the Lenape From Local History." https://hiddencityphila.org/2019/08

Silver, Peter. *Our Savage Neighbors: How Indian War Transformed Early America*. New York: W. W. Norton & Company, 2008.

Sipe, C. Hale. *The Indian Wars of Pennsylvania*, 2nd ed. Lewisburg, Pa.: Wennawoods Publishing, 1999.

Smith, C. Henry. *The Mennonite Immigration to Pennsylvania: In the Eighteenth Century*. Norristown, Pa.: Pennsylvania German Society, 1929.

Smolenski, John. *Friends and Strangers: The Making of a Creole Culture in Colonial Pennsylvania*. Philadelphia: University of Pennsylvania Press, 2010.

Soderlund, Jean R. *Lenape Country: Delaware Valley Society Before William Penn*. Philadelphia: University of Pennsylvania Press, 2014.

_____. Ed. *William Penn and the Founding of Pennsylvania 1680-1684: A Documentary History*. Philadelphia: University of Pennsylvania Press, 1983.

Spero, Patrick. *Frontier Country: The Politics of War in Early Pennsylvania*. Philadelphia: University of Pennsylvania Press, 2016.

Steel, James. MS Letterbook, 1730-41, in the Historical Society of Pennsylvania, Philadelphia.

Stockwell, Mary. *The Other Trail of Tears: The Removal of the Ohio Indians*. Yardley, Pa.: Westholme Publishing, LLC, 2016.

Stoughton, John. *William Penn, The Founder of Pennsylvania*. London: Hodder & Stoughton, 1882.

Strassburger, Ralph Beaver. *The Strassburger Family and Allied Families of Pennsylvania*. Gwynedd Valley, PA: "Printed for Private Circulation," 1922.

Street, Lucie. *An Uncommon Sailor: A Portrait of Admiral Sir William Penn*. New York: St. Martin's Press, 1988.

Stutzman, Ervin R. *The Hochstetler Story*. Harrisonburg, Va.: Herald Press, 2008.

_____. *Jacob's Choice: Return to Northkill, Book 1*. "Expanded Edition." Harrisonburg, Va.: Herald Press, 2014.

Sugrue, Thomas J. "The Peopling and Depeopling of Early Pennsylvania: Indians and Colonists, 1680-1720," *Pennsylvania Magazine of History and Biography*, 96 (January 1992), 3-31.

Tappert, Theodore G. and John W. Oberstein, tr. & ed. *From the Notebook of a Colonial Clergyman. Condensed from the Journals of Henry Melchior Muhlenberg*. Philadelphia: Muhlenberg Press, 1959.

Thayer, Theodore. "The Friendly Association," *Pennsylvania Magazine of History and Biography*, 67 (October 1943), 357-76.

Thomas, Gabriel. *An Historical and Geographical Account of Pennsylvania and West-New-Jersey in America*. London: A. Baldwin, 1698.

[Thomson, Charles]. *AN ENQUIRY INTO THE CAUSES OF THE ALIENATION OF THE DELAWARE AND SHAWANESE INDIANS FROM THE BRITISH INTEREST. And into the Measures taken for recovering their Friendship. Extracted from the Public Treaties, and other Authentic Papers relating to the Transactions of the Government of Pennsylvania and the said Indians, for near Forty Years . . . . Together with the remarkable journal of Christian Frederic Post, by whose negotiations, among the Indians on the Ohio, they were withdrawn from the interest of the French . . . . With notes by the editor explaining sundry Indian customs, etc. Written in Pennsylvania*. London: Printed for J. Wilkie, at the Bible, in St. Paul's Church-yard, 1759.

Tolles, Frederick B. *James Logan and the Culture of Provincial America*. Boston: Little, Brown & Company, 1957.

_____. *Meetinghouse and Counting House: The Quaker Merchants of Colonial Philadelphia 1682-1763*. Chapel Hill, N.C.: University of North Carolina Press, 1948.

Treece, Lorett. *The Storm Gathering: The Penn Family and the American Revolution*. Mechanicsburg, Pa.: Stackpole Books, 2002. (Originally published 1992 by The Pennsylvania State University Press.)

Trieb, Adolf. *Ibersheim am Rhein, Geschichte des Ortes seit den frühesten Zeiten, mit Berücksichtigung der Mennonitengemeinde*. Worms: n.p., 1911.

Trussell, John B. B., Jr. *William Penn: Architect of a Nation*. Harrisburg, Pa.: Pennsylvania Historical and Museum Commission, 1998.

Two Centuries of Nazareth 1740-1940. Nazareth, Pa.: Nazareth, Pennsylvania Bi-Centennial, Inc., 1940.

Uhler, Sherman P. *Pennsylvania's Indian Relations to 1754*. New York: AMS Press [1984]. (Originally presented as the author's doctoral thesis at Temple University, 1950.)

Ulle, Robert F. "The Original Germantown Families," *Mennonite Family History*, 2 (April 1983), 48-51.

Vaughan, Alden T. *Roots of American Racism: Essays on the Colonial Experience*. New York: Oxford University Press, 1995.

Wainright, Nicholas. "Plan of Philadelphia," *Pennsylvania Magazine of History and Biography*, 80 (April 1956), 164-170.

SELECTED SOURCES AND READINGS

Wallace, Anthony F. C. *Teedyuscung: King of the Delawares*. Philadelphia: University of Pennsylvania Press, 1949.

Wallace, Paul A. W. *Conrad Weiser: Friend of Colonist and Mohawk*. (Originally published Philadelphia 1945.) Reprint, Lewisburg, Pa.: Wennawoods Publishing, 1996.

_____. "Cooper's Indians," *New York History*, 35 (October 1954), 423-436.

_____. "Historic Hope Lodge," *Pennsylvania Magazine of History and Biography*, 86 (April 1962)., 115-142.

_____. *Indian Paths of Pennsylvania*. Harrisburg, Pa.: Pennsylvania Historical and Museum Commission, 1987.

_____. *Indians in Pennsylvania*. Harrisburg, Pa.: Pennsylvania Historical and Museum Commission, 1975.

_____. *Indians in Pennsylvania*, "Second Edition Revised by William A. Hunter." Harrisburg, Pa.: Pennsylvania Historical and Museum Commission, 1981.

Walton, Joseph Solomon. *Conrad Weiser and The Indian Policy of Colonial Pennsylvania*. Philadelphia: George W. Jacobs & Co., 1900.

Weidensaul. Scott. *The First Frontier: The Forgotten History of Struggle, Savagery, and Endurance in Early America*. Boston and New York: Houghton Mifflin Harcourt, 2012.

Weigley, Russell F., et al. *Philadelphia: A 330-Year History*. New York: W. W. Norton Company, 1982.

Weiser, Conrad. "Narrative of a Journey, Made in the Year 1737, by Conrad Weiser, Indian Agent and Provincial Interpreter, from Tulpehocken in the Province of Pennsylvania to Onondago . . .," tr. Hiester Muhlenberg, *Collections of the Historical Society of Pennsylvania*. Philadelphia: Historical Society of Pennsylvania, 1853, 1, 6-33.

Weslager, C. A. *Red Men on the Brandywine*. Wilmington, Del.: Hambleton Company, Inc., 1953.

_____. *The Delaware Indians: A History*. New Brunswick, NJ: Rutgers University Press, 1972.

_____. *The Delawares: A Critical Bibliography*. Bloomington, Ind., and London: Published for the Newberry Library by Indiana University Press, 1978.

White, Richard. *The Middle Ground: Indians, Empires and Republics in the Great Lakes Region, 1650-1815*. Cambridge, U.K.: Cambridge University Press, 1991.

Wildes, Harry Emerson. *William Penn*. New York: Macmillan Publishing Co., Inc., 1974.

Witthoft, John. *Indian Prehistory of Pennsylvania*. Harrisburg, Pa.: Pennsylvania Historical and Museum Commission, 1965.

Zeisberger, David. *History of the Northern American Indians in 18th Century Ohio, New York & Pennsylvania*. (Originally published 1910.) Reprint Lewisburg, Pa.: Wennawoods Publishing, 1999.

Index of Characters and Names

Agnes (indigenous wife of Frederick Post), 313
Allebach, Christian, 159, 168, 171, 249, 273, 283
Allebach, Elizabeth, 170, 213
Allen, William 179, 197, 226, 228, 230, 233-35, 237, 244, 252, 255-56, 260, 262, 270, 283
Altdörfer, Friedrich, 159, 222, 247, 273, 338
Alumapees (second name of Sassoonan), 182, 197-99, 202-05, 207, 217, 219, 225, 229, 233. 235-37, 239-42, 240-51, 253-57, 263-69, 272-73, 275, 277-85, 287-89, 293-94, 316-18, 328
Amherst, Sir Jeffery, 347-48
Antes, Henry, 253
Armstrong, John (General), 307
Armstrong, John (trader), 277
Asheton, Ralph, 171-72
Asheton, Robert, 99, 171-72
Aubrey, Laetitia (Penn), 46, 55, 84, 99-100, 145, 228
Bachman Family, 226
Baltimore, Lord (Cecil Calvert), 67-69, 74, 78, 89, 118
Bauer, Abraham, 290
Bebber, Mathias van, 91, 109, 123, 146, 163
Behr, Hans, 216
Beissel, Conrad, 231
Bergey, Hans Ulrich, 159, 273
Bezaillion, Peter and Ann, 82, 111
Biles, William, 232
Boehm, John Philip, 182, 185, 231-32.
Böhler, Peter, 252-53
Boone, Squire George, 182, 187, 236.
Bouquet, Henri Louis (General), 322, 348-50
Braddock, Edward (General), 297-99, 314
Brainerd, David, 262, 269, 178-80
Brechbühl, Benedicht, 125-26, 137-38, 260-61
Brechbühl, Ulrich, 251
Brown, Alexander, 245
Burckholder, Ulrich, 216
Burkholder, Hans, 153
Calhoun, Thomas, 330, 341-42
Canassetigo, 264, 266-68, 271.
Captain Bull (son of Teedyuscung), 315, 320
Captain Jacobs, 304, 307
Cassel, Henrich, 123.
Carpenter, Samuel, 88
Cassel, Yelles (Julius), 261
Chalkley, Thomas, 131
Chapman, John, 233, 244.
Charles I, 21-22
Charles II, 21, 24-25, 27-28, 32, 34, 36, 39, 41, 46-47, 49, 57, 71, 74-75, 92, 128

INDEX OF CHARACTERS AND NAMES

Clemens, Abraham (son of Gerhart and Anneli), 159, 170, 226, 273
Clemens, Anneli (Reiff), 73, 100, 102-03, 113, 116-17, 119, 123-24, 140, 155, 167, 170, 213, 223, 226.
Clemens, Barbara, 337-38
Clemens, Gerhart, 18, 42, 100, 102-03, 113, 115-17, 119, 123-24, 131, 136, 140, 146, 153, 155, 157, 159, 166, 170-71, 180, 185-86, 188, 197, 201-02, 213, 217, 221, 223, 226-27, 269, 272-73, 275, 363
Clemens, Gerhart (son of Jacob, grandson of Gerhart), 338
Clemens, Gerhart (son of Johannes, grandson of Gerhart), 242, 247
Clemens, Jacob (of Niederflörsheim, father of Gerhart), 42
Clemens, Jacob (son of Gerhart and Anneli), 123, 140, 155, 159, 170, 173, 247, 301-02, 337
Clemens, Johannes (of Kriegsheim), 36-37, 42
Clemens, Johannes (miller, son of Gerhart and Anneli), 123, 140, 159, 170, 173, 213, 227, 242, 247, 249, 273, 275, 283, 301, 303, 338, 340, 362
Clement, Gregory, of Toft, 51
Clemmer, Barbara (Detweiler), 247
Clemmer, Hans or Johannes, 213, 222-23, 247
Clemmer, Henrich, 213
Coale, George, 25, 32
Cock, Lasse ("Lawrence and Martha"), 26, 45-46, 52-53, 82
Combush, John, 244-45
Conguegas, 111, 142
Croghan, George (trader), 294, 346
Cromwell, Oliver, 21-23, 25, 34, 53, 99
Cromwell, Richard, 24
Custaloga, 332, 343, 347
Dährstein (Derstine), Michael 222, 283
Delaware George, 275, 289, 314, 316, 333
Denk, Christian, 339
Denny, William (Governor), 305, 307, 309, 313-15, 318-19, 334
Derstein, Johannes, 302
Derstine, Titus, 352
Dinwiddie, Robert (Governor), 294, 297
Dock, Christopher, 213, 301-02, 338
Dotterer Family, 169-70
Eastburn, Benjamin, 244-47
Eby, Theodorus, 125, 152
Elizabeth, Palatine Princess, 43
Evans, Hugh, 95
Evans, John (Governor), 105-09, 111, 121
Evans, Thomas, 95
Eyers (ship captain), 154-55
Fairman, Thomas, 45, 51-54, 56-57, 61, 64-68, 70, 78, 80, 85-86, 88-90, 95-97, 99, 103-08, 114, 123, 136, 141, 146-47, 212
Fairman, Thomas Jr., 141
Farmar, Edward, 136-37, 140, 146-48, 170, 186, 192-94

INDEX OF CHARACTERS AND NAMES

Fell, Gulielma (Penn), 238
Forbes, John (General), 313-15, 320-22, 327
Ford, Philip, 55, 84, 92, 106, 108, 112, 114
Fox, George, 25, 32, 35, 37-39, 41, 44, 74, 80
Franklin, Benjamin, 87, 213, 238, 251-52, 276, 282-83, 292, 297, 304, 308, 311-12, 325-26
Freed, Peter, 337
Freeman, Hannah, 178
Frey, Henry, 141-42
Funck, Anna, 291
Funck, Esther, 339
Funck, Henrich, of Bern and Kraichgau), 35, 151
Funck, Henrich (Bishop), 169, 173, 217, 260, 261, 276, 291, 302, 339-40
Funck, Martin, 318
Gaetschalcks, Gaetschalck, 171
Gaetschalcks, Jacob, 113, 116
Gaetschalcks, Jan, 171
Galle, Peter, 227
Geman, Benedict, 216
Geman, Christian, 216
Gist, Christopher, 287-89
Goetz, Frederich, 302, 339
Gookin, Charles (Governor), 121-22, 132, 136, 139, 148-50, 165, 190, 206
Gordon, Patrick (Governor), 182, 187-90, 192, 195-96, 205, 217, 236
Groff, Abraham, 269
Groff (Graff), Hans 131, 222
Gutt, Jacob, 216
Guy, Joseph (ship captain), 118-19
Hackman, Walton, 12, 355
Hagey, Henry, 352
Hallman, Lee, 15
Halteman, Nicholas, 159, 273
Hambright (Hambrecht), John, 345
Hamilton, Andrew, 192, 195
Hamilton, James (Governor), 330, 332-34, 344-46
Handel, Georg Friedrich, 154
Harrison, James (steward), 77
Heaney, Seamus, 168
Heckewelder, John, 6, 259, 281, 330, 340-43, 346
Herr, Abraham, 296, 349
Hershey, Benjamin (Bishop), 310-11, 317, 330
Hershey, Christian, 349
Hesselius, Gustav, 233
Hetkoquean, 58, 81-82, 209, 211
Hiestand, Küngold ("Kinget," wife of Hans Stauffer), 73-74, 83, 100-02, 226
Hill, Richard, 190, 195
Holme, Thomas (surveyor), 53-58, 64-65, 68, 71, 75-78, 85, 96, 106

Index of Characters and Names

Hochstetter, Oswald, 216
Hostetter, Nicholas, 312
Huber, Christian, 216
Huber, Hans, 216
Hunsecker, Valendine, 216
Hütwohl, Valentyn, 36, 42
James, Duke of York, 24, 28, 32, 4, 40-41, 467, 48, 69, 71, 75, 78-79, 101, 104
James Scott, Duke of Monmouth, 75
Janzen, Dirk, 197, 212
Jasper, Jan, 21
Jenkins, Howard, 85
Jennings, Francis, 318
Jennings, Solomon, 244
Johnson, Samuel, 329
Johnson, Sir William (agent), 331, 333-34
Jones, Griffith, 90
Kakawatchy, 185, 187, 189
Keith, William (Governor), 155, 160-61, 172, 180-81, 194-95, 210
Kelpius, Johannes, 94
Kendig, Martin, 152, 154
Kenny, James, 328, 330-31, 355, 357
Kerkes (Garges), Wilhelm, 227
Ketchum, Dee and Annette, 356-57
Keyser, Dirk, 78
King, Jacob (Jean Jacques LeRoi), 296
Kinsey, Elizabeth, 44-45, 56
Kinsey, John, 44
Kinton, Thomas, 340
Kolb, Agnes Schumacher, 102, 112
Kolb, Barbara, 123
Kolb, Henrich (Bishop),102, 113-17, 123, 140, 153, 201
Kolb, Isaac, 283
Kolb, Jacob, 227, 302
Kolb, Johannes, 113, 123, 140
Kolb, Martin, 102, 112-13, 123, 140, 201, 259-61
Kolb, Thielman Sr., 102
Kolb, Thielman Jr. (Dielman), 153-54, 157, 159, 168, 171, 173, 188, 197, 201, 217, 227, 251, 259, 261, 273, 275-76, 283, 301-02, 305, 309-10, 338
Kolb, Peter (Bishop), 102, 113, 115-16, 123-25, 153, 168
Kratz, Valentine, 159, 180, 221, 273
Landis, Abram, 353
Landis, Jacob, 273, 283
Langhorne, Jeremiah, 255
Lapapitton, 284-85
Lappowinzo, 179, 231, 233-35, 242, 245-47, 249, 352, 360
Lederach, brothers Andreas and Johannes, 157, 159, 247
Lehnman, Philip (Penn's personal secretary), 68

Index of Characters and Names

Letort, Ann, 111, 142
Loe, Thomas, 23, 31
Logan, James, 85-90, 96-97, 99, 103-08, 112, 114, 118-19, 122, 127-29, 131-33, 135-37, 139-41, 147-49, 154-56, 158, 160, 162-67, 172, 175-82, 186, 190-97, 202-08, 211-12, 219-22, 225, 228-31, 233-44, 246, 252-57, 263-68, 280, 282-83, 285, 308, 352, 359
Ludwig, Karl (Palatine Elector-Prince), 28, 36, 41, 114, 152
Maughoughsin, 69
Mananget or Manangy, 58, 95, 103, 107
Manawkyhickon, 242
Markham, William, 51-56, 58, 88
Marshall, Abraham, 176
Marshall, Edward, 244-46, 309, 361
Mathias, Joseph, 352
Metzler, Valentine, 349
Meyer, Christian, 291
Meyer, Elizabeth, 291
Meyer, Jacob, 291
Meyer, Samuel, 216
Michel, Franz Luis, 111-12, 125-26
Michael and Mary (Lenape couple), 349
Miller, Peter, 276
Milton, John, 33
Monmouth, Duke of, 75
Montour, Andrew, 275, 280, 294-95
Morris, Robert Hunter (Governor), 295, 304, 306
Moselman, Hans, 216
Muhlenberg, Henry Melchior, 284, 302, 333
Mushmeelin, 277-79
Nemacolin, 288-290, 297, 333
Neolin, 332, 347
Netawatwees (Newcomer), 332-33, 343, 356
Newlin, Nathaniel, 174-78
Norris, Isaac, 106, 127, 146, 155
Nutimus, 178-79, 221, 230-31, 233-34, 239, 242, 250, 256, 265-69, 282, 308, 347, 352
Oberholz, Jacob, 216
Op den Graeff, brothers Dirk, Herman, and Abraham, 65-66
Op den Graeff, Grietgen, 65
Op den Graeff, Isaac, 52
Opessah, 93, 132
Opekasset, 160, 191, 193, 202, 204, 206
Opplinger, Nicholas and Elizabeth (Meyer) 291, 304
Papunhank, 332
Pastorius, Franz Daniel, 64-66, 82, 157, 172, 212
Pearson, Enoch, 245
Pemberton, Israel, Jr., 255, 303, 305-07, 309-11, 313-14, 318-19, 325-28, 330-35, 344, 346

Index of Characters and Names

Pemberton, Phineas, 326
Penington, Edward, 85, 90, 96, 104
Penington, Isaac, 32
Penn, Giles, 21
Penn, Gulielma (Springett), 32, 35, 37, 55, 71, 73-74, 79, 84-85, 99
Penn, Hannah (Callowhill), 84, 86-88, 96-97, 100, 105, 114, 118, 142, 145-46, 165, 172, 178, 225
Penn, John (son of William), 88, 99-100, 145, 166, 178, 203, 227, 230, 233, 235, 240, 243, 246, 264-65, 296, 308
Penn, John (son of Richard), 349
Penn, Margaret (Jasper), 21
Penn, Richard, 227, 243, 246, 282, 349
Penn, Springett, 46, 55, 70, 84
Penn, Thomas, 178, 215, 216-18, 220-22, 226-30, 232, 235-39, 241-47, 249-50, 255-57, 262-65, 267-68, 271, 275, 288, 296, 305-08, 311-12, 356, 359
Penn, William, 9, 13, 15, 17, 22-28, 31-47, 49-58, 61-71, 73-101, 103-07, 111-14, 118-19, 121-22, 124-28, 131, 133, 135-36, 139, 141-42, 145-46, 148-49, 155-56, 158, 160-63, 165-67, 171, 173-76, 178-79, 190-93, 195, 198-200, 204, 208-11, 215-17, 219, 236, 256, 295, 301, 305, 326, 344, 349, 351, 353-56, 361, 363
Penn, William Jr., 22, 55, 81, 84, 87-88, 91-92, 98, 105-106, 112, 142, 145, 166, 172
Penn, William (Admiral),17, 21-24, 26-28, 34, 49
Percy, Hugh (ship captain), 216
Peter the Great, 86
Peters, Richard (Secretary), 271, 290, 295-96, 307, 315, 325-26, 334
Piselatulpe, 341
Pisquetomen, 202, 205, 207, 211, 219, 222, 242, 257, 263, 265-68, 275, 282, 284-85, 289, 296, 301, 303, 307, 309, 312, 314-16, 318-20, 322, 327-28
Plockhoy, Pieter Cornelisz, 25
Pontiac, 347-49.
Post, Christian Frederick, 313-22, 328, 330, 333, 340-41, 343, 346-47
Powell, David, 64-65, 80, 85, 90, 97, 99, 103-04, 108, 141, 146-47, 156-60, 163, 167, 170, 173, 186, 206, 221, 249
Preiss, Daniel, 169
Preiss, Johannes Jacob, 168-69
Preiss, Johannes (son of Johannes Jacob), 169
Preiss, Johannes (grandson of Johannes and Lenape wife), 302
Printz, John (Governor), 16
Pui, Nicholas du, 179
Rachel (indigenous wife of Frederick Post), 313
Reiff, Abraham, 291
Reiff, Anneli and Elizabeth (step-daughters of Hans Stauffer), 73
Reiff, Hans, 157, 159, 273
Reiff, Küngold ("Kinget") Hiestand, 73
Reiff, Michael, 73
Rementer, James, 355
Richardson, John, 97-98

INDEX OF CHARACTERS AND NAMES

Richmond (ship captain), 154
Rittenhouse, William, 78, 113
Roet, Hans (John Ruth), 287
Roth, Johannes, 168
Roth, Peter, 168
Ruth, Hans, 125, 151-52
Ruth, Henrich, 157, 159, 168, 171, 173, 188, 213, 249, 273, 283
Ruth, Magdalena, 157, 168, 173, 213, 249
Rutter, Thomas, 187-88, 190, 192, 194-95
Sassoonan (see also Alumapees), 18-19, 25, 38, 50, 58, 63, 82, 86, 95, 103, 119, 121-22, 136, 140, 147-51, 160-64, 167, 169, 172, 176, 179-83, 185, 187, 190-97, 199, 202-08, 211-13, 219-23, 226, 229-30, 234-36, 238, 265, 275, 282, 301, 303, 315, 319, 331-32, 338, 344, 347
Satcher, John and Mary, 104
Sauer, Christopher, 260, 275-76, 301, 303, 305, 313
Scherer, Hans, 216
Schijn, Dr. Hermanus, 123-25
Schnebele, Elizabeth (Kolb), 153, 227
Schnebele, Isaac, 302, 309
Schumacher, Agnes Kolb, 102
Schumacher, Peter, 74, 102, 109, 112-13
Schumacher, Peter Jr., 109, 112
Schwartz, Hans Andreas, 273
Scolitchy, 121, 136-38, 140, 147
Scull, Nicholas, 156, 212, 244
Shakatawlin ("Sam"), 190-91, 202, 204, 206
Shikellamy, 191-92, 202-04, 206-07, 211-12, 220, 277, 279-82, 284-85
Shingas, 202, 275, 285, 289, 296, 298, 301, 303-04, 307, 309, 312, 314, 316-17, 320-22, 328, 331-33, 341-43, 348-49
Shippen, Edward, 88
Shirk, Caspar, 215
Slave Sam, 104
Slaves ("Negroes"), Cuff, Hannah, Jane, Molle, Peter, 96
Snavely, John, 312
Souder, Jacob, 170
Springett, Gulielma (first wife of William Penn), 32, 35, 37, 55, 71, 73-74, 79, 84-85, 99
Smith, Timothy (sheriff), 233, 244
Stauffer, Ann Reiff (see Clemens, Anneli)
Stauffer, Christian, of Bern, 36-37
Stauffer, Christian, of Lower Salford, 171, 302
Stauffer, Daniel, 170, 186
Stauffer, Hans, 17-18, 28-29, 35-36, 39, 41, 43, 58, 69, 73, 85-86, 102, 111-12, 114-15, 124-26, 137, 151, 167, 225
Stauffer, Ulrich, 103
Steele, James, 221, 227
Still, Isaac, 316, 320-21
Strieper, Johannes, 91

Index of Characters and Names

Tamany (Tamanend), 6, 58, 61, 63, 68, 71, 76, 81-82, 99, 121, 136, 139, 163, 301, 344, 347, 351, 361-62
Tamaqua (Beaver), 202, 275, 289-90, 294-96, 304, 307, 312, 314, 316-17, 320-22, 328, 330-333, 341, 343-51
Tanacharison, 289-90
Tatamy, Moses Tunda, 231, 246, 249, 259, 262, 267, 269, 271, 280
Taylor, Jacob (surveyor), 104, 132, 171, 179
Teedyuscung (Gideon), 234, 282, 293, 303-04, 306-15, 319-20, 325, 331, 333-34, 345-49
Tenoughan, 67
Thomas, Gabriel, 82
Thomas, George (Governor), 250, 263
Thomson, Charles, 325-26
Tishekunk ("Captain John"), 179, 231, 233-34, 242, 245-47, 249, 253, 256, 259, 261-62, 267, 269, 271, 282
Tower (ship captain), 154
Trees, Abraham, 352
Tuneam, Joe, 244
Wägele, Georg, 227, 339
Walton brothers, 383
Wampler, Peter, 312
Washington, George, 287, 289-90, 292-94, 297, 299, 357
Watts, Isaac, 10, 364
Weiser, Conrad, 202-03, 212, 217, 219, 231, 237-41, 254-55, 263, 265-66, 269, 272, 275, 277
Weiss, Georg Michael, 231
Wesley, John, 252
Whitefield, George, 251-53, 259-60, 262
Wiegner, Christopher, 252, 260
William of Orange, 15, 46-47
Williams, Roger, 18
Winters, brothers John and Walter, 187-89, 191, 196
Wismar, Jacob, 138
Wistar, Caspar, 197, 212, 228, 241
Witmer, Hans, 216
Wood, Joseph, 232
Wright, Thomas, 183
Wyerman, Hans Sr. and Jr., 273
Yeates, James, 244-45
Ziegler, Andreas, 283, 302, 305, 327, 337-38, 340
Ziegler, Michael, 108, 227, 302, 310
Zinzendorf, Count Nicholas von, 259, 261-62, 269, 271

www.ingramcontent.com/pod-product-compliance
Lightning Source LLC
Chambersburg PA
CBHW020258240426
43673CB00039B/636